THIRD EDITION

The Strengths Perspective in Social Work Practice

Edited by

Dennis Saleebey

University of Kansas

Allyn and Bacon

Boston ▪ London ▪ Toronto ▪ Sydney ▪ Tokyo ▪ Singapore

Series Editor: *Patricia Quinlin*
Editorial Assistant: *Annemarie Kennedy*
Editorial-Production Administrator: *Joe Sweeney*
Editorial-Production Service: *Colophon*
Composition Buyer: *Linda Cox*
Manufacturing Buyer: *Suzanne Lareau*
Cover Administrator: *Kristina Mose-Libon*
Text Composition: *Omegatype, Inc.*

Between the time Website information is gathered and then published, it is not unusual
for some sites to have closed. Also, the transcription of URLs can result in unintended
typographical errors. The publisher would appreciate notification where these occur so
that they may be corrected in subsequent editions. Thank you.

Library of Congress Cataloging-in-Publication Data

The strengths perspective in social work practice / edited by Dennis Saleebey.—3rd ed.
   p.   cm.
Originally published: 2nd ed. New York : Longman, c1997.
Includes bibliographical references and index.
ISBN 0-8013-3310-5 (alk. paper)
1. Social service—Psychological aspects.   I. Saleebey, Dennis.

HV41 .S827 2002
361.3'2'0973—dc21

                                                                          2001033674

Printed in the United States of America

10 9 8 7 6 5 4 3 2 1   RRD-VA   02   03   04   05   06   07   08

To my family: My mother and father, June Hoff and Ted Saleebey, the seeds of my strength; my children, Jennifer, David, John, and Meghan, whose growth is the definition of possibility; and Ann, my wife, whose wisdom I count on, and whose shoulder I lean on.

In Memoriam

Bette A. Saleebey
Liane V. Davis
Howard Goldstein

Their strengths are found yet in the lives of others.

Affection! Thy intention stabs at the center:
Thou dost make possible things not so held,
Comunnicat'st with dreams.

—William Shakespeare (*A Winter's Tale*)

We confide in our strength, without boasting of it;
We respect that of others, without fearing it.

—Thomas Jefferson (Letter to William Carmichael and William Short)

CONTENTS

PART THREE   Strengths-Based Assessment and Approaches to Practice

9 The Strengths Model with Older Adults: Critical Practice Components   143

Becky Fast and Rosemary Chapin

FOREWORD

Let's begin with a real life story—albeit highly abbreviated—of the strengths perspective. The setting is a small town in northern Vermont about 6 years ago. The town is home to Martin, a man in his early twenties. Martin usually could be found hanging around the shops on Main Street much to the chagrin of the shopkeepers who, like many people in town, saw Martin as slovenly dressed, mentally deficient, moody, and irresponsible. Most agreed that Martin seemed headed for trouble. Fortunately, Martin met Nancy, a vocational counselor who was able to see past his appearance, social situation, and labels. Instead she saw someone who, despite many negative experiences and expectations, retained a sense of happiness, enjoyed people, and had a positive social outlook. She treated Martin with respect, took seriously his hopes and dreams, and worked with him to pursue them. After much hard work and additional support, Martin wound up as the proprietor of a discount store in town and a successful businessman.

When social work students first hear about the strengths perspective through stories like these, they tend to have two reactions: It makes good sense and it is straightforward. Both reactions likely stem from the congruence between the strengths perspective and social work beliefs and values. Martin's story, for example, illustrates the venerable tenet, "start where the client is," the belief that people can change, and the value that everyone deserves to be treated with dignity and respect. The seamlessness of this fit makes the strengths perspective appear to be simply the expression of fundamental, well-established qualities of good practice. Certainly there is nothing wrong about that, but it is hardly the fecund intellectual material to write books about. So why a third edition of this book in addition to an increasing number of articles on the strengths perspective?

I believe that the students' reaction (which also is common among practitioners) underestimates the complexity of the strengths perspective and the challenges involved in its implementation. Consider, for instance, that our observations and knowledge already are interpretations. Then consider, within the context of the human service system, the language that informs those interpretations. It is a language dominated by syndromes, addictions, pathologies, dysfunctions, disorders, and the like. These conditions form the context for our efforts to understand and help others. They define the field of possibilities that we or our clients can identify, consider, or imagine. Ironically, the very pervasiveness of this deficit language and its embedded assumptions make these interpretations hard to detect. Thus, we may overlook or fail to notice that the individuals, families, and communities we work with are in part constituted by medically or scientifically conferred labels. In fact, entry into the service system often requires such labels. Consequently, it is hard to see the person with mental illness or the child abuser as something other than their labels, or to consider crime-ridden, impoverished communities as wellsprings of resources. Negative situations seem to cry out for negative explanations—we want to know what is wrong when so little seems right.

Part of this difficulty stems from our culturally ingrained ethos of individualism. Even in cases like Martin's, it is the individual who overcomes negative expectations and stigma to achieve seemingly unreachable goals. Such achievements are then considered evidence of laudable internal qualities that were previously overlooked. While such individuals deserve praise, closer inspection reveals their achievements to be rooted not solely in personal, internal attributes, but in past and current relationships in which they learned to construe the world and themselves in ways that enabled them to endure and overcome adversity. Strengths from this standpoint are not simply personal traits or characteristics, but features of relationships. Such relationships are based in mutuality and connection. They express respect and affirm human dignity. They position social workers as allies with those they serve. In doing so, strength relationships invite people to identify and (re)connect with their personal and social resources, inspire them to bear hardships, overcome obstacles, resist oppression, and encourage action in accordance with their goals. Relationships have always been the heart of social work practice; the strengths perspective revitalizes and augments this feature.

When strengths are the starting point for discourses about people's lives, new realities are generated. Like an ultraviolet light that makes visible previously unseen parts of the spectrum, the strengths perspective reveals human potentialities and resources that could not be perceived in the light of current beliefs about human suffering. One consequence is the appearance of new areas for the development and application of practice. Some of these are explored in the present volume.

It takes courage for social workers to practice from a strengths perspective and not to acquiesce to the reified ideas of medical, social, economic, and legal institutions. Strengths-based practitioners are challenged not to deny the reality of disease and dysfunction, or to delay providing needed assistance. In a world in which many agencies depend on insurance payments that require formal diagnoses and in which poverty is considered a personal failing, resisting these challenges is difficult. However, the strengths perspective helps us understand that reality is equivocal: A world in which deficits are salient is one reality, one in which strengths prevail is another. This latter position need not deter practitioners from acting to relieve suffering or prevent harm. We can accept the reality of others' pain and respond to risk without assuming their disease and the social implications that such formulations entail. For the strengths-based practitioner or researcher, the key question becomes not what is Real (capital R intended), but what are the implications of the ways that we construct the real? For example, strength-based practitioners believe that when reality is constructed in collaboration with clients, when their stories are combined with, not subjugated to, professionals' stories, we generate useful realities. They also believe that focusing on the qualities and actions of people and communities that enabled them to surmount difficulties or even just get by in difficult circumstances leads to practices that are more in line with our professional values and beliefs than those developed from focusing on their deficits and failures.

Do not be fooled by the seeming simplicity of the strengths perspective; it has transformational potential. Indeed, if all of its tenets were adopted and put into practice, we would be living in a different world. Over the past several years the strengths perspective has been applied to different populations and areas of need, and its principles have been further refined. But while this instrumental work was proceeding, the strengths perspective has been quietly fostering a small revolution in which the hegemony of deficit explanations is beginning to weaken, belief in resilience is rebounding, and collaborative practice is growing. These changes are altering people's views of themselves and, as noted earlier, reinvigorating the social work relationship. It is a trend that I hope will continue.

This book, like all texts, is a palette on which we can reconfigure relations, develop ideas, or merely assimilate information into existing beliefs. My advice is to complicate the strengths perspective. Explore its possibilities, pursue its invitations, develop its language, and generate its relationships. The benefits to you and to those with whom you work will be substantial.

Stanley Witkin, Ph.D., professor, University of Vermont; editor-in-chief, Social Work

PREFACE

The interest in and work on the development of a strengths-based approach to case management, practice with individuals and groups, and community development continues not only at the School of Social Welfare, University of Kansas but around the country and even internationally. Much remains to be done, of course, with respect to inquiry and the further development of concepts and principles as well as techniques. But it is gratifying to witness, from the views of practitioners, their clients, students, and faculty how poignant the strengths perspective has been in their pedagogy and practice. It may be, too, that the strengths perspective will remain just that: a perspective, a way of thinking about and orienting yourself to your work and obligating yourself to your clients and their families and communities.

The responses to the first two editions of *The Strenths Perspective in Social Work Practice* have been gratifying. The authors are truly grateful for those reactions as well as the critiques that have been forwarded. In this edition, we kept some of the elements that have provoked positive responses, added some new ones that were thought to be essential, and responded to some of the criticism with revisions. You will find four brand new chapters by Margeret Waller and Michael Yellow Bird (Chapter 3), Edward Canda (Chapter 4), Jennifer Jones and Mary Bricker-Jenkins (Chapter 11), and Bonnie Benard (Chapter 12). And, for the most part, the other chapters have significant revisions. We have tried to be attentive to concerns about working with oppressed groups and remembering our professional commitment to social and economic justice. Spirituality is defined in this edition as a strength, and we have provided some new examples as well as some fresh ideas about practice.

We hope, of course, that this book will assist you in developing in your own professional work and pedagogy, a genuine strengths perspective. I have been privileged to travel around the country and, to a limited extent, abroad and consult with groups and organizations attempting to incorporate this perspective into their work or curriculum. Believe me, there are people doing some amazing things. But I also see that it is easy to think that one is using a strengths perspective when, in some ways, that isn't the case. The problem is that it requires a dedication and depth of commitment that, on the surface, does not seem warranted. Nonetheless, the authors of these chapters—who, by the way, are not of one mind about this perspective—hope that you see the enormity of the undertaking but also the joys that come from the use of a strengths approach.

Plan of the Book

The first part of the book, "The Philosophy, Principles, and Language of the Strengths Perspective" introduces you to the basic assumptions, the values, the guiding principles, and the lexicon of the strengths perspective. In Chapter 1, Dennis Saleebey lays out some of the assumptions and principles and contrasts them with the more dominant problem-based and medical models. In Chapter 2, Howard Goldstein not only examines the language and metaphorical struts of the perspective but takes us on an exciting journey into the literary and moral foundations of the strengths perspective.

Part two, "The Remarkable Strengths of People(s)," begins with Margeret Waller's and Michael Yellow Bird's dramatic and searing account of how the stark reality of oppression in the lives of Indigenous Peoples has promoted not just anguish and destruction, but a variety of cultural, tribal, and individual capacities and virtues that have helped people withstand the withering effects of genocide. In Chapter 4, Edward Canda details a qualitative study of how spirituality has sustained people confronting a serious chronic illness, cystic fibrosis. The struggle to come to terms with their illness led many people to form a bulwark of transcendent meaning and religion, a strength in the face of uncertainty and pain.

Part three, "Strengths-Based Assessment and Approaches to Practice," begins with Dennis Saleebey's overview of a strengths-based approach to practice as well as some ideas about how to discover and use strengths in practice. In chapter six Ann Weick and Ronna Chamberlain present their interesting and challenging take on how to understand and employ problems in the use of a strengths perspective. Their recommendations are down to earth and straightforward as they encourage turning problems into prospects. In the next chapter, Charles Cowger and Carol Snively provide an update on their thoroughgoing and useful strengths assessment quadrant model. They also issue some value-based and important cautions about not making assessment an oppressive one-sided process. Richard Rapp brings an update on his strengths-based case management model with people with substance abuse problems, a program that has been successful and ongoing at Wright State University for several years now. Rosemary Chapin and Becky Fast, in Chapter 9, discuss the employment of a strengths orientation with older citizens, along with some very practical guidelines. This is important for many reasons, not the least of which is the graying of America. In Chapter 10, Walter Kisthardt updates and expands his well-researched and well-received strengths-based case management principles and practices with people with severe and persistent mental illness. In the following chapter, Jennifer Jones and Mary Bricker-Jenkins present a stirring report of their work with the Kensington (Philadelphia) Welfare Rights Union as they work to end poverty and the war on the poor. This Union clearly understands the idea of building on strengths in the midst of trouble, and they have many ideas for us, as social workers, on being genuine partners in this kind of work.

Part four, "Strengths in Context," is intended to move the interests of the strengths perspective to the environment. In Chapter 12, Bonnie Benard, using the latest understandings of the resilience literature, offers practical guidelines for organizations and individuals who would foster the resilience and reserves of youth, especially those in difficulty. She provides a very helpful checklist at the end of the chapter. In the following chapter, Dennis Saleebey discusses how a strengths perspective plays out in community building with two examples of extraordinarily successful community-building programs. There are also some blueprints derived from the literature on what makes for a successful community-building effort. In Chapter 14, Patrick Sullivan and Charles Rapp, two of the foremost thinkers and developers of the strengths-based approach to case management, give us some ideas and directions about using the resources in the environment to foster and nourish the recovery process. They also regard policy as an important element of the environment.

In the final part, "Conclusion," Dennis Saleebey examines the consequences of taking on a strengths approach, answers some of the most commonly asked questions about it, and discusses its future as well as converging lines of thought and practice that seem consonant with the assumptions and outlook of the strengths perspective.

Acknowledgments

The authors who have contributed to this edition of the book have my deepest appreciation and gratitude. They are all very busy practitioners and scholars, but they are also committed to the strengths perspective. This, for them, was a labor of love—as you can tell from reading their work. I have derived great benefit and insight from reading their words, and I am sure you will too. These individuals do not just preach the sermon, they do the good work as well.

I would also like to thank the contributors to the first two editions: John Poertner, John Ronnau, Eloise Rathbone-McCuan, Julian Rappaport, Gary Holmes, and James Taylor. Their work on and dedication to the strengths approach continues. We would like to thank the reviewers for their suggestions: Robert Blundo, University of North Carolina at Wilmington; Julia B. Rauch, University of Maryland, Baltimore; LeAnne E. Silvey, Grand Valley State University; Richard Stagliano, Rutgers University; and Martha K. Wilson, Boise State University.

The editors at Longman, then Allyn and Bacon, have been extraordinarily supportive and patient. They have believed in this project from the inception of the first edition to this one. In particular, thanks to Janice Wiggins, Judith Fifer, and most recently, Alyssa Pratt and Karen Hanson. Without their encouragement, I am not at all sure that I would have attempted another edition of this book. Thanks, too, to Cheri L'Ecuyer at the School of Social Welfare. When I am floundering around with margins, fonts, headers, and footers, she sets it all straight and makes it look like a good manuscript should.

Finally, a word about two special people. Howard Goldstein died in 2000. He was one of the most intellectually audacious and bold scholars I have ever known. He also was a sensitive and skilled practitioner, and his concern for others always shone through. But his moral and intellectual vision for social work was unsurpassed in its clarity and reach. His chapter in this book is testament to the wondrous qualities of his mind and heart. We will miss him. The profession will miss him.

My wife, Ann Weick, is an exquisite partner in life and work. She is remarkable in the steadfastness of her belief in the strengths of others, her vision for this profession, and her love for those who have come to rely on her wisdom and caring.

CONTRIBUTORS

Bonnie Benard, M. S. W., is a nationally and internationally known figure in the field of prevention theory, policy, and practice. She is particularly recognized for introducing and conceptualizing resiliency theory and application beginning with her monograph, *Fostering Resiliency in Kids: Protective Factors in the Family, School and Community* (Northwest Regional Educational Laboratory, 1991). She holds a master's degree in social work. Bonnie has received many awards including the Award of Excellence from the National Prevention Network (1992), and the Spirit of Crazy Horse Award from the Black Hills Seminars (1997). She currently is the senior program associate with the Human Development Program at WestEd's Oakland, California, office.

Mary Bricker-Jenkins is a mother, farmer, writer, and social worker with a large public practice. As an academic, she is best known for her work and writings on feminist social work practice and public child welfare. She teaches social work practice at Temple University School of Social Work Practice and works as an ally in the growing movement to end poverty. She is an honorary member of the War Council of the Kensington Welfare Rights Union.

Edward R. Canda, Ph.D., is a professor and director of the doctoral program at the University of Kansas School of Social Welfare. He founded the Society for Spirituality and Social Work in 1990 and continues to serve on the advisory board. He has published more than 40 books, articles, and chapters on topics relating to spirituality and cultural diversity. His most recent books include *Transpersonal Perspectives on Spirituality in Social Work* (coedited with Elizabeth Smith, Haworth Press, in press) and *Spiritual Diversity in Social Work Practice: The Heart of Helping* (coauthored with Leola Dyrud Furman, Free Press, 1999).

Ronna Chamberlain, Ph.D., director of the office of Social Policy Analysis at the University of Kansas School of Social Welfare, first learned of the importance of a strengths perspective 20 years ago and has been a devotee since. One of the originators of the school's Strengths Model of Case Management, Dr. Chamberlain has continued to experiment with applications of the strengths model and is now particularly interested in its usefulness in developing social policy.

Rosemary Chapin, Ph.D., is an associate professor at the University of Kansas School of Social Welfare. She has extensive teaching, research, policy, and program development expertise in the long-term care area. She currently teaches social work and aging and social policy in the master's and doctoral programs at the School of Social Welfare. She also directs the Office of Aging and Long-Term Care at the school, and for the past 12 years has been involved in doing research and providing technical assistance to states to help craft long-term care policy. She has published widely in the area of long-term care policy and recently coauthored a handbook on strengths-based care management for older adults.

Charles D. Cowger, Ph.D., is the director of the School of Social Work at the University of Missouri, Columbia, where he also currently teaches a doctoral research course. International social development also occupies much of his time. He is president of the Inter-University Consortium for International Social Development. Formerly, he was on the faculty at the University of Illinois School of Social Work where he served in various administrative capacities. Other interests include woodworking, canoe backpacking, and pottery.

Becky Fast, M. S. W., is director of constituent casework services for U.S. Representative Dennis Moore (3rd Kansas congressional district). She joined Congressman Moore's staff after serving as an adjunct professor and manager of long-term care research and training at the School of Social Welfare, University of Kansas. She has presented nationally on the strengths perspective for case managers working with older adults and has recently published a manual entitled *Strengths-Based Care Management for Older Adults* (Health Professions Press, 2000).

Howard Goldstein, D. S. W., was active professionally and intellectually until his death in November 2000. Howard, never one to shirk from a challenge, was the editor of *Families in Society* at the time of his death and had just completed a monograph for the Council on Social Work Education, *Experiential Learning: A Foundation for Social Work Education and Practice.* He was a prolific author and a deft practitioner. He also was the intellectual and spiritual mentor to untold numbers of colleagues. His work in the cognitive and moral bases of practice, the promise of constructionist approaches, and, critically, on the esthetics of professional practice are unsurpassed in their audacity, clarity, and soundness. The profession and his friends will miss him deeply.

Jennifer C. Jones, M. S. W., L. S. W., is a recent graduate of Smith College School for Social Work. She is a member of the Kensington Welfare Rights Union's Education Committee, the Underground Railroad—Temple Depot, as well as the Social Welfare Action Alliance. She currently lives in Philadelphia and spends her time searching for the best ways to politicize her clinical practice through collective analysis and action.

Walter E. Kisthardt, Ph.D., is currently the interim program director and assistant professor with the Graduate Social Work Program at the University of Missouri, Kansas City. Dr. Kisthardt has provided training and technical assistance for human service programs in 39 states and in England. His original music and poetry have served to affirm and promote the principles of strengths-based practice.

Charles A. Rapp, Ph.D., is a professor at the University of Kansas School of Social Welfare. He holds a Ph.D. and M. S. W. from the University of Illinois and a B. S. from Milliken University. He is the codeveloper of the strengths model of case management and the client-centered performance model of social adminis-tration. His newest book, *The Strengths Model: Case Management with People Suffering from Severe and Persistent Mental Illness,* was published by the Oxford University Press in 1997.

Richard C. Rapp, M. S. W., L. I. S. W., is an assistant professor at the Wright State University School of Medicine, and clinical services developer and re-searcher with the Center for Interventions, Treatment, and Addictions Research at Wright State University. He is currently co-investigator and project director for two large treatment research projects. The Continuing Study of Case Manage-ment Treatment Enhancements project is a National Institute on Drug Abuse pro-ject examining case management as a way to improve treatment retention and outcomes. The Substance Abuse Treatment Continuum for Offenders Project is sponsored by the National Institute on Justice and the Ohio Department of Reha-bilitation and Correction.

Dennis Saleebey, D. S. W., is a Professor at the School of Social Welfare, Univer-sity of Kansas. He has been involved in a variety of small community-based pro-jects over the past 12 years that have had a strengths perspective as a core value and operating principles based on the inherent capacities of residents and local associations. He has written and lectured widely on the strengths perspective as well as alternative methods of professional knowing and doing, and the biopsy-chosocial nature of mental illness and health. His book, *Human Behavior and Social Environments,* was published by Columbia University Press in 2001.

Carol A. Snively, M. S. W., M. A., is an assistant professor of social work at the University of Missouri, Columbia. She is completing her doctorate at the Ohio State University. Her research focuses on youth involvement in community change, and addiction among adolescents and women, and effective helping strategies for minority youth. Carol is a registered/board certified art therapist and is exploring the use of art making as a tool in community organization.

W. Patrick Sullivan, Ph.D., is a professor at the Indiana School of Social Work, Indianapolis, and former director of the Indiana Division of Mental Health. His pri-mary interests are services to those facing serious and persistent mental illnesses, alcohol and drug treatment, and public policy. He was involved in the initial pilot case management projects that helped develop the principles and practices of the strengths model.

Margaret Waller, Ph.D., is an associate professor in the School of Social Work, Ari-zona State University, and has been a family therapist since 1982. She teaches human behavior, cultural diversity, and clinical practice with families. Her research and writing centers on intercultural understanding and resilience in individuals, families, and communities, with particular emphasis on Indigenous Peoples.

Ann Weick, Ph.D., is dean and professor at the University of Kansas School of Social Welfare. Her publications explore the philosophical underpinnings of social work practice from a variety of vantage points, including the continuing development of the strengths perspective. Her most recent essays probe the philosophical, historical, and metaphysical bases for current social work practice.

Michael Yellow Bird, Ph.D., is an associate professor in the School of Social Work, Arizona State University. He has held previous faculty appointments at the University of Kansas and the University of British Columbia. He teaches social work practice and cultural diversity. His current research and writing focus on the effects of colonialism on Indigenous Peoples in the United States, the politics of Indigenous People's racial identity labels, and theories of First Nations masculinity.

CHAPTER

1

Introduction

Power in the People[1]

DENNIS SALEEBEY

The idea of building on clients' strengths has achieved the status of adage in the lore of professional social work. Authors of textbooks, educators, and practitioners all regularly acknowledge the importance of this principle. Many of these calls to attend to the capacities and competencies of clients are little more than professional cant. So let us be clear: The strengths perspective is a dramatic departure from conventional social work practice. Practicing from a strengths orientation means this—*everything* you do as a social worker will be predicated, in some way, on helping to discover and embellish, explore and exploit clients' strengths and resources in the service of assisting them to achieve their goals, realize their dreams, and shed the irons of their own inhibitions and misgivings, and society's domination. This is a versatile practice approach, relying heavily on the ingenuity and creativity, the courage and common sense, of both clients and their social workers. It is a collaborative process depending on clients and workers to be purposeful agents and not mere functionaries. It is an approach honoring the innate wisdom of the human spirit, the inherent capacity for transformation of even the most humbled and abused. When you adopt the strengths approach to practice, you can expect exciting changes in the character of your work and in the tenor of your relationships with your clients.

Many of us believe (or have at one time believed) that we are building on client strengths. But sometimes we fall short. To really practice from a strengths perspective demands a different way of seeing clients, their environments, and their current situation. Rather than focusing exclusively or dominantly on problems, your eye turns toward possibility. In the thicket of trauma, pain, and trouble you can see blooms of hope and transformation. The formula is simple: Mobilize clients' strengths (talents, knowledge, capacities, resources) in the service of achieving their goals and visions and the clients will have a better quality of life on

---

[1]Part of this chapter is based on D. Saleebey, The strengths perspective in social work: Extensions and cautions. *Social Work, 41*(3), 1996, 295–305. With permission of the National Association of Social Workers.

their terms. Though the recipe is uncomplicated, as you will see, the work is hard. In the chapters that follow, you will encounter descriptions of the strengths approach used with a variety of populations, in a variety of circumstances. You will be exposed to schemes of assessment, methods of employment, examples of application, and discussions of issues related to moving from a concentration on problems to a fascination with strengths.

In the past few years, there has been an increasing interest in developing strengths-based approaches to practice, case management in particular, with a variety of client groups—the elderly, youth in trouble, people with addictions, people with chronic mental illness, even communities and schools (Benard, 1994; Clark, 1997; Kretzmann & McKnight, 1993; Miller & Berg, 1995; Mills, 1995; Parsons & Cox, 1994; Rapp, 1998). In addition, rapidly developing literature, inquiry, and practice methods in a variety of fields bear a striking similarity to the strengths perspective—developmental resilience, healing and wellness, solution-focused therapy, assets-based community development, and narrative and story to name a few. The impetus for these elaborations comes from many sources, but of singular importance is a reaction to our culture's continued obsession and fascination with psychopathology, victimization, abnormality, and moral and interpersonal aberrations. A swelling conglomerate of businesses and professions, institutions and agencies, from medicine to pharmaceuticals, from the insurance industry to the mass media, turn handsome profits by assuring us that we are in the clutch (or soon will be) of any number of emotional, physical, or behavioral maladies. Each of us, it seems, is a reservoir of vulnerabilities and weaknesses usually born of toxic experiences in early life. The *Diagnostic and Statistical Manual of Mental Disorders IV* (American Psychiatric Association, 1994) and its most recent iteration, DSM IV TR (Text Revision) (APA, 2000), have twice the volume of text on disorders as the previous edition DSM IIIR, with only seven years between the publication of DSM IIIR and DSM IV.

Not only are we mesmerized by disease and disorder, many of us have been designated as casualties by the ever growing phalanx of mental health professionals, turning mental health into a thriving and handsomely rewarding business. Prodded by a variety of gurus, swamis, ministers, and therapists, some of us are in hot pursuit of our wounded inner children and find ourselves dripping with the residue of the poisons of our family background. If you listen carefully, you can hear the echoes of evangelism in some of these current cultural fixations. And these are cultural preoccupations as well. The Jerry Springer show is no anomaly, except perhaps in regard to the level of schtick and tastelessness it exudes. Kenneth Gergen (1994) sees the result of this symbiosis between mental health professions and culture, as a rapidly accelerating "cycle of progressive infirmity" (p. 155). He wryly observes,

> How may I fault thee? Let me count the ways: impulsive personality, malingering, reactive depression, anorexia, mania, attention deficit disorder, psychopathia, external control orientation, low self-esteem . . . (p. 148)

To make these observations is not to callously disregard the real pains and struggles of individuals, families, and communities; neither is it to casually avert our glance from the realities of abuse of all kinds inflicted on children; nor is it to deny the tenacious grip and beguiling thrall of addictions. It is, however, to foreswear the ascendancy of psychopathology as society's principal civic, moral, and medical categorical imperative. It is to denounce the idea that most people who experience hurt, trauma, and neglect inevitably suffer wounds and become less than they might be. It is to return a semblance of balance to the equation of understanding and helping those who are hurting. The balance is hard to come by because the language of strength and resilience is nascent and just developing and, therefore, scant. Sybil and Steve Wolin (1997) say this about the two paradigms (risk and resiliency):

> As a result, the resiliency paradigm is no match for the risk paradigm, Talking about the human capacity to repair from harm, inner strengths, and protective factors, professionals feel that they have entered alien territory. They grope for words and fear sounding unschooled and naïve when they replace pathology terminology with the more mundane vocabulary of resourcefulness, hope, creativity, competence, and the like. . . . We believe that the struggle can be tipped in the other direction by offering a systematic, developmental vocabulary of strengths that can stand up to pathology terminology that is standard in our field. (p. 27)

Social work, like other helping professions, has not been immune to the contagion of disease- and disorder-based thinking. Social work has constructed much of its theory and practice around the supposition that clients become clients because they have deficits, problems, pathologies, and diseases; that they are, in some essential way, flawed or weak. This orientation leaps from a past in which the certitude of conception about the moral defects of the poor, the despised, and the deviant captivated us. More sophisticated terminology prevails today, but the metaphors and narratives that guide our thinking and acting, often papered over with more salutary language, are sometimes negative constructions that are fateful for the future of those we help. The diction and symbolism of weakness, failure, and deficit shape how others regard clients, how clients regard themselves, and how resources are allocated to groups of clients. In the extreme, such designations may even invoke punitive sanctions.

The lexicon of pathology gives voice to a number of assumptions and these in turn have painted pictures of clients in vivid but not very flattering tones. Some of these assumptions and their consequences are summarized below.

The person is the problem or pathology named. Diagnostic labels of all kinds tend to become "master statuses" (Becker, 1963), designations and roles that subsume all others under their mantle. A person suffering from schizophrenia *becomes* a schizophrenic, a convention so common that we hardly give it a thought. Once labeled a schizophrenic, other elements of a person's character, experiences, knowledge, aspirations, slowly recede into the background, replaced by the language of symptom and syndrome. Inevitably, conversation about the person becomes dominated by the imagery of disease, and relationships with the ailing person re-form around such representations. To the extent that these labels take hold, the individual, through a process of surrender and increasing dependence, becomes the once alien identification (Gergen, 1994; Goffman, 1961; Scheff, 1984). These are not value neutral terms, either. They serve to separate those who suffer these "ailments" from those who do not; a distinction that if not physical (as in hospitalization) is at least moral. Those who are labeled, in ways both subtle and brutish, are degraded—certainly in terms of social regard and status. However, these labels provide a measure of relief for some suffering individuals and their families—knowing, finally, what the matter is. In addition labels are certainly better than being thought of as possessed by demons. Nonetheless they do create a situation for far too many individuals of self-enfeeblement—moral, psychological, and civil (Gergen, 1994, p. 150).

The language of pessimism and doubt: Professional cynicism. Accentuating the problems of clients creates a wave of pessimistic expectations of, and predictions about, the client, the client's environment, and the client's capacity to cope with that environment. Furthermore, these labels have the insidious potential, repeated over time, to alter how individuals see themselves and how others see them. In the long run, these changes seep into the individual's identity. Paulo Freire (1996) maintained for many years that the views and expectations of oppressors have an uncanny and implacable impact on the oppressed. Under the weight of these once-foreign views, the oppressed begin to subjugate their own knowledge and understanding to those of their tormentors.

The focus on what is wrong often reveals an egregious doubt about the ability of individuals to cope with life's challenges or to rehabilitate themselves. Andrew Weil (1995) laments the profound pessimism and negativity in his own profession, medicine, about the body's innate inclination to transform, regenerate, and heal itself.

> I cannot help feeling embarrassed by my profession when I hear the myriad ways in which doctors convey their pessimism to patients. I . . . am working to require instruction in medical school about the power of words and the need for physicians to use extreme care in choosing the words they speak to patients. A larger subject is the problem of making doctors more conscious of the power projected on them by patients and the possibilities for reflecting that power back in ways that influence health for better rather than worse, that stimulate rather than retard spontaneous healing. (p. 64)

The situation is so bad that Weil refers to it as medical *hexing*—dire medical predictions and inimical attributions by physicians powerful enough to create anxiety, fear, depression, and resignation in patients. This is a common consequence of the biomedical model—a model that has profoundly influenced some fields of social work practice. The biomedical model and its more widely influential kin in the human service professions, the "Technical/Rationalist" model (Schön, 1983), are despairing of natural healing and people's capacity to know what is right. Extraordinarily materialistic, these models disregard the functional wholeness and fitness of anything under their scrutiny—including human beings. Social work's continuing emphasis on problems and disorders and the profession's increasing commerce with theories that focus on deficits and pathologies tend to promote the portrayal of individuals as sites of specific problems and as medleys of singular deficiencies. Such an attitude takes the social work profession away from its avowed and historical interest in the person-in-context, the understanding of the web of institutional and interpersonal relationships in which any person is enmeshed, and the possibility for rebirth and renewal even under dire circumstances.

Distance, power inequality, control, and manipulation mark the relationship between helper and helped. The idea that we have empirically grounded or theoretically potent techniques to apply is beguiling. But in some way it may create distance between clients and helpers. Distance itself, whether the distance of class, privileged knowledge, institutionalized role, or normative position, may imply a power inequality between helper and helped. In the end, the client's view may become fugitive or irrelevant. In discussing "resistant" clients, Miller and colleagues (1997) say this:

> If a therapist . . . suggests or implies that the client's point of view is wrong, somehow invalidates [sic], or upstages [sic] the client, 'resistance' may appear. After all, even if not already demoralized, who wants to be reminded of failure, criticized, and judged, or made to feel that you have to follow orders? What we come to call resistance may sometimes reflect the client's attempt to salvage a small portion of self-respect. As such, some cases become impossible simply because the treatment allows the client no way of 'saving face' or upholding dignity. (p. 12)

The surest route to detachment and a kind of depersonalization is the building of a case—assembling a portfolio on the client created from the identity-stripping descriptions of, for example, DSM IV TR or the juvenile justice code. Furthermore, the legal and political mandates of many agencies, the elements of social control embodied in both the institution and ethos of the agency, may strike a further blow to the possibility of partnership and collaboration between client and helper.

Context-stripping. Problem-based assessments encourage individualistic rather than ecological accounts of clients. When we transform persons into cases, we often see only them and how well they fit into a category. In this way, we miss important elements of the client's life—cultural, social, political, ethnic, spiritual, and economic—and how they contribute to, sustain, and shape a person's misery or struggles or mistakes. The irony here is that, in making a case we really do not individualize. Rather, we are in the act of finding an appropriate diagnostic niche for the individual, thus making the client one among many and not truly unique. All individuals suffering from bipolar disorder hence become more like each other and less distinctive. In doing this, we selectively destroy or at least ignore contextual information that, although not salient to our assessment scheme, might well reveal the abiding distinctiveness of the individual in this particular context. It might also indicate important resources for help and transformation as well as problem-solving.

The supposition of disease assumes a cause for the disorder and, thus, a solution. Naming the poison leads to an antidote. But in the world of human relationships and experiences, the idea of a regression line between cause, disease, and cure ignores the steamy morass of uncertainty and complexity that is the human condition. It also happens to take out of the hands of the person, family and friends, the neighborhood—the daily lifeworld of all involved—the capacity and resources for change. There are many cultural and spiritual avenues for transformation and healing. They, rightly enough, also suppose linkages between the nature of the problem (is it natural or unnatural? spiritual or mundane?) and its relief. But to bury these tools under the weight of a medico-scientific model is to inter a variety of familial and cultural media for change.

Remedies in the lifeworld usually begin with reinterpretations of the problem that come out of continuing dialogue with the situation and with clients. These renderings are mutually crafted constructs that may only be good for this client, at this time, under these conditions. Though they may have the power to transform clients' understandings, choices, and actions, these expositions are tentative and provisional. The capacity to devise such interpretations depends not on a strict relationship between problem and solution but on intuition, tacit knowing, hunches, and conceptual risk taking (Saleebey, 1989). Schön (1983) has characterized the tension between the usual conception of professional knowing and doing and this more reflective one as that between rigor and relevance. Relevance asks these questions of us: To what extent are clients consulted about matters pertinent to them? What do they want? What do they need? How do they think they can get it? How do they see their situation—problems as well as possibilities? What values do they want to maximize? How have they managed to survive thus far? These and similar questions, as answers draw near, move us a step toward a deeper appreciation of all clients' distinctive attributes, abilities, and competencies, and the world of their experience. They require of the social worker and the client a degree of reflection, the interest in making meaning and making sense. Iris Murdoch said that when we return home and share our day

> We are artfully shaping material into story form. So in a way as word-users we all exist in a literary atmosphere, we live and breathe literature, we are all literary artists, we are constantly employing language to make interesting forms out of experience which perhaps originally seemed dull or incoherent. (cited in Mattingly, 1991, p. 237)

Finding the words that shout the reality of the lived experience of people, and perhaps finding other words that reflect genuine possibility and hope is, in a modest and unscientific sense, finding cause for celebration—of promise.

The Strengths Perspective: Philosophy, Concepts, and Principles

I want to discuss two major philosophical principles as a way of staking out the claims of the strengths perspective, but in the context of the sometimes numbing and usually complex realities of daily life.

Liberation and Empowerment: Heroism and Hope

Liberation is founded on the idea of possibility: the opportunities for choice, commitment, and action whether pursued in relative tranquility or in grievous circumstance. We have fabulous powers and potentials. Some are muted, unrealized, and immanent. Others glimmer brilliantly about us. All around are people and policies, circumstances and conventions, contingencies and conceptions that may nurture and emancipate these powers or that may crush and degrade them. Somewhere within, and we may call it by different names, lies the longing for the heroic: to transcend circumstances, to develop one's own powers, to face adversity down, to stand up and be counted. All too often social institutions, oppressors, other people, some even with good intentions, tamp out this yearning or distort it so that it serves the interests and purposes of others. Nonetheless, however muted, this precious craving abides. It is incumbent on the healer, the humane leader, the shaman, the teacher, and, yes, the social worker to find ways for this penchant for the possible and unimaginable to survive and find expression in life-affirming ways. Of course, things go more smoothly if people simply play their roles and pay their taxes. Liberation exerts tremendous pressure on the repressive inclinations of institutions and individuals. Collectively, liberation unleashes human energy and spirit, critical thinking, the questioning of authority, challenges to the conventional wisdom, and new ways of being and doing. But liberation may also be modest and unassuming. We may try out new behaviors, forge new relationships, or make a new commitment. Hope and the belief in the possible is central to liberation. Before his death, the great pedagogue of liberation, Paulo Freire, wrote in his last book, *Pedagogy of Hope* (1996), that he had previously underestimated the power of hope.

> But the attempt to do without hope, in the struggle to improve the world, as if that struggle could be reduced to calculated acts alone, or a purely scientific approach, is a frivolous illusion. To attempt to do without hope, which is based on the need for truth as an ethical quality of the struggle, is tantamount to denying that struggler as one of its mainstays . . . [H]ope, as an ontological need, demands an anchoring in practice. . . . Without a minimum of hope, we cannot so much as start the struggle. (pp. 8–9)

Alienation and Oppression: Anxiety and Evil

The circumstances around us will not let us deny the existence of harsh and tyrannical institutions, relationships, circumstances, and regimes. Bigotry, hatred, war, slaughter, repression, and, more quietly but no less devastating, setting people aside, treating them as the despised other, and acting as though they are not fully human, are all daily reminders of the existence of evil, brutality, and despotism. But why is the capacity for evil the seeming companion to the urge to the heroic?

How often do we stand, agape, horrified at what we see or hear about or read about? Vicious acts of cruelty, violence born of intolerance and hate—how can they happen, we cry? Yet, aren't there times when we have been propelled to act or been a party to actions that have inflicted emotional or physical pain on others, often those who are different from us? Why?

We are small, and vulnerable. The cosmos is enormous. We tremble at the insignificance and frailty of our being when cast against the magnitude of time and the vastness of space. At times, our fear and trembling is best handled by taking matters into our own hands, individually or collectively, and dealing the instrumentalities of fear and loathing onto others. Thus we subdue our own uncertainties and obscure our very paltriness. It may even be that some of these acts of violence or marginalizing are "immortality projects" designed to blind us to the reality of our own organismic vulnerability and eventual demise (Becker, 1973; Fromm, 1973; Rank, 1941).

But from the ashes of destruction, mayhem, and oppression may emerge the human spirit, the capacity for the heroic. So we can never dismiss the possibility of redemption, resurrection, and regeneration. However, the sweep of history, the grandeur of wholesale creation and destruction eventually find their way into the nooks and crannies of our lives. These sweeping generalities occur in the small confines of daily life as well. You see a single mother and her 10-year-old daughter. They have come to the family service agency you work for. The mother is worried. Her daughter, once sweet and compliant, a joy to be around, is becoming morose, uncommunicative, anxious, and weepy. The quality of her work at school is plummeting, and friends seem unimportant to her. Father left the family suddenly and left them in dire financial straits. It had been a marriage of youthful misjudgments the mother allows, but, she says, in spite of the financial hardships maybe it is better that he has gone. The mother wonders if her daughter's current woes aren't related to his leaving about 6 months ago. You spend considerable time over the next weeks exploring the situation with the mother and daughter. Eventually you discover that for a period of almost 2 years the young girl had experienced physical and sexual depredation and brutality at the hands of her father. She had vowed never to tell anyone—to herself! Never let him know how much he had hurt her. Never! And she maintained her vow until he left. Now she was falling apart, grieving, experiencing rage, and feeling the wounds of violation. But in the ashes of devastation, this young girl's spirit, against all odds, flourished. Now the mother and the social worker must make an alliance with this tiny, amazing soul.

We have seen that the preoccupation with problems and pathologies, while producing an impressive lode of technical and theoretical writing, may be less fruitful when it comes to actually helping clients grow, develop, change directions, realize their visions, or revise their personal meanings and narratives. What follows is a brief glossary of terms supporting an orientation to strengths as well as a statement of the principles of practice central to a strengths perspective. These are meant to give you a vital sense of what a frame of mind devoted to the strengths of individuals and groups requires.

The Lexicon of Strengths

"We can act," wrote William James (1902) in reflecting upon Immanuel Kant's notions about conceptions, "as *if* there were a God; feel as *if* we were free; consider nature as *if* she were full of special designs; lay plans as *if* we were to be immortal; and we find then that these words **do** [emphasis added] make a genuine difference in our moral life" (p. 55). Language and words have power. They can elevate and inspire or demoralize and destroy. If words are a part of the nutriment that feeds one's sense of self, then we are compelled to examine our dictionary of helping to see what our words portend for clients. Any approach to practice speaks a language that, in the end, may have a pronounced effect on the way that clients think of themselves and how they act. Not only that, our professional diction has a profound effect on the way that *we* regard clients, their world, and their troubles. In the strengths approach to practice, some words are essential and direct us to an appreciation of the assets of individuals, families, and communities.

Empowerment.   Although rapidly becoming hackneyed, empowerment indicates the intent to, and the processes of, assisting individuals, groups, families, and communities to discover and expend the resources and tools within and around them. Stephen Rose (2000) says this about empowerment practice as he came to understand it in his career:

> Central to this [empowerment] practice was understanding the notion as a relational expression, not a technique or instrument. In empowering relationships, meaning was restored to each person; earned trust was built into the explicit acknowledgement of the purpose of the practice; interactions were explored for their links to social structures and their interests; and clients' lives were envisioned simultaneously as unique in terms of meaning, but collective or population-based in terms of patterns of domination and system barriers to validity. (p. 412)

To discover the power within people and communities, we must subvert and abjure pejorative labels; provide opportunities for connections to family, institutional, and communal resources; assail the victim mind-set; foreswear paternalism; trust people's intuitions, accounts, perspectives, and energies; and believe in people's dreams. Barbara Levy Simon (1994) builds the concept of empowerment with five necessary ideas: collaborative partnerships with clients and constituents; an emphasis on the expansion of client strengths and capacities; a focus on both the individual or family and the environment; assuming that clients are active subjects and agents; and directing one's energies to the historically disenfranchised and oppressed. Pursuing the empowerment agenda requires a deep conviction about the necessity of democracy. It requires us to address the tensions and conflicts, the institutions and people that subdue and limit those we help, and compels us to help people free themselves from these restraints (Pinderhughes, 1994). Too often, helping professions (although social work has been very wary of falling into this trap) have thwarted this imperative by assuming a paternalistic posture, informing people about what is good for them, and exhorting people to do the right thing. The strengths approach imposes a different attitude and commitment. The strengths of individuals and communities are renewable and expandable resources. Furthermore, the assets of individuals almost always lie embedded in a community of interest and involvement. Thus, the ideas of community and membership are central to the strengths approach.

Membership.   To be without membership, writes Michael Walzer, is to be in a "condition of infinite danger" (1983, p. 32). To be without membership is to be alienated, to be at risk for marginalization and oppression. People need to be citizens, responsible and valued members of a community. To sever people from the roots of their "place" subverts, for all, civic and moral vigor. The strengths orientation proceeds from the recognition that all of those whom we serve are, like ourselves, members of a species, entitled to the dignity, respect, and responsibility that comes with such membership. But, too often, people we help have either no place to be (or to be comfortable) or no sense of belonging. The sigh of relief from those who come to be members and citizens and bask in the attendant rights and responsibilities, assurances and securities, is the first breath of empowerment. There is another meaning of membership and that is that people must often band together to make their voices heard, get their needs met, to redress inequities, and to reach their dreams. Jonathon Kozol writes eloquently about the lived experience of people, especially children, who are poor and struggle with the ignorance, hostility, lack of regard, and destructive policies of the outside world. He describes places of refuge, resurrection, and membership. St. Ann's Church and School in the South Bronx is one such place. Here, Mother Martha, the pastor, invites the membership of children and adults. The reality of segregation and separation from the mainstream is never very far from the halls of St. Ann's.

> Despite the isolation and betrayal that may be suggested by these governing realities, St. Ann's is not a place of sorrow, but at least during the hours when children fill its corridors and classrooms with their voices and their questions and their paperpads and their notebooks and their games, it is a place of irresistible vitality and energy and sometimes complicated hope, and now and then uncomplicated joy. For grown-ups in the neighborhood, it is an energizing place as well, although the burdens that they bring with them when they come here in times of crisis to seek out the priest can often seem at first overwhelming. (2000, p. 33)

The same kind of trustful energy is poured into community-building and neighborhood development projects all over this country. In her investigation of programs that work Lisbeth Schorr (1997) says this about successful community building programs:

> Community building . . . is more an orientation than a technique, more a mission than a program, more an outlook than an activity. It catalyzes a process of change grounded in local life and priorities. Community building addresses the developmental needs of individuals, families, and organizations within the neighborhood.

It changes the nature of the relationship between the neighborhood and the systems outside its boundaries. A community's own strengths—whether they are found in churches, block clubs, local leadership, or its problem-solving abilities—are seen as central. (pp. 361–362)

You can see that the ingredients of the strengths perspective abound in this definition of community building—empowerment, membership, and, certainly, indigenous resilience.

Resilience.   There is a growing body of inquiry and practice that makes it clear that the rule, not the exception, in human affairs is that people do rebound from serious trouble, that individuals and communities do surmount and overcome serious and troubling adversity.

> At best or worst, depending on one's perspective, only about a third [of children who face dramatic stress] generally succumb; approximately two thirds do not. The purpose of resilience research is to learn how and why [this two thirds] beat the odds. (Wolin & Wolin, 1996, p. 246)

Much of this literature documents and demonstrates that particularly demanding and stressful experiences, even ongoing ones, *do not lead inevitably to vulnerability, failure to adapt, and psychopathology* (Katz, 1997; Werner & Smith, 1992; Wolin & Wolin, 1996). Resilience is not the cheerful disregard of one's difficult and traumatic life experiences; neither is it the naive discounting of life's pains. It is, rather, the ability to bear up in spite of these ordeals. Damage has been done. Emotional and physical scars bear witness to that. In spite of the wounds, however, for many the trials have been instructive and propitious. Resilience is a process—the continuing growth and articulation of capacities, knowledge, insight, and virtues derived through meeting the demands and challenges of one's world, however chastening.

Healing and Wholeness.   Healing implies both wholeness and the inborn facility of the body and the mind to regenerate and resist when faced with disorder, disease, and disruption. Healing also requires a beneficent relationship between the individual and the larger social and physical environment. The natural state of affairs for human beings, evolved over eons of time and at every level of organization from cell to self-image, is the repair of one's mind and body. Just as the resilience literature assures us that individuals have naturally occurring self-righting tendencies, even though they can be compromised (Werner & Smith, 1992), it seems also the case that all human organisms have the inclination for healing. This evolutionary legacy, of course, can be compromised by trauma, by environmental toxins, by bodily disorganization, and, not the least, by some of our professional intervention philosophies and systems. But, the bottom line is this: If spontaneous healing occurs miraculously in one human being, you can expect it to occur in another and another. Such organismic ingenuity only makes common sense. Otherwise, how could we have survived as a species for hundreds of thousands of years without hospitals, HMOs, physicians, psychiatrists, pharmacists, or talk show hosts? Healing occurs when the healer or the individual makes an alliance with, or instigates the power of, the organism to restore itself (Cousins, 1989; Pelletier, 2000; Weil, 1995). So healing and self-regeneration are intrinsic life support systems, always working and, for most of us, most of the time, on call. Such a reality has dramatic implications, not just for medicine but for all the helping professions. At the least, it challenges the assumption of the disease model that only experts know what is best for their clients and that curing, healing, or transformation comes exclusively from outside sources. At some level of consciousness, as Roger Mills (1995) reminds us, we have a native wisdom about what is right for us and what we should do when confronted with organismic or environmental challenges.

Dialogue and Collaboration.   Humans can only come into being through a creative and emergent relationship with others. Without such transactions, there can be no discovery and testing of one's powers, no knowledge, no heightening of one's awareness and internal strengths. In dialogue, we confirm the importance of others and begin to heal the rift between self, other, and institution.

Dialogue requires empathy, identification with, and the inclusion of other people. Paulo Freire (1973) was convinced, based on his years of work with oppressed peoples, that only humble and loving dialogue can surmount the barrier of mistrust built from years of paternalism and the rampant subjugation of the knowledge and wisdom of the oppressed. "Founding itself upon love, humility, and faith, dialogue becomes a horizontal relationship of which mutual trust between the dialoguers is the logical consequence" (pp. 79–80). A caring community is a community that confirms otherness, in part by giving each person and group a ground of their own, and affirming this ground through encounters that are egalitarian and dedicated to healing and empowerment.

The idea of collaboration has a more specific focus. When we work together with clients we become their agents, their consultants, stakeholders with them in mutually crafted projects. This requires us to be open to negotiation and to appreciate the authenticity of the views and aspirations of those with whom we collaborate. Our voices may have to be quieted so that we can give voice to our clients. Comfortably ensconced in the expert role, we may have great difficulty assuming such a conjoint posture.

Suspension of Disbelief.   It would be hard to exaggerate the extent of disbelief of clients' words and stories in the culture of professionalism. While social work because of its enduring values may fancy itself less culpable in this regard than other professions, a little circumspection is warranted. As just one example (and probably somewhat unfair because this is a brief excerpt from a text on social work practice that generally assumes a positive view of clients), Hepworth and Larsen (1990) wrote:

> Though it is the primary source of information, verbal report is vulnerable to error because of possible faulty recall, distorted perceptions, biases, and limited self-awareness on the part of clients. It is thus vital to avoid the tendency to accept clients' views, descriptions, and reports as valid representations of reality. Similarly,

it is important to recognize that feelings expressed by clients may emanate from faulty perceptions or may be altogether irrational. (p. 197)

Two observations: First, the idea that there are valid representations of reality is questionable. That is, there are many representations of the real world. Is, say, a Lakota understanding of fever any less relevant in context than a Manhattan internist's? Second, to begin work with clients in this frame of mind would seem to subvert the idea that clients often do know exactly what they are talking about and that they are experts on their own lives. And, are social workers own interpretations less subject to faulty recall, or their own interpretive forestructures less likely to be slathered over clients' own understanding? Perhaps, the suspension of belief in clients' accounts comes from the radiation of scientific thinking throughout our culture and into the professions. The ideal of the scientific investigator as objective and dispassionate observer has been transfigured into a certain incredulity about, and distancing from, clients. If the rise of the professions (and the ideology of professionalism) was part of the extension and reinforcement of the institutions of socialization and social control during the Victorian era, then a certain detachment and restraint in accepting clients and their stories made sense (Bledstein, 1978).

Professionals have contained the affirmation of clients in a number of ways:

- by imposing their own theories over the theories and accounts of clients
- by using assessment in an interrogative style designed to ascertain certain diagnostic and largely preemptive hypotheses that, in the end, confirm suspicions about the client
- by engaging in self-protective maneuvers (like skepticism) designed to prevent the ultimate embarrassment for a professional—being fooled by or lied to by a cunning client

The frequent talk about manipulative and resistant clients in many social agencies may stem from the fear of being made the fool. To protect self-esteem, nonnormative lifestyles, self-interests, or benefits, clients may have a vested interest in not telling the truth. But we must consider the possibility that avoiding the truth may be a function of the manner in which the professional pursues and/or asserts the truth. The professional's knowledge, information, and perspective are privileged and carry institutional and legal weight. The client's do not.

In summary, the lexicon of strengths provides us with a vocabulary of appreciation and not aspersion about those with whom we work. In essence, the effort is to move away from defining professional work as the articulation of the power of expert knowledge toward collaboration with the power within the individual or community toward a life that is palpably better—and better on the clients' own terms.

Principles of the Strengths Perspective

The principles that follow are the guiding assumptions and regulating understandings of the strengths perspective. They are tentative, still maturing, and subject to revision and modulation. They do, however, give a flavor of what practicing from a strengths appreciation involves.

Every Individual, Group, Family, and Community Has Strengths.   While it may be hard at times to invoke, it is essential to remind oneself that the person or family in front of you and the community around you possess assets, resources, wisdom, and knowledge that, at the outset, you probably know nothing about. First *and* foremost, the strengths perspective is about discerning those resources, and respecting them and the potential they may have for reversing misfortune, countering illness, easing pain, and reaching goals. To detect strengths, however, the social work practitioner must be genuinely interested in, and respectful of, clients' stories, narratives, and accounts—the interpretive slants they take on their own experiences. These are the most important "theories" that guide practice. The unearthing of clients' identities and realities does not come only from a ritual litany of troubles, embarrassments, snares, foibles, and barriers. Rather, clients come into view when you assume that they know something, have learned lessons from experience, have hopes, have interests, and can do some things masterfully. These may be obscured by the stresses of the moment, submerged under the weight of crisis, oppression, or illness but, nonetheless, they abide.

In the end, clients want to know that you actually care about them, that how they fare makes a difference to you, that you will listen to them, that you will respect them no matter what their history, and that you believe that they can build something of value with the resources within and around them. But most of all, clients want to know that you believe they can surmount adversity and begin the climb toward transformation and growth.

Trauma and Abuse, Illness and Struggle May Be Injurious but They May also Be Sources of Challenge and Opportunity.   The Wolins (1997) point out that the "damage model" of development so prevalent in today's thinking only leads to discouragement, pessimism, and the victim mind-set. It also foretells a continuing future of psychopathology and troubled relationships. Individuals exposed to a variety of abuses, especially in childhood, are thought always to be victims or to be damaged in ways that obscure or override any strengths or possibilities for redemption or rebound. In the Wolins' "challenge model," children are not seen as merely passive recipients of parental unpredictability, abuse, disappointment, or violence. Rather, children are seen as active and developing individuals who, through these trials, learn skills and develop personal attributes that stand them in good stead in adulthood. Not that they do not suffer. They do. Not that they do not bear scars. They do. But they also may acquire traits and capacities that are preservative and life affirming. There is dignity to be drawn from having prevailed over obstacles to one's growth and maturing. The Wolins (1993) refer to this as "survivor's pride." It is a deep-dwelling sense of accomplishment in having met life's challenges and walked away, not without fear, even terror, and certainly not without wounds. Often this pride is buried under embarrassment, confusion, distraction, or self-doubt. But when it exists and is lit, it can ignite the engine of change.

Individuals, groups, and communities are more likely to continue development and growth when they are funded by the currency of capacities, knowledge, and skills (Delgado, 2000; Kretzmann & McKnight, 1993). While the strengths perspective is powered by a similar belief, the observation of many who practice using a strengths approach is that many people who struggle to find their daily bread, a job, or shelter are already resilient, resourceful, and, though in pain, motivated for achievement on their terms. Kaplan and Girard (1994) put it this way:

> People are more motivated to change when their strengths are supported. Instead of asking family members what their problems are, a worker can ask what strengths they bring to the family and what they think are the strengths of other family members. Through this process the worker helps the family discover its capabilities and formulate a new way to think about themselves. . . . The worker creates a language of strength, hope, and movement. . . . (p. 53)

Assume That You Do Not Know the Upper Limits of the Capacity to Grow and Change and Take Individual, Group, and Community Aspirations Seriously.

Too often, professionals assume that a diagnosis, an assessment, or a profile sets the parameters of possibility for their clients. In our personal lives, looking back, we sometimes marvel at the road we traveled—a road that we, at the outset, might not have even considered taking—and the distance that we have come. For our clients, too often, we cannot imagine the prospect of similar dizzying and unanticipated destinations. The diagnosis or the assessment becomes a verdict and a sentence. Our clients will be better served when we make an overt pact with their promise and possibility. This means that we must hold high our expectations of clients and make allegiance with their hopes, visions, and values. In speaking of people struggling with serious addictions, most of whom recover on their own, Peele and Brodsky (1991) say,

> More often than not people rise to the occasion when they are given positive options. People typically strive to set their lives straight, and given time, usually succeed. Age tends to ameliorate or eliminate bad habits while bringing greater self-contentment and improved coping. Nearly all people have values that are incompatible with their addictions—the most remarkable cases of "instantaneous" cure occur when these values [and, I might add, visions] crystallize so that people reject the addiction. (pp. 162–163)

It is becoming increasingly clear that emotions have a profound effect on wellness and health. Emotions experienced as positive can activate the inner pharmacoepia, those chemicals that relax, help fight infection, and restore. This is undoubtedly part of our evolutionary success; our ability to adapt to situations, even highly toxic ones, that were not foretold in our genome (Damasio, 1994). When people believe that they can recover, that they have prospects, that their hopes are palpable, their bodies often respond optimally. That does not mean that people do not get sick. It does mean that when people are sick, healers can make an alliance with the body's regenerative powers and augment them with real but nonetheless fortifying and uplifting expectations (Weil, 1995). Roger Mills's (1995) health realization/community empowerment projects (detailed in Chapter 13) are based on similar principles. Mills's idea is that everyone has innate wisdom, intelligence, and motivating emotions and that these, even if muted by circumstance, are accessible through education, support, and encouragement. The goals of his projects are to "reconnect people to the [physical and mental] health in themselves and then direct them in ways to bring forth the health of others in their community. The result is a change in people and communities which builds up from within rather than [being] imposed from without" (Mills, 1993, cited in Benard, 1994, p. 22). So it is that individuals and communities have the capacity for restoration and rebound.

We Best Serve Clients by Collaborating with Them.   The role of expert or professional may not provide the best vantage point from which to appreciate clients' strengths and assets. A helper may best be defined as a collaborator or consultant: an individual clearly presumed, because of specialized education and experience, to know some things and to have some tools at the ready but definitely not the only one in the situation to have relevant, even esoteric, knowledge and understanding. Ms. Johnson knows more about thriving in a public housing project than anyone I can think of. Over the course of 35 years, she successfully raised 11 children. She maintained a demeanor of poise, and she demonstrated intelligence and vigor, even as her community underwent dramatic, often frightening changes. Her contributions to the community are, simply put, amazing. She has much to teach us and other residents of her community. I certainly would not presume to work on Ms. Johnson but would be privileged to work with her.

We make a serious error when we subjugate clients' wisdom and knowledge to official views. There is something liberating, for all parties involved, in connecting to clients' stories and narratives, their hopes and fears, their wherewithal and resources rather than trying to stuff them into the narrow confines of a diagnostic category or treatment protocol. Ultimately a collaborative stance may make us less vulnerable to some of the more political elements of helping: paternalism, victim-blaming (or, more currently, victim-creating), and preemption of client views. It is likewise important to get the stories and views of clients out to those who need to hear them—schools, agencies, employers, local governments, churches, and businesses. This is part of the role of advocacy. The policies and regulations that affect many of our clients are crafted in the halls of Congress and are often far removed from the daily reality of clients. Furthermore, these policies do not take advantage of the wisdom and resources of their intended beneficiaries and recipients.

Every Environment Is Full of Resources.   (See Chapters 11, 12, 13, and 14.) In communities that seem to amplify individual and group resilience, there is awareness, recognition, and use of the assets of most members of the community (Kretzmann & McKnight, 1993). Informal systems of individuals, families, and groups, social circuits of peers, and intergenerational mentoring work to assist, support, instruct, and include all members of a community (Schorr, 1997). In inclusive communities, there are many opportunities for involvement, to make contributions to the moral and civic life of the whole; to become, in other words, a citizen in place. No matter how harsh an environment, how it may test the mettle of its inhabitants, it can also be understood as a potentially lush topography of resources and possibilities. Such an idea runs counter to conventional social work wisdom and public policy. However, in every environment, there are individuals, associations, groups, and institutions who have something to give, something that others may desperately need: knowledge, succor, an actual resource or talent, or simply time and place. Such resources usually exist outside the usual matrix of social and human service agencies. And, for the most part, they are unsolicited and untapped. Melvin Delgado (2000), in his articulation of the capacity-enhancement approach to urban social work practice, describes the five critical assumptions of that approach: " (1) The community has the will and the resources to help itself; (2) it knows what is best for itself; (3) ownership of the strategy rests within, rather than outside, the community; (4) partnerships involving organizations and communities are the preferred route for initiatives; and (5) the use of strengths in one area will translate into strengths in other areas . . . a ripple effect" (p. 28).

Such a view of the environment, while seeming to comfort those who believe that people(s) should pull themselves up by their collective and individual bootstraps, *does not* abrogate the responsibility for working for social and economic justice. It does, however, recognize that while we await the energizing hand of political transformation, there are reservoirs of energy, ideas, talents, and tools out there on which to draw. To regard the environment as only inimical or toxic moves us to disregard these resources or mistakenly judge them as disreputable. When justice comes, the community that is aware of and employing its human and social capital to the degree possible is in a much better position to drink the cooling waters of that justice.

Caring, Caretaking, and Context. The idea that care is essential to human well-being does not sit well in a society beset by two centuries of rugged individualism. Deborah Stone (2000) says that we have three rights to care. First, all families must be permitted and assisted in caring for their members. Second, all those paid caregivers need to be able give the support and quality care that is commensurate with the highest ideals of care without subverting their own well-being. Finally, a right to care boils down to this: that all people (and there may be 38 million children under the age of 10 who clearly need care and anywhere between 30 and 50 million adults who need some degree of care) who need care get it. We do have a horror of dependence. But, as Stone says,

> Caring for each other is the most basic form of civic participation. We learn to care in families, and we enlarge our communities of concern as we mature. Caring is the essential democratic act, the prerequisite to voting, joining associations, attending meetings, holding office, and all the other ways we sustain democracy. (p. 15)

In one sense, social work is about care and caretaking. Ann Weick (2000) makes the case that social caretaking as an activity is the profession's hidden (and first) voice, hidden because it is also woman's voice. Caretaking is, in a diffuse sense, also the work of the strengths perspective.

> Recognizing the capacity for toughness and tenderness, for clear reason and fluid intuition, for radical hope and dry-eyed reality brings us back to the challenges of caretaking. But rather than discounting its demands and possibilities, the lesson of our first voice tells us to pay attention to every dimension it encompasses. Social work is social caretaking. . . . We need to turn our attention to the humblest activities of social caretaking and offer our boldest ideas about strengthening the social web connecting us all. (p. 401)

Like social caretaking, and social work, the strengths perspective is about the revolutionary possibility of hope; hope realized through the strengthened sinew of social relationships in family, neighborhood, community, culture, and country. That contextual sinew is fortified by the expression of the individual and communal capacities of all.

Some Preliminary Thoughts

Social work has had something of a dissociative history with regard to building on client strengths. From its inception as a profession, the field has been exhorted to respect and energize client capacities. Bertha Capen Reynolds(1951) looked at the issue in terms of workers' obligations:

> The real choice before us as social workers is whether *we* are to be passive or active. . . . Shall we be content to give with one hand and withhold with the other, to build up or tear down at the same time the strength of a person's life? Or shall we become conscious of our own part in making a profession which will stand forthrightly for human well-being, *including the right to be an active citizen?* (p. 175, emphasis added)

The historical and continuing tension between the desire to become more professional, more technically adept, to focus on "function" rather than "cause" (Lee, 1929), to elevate social work to a new level of respect and comparability among the professions, and, on the other hand, to retain the interest in social action and the redress of social inequities seems to have been resolved recently in favor of the former. The writing, lexicon, and perspective of, say, clinical social work and those of social action or community development are quite different, maybe even at odds. While there is no implacable conflict between the interests of social work practice and social action, the infusion of psychodynamic thinking, the rise of private practice and vendorship, the mass appeal of DSM IV TR among other factors have driven social work toward a model of practice that is more heavily aligned with psychological thinking and psychopathology theories (Specht

& Courtney, 1993). The theories that define such an alignment are typically oriented toward family and individual dysfunctions and disorders. While we must respect the impact of problems on the quality of life for our clients, we must also exercise extraordinary diligence to assure that the resources and positive attributes of clients draw our attention and define our efforts.

Although today's social work practice texts typically nod in the direction of client strengths but provide little guidance to the student or worker about how to make an accounting of strengths and how to employ them in helping, we are currently seeing movement away from the problem or pathology perspective. The solution-focused approach is one example. In essence, it regards clients in the light of what they have done well, those times that the problem has not been apparent, or those times when exceptions to difficulty have occurred. Furthermore, client goals and visions are the centerpiece of the work to be done. It is not unusual for solution-focused practitioners to ask how things would be positively different if a miracle occurred overnight and the problem no longer held (Miller & Berg, 1995; Miller et al., 1997). The literature on resilience, discussed briefly earlier in this chapter, also provides conceptual and clinical ground for employing client strengths as a central part of the helping process. In the words of Benard (1994; see also Chapter 12), "Using resilience as the knowledge base for practice creates a *sense of optimism and hope*. It allows anyone working with troubled youth to, as poet Emily Dickinson urges, "dwell in possibility," to have confidence in their futures and, therefore, to convey this positive expectation to them" (p. 4).

Finally, the research on the effectiveness of a strengths approach, although very preliminary, suggests that it may be an effective and economical framework for practice or case management (Rapp, 1998). Related research on power of mind/health realization; resilience-based practice; solution-focused therapy; community-building; and the research done on the critical factors in successful therapy provide some associated support for the elements of a strengths perspective that make a difference. Research actually done from the vantage point of a strengths approach includes the views and concerns of the stakeholders (subjects and clients) from the outset. The results of the research are to be used to achieve stated objectives of the stakeholders and/or to aid in the solving of identified problems.

In Chapter 15, I will discuss in more detail some of the converging lines of research and practice that are reinforcing the strengths perspective. I will also address some of the persistent and significant criticisms of it.

Conclusion

This third edition is intended to extend our knowledge of a subject that has been part of social work lore for decades, namely, the importance of building on client strengths. Such an endeavor affirms the core values of the profession; it brings together clients, communities, and helpers in a relationship that exploits the best in all; and it restores a sense of hope and optimism in working with clients.

The strengths perspective is not yet a theory—although developments in that direction become bolder (Rapp, 1998). It is a way of thinking about what you do and with whom you do it. It provides a distinctive lens for examining the world of practice. Any approach to practice, in the end, is based on interpretation of the experiences of practitioners and clients and is composed of assumptions, rhetoric, ethics, and a set of methods. The importance and usefulness of any practice orientation lies not in some independent measure of its truth, but in how well it serves us in our work with people, how it fortifies our values, and how it generates opportunities for clients in a particular environment to change in the direction of their hopes and aspirations. The authors believe and hope that you will see the fertility of the strengths perspective in initiating such opportunities for clients and the workers who serve them.

DISCUSSION QUESTIONS

1. What are the most significant contrasts between a strengths approach and a problem-focused one?

2. If you were to employ the strengths perspective in your practice, how would your approach to clients change?

3. What are the barriers you or any other practitioner might face in approaching your practice with individuals, families, groups or communities from a strengths vantage point?

4. What do you consider to be your strengths? How do they energize your practice? How do they shape your personal life?

5. Think of a client you have worked with. Did you ever account for some of the client's (whether an individual or community) capacities and assets? Did you use them in practice? How?

REFERENCES

American Psychiatric Association. (2000). *Diagnostic and statistical manual of mental disorders IV TR.* Washington, DC: American Psychiatric Association.

Becker, E. (1973). *The denial of death.* New York: Free Press.

Becker, H. (1963). *Outsiders: Studies in the sociology of deviance.* New York: Free Press.

Benard, B. (1991). *Fostering resiliency in kids: Protective factors in the family, school, and community.* San Francisco: Western Regional Center.

Benard, B. (1994). *Applications of resilience.* Paper presented at a conference on the Role of Resilience in Drug Abuse, Alcohol Abuse, and Mental Illness. Dec. 5–6. Washington, D.C.

Bledstein, B. (1978). *The culture of professionalism.* New York: Norton.

Clark, M. D. (1997, April). Strengths-based practice: The new paradigm. *Corrections Today, 165,* 110–111.

Cousins, N. (1989). *Head first: The biology of hope.* New York: Dutton.

Damasio, A. R. (1994). *Descartes' error: Emotion, reason, and the human brain.* New York: Grosset/ Dunlap Books.

Delgado, M. (2000). *Community social work practice in an urban context: The potential of a capacity-enhancement perspective.* New York: Oxford University Press.

Freire, P. (1973). *Pedagogy of the oppressed.* New York: Seabury.

Freire, P. (1996). *Pedagogy of hope: Reliving pedagogy of the oppressed.* New York: Continuum.

Fromm, E. (1973). *The anatomy of human destructiveness.* New York: Holt, Rinehart & Winston.

Gergen, K. J. (1994). *Realities and relationships: Soundings in social construction.* Cambridge: Harvard University Press.

Goffman, E. (1961). *Asylums: Essays on the situation of mental patients and other inmates.* Garden City, NY: Anchor/Doubleday.

Hepworth, D. H., & Larsen, J. (1990). *Direct social work practice: Theory and skills* (3rd ed.). Chicago: Dorsey Press.

James, W. (1902). *The varieties of religious experience.* New York: Modern Library.

Kaplan, L., & Girard, J. (1994). *Strengthening high-risk families.* New York: Lexington Books.

Katz, M. (1997). *On playing a poor hand well: Insights from the lives of those who have overcome childhood risks and adversities.* New York: Norton.

Kozol, J. (2000). *Ordinary resurrections: Children in the years of hope.* New York: Crowne Publishers.

Kretzmann, J. P., & McKnight, J. L. (1993). *Building communities from the inside out: Toward finding and mobilizing a community's assets.* Evanston, IL: Northwestern University, Center for Urban Affairs and Policy Research.

Lee, P. R. (1929). Social work: Cause and function. *Proceedings of the National Conference of Social Work,* 3–20.

Mattingly, C. (1991). Narrative reflections on practical actions: Two experiments in reflective story-telling. In D. A. Schön (Ed.), *The reflective turn: Case studies in and on educational practice.* New York: Teacher's College Press.

Miller, S. D., & Berg, I. K. (1995). *The miracle method: A radically new approach to problem drinking.* New York: Norton.

Miller, S. D., Duncan, B. L., & Hubble, M. A. (1997). *Escape from Babel: Toward a unifying language for psychotherapy practice.* New York: Norton.

Mills, R. (1995). *Realizing mental health: Toward a new psychology of resiliency.* New York: Sulzburger & Graham.

Parsons, R. J., & Cox, E. O. (1994). *Empowerment-oriented social work practice with the elderly.* Newbury Park, CA: Sage.

Peele, S., & Brodsky, A. (1991). *The truth about addiction and recovery.* New York: Simon & Schuster.

Pelletier, K. R. (2000). *The best alternative medicine: What works? What does not?* New York: Simon & Schuster.

Pinderhughes, E. (1994). Empowerment as intervention goals: Early ideas. In L. Gutierrez & P. Nurius (Eds.), *Education and research for empowerment practice.* Seattle, WA: University of Washington School of Social Work, Center for Policy and Practice Research.

Rank, O. (1941). *Beyond psychology.* New York: Dover Books.

Rapp, C. A. (1998). *The strengths model: Case management with people suffering from severe and persistent mental illness.* New York: Oxford University Press.

Reynolds, B. C. (1951). *Social work and social living: Explorations in philosophy and practice.* Silver Spring, MD: National Association of Social Workers.

Rose, S. M. (2000). Reflections on empowerment-based practice. *Social Work, 45,* 401–412.

Saleebey, D. (1989). Professions in crisis: The estrangement of knowing and doing. *Social Casework, 70,* 556–563.

Scheff, T. J. (1984). *Being mentally ill: A sociological theory* (3rd ed.). New York: Aldine.

Schön, D. A. (1983). *The reflective practitioner.* New York: Basic Books.

Schorr, L. B. (1997). *Common purpose: rebuilding families and neighborhoods to rebuild America.* New York: Anchor/Doubleday.

Simon, B. L. (1994). *The empowerment tradition in social work: A history.* New York: Columbia University Press.

Specht, H., & Courtney, M. (1993). *Unfaithful angels: How social work has abandoned its mission.* New York: Free Press.

Stone, D. (2000). Why we need a care movement. *The Nation, 270,* 13–15.

Walzer, M. (1983). *Spheres of justice.* New York: Basic Books.

Weick, A. (2000). Hidden voices. *Social Work, 45,* 395–402.

Weil, A. (1995). *Spontaneous healing.* New York: Knopf.

Werner, E., & Smith, R. S. (1992). *Overcoming the odds.* Ithaca, NY: Cornell University Press.

Wolin, S. J., & Wolin, S. (1993). *The resilient self: How survivors of troubled families rise above adversity.* New York: Villard.

Wolin, S., & Wolin, S. J. (1996). The challenge model: Working with strengths in children of substance abusing parents. *Adolescent Substance Abuse and Dual Disorders, 5,* 243–256.

Wolin, S., & Wolin, S. J. (1997). Shifting paradigms: Talking a paradoxical approach. *Resiliency in Action, 2,* 23–28.

CHAPTER

2

The Literary and Moral Foundations of the Strengths Perspective

HOWARD GOLDSTEIN

Bertha

I would never have been a victim. I think I was born with a chip on my shoulder. To think my mother had to die and we were taken and put in that place. Now I understand it was a matter of necessity, my father couldn't help himself. So in a way it was a blessing that there was a place to go because our aunts who were poor had their own kids and you know goddam well that they cater to their kids before they give you anything. So in a way it was a Godsend and it was what you made of it. You could either be a sniveling little nothing or you could be mischievous and upset people around you. You had to have a sense of humor or you'd be creamed. I'm not bitter. What saved me were the tricks I pulled on the superintendent. If I could outwit him, I could overlook a lot of other stuff.

These are Bertha's words—her response to my request that she tell me what it was like to have been a ward in a bygone orphanage, to have spent most of her first 16 years in an institution. Bertha was one of almost 40 elders, alumni of the Children's Home who eagerly shared the stories of their lifetimes with me (Goldstein, 1996).

A widow on the outer edge of her seventh decade, she was still mischievous, funny—but now in ways tempered by irony. Although the setting of our conversation was the kitchen of Bertha's small, modest Florida retirement condo, I had the sense of speaking with a larger and older version of a younger Bette Davis; she was in command, with well-practiced hauteur, the smoke of Bertha's poised cigarette dramatized her answer to my question, "What was it really like growing up in the old orphanage?"

Nowadays, stories about survival have become so common as to wind up as fillers for the back pages of newspapers unless the latest cataclysm could be described in comparative and superlative terms—as a *more* devastating flood, *more* heinous killings, a *fiercer* fire. The world becomes a more threatening place and the numbers of remarkable people who have had to show the buoyancy, the immense vitality to overcome, outlast, and master their catastrophes increases. Still, traditional psychological thinking prevails: These signs of health and strength in the face of hardship are overlooked by a morbid interest in the defects, limitations, illness, and other presumed consequences of these traumas. In other words, if one fails to adjust it is obviously *because of* such insults to mind and body; but if one overcomes, it is explained that one does so *in spite* of these traumas. And so, human triumphs stand as oddities, exceptions to the received wisdom, and are converted into the substance of Sunday supplements. I will give my attention to the reasons for this paradox.

I use Bertha's rejoinder as an introduction to this endeavor. Her life is not the journey of a heroine, the chronicle of a victor. I came to learn that her many years were scarcely exceptional: Married to Ed—it seemed to her like forever—she frequently had to take charge of his trucking business because of a chronic illness that finally left her a widow. They raised four children who had to make it through college on their own; money was never in excess. But what Bertha truly felt pride and success about was her many years of volunteer work with handicapped children. She poked me in the ribs to take a close look at her living room wall adorned with framed citations, honors, news clippings expressing gratitude for the difference she made in the lives of these children.

Consider this: It is the fact that Bertha (and the other graduates of that children's institution) succeeded, *did* live an ordinary life as a wife, mother, and citizen that distinguishes her. By most accepted psychosociological theories and expositions Bertha's life should have been otherwise. The inventory of her early years in the home includes large servings of the classic maltreatment and trauma used to predict a less than ordered and secure adulthood. Not only did she openly deal with the obvious wounds of separation from and loss of a parent but resisted what could have been a more insidious affliction, an entire childhood as a ward of an archetypal orphanage.

Let me put this account in other terms to point to where this essay is heading. We know that a story like Bertha's is at risk because it can be interpreted, given meaning, to fit the presumptions of the reader. On telling this story, as I have done, to an ordinary audience of, say, friends or family, the listeners typically react in buoyant and affecting ways: "What spirit and perseverance," one says; another, "She reminds me of my dear old aunt who outlived two wars and four husbands"; and a third, "And she didn't have anything like the safety net we have."

Tell this story to professionals, however, and the reaction is quick and critical: "She reminds me of a really difficult patient who always avoided the facts"; "Look, this is just denial in action"; or, "Read Bowlby's book about early loss. There is lots more she isn't saying."

There is a third group—not easy to define or label—who, in plain talk, allude to something like the strength and resilience (terms I will use interchangeably) of spirit and self. They are neither Pollyannish about nor are they blind to the reality of vulnerability, frailty, adversity, and suffering. But what they are attuned to are the many paths that people seek out, alone or with help, that lead to, not away from, remarkable resources and talents, visions and beliefs that allow for much more than just survival. Responses from this group to Bertha's account take such forms as: "How remarkable that she could experience and live with both sorrow and joy"; "She could have used the same recollections to justify most any human failing"; "It's refreshing to hear about someone who is not a blamer, a victim"; "No question, life for her was a matter of choices—and tough ones, too."

Here we have three of the distinct and familiar perspectives on the same story. The first might be called "folk talk," in sympathy with what Jerome Bruner (1990) refers to as "folk psychology . . . or culture's account of what makes human beings 'tick' [including] a theory of mind, one's own and others [and] a theory of motivation." "Folk talk" is just another way of alluding to the manner in which people, like Bertha, define themselves and their worlds in what we now call narrative terms. The second perspective, the *psychosociological* or *medico-scientific model*, is used to sort out the presumed causes, deficits, and implications of a particular human condition. The third is the *strengths* perspective, which takes account of one's capabilities and powers.

There is yet a fourth perspective, one that is inherent to the strengths approach. It is the *moral* foundations or the *moral center of gravity* of one's endeavors to live the best life possible. Morality (or its absence) is not as clearly evident as the other personal characteristics just noted: It is found in the essence of the stories people tell, the overtones of goodness or badness, of right or wrong, or of evil or virtue that storytellers seem to attribute to their thoughts and actions. Bertha's account offers many examples: She implies that being a victim would be unpardonable; that it became important to her to free her father from blame; that it was right to defy authority when her self-esteem was at stake; that it was her obligation to support her husband and children; and to volunteer to help handicapped children meant that one could be a decent human being.

As I will show later in this chapter, it is not the staid human sciences but the vital humanities and its literature—the novel, autobiography, poetry, and drama—that best tells us about the resilience and strength and their implicit moral persuasions that one calls on to become a person. We need only consider, for example, how the powerful literature of the Holocaust and the civil rights movement or fictional and dramatic tales of earthy, ordinary lives can enrich our understanding and appreciation of the personal and shared struggles of our clients, thus helping us become more effective in our work.

For now, it is important to sketch some of the critical differences between the two major perspectives on or interpretations of the human situations encountered in practice. The first is the medico-scientific or psychosociological approach that, for the sake of brevity, I will call a deficit approach in contrast with the second, the strengths approach. The former uses the formal and customary terminology of textbooks and manuals; the latter embodies the significance of folk talk, the language and perceptions of clients, and its moral essence. Contrasting the two is not a matter of word play or an argument for the sake of argument: At stake is the well-being of our clients (however it is defined) since each perspective is itself a prescription of sorts for how we are required to understand and therefore work with problems of living. Both approaches rely on all sorts of metaphors, allusions, and idioms. Lofty and impressive terms such as "transference," "object relations," or the various diagnostic categories found in textbooks or diagnostic and statistic manuals are indeed inventions, as figurative and free of specific referents as are the more earthy terms used in the more humanistic approaches to practice—they mean only what the speaker intends them to mean. Simply, the language of the theories, concepts, and philosophies we choose to use to describe, explain, or classify our clients will, by definition, influence the character, focus, style, and goals of the helping process and, not the least, the expected roles of the participants.

Stated another way, any theoretical approach we employ to study and treat our clients' troubles is a creation of the mind, a shared collection of beliefs and assumptions selectively designed to interpret and explain the particular phenomenon. In choosing, for whatever reason, one theoretical approach over another we are, as the novelist Saul Bellow (2000) observes, assuming in advance what the general outcome of that approach will be. The disability or deficit version of human behavior predicts dire consequences; the strengths' narrative is far more optimistic and hopeful about how life will turn out. Although Bellow speaks about storytellers and writers, his words also apply to helping professionals: Despite our scientific, objective pretensions, we turn "the human condition into a sequential narrative of how it came to be" (p. 65). And if this is the case, we cannot help but intrude in the moral and ethical domain of our clients' lives, the often entangled, confused, and painful web of moral strains for which right answers are not always visible.

In our efforts (if not our need) to make sense of clients' confused circumstances by ordering them into one or another assumptive approach to practice there is the risk that we will overlook the more subtle moral conflicts and ironies that weave the tangled skein of clients' lives. The stories clients present about themselves—the problem, or some experience or recollection—are told in figurative rather than factual or evidentiary terms. We hear an account or an impression that often is seasoned with all sorts of images. It might include similes ("Sure, I got away with it but I feel like an escaped con."); symbols ("An A, number one failure, that's me as a father."); irony ("You try so hard to be the best and where does it get you?"); or euphemisms ("Sometimes you just have to tell a white lie."). Equally, the client's story may protect immoral or amoral feelings: "You can't blame me. If you had the childhood that I did, you'd know I couldn't help it," or "I'm sure you know that alcoholism is a disease." It is literature that teaches us how metaphors enrich our understanding of lives.

To rephrase this overview, I propose that our professional activities are not, as we would prefer to believe, rational consequences of a set of established and tested theories, constructs, and techniques similar to those of the hard sciences. Rather, we have inherited (and are taught) sets of abstractions, concepts, and theories that are made up of value-laden metaphors and idioms. Such constructions embody philosophic assumptions about the human state (Is human behavior a consequence of certain past causes or is it always in the process of adapting to uncertainties about the future?); ideologies of professionalism (Are we purveyors of the scientific method or social humanists?); and, not the least, the politics of practice where theories and schools of thought compete with one another for ascendance. The rhetoric of the professional's chosen perspective inevitably dictates (at least in broad terms) the helpers role vis-à-vis that of the client's. Thus, in choosing a perspective, unavoidable ethical questions come forward about the allocation of power and authority (and the matter of self-determination) in the helping experience. As it happens with a medico-scientific approach to practice, the weight of influence is measured by the expertise of the practitioner. In the case of the humanistic, strength-oriented approach, the issues of power and authority are the natural interpersonal conditions of the helping process that, optimally, should be shared by client and worker.

A useful way of pursuing the issues and questions raised thus far would be to redefine the two perspectives on practice as the social constructions they are, expressing public and professional attitudes and beliefs. It is here that the question of plausibility comes forth. How well does each of these perspectives and their constructions serve us in our work with people? To what extent do they approximate and reflect the real-life human circumstances we encounter in practice? In what ways does the influence of these orientations intrude into the ethical and political climate of the helping relationship? How do they deal with the inescapable moral dimensions of practice? For purposes of argument and contrast the commentary will need to be framed in polar terms.

Strength/Resilience and Pathology as Social Constructions

As defined by Gergen (1985) social constructionist inquiry attempts to understand the processes by which people explain and define themselves and their world. Questioning the notion that there is a firm and objective basis for conventional knowledge and language, social constructionism argues that the terms in which the world is understood are social artifacts, the products of cultural, symbolic, and historical interchanges among people. Such artifacts have currency only as long as there is consensus about their value: Simply put, we continue to depend on the conventional knowledge and language. As long as they serve our varied social, adaptive, and professional purposes we have no need to question the verity of such truths.

As social constructions, the language of each perspective attributes its own meaning to the human condition. By definition, *strength* and *psychopathology* denote what might be thought of as complementary states of being. That is, health makes sense in its relation to illness. According to *Webster's 3rd New International Dictionary* (1993), the former refers to moral courage, fortitude, physical force, and vigor among other virtues; psychopathology covers abnormality, disorder, and disease.

As an inherited construct, how did it happen that the seemingly precise biomedical term *pathology* came to be applied to something as ambiguous as human mental states? Although the term has a long history in general medicine, it did not come into usage by medical psychiatry until the mid-19th century. At that point, its adoption as a medical classification and its consequences were as political as medical.

By mid-century the study of brain anatomy took over and the positivistic sciences came into ascendance. Within this scientific revolution, medicine became institutionalized and standardized. Swept along with this change was the formal medicalization of mental disorders (Ellenberger, 1970).

> Ernest Becker sums up the rise of the medical prerogative: Nineteenth-century diagnosticians redoubled efforts to keep man under medical wraps and dress his behavior disorder in Greco-Latin cant. Thus the science that knew least about total symbolic man and most about the animal body fully established its sacrosanct domain. We are coming to know that it had no business there. . . . The result of this lopsided jurisdictional development was that human malfunction has continued to be treated largely in nineteenth century disease categories up to the present day. (pp. 9–10)

There is one special consequence of the medicalizing or mechanizing of what, as a catchall of human distress and conflict, is called "mental disorders": The medical model as a rational, empirical, scientific method for diagnosis and treatment and its theories have little room for the intangible, immeasurable spectrum of personal beliefs and moral (or immoral) convictions. Such beliefs might include images as varied as personal faith, myths—both private and cultural—a spiritual sense of trust, whether secular or religious, that offers the hope and promise of divine intercession. Other images and projections picture the self in a more sympathetic future, or as a moral compass that points to judgments of virtue or bad faith, personal responsibility and obligation versus indifference to others' needs and rights. Falling outside psychological taxonomy, such exclusively human propensities are at risk of being considered irrational or metaphysical. Fairness demands that I not be overly wholesale in such judgments: Certainly the empirical practitioner, the precise behaviorist, even the organically oriented professional are sentient beings in their own right who respect and value such transcendent levels of existence. Whether they are used as credible motivations in practice is another question.

Strength and resilience are social constructions with some vintage, built into, over time, the ordinary, civil, or folk vocabulary. Terms—or really subjective value judgments—such as virtue, willpower, integrity, and fortitude, are common, culturally defined ways of referring to what was once called one's character and worth. We recognize their presence when they are energized in response to the travails of living. Ironically, psychological opinions are sometimes easier to handle for I am less responsible for my behavior when I am considered as depressed, anxious, or compulsively driven rather than, say, awful moody and sour, a chronically unhappy worrier, or controlling and domineering. Where the former are face-saving, implying that "something made me do it," the latter are, of course, judgments of character, reproaches about our attitudes and behavior to others.

Thus, perspectives on strength and resilience do not ignore the dark side of what it means to be human. Even so, well-deserved feelings—failure, inadequacy, or self-esteem—are not judged as defects but as a possible starting point at which clients (or any of us) can begin to explore where, psychologically, interpersonally, and morally, they have failed to achieve their or society's standards for personal responsibility, growth, and realization. The strengths perspective encourages and implies an expansive (rather than a reductionistic) and inclusive mode of understanding. Whether resilience is an inborn attribute is uncertain; even if it were, its force is most evident in our vital relationships with others. We learn this by listening closely to the client's definition of what life has been and is all about; by our regard for latent potentials, expectations, visions, hopes, and desires; by the *meanings* one gives to or finds in his or her circumstances, and not the least, by the quality and extent of one's *relationships*. Still, no matter how well we succeed in deepening our understanding, humility must be ever-present. The human situation remains open-ended.

Implications for Social Work Practice

Let us consider, first, the shape practice would take should it adopt either the deficit or strengths persuasion. I have already mentioned that the logical follow-through of a perspective that one learns, elects, or finds sympathetic to his or her world view should result in a peculiar social arrangement (whether it is called a psychotherapy, casework, counseling, or advocacy relationship). The nature of this arrangement or structure with its procedures and ground rules will quickly— but perhaps subtly—inform the client about how to be, what to expect, where he or she stands, and other undercurrents of the human relationship.

Specifically, if my metaphor for practice is the medical model, the logic of this model will lead me from the general to the specific—as might occur in a visit to a family physician who seeks to grasp the original causes of the specific symptom. I will want to know from the outset as much as possible about you, the presenting problem, and perhaps what it is like for you to be in this situation. But as we proceed together, my intent to reach a diagnosis (or assessment or evaluation) of what is wrong (and, hopefully, the cause) will lead me to narrow the inquiry if I intend to arrive at a plan of action or treatment. Along the way, I will do my best to involve you in all stages of the event.

Certain pitfalls are encountered when I, the practitioner, endeavor to assess you, your problem, and its cause. There is a suggestion in this process that I, as the human relations expert, can in certain respects know you better than you can understand yourself. This being the case, the client learns quickly about who in this relationship has earned the special knowledge and authority of professionalism, who is in charge. Let us not overlook the possibility that there are some rewards—certain comforts and relief—when one is in the hands of a maestro who promises to lead the way. Such comfort does not come without risk: In an asymmetrical relationship where power is unevenly held, critical moral and ethical questions about responsibility, rights, and informed consent may not receive their proper due.

At any rate, my commentary is surely an oversimplification of a complex and convoluted process. But however this mode of practice unfolds, keep in mind that it is *linear* in its logic: Causes will bring about effects; diagnosis will lead to treatment that should effect cure; development is sequential, one stage following another, and so on.

In thinking about the alternative approach of the strengths/resilience perspective it is impossible to make a one-to-one comparison with the medical model or to talk about which works better. Since each is based on its own unique assumptions about the human condition, any judgment or comparison would be as pointless as trying to say that the English language is better than the Japanese, that, geographically, oceans are better than mountains. True, both perspectives have similar purposes; both are centered in a sentient, human relationship. Beyond these essential commonalties their world views diverge considerably.

Strength and Resiliency

Although I have used strength and resilience interchangeably, it is time now to denote what they illuminate in the larger picture. As a perspective on human problems of living, I have referred to the strength perspective as an organizing construct that embraces a set of assumptions and attributes about health and potential. Although I am not sure there is consensus about this definition, I see resilience as the attribute that epitomizes and operationalizes what the strength perspective is all about.

Only recently has the theory of resiliency claimed a small corner of the literature of the behavioral sciences. George Vaillant (1993) defines resilience as the "self-righting tendencies" of the person, "both the capacity to be bent without breaking and the capacity, once bent, to spring back" (p. 284). Reflecting on a 50-year longitudinal study of men whose childhoods were marked by severe risk, Vaillant tells how he was struck with their ability to "spin straw into gold, laugh at themselves, display empathy . . . and worry and plan realistically," characteristics that apply equally to Bertha and her colleagues. Gail Sheehy (1986) carries this definition a step further in her tribute to what she calls the "victorious personality":

> One may be born with a naturally resilient temperament, but one develops a victorious personality. Those who do often come to believe they are special, perhaps meant to serve a purpose beyond themselves. Among the elements that contribute to a victorious personality are the ability to bend according to circumstance, self-trust, social ease . . . and the understanding that one's plight is not unique. (p. 267)

The concept of resiliency might not strike everyone as particularly novel, enlightening, or as a breakthrough in the field of psychology. It is, after all, merely an intellectualized version of what our culture and its folk psychology has always admired—and often expected—about the hardiness and pliability of the human spirit. While Social Darwinism has taken this standard to an extreme, in a more kindly sense, society as a whole has always assumed that, perhaps with some help and support, its members will literally stand up and be counted. Nevertheless, when Anthony and Cohler (1987) set out to edit a text on resilience, they were astonished at the sparseness of the literature on this topic:

> One would have thought that the picture of children triumphing over despairing, degrading, depressing, depriving, and deficient circumstances would have caught the immediate attention of both clinicians and researchers, but the survivors and thrivers appear to pass almost unnoticed amidst the holocaust of disadvantage and the tragedies of those who succumbed to it. (p. 28)

As was the intent of my study of the graduates of the Children's Home, previous behavioral scientists sought to sort out the characteristics of people who appear to be of the resilient mold, those who, as children, struggled with adversity without special help and eventually found their way into rewarding adulthood. There is agreement about one thing: As children, they were not exceptional "superkids."

These investigators focused largely on the personality characteristics of resilient children such as temperament, cognitive skills, self-esteem, and their social skills involving curiosity about people, cooperativeness, and friendliness. These features, however, tend to perpetuate the myth of causality: *If* one has any of these characteristics *then* certain resilient behaviors should follow. Even accepting this formula, it is, of course, hard to know what came first—whether these personal and social attributes begot resiliency or whether resiliency itself was the outgrowth of experience and trial. The researchers also allowed that the traits of resiliency do not add up like collecting grades or varsity points. Rather, they tend to swell exponentially. When a child or adult takes risks or survives a serious threat, new skills and greater self-confidence accrue. These gains fuel the individual to dare and test herself in other venues of her life; and so the successful adventures of living multiply.

From an implied feminist standpoint, Judith Jordan (1992) also contests the causal idea, saying that the roots of resilient attitudes and behavior are not entirely located within the person or his social supports. More in line with the experience of the home's children and the importance of the social context mentioned earlier, the sources of mastery and resilience are seen as the shared give-and-take, the dialectics, mutualities, and moral obligations essential to good interpersonal relationships. The former wards put this explanation in homelier terms: "it was camaraderie . . . my group"; "there was always someone among us who cared what happened"; "by my rules, I never put myself first"; "other kids came to me for help and advice"; "I had to be the mother and fight for my sibs." In these terms, resilient behavior is not effected by something or someone: As a complex form of flexibility and mastery, it arises up out of and is nourished by interpersonal and social processes.

In this view, Jordan argues that current studies of the psychology of resilience are too limited since they focus largely either on the *individual's* acculturation or the gains of social support. Concentration either on personality (how one turns inward to find strength) or social support (turning outward for assistance and comfort) is a "separate self" model of development that works in one-directional ways. Jordan contends that this model is an *individualized*—even isolated—conception of what it means to be resilient and, for that matter, what it means to be a person. Resilience, in her terms is a relational dynamic nurtured by a two-way process of mutuality and empathy—a process of "sharing with" more so than "getting from." As Bertha told me, "we all took an interest in each other . . . took up for each other." This unspoken bond did more than ease one's misfortune and sadness—the penalties of orphanage life: Such fellowship (often with irony or comedy) encouraged and applauded any show of talent for battling with trial and hardship, rewarded even a flicker of courage and self-confidence, and set the norms for how people were supposed to be with one another. Although trust and caring perhaps were not substitutes for the affection and intimacy of a family, such sympathies could be depended on as proofs that someone was there, that trust among people was possible, that security was possible.

In case I am giving the impression that institutional life, as described by its graduates, was altogether a children's garden of delight I must report on its larger and darker side—a harsh and crude pecking order meant that there were lots of bloody battles. Kids stole, cheated, lied, and played mean tricks. There were snotty-faced kids, whiners, bedwetters, complainers, blamers—the unkempt, pimply, unwashed kids.

This suggests that it is vital that we look beyond the resilient and moral character of the individual to the kind of moral (and often amoral) world within which the individual is located—what he or she is up against in the struggle to define one's self. In these times, how does one adjust one's moral compass to determine how, in moral terms, one ought to be or what one ought to avoid being? Why should personal obligation and responsibility deserve any consideration when people are enmeshed in a social order in which moral questions are deadened by indifference to political guile, where both obscene wealth and degrading poverty accelerate on both ends of the economic spectrum, where deprivation of deserved health care and security become facts of life, and where the manipulation, greed, and power of special interest groups dominate public life?

As we face our clients, we still have to figure out how to help them find ways to discover their potentialities for strength, resilience, and moral responsibility and where they are in their particular circumstances. Primarily, the basic principles of helping are set in motion with a primary focus on—or, better, a commitment to—how clients perceive their world. The sensitivity, optimism, and goodwill of the helper are by no means contagious: Clients—like all other undesignated human beings—will necessarily concede to or adopt this attitude. We are persistent in how we cling to our realities, our beliefs about how we see our lives within the world we occupy: They are our truths, and often, our raison d'etre. Still, the beginnings of trust and hope offer at least some probability that narrow self-consciousness might gradually give way to greater openness.

It is relationships of this kind and quality that makes the difference. Patients (subjects in a study) who believed they benefited from the services of a mental health center attributed the primary reason for their improvement to their thera-pists' genuine acceptance of their real-life worth and strength (Kunin, 1985). Mahoney (1991) in his authoritative book on change puts it in more sober terms:

> The optimal therapeutic relationship creates a special human context—a context in and from which the client can safely experiment with and explore familiar and novel ways of experiencing self, world (especially interpersonal), and possible rela-tionships. Such experiments and explorations—which are individualized to match the client's current competencies and experiential horizons—are constrained only by the requirements that they be self-caring and socially responsible. . . . "Optimal helping respects the power and resilience of the human spirit." (pp. 267, 271)

Unquestionably, every model of practice is guided by an externally shaped code of ethics, its rules for avoiding any transgression that might prove harmful or insidious. It seems to me that a strengths perspective is by its very nature an ethical and moral enterprise. Where all forms of treatment are committed to helping the individual or family or group per se, the strengths approach is distinctive in how it is, at the same time, focused on how people live in and make sense of their world of experience. It is often a world beset by value issues and moral conflicts that are evident in what people will or will not settle for when it comes to their conditions and qualities of living, their essential relationships, and their prospects for the future. Although such questions are inescapable in the ordinary, daily demands of living, they are painfully aggravated when, for whatever reason, life becomes too chaotic—perhaps out of control—when one is deprived of basic needs—both mate-rial and relational, when the integrity of self is at risk, when one's moral obligations are in doubt, and when former values and beliefs seem no longer reliable.

Preparation for a Strengths Approach to Practice

Although I don't have even an approximate estimate of the number of programs that teach a strengths model, judging by the increasing quantity of articles dealing with applications of a strengths approach to various populations and problems that cross my desk as the current editor of the journal *Families in Society,* it is appar-ent that this orientation has taken hold in many settings. Despite its growing pop-ularity, references to how it should be taught and learned are indeed scarce: For example, no mention of education for practice can be found in the indexes of pre-vious editions of this book.

Saleebey (1997) and Cowger (1997), among other authors in the previous edition of *The Strengths Perspective in Social Work Practice,* sketch plans for assessment and action that are instructive. Still, it seems to me that, without a more formal and relevant educational foundation, there is the risk that the strengths approach could be applied by some social workers prescriptively, or as a recipe for practice—as more of a tool or technique than as a humanistic means of joining with clients in the pursuit of growth. Perhaps more important, without such foundations it would be difficult to articulate and build this valuable approach into the knowledge base of the profession. In many ways the attractiveness of the strengths perspective seems to be based not entirely on its own conceptual coherence and merits than as a welcome alternative (for some) to the biomedical or pathological models of practice described previously. And, not the least, this perspective has a very human appeal insofar as it can serve as a prototype for the kind of civility, regard, and caring that nurtures *all* meaningful relationships.

At this point, I would not undertake a task as ambitious as devising a curriculum for the strengths perspective. Yet, it is possible to suggest certain resources for teaching and learning that are suggested by the two major constructs discussed earlier—social constructionism and morality—that are implicit in the strengths perspective. Both call for some revisions in and alternatives to the traditional educational content of social work. The former proposes that we cross disciplinary boundaries to explore what fields concerned with social discourse, language and metaphor, and postmodern theory would enable practitioners to better grasp how, historically, situationally, and culturally, people create their personal realities and worldviews. Complementing this pursuit, questions about the role of morality requires a more radical venture into the literature of the humanities—novels, autobiographies, and drama, for example—that offers intimate and vicarious understandings of the deep-set influence of morality, courage, and virtue. The modern novelist Salman Rushdie says with eloquence, "Literature is where I go to explore the highest and lowest places in human society and the human spirit, where I hope to find not absolute truth but the truth of the tale, of the imagination and of the heart."[1]

Social constructionism (and its alternative term, constructivism) has, in recent years, become a contender in the mainstream of social work thought and education. It has been addressed from many perspectives in many articles and in two major texts, *Revisioning Social Work Education: A Social Constructionist Approach* (1993) and *Constructivism in Practice: Methods and Challenges* (1998). Laird (1993), the editor of the first text, tells us how social constructionism has become a prominent principle in many social agencies and in teaching and practice. Crossing many boundaries, it combines ideas from anthropology, postmodern theory, and feminist theory. One can also add cognitive theory, linguistics, and narrative theory. Social constructionism has also effected the use of ethnographic research (as exemplified in my 1996 study *The Home on Gorham Street and the Voices of Its Children*) to capture the firsthand, personally experienced nature and meaning of lives.

Moral Values and Literature

Turning to literature of the humanities as a source of knowledge—or more specifically, to the kind of wisdom that informs our work with people—is of a very different order than usual forms of knowledge building. The pursuit of this kind of

[1]Quoted in *Observer*, (1989, February 19).

learning is not a sophisticated quest for new horizons of erudition, new theories or research that expand our perceptions and understanding. In a manner of speaking, it is a return to our more naive and primal ways of learning about the world, its people, and about what life is all about. Before most of us ever thought about becoming a social worker, a firefighter, or a teacher we read stories that in their peculiar way imprinted on or created networks in our minds ways of knowing—certain ways of thinking about phenomena that often were very distant from the tiny corners of the world we inhabited. We learned about foreign culture and customs, about how and why some people acted and thought in, for us, rather alien ways, about what it meant, felt like, to be courageous, to take a brave stand, to make an honest choice. Likewise, we learned about the penalties for less than virtuous behavior. As Angela Carter, the British author once suggested, reading deepens your understanding of yourself. In her words, "Reading a book is like rewriting it for yourself. . . . You bring to a novel, anything you read, all your experiences of the world. You bring your history and you read it in your own terms."[2]

Literature as a flowing spring from which we can draw the sustenance of understanding of the human dilemma crosses many disciplinary boundaries. Sigmund Freud himself once complained that it did not fail that when he thought up a new idea he discovered that some poet had said it all before. We have been enlightened not only by poets and writers (and even by our clients with more modest literary ambitions) but also by scholars in other fields. An unexpected example is Richard Posner (1997), the conservative jurist and author of several books on a broad range of legal and ethical issues. In his essay "Against Ethical Criticism" he tells of the "empathy-inducing" role of literature that helps bridge the gap between separate lives and their experiences:

> In reading literature we are also learning about the values and experiences of cultures, epochs, and sensibilities remote from our own, yet not so remote as to be unintelligible. We are acquiring experience vicariously by dwelling in the imaginary worlds that literature creates. We are expanding our emotional as well as our intellectual horizons. An idea can usually be encoded straightforwardly enough and transferred more or less intact to another person. It is different with emotions. I do not *feel* your pain, your losses. You can *describe* a pain, its origins, and its consequences in as comprehensive detail as you like and I still will not experience them. And likewise with describing your feelings about getting old, falling in love, losing a friend, failing in business, succeeding in politics. Imaginative literature can engender in readers emotional responses to experiences they have not had. (p. 19)

Gary Saul Morson (1988), a professor of Russian literature, unfolds a credible appeal to reason as to why literature—the novel in particular—offers the most reliable understanding of the psyche and the social world. The good novel or the autobiography that chronicles a moral struggle does not just tell *about* the nature of the moral experience but draws the reader into the narrator's real-life experience in which certain moral convictions are the resources that embolden acts of

---

[2]Quoted in *Marxism Today*, (1985, January).

strength and resilience. One gains more than an understanding of other people and their moral decisions in everyday life: While reading, one vicariously grapples with moral values from moment to moment. Thus, within a particular piece of literature, the reader experiences not what ought to be right morally and ethically but what truly concerns a real person, the moral decisions made moment by moment "by inexhaustibly complex characters in unrepeatable social situations at particular historical times." Thus we learn again that one's power to, in effect, make it in life—as did Bertha—is not a universal virtue but a curious and intricate combination of personal talents.

The field of mental health has generated a number of books that show how literature can illuminate and amplify our understanding of various disorders.[3] Although I have talked with many colleagues who do use the literature of the humanities—as various as *Winnie the Pooh* and autobiographies of women—to round out their more typical reading lists, one finds little in social work publications that credits such literature as a valuable medium for a richer grasp of human behavior. Apparently unread were the words of Maxine Greene (1966), a professor of English at the Teachers College, Columbia University, who, in her article "The Humanities and Social Work Education" proposed that literature offers the opportunity to become engaged in critical life situations in symbolic ways and to discover what they mean: It is the kind of experience that stirs one to turn back into herself and her "reality." She asked: Where else can one look for ways of pondering questions not answerable by factual statements, nor soluble through formal or empirical inquiry? And these questions, of course, have largely to do with ethical and moral choice where judgments do not neatly fall into right or wrong categories. She spoke of times when, in working with clients, the helper cannot take refuge in methods, anonymity, and distance, when dependable understanding seems just beyond reach, when one has to take the risk of choice and assert ones identity and values without certainty or verification. Thus, she advised educators:

> In the student's preparation for the dangerous world where there will be no one to give him orders, he [sic] requires the development of his sensibilities that the arts can provide. He needs opportunities to participate imaginatively in the kinds of formed experiences that engages him wholly as an intelligent and emotional being, that possess the special potentiality of revealing him to himself. . . . He needs to dredge up the queer, unanswerable questions which are philosophical, so that he can orient himself in the days to come, find his own perspective. . . . This is what it means to be enlisted in the search for meaning at a moment when meanings are no

---

[3]See, for example, *The World Within: Fiction Illuminating Neuroses in Our Time,* edited by Mary Louise Aswell (New York: McGraw-Hill, 1947); *The Inner World of Mental Illness: A Series of First-Person Accounts of What It Was Like,* edited by Bert Kaplan (New York: Harper and Row, 1964); *The Abnormal Personality Through Literature,* edited by A. A. Stone & S. S. Stone (Englewood Cliffs, NJ: Prentice-Hall, 1966); *The Age of Madness: The History of Involuntary Mental Hospitalization Presented in Selected Texts,* edited by Thomas Szasz (New York: Jason Aronson, 1974); and *Madness and Sexual Politics in the Feminist Novel: Studies in Brontë, Woolf, Lessing and Atwood,* edited by Barbara Hill Rigney (Madison: University of Wisconsin Press, 1978).

longer fixed. This is what it means to be enlisted in the quest for principle and ideal, when the codes are no longer "given." (p. 31)

When it comes to the question of which and what kind of literature might be instructive in class and field teaching we run into the problem of selection of appropriate readings. The task is much simpler when it comes to the usual run of knowledge and theory. If we think that students need to learn about social constructionism, for example, there are many resources and indexes we can turn to. The social and psychological sciences offer persuasive and categorical explanations of and theoretical structures for systematizing human behavior in accord with the methods of science. But every day experience also tells us that every human instance is, by the fact that it is indeed human, an exception to, a variation on, or a deviation from these scientific propositions. Thus, to discover the literature we must cross many boundaries of understanding. This is especially the case if we want to open learners' minds to the autobiographic, moral, epic, and lyric character of lives that will inform and expand what we gain from our scientific studies but also to, at times, transcend the knowledge of the sciences.

In addition, it would be gratuitous even to suggest the specific examples of literature that you, the reader, should select or would be appropriate for teaching. What we choose to read for our pleasure or purpose is most personal, depending on our interests, past experiences, world view, and taste. Typically, what we gain from the experience of reading the novel, drama, or poem is largely serendipitous: Suddenly, we turn a page and discover the words that enlighten or drive home a grand idea. For example, I cherish the works of past and contemporary Jewish writers who capture, recall, or deepen my understanding of aspects of my own life or my outlook on the world. I find again the moral idioms of my existence and thereby deepen my sensitivities to the eloquent idioms that mark all that is meaningfully right for others' lives.

With that said, it is still necessary to think in terms of categories if I intend to illustrate how literature in its various forms might inform our understanding of strength and resilience and their moral connotations. Although the humanities offer archetypes of the human experience in its myriad if not infinite forms, for our purposes I choose to be more pragmatic: I offer a few excerpts from autobiographical, confessional, and poetic writings that serve as commentaries on what has been called, "The Other Side of the Desk." Given that so much of the professional literature centers on the expert activities of the practitioner, what it's like for the client should be of considerable interest to those of us who enter into another's life circumstances. Although one can find various formal client satisfaction studies and interviews, we rarely encounter the unbidden impressions of consumers about their therapeutic experiences. And, an essential difference between formal studies of clients' reports and their personal literary versions is that, as we will see in the following excerpts, the latter are expressed within the contexts of and meanings for their social and personal lives as a whole. In other words, the literature of being helped will often tell us more intimately how strengths might be kindled not only as a result of treatment but in defiance of it. Keeping in mind Bertha whose moral convictions prevailed over institutional care, let us consider other examples.

I start with *Rose's Story* (1991), a narrative autobiography written in the kind of plain prose any client might use. Rose (a pseudonym) wrote this account in her thirties at the suggestion of her last therapist, Diane, who truly made a difference. Thus it is not an epic in its full literary or Homeric sense since Rose is by no means the tragic heroine. She might be just another plain woman who passes unnoticed in the doorway of a welfare office or mental health center. Yet, the journey she describes into and out of the backwoods of our social welfare system stands for the endurance and strength it takes to overcome some of the worst (and fortunately, the occasional best) the system imposes on those who occupy the ragged margins of society. She is a woman of considerable mettle and spirit. She found within herself the ability to rise above the devious modes of psychological labeling, institutionalization, and discrimination that passes for professional expertise and coldly violates social justice and moral responsibility. It is worth noting that this guileless, autobiographical account of one's life as a client was published with the hope that "educators might use it as a complement—if not as an antidote—to the standard abstract, formulaic textbooks on methods of helping." Such autobiographical—as well as other literary forms—invite, if not entice, the reader to, in effect, read between the lines of the text. In so doing, one might appreciate that within the dense jungle of dysfunction it is possible to find a small clearing where spirit, aspiration, and hope still endure. Here is where relationship counts.

A few brief excerpts of Rose's narrative in which she recalls her first years as a foster child and, without malice or reproval, traces her struggles over the next 30 years with professionals—many just "doing their jobs" as she saw it, as well as the few who made a difference.

When she was 11 years old that she was taken to court. After beatings by her stepmother, she had been placed in a religious girls school from which she ran away because she was whipped. "I didn't even know I was in a courthouse much less sitting outside my own trial." She learned many years later that doctors were testing her at her probate hearing.

> The next day, a welfare worker came to the orphanage and said she was taking me to a new and beautiful home with plenty of kids and a nice school and all new clothes. I was a little confused and happy that at last I was going to get adopted by a nice family.
>
> Something was certainly wrong with this worker's story. She had to be the world's greatest liar because she took me instead straight to Chatwood Psychiatric Hospital where I was locked up with a bunch of screaming old ladies that scared me to death. They put me in a bathtub and scrubbed me from head to foot with some smelly soap. They told me I was here to stay and I had to take four shots [probably Thorazine] a day. Then I said I wasn't going to stay or take any shots because I wasn't sick. They threw me on the floor and gave me a shot right then. I still knew I was right, but after that I sure didn't argue with them about anything. I just took whatever came my way. (p. 13)

Other terrible hardships followed in the succeeding years—brutal foster homes, abuse of many kinds. Nonetheless, she was proud that she did well in high school where she met a kind and loving young man (both were 16). They eventually were partners in their graduation class and both won art scholarships at a college they planned to attend after they were married. But it was not to be: Her fiancé was killed in an auto accident even as he was working out plans for their future. Later she was pressured into marrying a man 20 years older "at the cheapest wedding" her father could put together in his living room. "Living with Elton was never having anything in the house to eat, not being allowed to talk to anyone much, or have any friends." Divorce, depression, the eventual birth of two children (including her daughter whom she refused to abort and for whom she fought bitter fights to retain custody), and other travails followed. But let us leave this litany of despair and find Rose, now well into her thirties and reflecting on the caring help she finally found and her still undimmed hopes:

> I am really looking forward to the future, since I have made several great accomplishments in the last few years. I went back to college two years ago and tried to get a degree in social work and psychology. I was making all A's but had to quit because I could not keep up the pace and they only offer grants for full time or nothing. This really broke my heart . . . I know I have a lot of common sense as well as intelligence. (p. 107)

Programmed as we are by the conventional wisdom and theories that proclaim the inescapable costs of an abused and neglected childhood, we wonder, Are these strengths real? Rose offers her explanation.

> I have been in counseling with Diane for five years now. . . . I am still seeing Dr. Bergmann [a psychiatrist] and he is happy with my progress. Although I always looked to him and trusted him, what I really needed in my life was a good, decent woman I could learn to love and trust as well. I know this was the hardest part of my treatment. I not only started trusting Diane but also learned to love her as the mother I never had. (p. 101)

In a book jointly written by a therapist and her client about the experience of therapy (Fibush & Morgan, 1977), Martha is a client and a professional writer who is somewhat more sophisticated and reflective. Her words reveal how literature can serve a monitory or cautionary purpose that the helping professions themselves cannot provide. She discloses the costs of misunderstanding, what can go wrong when the best-intentioned people miss the boat, are lead astray by their presumptive theories, or otherwise blunder in their endeavor to do good. For example, Martha explains her remark on being "done wrong" by the Mental Hygiene Clinic with this question:

> How do social workers, technicians, psychiatrists, or whatever in an intake position distinguish between a person with relatively weak defenses in a minimal pressure life situation and someone with rather great strengths in a maximal pressure life

situation? After all, they can't evaluate the situation itself from their place in the consulting room. And the misestimation of his own life situation is frequently part and parcel of the patient/client's problem/illness.

Then, after learning from her experience with Esther, her therapist, what therapy can indeed accomplish, Martha looks back at the misdirections of her previous therapists to underscore this vulnerability of the client when moral strengths are disregarded:

> My past therapists wanted to help me make "realistic" plans for my future: "Don't try to function on a normal level. Don't, for example, try to take a job outside the home in the normal workaday world." But my problem wasn't schizophrenia, as they thought, but inexperience or deprivation or underdevelopment of a sort. And testing myself in new and difficult situations turned out not only *not* to be destructive but just exactly what I most needed to do, and my best kind of learning and growing experience.

And she adds ruefully:

> I have really been encouraged by several previous therapists to use insights gained in therapy to lacerate myself. They seem to equate that process with "facing the reality of my illness." The more I pleaded guilty to being sick, sick, sick and the cause of the mess around me, the more they told me what good work I was doing. I wonder why they never noticed that all the good work made me a lot sicker.

Now we hear the voice of Kate Millett who autobiographically chronicles the experience of a "mad" patient. An academic turned activist, Millett's radical bravura culminated in her 1970 book, *Sexual Politics,* a major text of feminist and culture studies. Twenty years later, after teaching philosophy and literature at various universities and writing essays and autobiographies, she writes *The Loony-Bin Trip* (1990), which she describes in her preface as

> an account of a journey into that nightmare state ascribed to madness: that social condition, that experience of being cast out and confined. I am telling what happened to me. Because the telling functions for me as a kind of exorcism, a retrieval and vindication of the self—the mind—through reliving what occurred. It is a journey many of us take. Some of us survive it intact, others only partially survive, debilitated by the harm done to us: the temptation of complicity, of the career of "patient," the pressures toward capitulation. I am telling this too in hope that it may help all those who have been or are about to be in the same boat, those captured and shaken by this bizarre system of beliefs: the general superstition of "mental disease," the physical fact of incarceration and compulsory drugs . . . stigmatized throughout the rest of one's life. A fate, after all, held before all of us throughout the whole course of our lives, the notion of "losing one's mind." An eventuality I once would have regarded as absurd, impossible, someone else's bad luck but not mine. (p. 11)

The heart of her book is her forced hospitalization in the United States and Ireland by her family and, subsequently, with the support of her lover, her fight against resuming lithium treatment. One excerpt of her memoir toward the end of her struggle with the drug is her collision in New York with Dr. Foreman, her psychiatrist:

I am going to Dr. Foreman's office for myself alone, to save my life, I say, nauseate. I surrender my capacity—proclaimed so willfully, foolishly—to control my fate through my own unaided mind. My mind on its own was not sound. Being of unsound mind then . . . here is the remedy, lithium; take it and you are healed. Bullshit . . .

Foreman is by no means glad to see me, though my coming at all must be a satisfaction: hadn't I been fool enough to go off the medication, and wasn't I here just as prophesied in serious depression? The punishment, the inevitable punishment of mania.

But it is the mania that really interests the doctors, that must be stamped out. Depression is your own problem; get out of it however you can. Wait out the months, a year maybe, until it goes away. Only you must not commit suicide—that is absolutely forbidden. Your life does not belong to you but to the doctors, the relatives, the state: the social circle. Show any symptoms of suicide, and they'll pick you up like a thief. I show none. Am not even admitting the extent of my depression—only my surrender to the medication, to anything that will give me the will to live . . . All I had to do was swallow four simple capsules a day. I would have been all right the rest of my life: my career, my farm, my friends, my reputation. I wouldn't be broke and unable to write. The six years I took the stuff were fine and productive. I did three books in that period and a great many exhibitions. Fool. Fool, to think you knew better. I squirm before Foreman while he regards me, probably amused. . . .

Foreman would be more than right; he is merciless, laying down the law about my disease, infirmity, blight: "No doubt about it, no way around it, Kate, you're a manic-depressive, that's you, Kate." How I hate his use of my first name in this condescending sentence. He called me Kate, I call him doctor. "Get used to that, you're just going to have to live with it," he says, leaning back in his chair smiling. "Of course we've got a new name for it now: bipolar affective illness." The boyish haircut, the perfect good looks, his shirt stretched tight against his perfect chest. The walkie-talkie at his belt, the office humming behind him, full of patients waiting. His avaricious assistants are consummately rude to me—a crumpled, has-been writer, condemned by this diagnosis to a life time of insanity. Would it were over already; I can't last through another depression. . . .

You must say you are crazy, say it, kiss the rod. Unless you repent to this stuffed shirt there is no lithium pill, no chemical cure, the precious prophylactic against your ups and downs, the vicious cycle of manic episode and depression. (pp. 258–262)

But when we jump from Millett's moment of almost unutterable despair to the last pages of her memoirs—her conclusion and retrospection—we find a possible answer to the question: Why do some people do more than just survive and actually discover their strengths?

I wrote *The Loony-Bin Trip* between 1982 and 1985. . . . Now, when I reread it, I find something in it rings false. True, it describes depression: the giving in, the giving up, the abnegation so complete it becomes false consciousness. But typing it over I want to say, Wait a moment—why call this depression?—why not call it grief? You've permitted your grief, even your outrage, to be converted into a disease. You have allowed your overwhelming, seemingly inexplicable grief at what has been done to you—the trauma and shame of imprisonment—to be transformed into a mysterious psychosis. How could you? (p. 309)

One last example, drawn from a multitude of other literary works that portray various takes on the other-side-of-the-desk experience.[4]

I am alone here in my own mind.
There is no map
and there is no road.
It is one of a kind
just as yours is.

This is the start of one of Anne Sexton's poems, written in her forties, a few years before she took her life but at a time when her mètier as a poet was at its crest—a time when she recieved countless accolades, honors, and awards. And what could give her greater reward than gaining a professorship at a prestigious university, considering she had not attended college? Sexton's life and work proves that whatever we call madness, psychosis, or mental illness cannot be bracketed into one category or another, cannot be subtracted, disengaged from life itself, from our sense of who and where and why we are in our world of being. And as part of life's story, it has its own genre, style, variety, and grade.

Indeed, she was endowed with a mixed bag of pathological labels during her endless psychotherapies and frequent hospitalizations. One may be tempted to speculate about the chimerical link of madness and creativity, but we will see that connection as too simple. Sexton had a vigorous, full-blooded life. She was wife and mother, insistently developed her craft, held lasting and deep friendships, worked closely with other noted artists—Tillie Olsen, Stephen Spender, Robert Lowell, Philip Rahv, and others—negotiated with publishers and editors, taught and launched other writers in their careers, and more. She suffered many losses—the death of both her parents in one year was the most grievous. She was not entirely a gentle poet: She was at times manipulative, demanding, dependent—generally difficult.

I encourage the curious reader to savor her writing not only as the legacy of an artist but as yet another unique example of the power of literature to enrich understanding of the human condition. The excerpts offered here are a very incomplete sample of the changing texture of the last decades of her life, braided by her therapy, creativity, anguish, and joy in the ordinary and imaginative moments of her life.

[4]See, for example, Neugeboren, J. (1997). *Imagining Rober: My brother's madness and survival—a memoir.* New York: William Morrow; Elkin, S. (1994). Out of one's tree. In T. Kidder & R. Atwan, (Eds.), *Best American essays* (pp. 92–109). Boston: Houghton Mifflin, 92–109; Krim, S. (1991). The insanity bit. In S. Krim, *What's this cat's story?* (pp. 40–52). New York: Paragon House.

While trying to care for her daughter and balance her relationship with her husband, her mother developed breast cancer, moved in with the Sexton family, and, in a few months, died. Three months later her father suffered a fatal cerebral hemorrhage. Nonetheless, the next 4 years were prolific and exciting for Anne. She began to refine her gift. Although her sporadic outbreaks of mental illness continued, as did her therapy, the family learned to ride out the episodes. Her collection of poetry *To Bedlam and Part Way Back* (1960) received many favorable reviews, but, though she enjoyed her new status, the more notice she received, the more exposed and vulnerable she felt. Nevertheless, she plunged on, determined to explore and experience and record.

To Bedlam opens with a poem for her psychiatrist, "You. Doctor Martin." An excerpt:

> *You, Doctor Martin, walk*
> *from breakfast to madness. Late August*
> *I speed through the antiseptic tunnel*
> *where the moving dead still talk*
> *of pushing their bones against the thrust*
> *of cure. And I am queen of this summer hotel*
> *or the laughing bean on a stalk*
> *of death. We stand in broken*
> *lines and wait while they unlock*
> *the door and count us at the frozen gates*
> *of dinner. The shibboleth is spoken*
> *and we move to gravy in our smock*
> *of smiles. We chew in rows, our plates*
> *scratch and whine like chalk.*

A patient in a mental hospital wrote to Anne Sexton, feeling Anne was a kindred spirit. Anne wrote back, the beginning of an ongoing correspondence:

> The sun will come back, I promise. I don't know when . . . but it will, it did for me. True, it hides from me now and then and those are bad days and sometimes even months. Still, I am much better. Your letter evokes my feelings of the past and how well I know how it is with you! . . . Yes, you can go far down—but you can come back up . . . you don't need to die down there . . . but at least you can reach out to me and your doctor . . . I used to say to my doctor "You're not crazy if you can find one sane person who you can talk to."

Later she taught a poetry class at a private mental institution where a number of well-known artists had been patients. She said in a letter to a student, "Poetry led me by the hand out of madness. I am hoping I can show others that route."

The intent of this chapter is to offer a position on the strengths perspective that defines it as a humanistic enterprise and thus intimately ties it to the threads of moral distress that are woven into the texture of social work practice. I marked out the differences distinguishing the traditional defectological model from the strengths perspective, showing that the former is concerned with what's wrong—that which needs fixing—and the latter engaged with what's right—that which can be the foundation for enhancing strength, resilience, and moral responsibility. To put it in the now familiar Jewish idiom, the strengths perspective focuses on how to become a *mensch*. Beginning with Bertha's words, her autobiographical account of her fight against victimhood, I showed both through rhetoric and example how the humanities and its literature—the novel, autobiography, poetry, and drama—can enrich and profoundly deepen the empathic understanding needed for an effective strengths approach to practice.

I am compelled to admit that my argument is handicapped by the fact that I am not a litterateur, a scholar, or literary critic intimately familiar with the literature and letters of the humanities. Rather, I write as a social worker, one who just happens to be an avid reader who searches for the links between creative expression and the essence of ordinary lives. Certainly, I have overlooked countless other literary resources that would more passionately reaffirm these links. Thus I suggest that, just as social work has crossed disciplinary boundaries into philosophy, moral theory, and the social and behavioral sciences to draw from the valuable knowledge of certain writers and consultants, it would be opportune to do the same with regard to the humanities.

In this vein, Jerome Bruner's (1996) observations on the significance of stories helps me bring this chapter to its close. In his essay, "The Narrative Construal of Reality," he asks:

> What, in fact, is gained and what is lost when human beings make sense of the world by telling stories about it—by using the narrative mode for construing reality? The usual answer to this question is a kind of doxology delivered in the name of "the scientific method": Thou shalt not indulge in self-delusion, nor utter unverifiable propositions, nor commit contradiction, nor treat mere history as cause, and so on. Story, according to such commandments, is not the realistic stuff of science and is to be shunned or converted into testable propositions. If meaning making were always dedicated to achieving "scientific" understanding, such cautions might be understandable. But neither the empiricist's tested knowledge nor the rationalist's self-evident truths describe the ground on which ordinary people go about making sense of their experiences. . . . These are matters that need a story . . . to get successfully from what somebody said to what he means, from what *seems* the case to what "really" *is*. Although the scientific method is hardly irrelevant to all this, it is certainly not the only route to understanding. (p. 130)

Whether stories are contrived—for literary purposes or to preserve self-esteem—or are responsive to another's inquiry, or are casually told to inform, amuse, brag, defy, or otherwise make a point, they contain and make sense on many levels—that is, if one really listens. And if one listens, what might be caught are voices that are unheard by the more objective, linear, and categorical modes of inquiry. Such schemes—diagnosis and assessment, for example—are like the blueprints of a home: They capture the outlines and structure of the place but cannot say what its lived-in qualities are like. And so revealing are these voices of the inevitable ironies and paradoxes of what it means to be human and, even more so, to share in human dialogue.

And so, returning to the literary examples in the previous pages as well as the scope of the humanities itself, let me identify just a few of the voices that may surface in our reading.

The Voice of Social Conscience, Criticism, and Commentary. This voice pleads to be heard about the inequities and bureaucratic rigidities that impair—if not cancel out—even the best intentions to do good. A poignant example is Rose's documentary of the sorry backwaters of the social welfare system. Even though her plain words are without passion or blame, they compel us to resist our idle tendencies to excuse or accept as a given the all too common institutional failures. Nor can we excuse the officials and professionals whose indifference to or rigid clutch on the rules, policies, and exclusions deny the mission they are obligated to fulfill. Far more persuasive than outcome studies or client surveys, the personal account of encounters with such putative helpers should trouble our professional conscience and responsibilities.

The Voice Challenging Conventional Wisdom. We are by nature captives of our narrow, finely structured worlds—but comfortable captives since, if we don't question them too much, the pieces fit so nicely together in the form of the theories, realities, truisms, and platitudes we live by. Heeding narrative lives and literature, we might, at times, allow ourselves to reconsider who we are, what we know, and what we do when we presumptively enter into and attempt to define the our clients' problems and lives. We might even disclaim the simplistic solutions and classifications that are dealt out by experts and specialists in the attempt to demystify what is essentially enigmatic.

The Voice of Contradiction. Similarly, the literature of the humanities and narrative insistently prod us to consider that, when it comes to the human condition, things aren't as rational, predictable, linear, or explicable as we wish they were: Discontinuity is the mirror of reality. Or we might say that from our explorations in the humanities, a certain insight and maturity can be gained that would allow for informed dissent. Scarcely as definitive as a psychological treatise, nonetheless, Anne Sexton's poetry makes the plain statement that truth varies, that seeming opposites—fear and courage or hope and dread—naturally, albeit painfully. Such incongruities are the inescapable ironies of a full-blooded life. Sexton tells us that madness is not absolute, a final judgment: Rather it is an experience in time and place in which the self—however we define it—may be stretched to its most absurd extremes.

The Moral Voice and Its Values. Beyond or below the more obvious moral shoulds and musts that guide the sensible approach to work, love, and life in general are the discrete and determining choices that betray the suffering and struggle about what is truly at stake in one's situation. We find them in epics and autobiographies not necessarily labeled there as moral or ethical choice; yet they unmistakably mark one of life's significant crossroads. Whether one chooses or refuses to commit the moral act, there is a price. To my mind, we get a better understanding of what the elusive ideas of strength and resilience mean when we have a sense of the inner invincible moral voice that insists on a moral bearing. Consider that it was this kind of moral voice that compelled Kate Millet to redis-cover or reinvent the virtues that, within the ruination of her illness, were pow-erful enough to allow her to reclaim sanity and its moral obligations.

Art, as it is expressed through its many humanistic genres, is the foundation for a narrative approach to helping people grapple with their ordeals of living. This premise was the basis of the intent of this chapter—to show how the humanities open pathways of thought and understanding that expand our grasp of the raw data of human experience, the stories people tell.

DISCUSSION QUESTIONS

1. How might you use the arts, the books you've read, the poetry, the essays, or films and plays that you have seen, or the music that you listen to, to inform your under-standing of the clients you see?

2. What does it mean to say that resilience is primarily an interpersonal phenomenon?

3. How are both the medical/scientific perspective and the strengths/resilience per-spective social constructions? What difference does that idea make to you?

4. What does *The Looney Bin Trip* suggest about the current medical constructions of practice?

REFERENCES

Anthony, E. J., & Cohler, B. J. (Eds.). (1987). *The invulnerable child.* New York: Guilford Press.

Bellow, S. (2000). *City of God.* New York: Random House.

Bruner, J. (1990). *Acts of meaning.* Cambridge: Harvard University Press.

Bruner, J. (1996). The narrative construal of reality. In J. Bruner *The culture of education* (pp. 130–149). Cambridge: Harvard University Press.

Cowger, C. (1997). Assessing client strengths: Assessment for client empowerment. In D. Salee-bey (Ed.), *The strengths perspective in social work practice* (pp. 59–73). New York: Longman.

Ellenberger, H. (1970). *The discovery of the unconscious.* New York: Basic Books.

Fibush, E., & Morgan, M. (1977). *Forgive me no longer: The liberation of Martha.* New York: Family Service Association of America.

Franklin, C., & Nurius, P. S., (Eds.). (1998). *Constructivism in practice: Methods and challenges.* Grimsby, Ontario, Canada: Manticore.

Gergen, K. J. (1985). The Social Constructionist Movement in modern psychology. *American Psy-chologist, 40,* 266–275.

Goldstein, H. (1996). *The home on Gorham Street and the voices of its children.* Tuscaloosa, AL: Uni-versity of Alabama Press.

Gove, P. B., & Merriam-Webster. (1993). *Webster's 3rd new international dictionary.* Springfield, MA: Merriam-Webster.

Greene, M. (1966). The humanities in social work education. *Journal of Education in Social Work, 2*(1), 21–31.

Jordan, J. V. (1992, April). *Relational resilience.* Paper presented as part of the Stone Center Collo-quium Series, Wellesley, MA: Wellesley College.

Kunin, R. (1985). *A study of clients' self-reports of their experience of personal change in direct practice.* Unpublished doctoral dissertation, Case Western Reserve University.

Laird, J. (1993). Family centered practice: Cultural and constructionist reflections. In J. Laird (Ed.), *Revisioning social work education: A social constructionist approach* (pp. 31–54). New York: Haworth.

Laird, J. (Ed.). (1993). *Revisioning social work education: A social constructionist approach.* New York: Haworth.

Mahoney, M. J. (1991). *Human change processes.* New York: Basic Books.

Millett, K. (1990). *The loony-bin trip.* New York: Simon & Schuster.

Morson, G. S. (1988, Autumn) Prosaics: An approach to the humanities. *American Scholar, 57,* 515–528.

Posner, R. (1997, April). Against ethical criticism. *Philosophy and Literature, 21,* 1–27.

Rose. (1991). *Rose's story: From client to individual.* Milwaukee: Family Service America.

Saleebey, D. (1997). The strengths approach to practice. In D. Saleebey (Ed.), *The strengths perspective in social work practice* (pp. 49–58). New York: Longman.

Sass, L. A. (1992). *Madness & modernism.* New York: Basic Books.

Sexton, A. (1960). *To bedlam and part way back.* Boston: Houghton Mifflin.

Sheehy, G. (1986, April 20). The victorious personality. *New York Times Magazine,* p. 26.

Vaillant, G. E. (1993). *The wisdom of the ego.* Cambridge: Harvard University Press.

3

Strengths of First Nations Peoples[1]

MARGARET WALLER

MICHAEL YELLOW BIRD

When Europeans crossed the Atlantic beginning in the late 15th century, they found two continents populated by 30 million people from many independent Nations (Marger, 1994). Evidence indicates that North America had been inhabited by Indigenous Peoples for 75,000 years (Josephy, 1991). However, traditional creation stories of many North American tribes teach that Native Peoples have been in this area since the beginning of time. Indigenous Peoples included hundreds of cultures, as different from one another as they were from Europeans.

Since first contact, the well-being of Indigenous Peoples has been continuously challenged by internal colonialism.[2] Europeans interpreted Indigenous Peoples' unfamiliar physical appearances, beliefs, and practices as signs of biological, intellectual, cultural, and moral inferiority. In the minds of European colonizers, this interpretation was justification for exploitation, appropriation of land and resources, and genocide (Marger, 1994), all of which were, according to the Europeans, "God's will" (Thornton, 1987).

---

[1] The terms *First Nations Peoples, Indigenous Peoples,* or *Native Peoples,* describe North American tribes more accurately than *Native Americans* or *American Indians,* both of which are misnomers, since Indigenous Peoples long predated America; and *Indians* is an artifact of Christopher Columbus's geographical confusion. While First Nations and Indigenous Peoples are generic labels for more than 660 different tribal groups, they are used as empowering descriptors. The terms are plural and uppercase acknowledging the distinctness and sovereignty of Indigenous Peoples. The generic label Indigenous Peoples prefer to be called varies. What is most respectful and appropriate is to refer to Indigenous Peoples by their tribal Nation or Indigenous affiliation. Often this means using a name that each group has selected for itself from its own Indigenous language. We will use Indigenous Peoples and Native Peoples in this chapter.

[2] Internal colonialism refers to a form of domination in which one ethnic group within a country imposes its political, economic, social, and cultural institutions and will on an indigenous people (Ferrante & Brown, 2001).

Between 1500 and 1900, slavery, disease, the introduction of alcohol, warfare, and forced removal from traditional lands all contributed to genocide that destroyed between 95% and 99% of the Indigenous population (Stiffarm & Lane, 1992). As a continuing consequence of the centuries of internal colonialism and oppression, Indigenous Peoples today contend with more severe problems related to income, education, occupation, employment, health care, mortality, and housing, than any other population group in the United States (Marger, 1994).

Nevertheless, Indigenous populations have survived, and are among the youngest and fastest growing population groups in the United States (Locke, 1992). The average age of the Indigenous population is 16. In 1990 there were an estimated 2 million Indigenous people in the United States. This is a 38% increase over the recorded 1980 population, and 4 times the 1960 population estimate (Marger, 1994). There are 660 federally recognized tribes in the United States. An additional 200 tribes are still struggling with legal and government agencies to gain federal recognition (Wright, et al. 1997). This chapter highlights some of the strengths that have made it possible for Indigenous Peoples to survive and adapt despite centuries of oppression.

Historical Distortion of Strengths of Indigenous Peoples

Historically, the strengths of Indigenous Peoples have often been viewed as deficits and used against them. For example, although sharing and generosity have been regarded as core values and economic strengths of Indigenous Peoples, these virtues have been regarded as cultural deficiencies and anomalies by whites (Meyer, 1977). In one case, a religious missionary working among the Mandan, Hidatsa, and Arikara in the late 1800s declared, "they are a generous people and feel their responsibility toward their brother. But the mission work is gradually overcoming this" (Meyer, 1977, p. 128). In 1493, Christopher Columbus, on his second voyage to the "new world," used the generosity, kindness, cooperation, and peacefulness of the Arawaks against them. When the Arawaks first encountered Columbus, they ran to greet him and his sailors, bringing them food and gifts. In his journal he wrote, "They . . . brought us parrots and balls of cotton and spears and many other things, which they exchanged for the glass beads and hawks' bells. They willingly traded everything they owned. . . . They do not bear arms, and do not know them, for I showed them a sword, they took it by the edge and cut themselves out of ignorance. . . . They would make fine servants. . . . With fifty men we could subjugate them all and make them do whatever we want" (Akwesasne Notes, 1972, p. 22).

The social work profession has historically identified itself as a profession that focuses on strengths (Hepworth & Larsen, 1982; Towle, 1945). However, stories about Indigenous Peoples in the social work literature have generally been deficit focused. Such problem-focused stories perpetuate oppressive societal stereotypes and constrict vision in both service recipients and helping professionals (Waller,

Risley-Curtiss, Murphy, Medill, & Moore, 1998). Like Columbus, early missionaries, and other European colonizers, social workers' accounts have obscured the strengths of Indigenous Peoples.

Strengths of Indigenous Peoples

A vibrant, colorful tapestry of strengths has made it possible for Indigenous Peoples to persevere despite the ongoing assaults of internal colonialism. The following section provides a sampling of strengths important to some. Given the wide diversity among Indigenous Peoples, it is not possible to generalize these strengths across cultures. In working with particular clients, social workers may identify and draw upon these strengths and may discover many others.

Resistance

While European Americans have persistently attempted to destroy Indigenous cultures and remold Native people in the image of the white man, Indigenous people have steadfastly struggled to preserve their cultural integrity (Wright & Tierney, 2000). One of myriad examples is resistance to the government's use of boarding schools to force assimilation. Until the last of these government-run schools was closed in the 1970s, children were forcibly removed from their homes and relocated to off-reservation boarding schools where they were forced to look and act European, and were severely punished for speaking their own languages or exhibiting any other reflection of their Native identities. Children were often neglected and/or abused sexually, physically, and emotionally. In some cases, they were killed for infractions, and their deaths were recorded as accidents or suicides (Anderson, Putnam, Sinclair-Daisy, & Squetimkin-Anquoe, 1999). Native children and their families resisted this attempted ethnocide from the beginning and the experiment was ultimately abandoned. Luther Standing Bear attended the first boarding school, established in Carlisle, Pennsylvania, in 1879. He recalled,

> I remember when we children were on our way to Carlisle School, thinking that we were on our way to meet death at the hands of the white people. The older boys sang brave songs, so that we would meet death according to the code of the Lakota. (Aguirre & Baker, 2000, p. 95)

In another example, a Diné social worker related the following story (personal communication, C. Endischee, July 31, 1999).

> My grandmother lived in the mountains in the traditional way. I loved visiting my grandmother but it was hard for me to help out with the sheep and chores, since I had grown up in the city. I felt ignorant next to the "rez" kids who seemed to know how to do everything. Sometimes my grandmother would see me getting discouraged and she would stop her work, sit me down, and tell me a story. One afternoon, she called me over and handed me a small ball of dried adobe. "Go

ahead, break it open and look inside," she said. I cracked open the ball and found fresh bread inside. "Go ahead and eat it," she said. I made a face. This bread with dried mud on it didn't look very appetizing to a city girl. Seeing my disgust, my grandmother told me this story. "When I was a child, the federal agents would come to everyone's house, trying to steal our children and send them off to boarding schools. Sometimes, after years of abuse, our children would return home forever changed. Sometimes they never came home at all. So we escaped to the mountains to hide, but they kept coming after us, taking our children. It wasn't safe to stay in one camp too long because they would see the smoke from our fires and find us. So we learned to make a fresh dough, cover it with wet adobe, and bury it under the coals from the fire. Then, at day break, we left and hid somewhere else. Pretty soon, the white men would see the smoke and find our camp, but we would be gone, so they would leave. After a while, we would circle back around and there our bread was, already baked and ready to eat. That's how we outsmarted them."

The grandmother blessed the bread and she and her granddaughter ate it together.

Sovereignty

Unlike any other ethnic or racial group in the United States, First Nations Peoples are a political entity. The U.S. government recognizes Indigenous Peoples as having a special, legal government-to-government relationship with the United States (Pevar, 1992). By law, they are "distinct, independent political communities possessing and exercising the power of self government" (Worcester v. Georgia, 1831). As a consequence of sovereignty, Indigenous Peoples may participate in three levels of citizenship: Indigenous, state, and United States. Indigenous families who belong to federally recognized tribes are eligible to receive federal services such as health care, education, and social services.

Sovereign Indigenous Nations have inherent powers of self-government. They have the right to make, pass, and enforce laws, implement taxation, create tribal constitutional codes, license social workers, declare war, and seek remedy in international courts of law. They also possess aboriginal territories (lands) that are protected under trust agreement with the United States. Social workers who work with and on behalf of Indigenous Peoples must respect Indigenous sovereignty. They must agree to abide by all laws of the nations just as they would in any other country. Any issues regarding the welfare and protection of Indigenous children falls under the province of Indigenous nations. Sovereignty is essential to the preservation of the rights and resources of Indigenous Nations and is a powerful protective factor. No other racial group in the United States has a similar sovereign political and legal standing.

Separation

The most resilient Indigenous cultures have recognized the importance of maintaining physical, social, psychological, and spiritual distance between themselves and the rest of the United States (Weaver, 1999). Reservations, for many people, are protected homelands that make it possible to preserve the parts of their traditional culture that contrast with the surrounding European culture (Elsass, 1992; Wilkinson, 1987). Traditionalists believe that maintaining cultural survival is just as important as physical survival, and that this can only be achieved with separation. In the Taos Pueblo, for example, while tourism is an important part of the economy, contact with outsiders is strictly regulated. Although visitors are allowed to visit the plaza during certain hours and may observe some seasonal dances, most of the Pueblo land and the most sacred ceremonies are closed to the public.

Another powerful strategy for preserving Taos culture is the 18-month period in which Taos boys reside in the Kiva and are steeped in Taos language, beliefs, and practices. During this time the boys wear traditional clothing, speak only Tewa, the Taos language, and eat only traditional foods prepared by family members. They receive daily instruction from tribal elders, preparing them to fulfill traditional roles in their families and clans. During the Kiva time, a boy has contact only with Taos people and culture. No contact with European or any other outside culture is permitted. At the end of a boy's time in the Kiva, he is fluent in his native language, knowledgeable about traditional beliefs and practices, and ready to take his place as a man in the Taos community.

Although no Indigenous person can escape the influence of European American culture, separate and protected tribal lands allow Indigenous cultures to preserve their integrity. Given that the Indigenous population is split between those living on and off reservations (Marger, 1994), many Indigenous people lack knowledge of their traditional lifeways. Many people have been brought up in boarding schools or raised in urban areas. Nevertheless, separate and protected tribal lands where traditional lifeways continue, provide them with spiritual and psychological homes apart from the hostile dominant culture. Teles (Waller & McAllen-Walker, in press), a Diné university student who lives in Phoenix, Arizona, 3 hours away from his home community, describes his connection with his tribal home this way.

> I think that we are such a close family, I mean we've become actually closer, even though we don't see each other for quite some time, you know, a month, or two months. But still, I feel a connection to everybody back home in a sort of sense to where it will infiltrate my dreams, my thought processes, and sure enough, I'm right. If something's going on. Like for example, my sister . . . for some reason or another, I'll just pick up the phone to call, and it so happens that at that moment, you know, she will be trying to call me. We'll pick up the phone at the same time and we both get a busy signal. You know, that kind of thing. And so, and with my mom and dad it's that way too. And so in that sense, that I don't see them often but still feel this, I don't know, huge waves of something or another I feel like emanating from the North. . . . And sure enough, when it's with me, I just know.

Positive Cultural Identity

Many Indigenous people have, by force or by choice, to varying degrees, taken on values and ways of the dominant society. Nevertheless, a strong, positive identification with one's Native culture, reinforced by continuing participation in traditional lifeways, can buffer against the negative impact of interactions with the dominant culture and promote a sense of well-being (Oetting & Beauvais, 1991). Esther, for example, grew up in the Taos Pueblo community, participating in traditional lifeways. Because of economic necessity, for the past 30 years she has lived, worked, and raised her children in Albuquerque, 3 hours away from her home community. Esther maintains her cultural identity by returning regularly to her home community to spend time with family and friends and participate in seasonal dances and feast days. Though she lives in Albuquerque, she considers the Taos Pueblo to be her home.

Tribal Colleges

The ongoing legacy of internal colonialism is inextricably intertwined with the experience of Indigenous Peoples in the United States educational system. Most Native grandparents and many parents today are survivors of educational environments in which they were taught that they were inferior to white people and that their traditions were savage and immoral. These historical factors continue to influence the experience of Native students in mainstream educational institutions (Hurtado, 1992) and are evident in educational outcomes. For example, if 100 Native students enter the ninth grade, only 60 will graduate from high school. Of these graduates, only 20 will enter a mainstream college and only 10 will receive a 4-year degree (Aguirre & Baker, 2000, p. 97).

In response to this problem, tribal colleges—usually two-year community colleges—have evolved over the past 30 years. Tribal colleges offer culturally relevant curricula that include emphasis on tribal history, Native languages, and fostering a strong, positive cultural identity (Harjo, 1993). The Navajo Community College, established in 1968, was the first tribal college. By 1996, there were 29 tribal colleges nationwide. These institutions serve about 10,000 Native students. In contrast to the experience of Native students in mainstream colleges, 35% of students entering tribal colleges go on to complete their bachelor's degrees, more than 3 times the success rate of those students in mainstream colleges.

Suspicion and Mistrust

Indigenous Peoples in all parts of the world experience the legacy and continuing trauma of colonization. Genocide and ethnocide are omnipresent threats for Indigenous Peoples. Suspicion and mistrust are healthy responses under these conditions and have helped Indigenous Peoples in the United States to survive the relentless onslaught of the dominant culture (Schaefer, 1998; Weaver, 1999). In dealing with non-Native clinicians, Indigenous clients coping with presenting problems often have the added challenge of dealing with the clinician's distorted perceptions of Indigenous people. As Modoc novelist Michael Dorris (1987) puts it,

> The Indian mystique was designed for mass consumption by a European audience . . . it is little wonder then, that many non-Indians literally would not know a real Native American if they fell over one, for they have been prepared for a

well-defined, carefully honed legend. . . . For most people the myth has become a real and a preferred substitute for reality. (p. 99)

Suspicion and mistrust pose a special problem for professional helpers, both Native and non-Native. If helpers are Native, clients may wonder if they can be truly empathic or whether they have sold out and become *apples,* a colloquial term for a person who is red on the outside, but white on the inside. Mainstream professional helpers who have not lived the experience of internal colonialism, may misunderstand a Native client's reticence, and may interpret it as a personal or cultural liability. Reasonable doubt, and questions about the helpers' intentions are likely to occur. If helpers are non-Native, how do they perceive Native people? Do they see stereotypes or individuals? What are their motivations? Do they romanticize Native cultures? Are they hoping to appropriate Native worldview and lifeways and use them to derive a sense of identity, spiritual connectedness, and social status (Waller & McAllen-Walker, in press)? If so, they are perpetrating a new-age form of colonialism, more insidious in some ways than straightforward genocide and appropriation of land and resources, because it is spiritual resources that are being distorted, exploited, and appropriated. Indigenous clients are particularly vulnerable in relationships with such people because positive regard is seductive, particularly when the client is in pain. As one Diné college student put it:

> So back to spirituality and exploitation, so that's why I think all of that does a lot of damage. A lot of it has to do with the dominant value system changing. I see it more as an assault, appropriating Native values, practices, etc., and what exactly is that going to do? You know, I mean, I think there are a lot of people who think that Indian people, Indian cultures, are like living saviors, you know . . . I think [white] people are searching, and when it comes to Indian people, we are now expected to be above all of this, you know? I think that does damage as well. Like with all these New Agers, it's just like it leaves a wide open space for exploitation, I mean, I mean believe me, I see that. And I see people who are totally, you know, who shouldn't be doing that [e.g., assuming "Indian sounding" names, marketing healing practices such as the Sweat Lodge, burning sage, using ceremonial fans, etc.]. You know, they're messing with our, our universe . . . messing with our spirituality, our ceremonies and all of that. And people are making money off of it. And what if a young person is trying to find their place, you know, and starts seeing that. It's totally wrong in most cases. (Waller & McAllen-Walker, in press)

For these reasons, initial suspicion and mistrust of professional helpers are important protective factors for Indigenous clients. It is advisable for the professional helper to embrace them as the coping resources that they are.

An alternative way of viewing a Native client's suspicion and mistrust is as an invitation for the professional helper to reflect on her own attitudes and motivations in working with Indigenous clients. The need for this introspection on the part of non-Native professional helpers is illustrated in this poem written by Nancy Wood in 1974.

> *You know how it is.*
> *People come here and they want to know our secret of life.*
> *They ask many questions, but their minds are already made up.*

They admire our children but they feel sorry for them.
They look around and they do not see anything except dust.
They come to our dances but they are always wanting to take pictures.
They come into our homes expecting to learn about us in five minutes.
They are glad they do not live here.
Yet they are not sure whether or not we know something which is the key to all
  understanding.
Our secret of life would take them forever to find out.
Even then, they would not believe it.

Intertribal Celebrations

Intertribal celebrations such as powwows and gourd dances have evolved over the past 100 years into gatherings where people from many tribes come together to visit, catch up with friends from different communities, pray together, and share traditional dances and songs. Currently, Native Peoples collaborate to organize events with prizes and competitions in more than 1,000 locations across the United States. Such celebrations foster solidarity among tribes, and facilitate coming together to seek solutions to common grievances. These intertribal celebrations amplify the voice of Indigenous Peoples, and demonstrate the power and richness of contemporary Native cultures (Parfit, 1994).

Kinship, Mutual Assistance, and Distributive Justice

In many Indigenous societies, human beings are inextricably interconnected through a complex web of relationships, including relatives by blood, clan, tribe, and adoption. Among the Diné, for example, mutual dependence and cooperation are givens, and individual standing in the community is largely related to the extent to which a person is helpful to others. To be Diné is to fulfill one's responsibility to one's relations. This is why one of the harshest forms of retribution is to be told, "You act as if you have no relatives" (Austin, 1993). The following vignettes illustrate the importance of mutual assistance and distributive justice in one Diné community (Waller & Patterson, in press). Here a 30-year-old woman describes how she and her husband helped his 27-year-old sister and her children.

> She had been left by her husband. . . . so she had no place to go and she brought her [four] kids here. And on top of that, she had a handicapped child. She was carrying more load than we were, so we accepted her in and we did our part. We helped her pull some of the load she was carrying. We spent the whole winter with her and about half of the summer. (p. 9)

In the next instance, a 58-year-old man describes helping his elder neighbor.

> Well this neighbor lives by himself. He's a widow and he's eighty years old. He has sheep, goats, about five dogs and about thirteen cats. And then he always needs my help. So I really help this man because he used to help me a lot when I used to be in problems. He talked to me a lot. How to straighten up. So, he's a really strong believer. So that's why me and him are really close. We help each other. (p.11)

In many Indigenous cultures, every individual is expected to fulfill prescribed relationship roles. One earns respect by giving priority to the needs and welfare of others—seeing that they are fed, housed, and cared for. Those who refuse to help, or think of themselves before others are not held in high esteem (Nofz, 1988). Among the Diné, for example, the maternal uncle is expected to be a father figure. Roland, for example, is the first in his extended family to complete college. He has a law degree as well and is currently a college professor in Phoenix. As soon as Roland became professionally settled, he bought a home large enough to accommodate the next generation of college students in his family. He currently provides housing, food, tuition, books, and many other necessities for his three nieces, all students in a local college, along with one niece's baby. He will continue to support them throughout their college education. Kinship relations and expectations in Roland's family promote a sense of belonging and security. No one is expected to stand alone.

Similarly, love for children is unconditional. Traditionally, children have grown up in extended family households under the care of members of multiple generations. They are claimed, cherished, and cared for, not only by their parents but by all of their relations. In many Indigenous languages, for example, there is no term for cousin, niece, or nephew. This child is addressed by the entire clan as brother, sister, son, or daughter—terms generally reserved for immediate family in the dominant culture (Cross, 1986; Red Horse, 1980).

When kinship systems are intact, children born to young, single mothers are not subject to the prejudices and hardships that they would be likely to encounter in the American mainstream. Similarly, elders in traditional households are respected and have active roles and influence in the raising of children, and in family and community decision making.

In some traditions, distributive justice is formalized, for example, through giveaways in which families honor a particular member by distributing food, clothing, linens, and other household items to other families, or by giving gifts to community members and traditional practitioners who have gathered to pray for a family member. In many communities, a family's wealth and status is measured not in terms of what family members possess, but by their generosity to others.

The social worker seeking to assist a Native family should understand that professional helpers typically are not the first line of defense in many communities and, in fact, may not have ever been used. For example, in one study of 100 helping episodes in a Diné community, researchers found that informal helpers had never consulted professional helpers and were never consulted by them. In communities such as this one, in which the standard practice is to rely on informal helping systems, an effective social work intervention might be to assist the client in accessing informal helpers. It would also be useful to collaborate with informal helpers within the community (Waller & Patterson, in press).

Traditional Spirituality and Healing Practices

Indigenous Peoples continue to practice many sacred and secular rituals rooted in diverse ontological beliefs and cosmologies. Spiritual practices and beliefs have great importance in many people's lives and are an important source of comfort, strength, meaning, self-renewal, and connectedness. Beliefs and practices are often deeply connected to the lands that people occupy or have come from and may feature sacred mountains, waters, forests, stories, songs, plants (medicines), dances, and symbols. Generations of repression and pressure to forsake their religions for European Christianity, have led some people to reject their ancient traditions and replace them with Christian beliefs and practices. Others combine Christianity with traditional beliefs and practices. Some Indigenous groups have borrowed ceremonies from other groups in an effort to help their people. Examples are the use of the Sundance and the Sweat Lodge, both of which are thought to have originated with the plains tribes but are currently widely practiced. Similarly, the Native American Church, organized in 1918, began in the Southwest, but now has members from many tribes across the United States.

Following generations of religious and legal repression of Indigenous beliefs and practices, the 1978 American Indian Religious Freedom Act declared the U.S. government's commitment to "protect and preserve the inherent right of American Indians to believe, express, and practice their traditional religions" (Schaefer, 1998). Drawing on this legislation, Native Peoples are seeking to reclaim sacred areas and are gaining protection for conducting traditional ceremonies for military personnel and individuals confined to treatment centers and prisons. In past and present times, Indigenous Peoples have used spirituality to overcome despair and to cope with the oppression. Many also use spirituality to celebrate who they are, what they know and believe, and to give thanks for the triumphs and good fortune that they experience in life. For many Native people, spiritual beliefs, ceremonies, and practices were, and remain, a major defense against European colonization.

Storytelling and Legends

Storytelling among Indigenous Peoples has a long and rich tradition and is an important source of cultural strength. It is the principal means by which Indigenous Peoples remember who they are and where they come from, and gain insight into where they are going. Storytelling also gives meaning to experience and provides perspective. Laguna poet Leslie Marmon Silko, for example, describes having often returned to Laguna Pueblo, seeking respite from life in the American mainstream. Her elder relatives would listen to her descriptions of situations and events and would wrap her experiences in ancient stories or humorous anecdotes that invariably comforted her and gave her a sense of shared experience, perspective, and direction.

Tribal and personal narratives also serve to convey important messages about how to conduct oneself in the world and are the principal means of teaching, correcting, and guiding children. For example, among the Sahnish, storytelling includes myths of ancient times, legends of supernatural power bestowed on selected individuals, historical accounts, anecdotes of mysterious incidents, and fictional tales (Parks, 1996). Tribal narratives depict situations, places, persons, or events that enable Sahnish individuals to understand who they are, how they should behave, what they should know and value, and where they come from (Yellow Bird, 1995). Among the Diné, "legends are not only the basis of the complex ceremonials, they are also the history of the people, much as the Old Testament is both the Judaic religious base and the history of the ancient Jews" (Locke, 1992, p. 55).

From generation to generation, Indigenous Peoples have used storytelling to pass down traditional teachings and guidance, to recount history, strengthen identity, instill pride, transform individuals and the community, strengthen relationships, and provide enjoyment. Storytelling is a primary means of transmitting tradition and history across generations, and, as such, sustains cultures. Storytelling can also nurture cultural pride and can be a form of resistance. For example, there are many humorous stories that give encounters with Custer, Columbus, and the Pilgrims a new twist. While the storytelling of Indigenous Peoples is often done in the context of enjoyment and entertainment, it is far from being a frivolous event. Among many nations there is a strict protocol about who can tell stories and when, where, what, why, and how stories can be shared.

Humor

Humor is cherished and cultivated in many Indigenous cultures, and permeates peoples' spiritual, social, and political lives. For example, sacred clowns are key players in many ceremonies. They delight young and old with their oratorical talents and use humorous stories to convey important cultural knowledge. No one is exempt from the exaggerated acts and mimicking behavior of the sacred clowns, including governors and other tribal officials. The clown's disregard for authority provides another layer of enjoyment for the group (Shutiva, 1997). At powwows, emcees are chosen, in part, because of their ability to combine speaking knowledgeably about tradition with charming audiences with humorous stories, jokes, and puns (Giago, 1990). During gatherings, no one escapes playful teasing. Relatives and friends have reservoirs of jokes and funny stories that predictably surface at every get-together. These exchanges transport members of the group to a common place that lifts spirits and is comforting in its familiarity. The Navajo language, for example, is full of subtle meanings and words that may be slightly modified for humorous effect. Since the Diné culture possesses no system of social stratification, anyone can engage in playful humor. "A respected elder can act the fool without losing dignity. Too, children can tease their parents or even their grandparents unmercifully and to a degree that would never be accepted in white society" (Locke, 1992, p. 28).

Humor can be used as a means of socialization and social control. For example, it may be employed to correct inappropriate behavior in children or adults in a way that gets the point across without shaming or embarrassing the person who is out of step. In one Diné family, for example, an uncle living away in the city would occasionally break with the family protocol and stay out of touch with family members for weeks at a time. Family members began to playfully refer to him as "Hides A Lot. " He started calling home more often.

Another use for humor is as a survival mechanism in dealing with the complexities of living simultaneously in Native and non-Native worlds, and as a means of resistance against oppression by the dominant society. For example, a Diné woman tells a joke about an old Diné man who was walking slowly and thoughtfully along the road. A young, abrasive, loud white guy, oblivious to the protocol for addressing elders, pulls his truck over and yells, "Hey old man, do I take this road to Flagstaff?" The old man, without looking up, replies, "No, you can go on yourself, but you better leave the road here."

Political Activism

Political activism has contributed greatly to the preservation of Indigenous culture, language, religious freedom, traditional healing practices, and self-determination (Deloria & Lytle, 1984; Morris, 1992). The National Congress of American Indians (NCAI), founded in 1944, in Denver, Colorado, was the first national organization representing First Nations Peoples. The NCAI uses strategies similar to those of the NAACP and continues to play an important role in protecting the rights of Native People. The 1960s and 1970s were marked by political organizing and increasingly militant protests by Indigenous Peoples. The American Indian Movement (AIM), founded in 1968, is nationally known for the use of confrontational tactics to challenge inequities perpetrated by the Bureau of Indian Affairs (BIA) and law enforcement agencies. Recently, AIM has brought attention to contemporary racist practices such as the commercial use of racial slurs, as in the Washington Redskins, or Squaw Valley, or the use of Indian mascots for sports teams. The Alaskan Federation of Natives (AFN) was organized in 1967 to stop the state of Alaska from illegally appropriating oil-rich Native land. As a result of the efforts of the AFN, legislation granted control and ownership of 44 million acres to Alaska's native Inuits, Aleuts, and other peoples, and gave them a cash settlement of nearly $1 billion (Schaefer, 1998). Another legislative milestone resulting from political activism was the Indian Child Welfare Act of 1978. Prior to this legislation, up to 35% of all Indigenous children were removed from their homes and placed in non-Native foster care or adoptive placements, or in institutional care. As a result of this legislation, placement of Native children is at the direction of tribal social service and court systems and, to the extent possible, placement is with Indigenous families who can foster the development of a strong, positive, cultural identity (Goodluck, 1993).

Conclusion

This chapter provides only a small sampling of the many strengths of First Nations Peoples. However, we hope to have contributed to a much needed shift in professional discourse from a deficit focus, to a focus on the strengths that have contributed to the resilience of these many, diverse peoples. In the words of Suzan Shown Harjo (1993), Cheyenne and Hidalgo Muskogee president of the Morning Star Institute,

At this time, under new laws that we have crafted, our relatives and sacred objects are returning home from museums and educational institutions nationwide. We have the privilege of settling the spirits. For many of our ancestors of the not-so-distant past, commemorating and mourning ceremonies were a luxury of life on the run. We today are mourning for them and for ourselves, learning the mighty power of grief, using ceremonies that honor the dead and revitalize the living.

We today are celebrating the recovery of much of our history. We are greeting sacred, living beings who have been "museum pieces" during all our lifetimes, honored in our memories and customs, but never seen in their context by anyone living. With their return to the Native Peoples who have the collective knowledge and wisdom to feed and care for them properly comes information about yesterday and tomorrow—how to reconcile the past, prepare for the future, avoid the voices of distraction.

This is the spiritual and tangible equivalent of the buffalo coming back.

They bring strength over a long journey, confidence in the longer one ahead. They fill the heart with joy and give assurance as real as a healthy birth. We are so fortunate to be the ones here at this place and moment.

This is a good day to live.

DISCUSSION QUESTIONS

1. How does strength come from the pains and anguish of oppression, violence, and discrimination?

2. Can you see a similar development of capacities and residencies in other groups (class, race, ethnicity, age, physical status, sexual orientation) who historically have been oppressed? What are these groups and what are the strengths that you have seen?

3. In working with, say, a Diné youth who is having trouble with alcohol abuse and school performance, how would you go about helping him discover and use the strengths of his people that he may possess?

REFERENCES

Aguirre, A., & Baker, D. V. (2000). Structured inequality in the United States: Critical discussions and the continuing significance of race, ethnicity, and gender. Upper Saddle River, NJ: Prentice Hall.

Anderson, L., Putnam, J., Sinclair-Daisy, F., & Squetimkin-Anquoe, A. (1999). American Indian and Alaskan Native single parents. In C. L. Schmitz & S. S. Tebb (Eds.), *Diversity in single-parent families: Working from strength* (pp. 33–68). Milwaukee, WI: Families International, Inc.

Akwesasne Notes. (1998). Columbus a trader in Indian slaves. In R. T. Schaefer, *Racial and ethnic groups* (7th ed. p. 22) New York: Longman.

Austin, R. (1993, Spring). Freedom, responsibility and duty: ADR and the Navajo Peacemaker Court. *The Judges Journal, 32* (2), 8–11, 47–48.

Cross, T. L. (1986). Drawing on cultural tradition in Indian child welfare. *Social Casework, 67,* 283–289.

Deloria, V., Jr., & Lytle, C. (1984). *The nations within: The past and future of American Indian Sovereignty.* New York: Pantheon Books.

Dorris, M. (1987). *Indians on the shelf*. In C. Martin (Ed.), *The American Indian and the problem of history* (pp. 98–113). New York: Oxford University Press.

Elsass, P. (1992). *Strategies for survival: The psychology of cultural resilience in ethnic minorities*. New York: New York University Press.

Ferrante, J., & Brown, P. (2001). *The social construction of race and ethnicity in the United States* (2nd ed.). Upper Saddle River, NJ: Prentice Hall.

Giago, T., Jr. (1990). My laughter. *Native Peoples: The Arts and Lifeways, 3* (3), 52–56.

Goodluck, C. (1993). Social services with Native Americans: Current status of the Indian Child Welfare Act. In H. P. McAdoo (Ed.), *Family ethnicity: Strength in diversity* (pp. 217–226). Newbury Park, CA: Sage Publications.

Harjo, S. S. (1998). This is a good day to live. In R. T. Schaefer, *Racial and ethnic groups* (7th ed., pp. 167–168). New York: Longman.

Hepworth, D., & Larsen, J. (1982). *Direct social work practice*. Homewood, IL: Dorsey Press.

Hurtado, S. (1992). The campus racial climate: Contexts for conflict. *Journal of Higher Education, 63* (5), 539–569.

Josephy, A. (1991). *The Indian heritage of America*. New York: Houghton Mifflin.

Locke, R. F. (1992). *The book of the Navajo*. (5th ed.). Los Angeles, CA: Mankind Publishing Company.

Marger, M. N. (1994). *Race and ethnic relations: American and global perspectives* (3rd ed.). Belmont, CA: Wadsworth Publishing Company.

Meyer, R. W. (1977). *The village Indians of the Upper Missouri*. Lincoln, NE: University of Nebraska Press.

Morris, G. T. (1992). International law and politics: Toward a right to self-determination for indigenous peoples. In M. A. Jaimes (Ed.), *The state of Native America: Genocide, colonization, and resistance* (pp. 55–86). Boston: South End Press.

Nofz, M. P. (1988, February). Alcohol abuse and culturally marginal American Indians. *Social Casework, 69* (2), 67–73.

Oetting, E. R., & Beauvais, F. (1991). Orthogonal cultural identification theory: The cultural identification of minority adolescents. *International Journal of Addictions, 25,* 655–685.

Parfit, M. (1994). Powwows. *National Geographic, 185* (June), 85–113.

Parks, D. (1991). *Traditional narratives of the Arikara Indians*. (vol. 3). Lincoln, NE: University of Nebraska Press.

Pevar, S. (1992). *The rights of Indians and tribes: The basic ACLU guide to Indian and tribal rights* (2nd ed.). Carbondale and Edwardsville, IL: Southern Illinois University Press.

Red Horse, J. G. (1980). American Indian elders: Unifiers of Indian families. *Social Casework, 61,* 490–493.

Schaefer, R. T. (1998). *Racial and ethnic groups* (7th ed.). New York: Longman.

Stiffarm, L. A., & Lane, P., Jr. (1992). The demography of native North America: A question of American Indian survival. In M. A. Jaimes (Ed.), *The state of Native America: Genocide, colonization, and resistance* (pp. 23–53). Boston: South End Press.

Shutiva, C. (1997). Native American culture and communication through humor. In A. Gonzalez, M. Houston, & V. Chen (Eds.), *Our voices: Essays in culture, ethnicity, and communication* (pp. 113–118). Los Angeles, CA: Roxbury Publishing Company.

Thornton, R. (1987). American Indian holocaust and survival: A population history since 1492. Norman, OK: University of Oklahoma Press.

Towle, C. (1945). A social work approach to courses in growth and behavior. *Social Service Review, 34,* 402–414.

Waller, M., & McAllen-Walker, R. X. X. (in press). One man's story of being gay and Diné: A study in resiliency. In M. Bernstein (Ed.), *Queer families, queer politics*. New York: Columbia University Press.

Waller, M., & Patterson, S. (in press). Natural helping and resilience in a Diné community. Manuscript submitted for publication.

Waller, M., Risley-Curtiss, C., Murphy, S., Medill, A., & Moore, G. (1998). Harnessing the positive power of language: American Indian women, a case example. *Journal of Poverty, 2* (4), 63–81.

Weaver, H. (1999). Indigenous People in a multicultural society. In P. L. Ewalt, E. M. Freeman, A. E. Fortune, D. L. Poole, & S. L. Witkin (Eds.), *Multicultural issues in social work: Practice and research*. Washington, DC: NASW Press.

Wilkinson, C. F. (1987). *American Indians, time and the law*. New Haven, CT: Yale University Press.

Worcester v. Georgia, 31 U.S., [6 Pet.] 515 (1831).

Wright, B., & Tierney, W. G. (2000). American Indians in higher education: A history of cultural conflict. In A. Aguirre, Jr., & D. Baker, *Structured inequality in the United States: Critical discussions on the continuing significance of race, ethnicity, and gender*. Upper Saddle River, NJ: Prentice Hall.

Wright, J., Lopez, M., & Zumwalt, L. (1997). That's what they say: The implications of American gay and lesbian literature for social service workers. In L. Brown (Ed.), *Two-spirit people* (pp. 67–82). New York: Hayworth.

Wood, N. (1974). *Many winters*. New York: Doubleday.

Yellow Bird, M. J. (1995). Spirituality in First Nations story telling: A Sahnish-Hidatsa approach to narrative. *Reflections: Narratives of Professional Helping 1* (4), 65–72.

4

The Significance of Spirituality for Resilient Response to Chronic Illness[1]

A Qualitative Study of Adults with Cystic Fibrosis

EDWARD R. CANDA

This chapter is dedicated to Lisa McDonough, consultant to this study, who died awaiting a lung transplant as this book went to press. She graced many by her wonderful spirit.

Spirituality is not escapism. It is who we are. It is our daily life. It's everything rolled into one.

—Doug (study participant)

[1]The author wishes to thank the following people: Robert C. Stern, M.D., and Carl F. Doershuk, M.D., of the Department of Pediatrics, Case Western Reserve University and Rainbow Babies and Childrens Hospital, Cleveland, Ohio, for significant assistance throughout the study; Ms. Lisa McDonough, columnist for the newsletter *CF Roundtable,* for kind help and numerous insights regarding findings and implications of this study; and Paula K. Duke, M.A., for going well beyond the call of duty as research assistant. The research was supported in part by a Graduate Research Fund Faculty Development Grant from the University of Kansas School of Social Welfare.

Interest in spirituality as a source of strength for people facing serious life challenges is growing rapidly among social workers. This interest connects four types of theoretical and empirical studies: formulations of definitions of spirituality (e.g., Bullis, 1996; Canda & Furman, 1999; Derezotes & Evans, 1995; Ellor, Netting, & Thibault, 1999; Joseph, 1987); research on sources of people's strengths and resiliency (e.g., Palmer, 1999; Saleebey, 1997); medical studies on the role of religion and spirituality in supporting health (e.g., Dossey, 1993; Hawks, Hull, Thalman, & Richins, 1995; Matthews, Larson, & Barry, 1993); and studies of people's growth through crisis and illness (e.g., Dunbar, Mueller, Medina, & Wolf, 1998; Sidell, 1997; Smith, 1995; Young & McNicoll, 1998). However, previous studies of the impact of spirituality on people experiencing crisis, illness, and disability were guided mainly by assumptions formed by scholars and professional helpers, rather than the views of service consumers.

Accordingly, this qualitative study had three purposes: to identify the views of adults with cystic fibrosis (CF), which is a genetic, chronic, and usually terminal illness, concerning their usage and definitions of spirituality and related terms; to describe their accounts of the contributions of spirituality to their resilient response to having CF; and to convey their recommendations for social workers and health care professionals. The situation of people with CF serves as an especially strong example of how spirituality can be a source of strength in adverse circumstances, since the illness is presently incurable.

Methodology

To develop interview questions, the author first reviewed transcripts from 1 year of discussion on the Cystic-L on-line internet group, 5 years' material from the mutual support newsletter *CF Roundtable,* and books about the lives of people with CF (Deford, 1983; Lab & Lab, 1990; Staunton, 1991; Woodson, 1991). The author then identified 16 adult respondents from the patient population of a national CF medical treatment center. A previous quantitative survey there of all 402 patients revealed use of spiritually oriented health support activities among approximately 60% of patients, but did not give details of the performance, meaning, and impact of these practices (Stern, Canda, & Doershuk, 1992). The most commonly reported of these were group prayer, faith healing using religious healing objects (such as a religious medal), meditation, and pilgrimage. Most patients or their adult representatives reported self-perceived benefits from all practices, including amelioration of symptoms and providing a sense of care and comfort for patient and loved ones. No injury or significant costs were incurred.

To explore these people's views in more detail, the author used a purposive sampling strategy to select adult respondents who demonstrated a high level of interest in spirituality as a source of strength in the previous survey and whose status reflected a variety of characteristics, including health status (mild symptoms to lung transplant candidates and lung transplant recipient), gender (8 male; 8 female), age (range 22–45), ethnicity (2 African American, 14 European

American), religious affiliation (6 mainline Protestant, 6 evangelical Protestant, 2 Catholic, 1 Catholic/Buddhist; 1 agnostic), and other variations of educational level, marital status, geographic residency, occupation, and employment. In accord with empowerment-oriented research, people with CF were involved in all phases of the study from the very beginning and findings are being used to contribute to service improvements on their behalf (Chamberlain, Stephens, & Lyons, 1997; Chesler, 1991; Lincoln, 1992, 1995; Rapp, Shera, & Kisthardt, 1993). This research approach recognizes that the insights of participants, gleaned from their long perseverance, soul searching, and personal growth, are important assets for their own resilience and for sharing with others.

Respondents received a list of topics prior to the interview so they could pre-pare responses. Topics included the meaning of spirituality and related terms, impact of illness on daily living, use of spiritual activities and supports to deal with CF, and advice for professional helpers. Telephone interviews (1½–2 hours) were transcribed verbatim and coded, sorted, and analyzed by the constant comparative method to identify patterns of themes and variations within themes with the assis-tance of a word processing program (MS Word) (Berg, 1997; Lincoln & Guba, 1985).

In accordance with empowerment, ethnographic, and phenomenological approaches to research, the researcher (who has CF) included himself as a participant/observer in the study, while bracketing his own assumptions so that they did not distort the first 15 interviews nor the analysis of their transcripts (Agar, 1996; Braud & Anderson, 1998). The researcher used his personal experi-ence and professional study of this topic to enhance empathic interviewing, to support realism in portrayal of CF, and to deepen nuances in analysis and inter-pretation of data. The researcher trained an assistant to interview him according to the same interview guide as was used for the first 15 interviews. The resulting transcript was set aside until all other transcripts were analyzed. Then, the researcher analyzed his transcript and compared it with those of the other 15 interviewees. This was helpful in checking the tentatively derived patterns of themes, because the researcher had a significantly different vantage point from most of the other participants by virtue of his role as researcher as well as unusual features of his spiritual perspective and health status. The themes that emerged from analysis of the first 15 participants were supported through this comparison.

To check the credibility of conclusions with participants, a draft of this man-uscript was sent to all participants to give an opportunity for response. Of the 14 respondents who could be reached, none expressed objection to the content. Four wrote to emphasize support for it.

To seek confirmation of the relevancy of observations to other adults with CF (i.e., transferability) and to caution against researcher bias, findings were shared in detail with a consultant with CF, Ms. Lisa McDonough, who is a nationally known columnist (for *CF Roundtable*) on spirituality. This consultant had no involvement with the design of the study or prior contact with the researcher. Feedback from this consultant supported the broad relevance of themes and implications for peo-ple with CF and professional helpers. Further, the findings from this sample of the

402 participants in the original survey are consistent with the themes identified for those 60% who used spiritually oriented healing, though much more detailed. In addition, the consensus statement (in the following section) was distributed, with a request for response, to hundreds of people with CF, including all readers of *CF Roundtable* and subscribers to two internet discussion groups for people with CF (CYSTIC-L@HOME.EASE.LSOFT.COM and cysticfibrosis@conncoll.edu). No one expressed objection to the content; all responders supported it.

Finally, to support the dependability of procedures and to confirm accurate inferences from data analysis, periodic self audits of a detailed methodological audit trail and checks with medical and social work colleagues were performed.

In the following presentation of findings, words in quotation marks represent exact quotes or close paraphrases from respondents' interview transcripts. First, patterns of similarity and difference among the participants as a group will be presented. Then, to illustrate the distinct voices of participants, two contrasting participants' stories will be summarized, mostly in their own words.

Summary of Findings

Understandings of Faith, Religion, and Spirituality

None of the preestablished demographic or personal characteristics appeared to influence variations on the themes. Although religious affiliation itself was not a distinguishing feature, differences of spiritual propensity (Canda & Furman, 1999) were important in relation to metaphors and key terms used to describe the process of dealing with CF. Participants could be divided into two groups: those who were evangelical, exclusively committed Christians (n = 6) and those with an ecumenical viewpoint, that is, inclusive of multiple spiritual perspectives. The ecumenical group included Christians (n = 9) and an agnostic (n = 1). All of the members of the evangelical group affiliated with Protestant non-mainline denominations and small local church groups. They described themselves by expressions such as "Bible-based," "born-again," "nondenominational," and "accepting Jesus as Lord and Savior." If they referred to other religions, they indicated the belief that everyone should accept Jesus as their Lord. This was stated in the context of wishing to share the benefits of faith that they receive with other people who have CF and their professional helpers.

Most members of the ecumenical group affiliated with mainline Protestant (e.g., Lutheran or Methodist) and Catholic denominations; one agnostic developed a personally tailored humanistic spiritual perspective. The ecumenical Christians emphasized the importance of their faith in Christ and their membership in Christian communities, as did the evangelical Christians. However, when referring to other religions, they said that there are many ways of approaching spiritual life that can be valuable. Some of the ecumenical Christians participated in other religions, including a Catholic who practiced Zen Buddhist meditation and a Protestant who shared worship services with his Catholic wife. The ecumenical agnostic described herself as a former Catholic who attends a Protestant church according to her husband's preference. She is open to the possibility of God's existence, but focuses on expressing spirituality through a sense of "brotherhood with all people" and "oneness with the universe."

All respondents distinguished spirituality and faith from religion. They described religion to be associated with institutionalized formal patterns of beliefs, rituals, and symbols related to faith and spirituality. Participants commonly described religion by terms such as "ritualistic, organized, institutional, relating to membership in a group, based on rules and regulations." All evangelical Christian respondents and the ecumenical agnostic respondent used the term religion with some ambivalence and negative connotations, reflecting the idea that institutionalized "man-made" religions can become overly rigid, conformist, or authoritarian, thus distracting from the core experiences of faith and spirituality. The ecumenical Christian respondents recognized that religions can sometimes divert attention from spirituality, but they referred to the positive contributions of religion without ambivalence. On all other matters, the ecumenical agnostic and the ecumenical Christians were more similar in their views in contrast to the evangelical Christians.

All respondents described spirituality as a way of life involving a search for meaning oriented toward a sacred realm (e.g., supernatural powers such as God, Jesus, angels, and heaven, or, for the agnostic, nature and the oneness of the universe) as well as primary motivating values (such as love, compassion, and service). The participants conceived of spirituality as an integration of core personal beliefs, values, and religious activities together with experience of the sacred within daily life, social relationships, and strategies for dealing with CF.

All participants, except the agnostic, frequently used the term *faith*. Faith referred to personal relationship and experience with divinity and the associated contents of beliefs in God. Faith was occasionally used in the sense of trust and confidence, especially in God and the promise of "eternal life with Jesus." For the evangelical Christian participants, faith was given greatest importance and was closely associated with spirituality. For the ecumenical Christians, all three terms (*faith, religion,* and *spirituality*) were closely interconnected. The agnostic respondent did not view faith as important to her, because she defined it in Christian terms that did not fit her belief system. Overall, 75 percent of respondents rated faith and spirituality as much more important and fundamental to them than formalized religion.

Beyond the differences between the two groups (evangelical and ecumenical) in theological language, both shared the conviction that faith and spirituality (and religious participation as a secondary expression of them) are sources of great strength. They are important for practical management of symptoms of CF, for achieving a sense of personal and social well-being, and for discovering meaning that infuses and transcends confrontation with physical limitations and death. As the implications section will discuss, most current social work literature uses the term *spirituality* to include matters of faith and religious and nonreligious spiritual perspectives. In this sense, participants' shared strategy of using spirituality to deal with CF created a commonality of outlook that was stronger than differences of spiritual propensity and demographic characteristics.

Ideas about Impacts of CF on Participants

Since CF is presently an incurable illness, it is not surprising that all participants identified severely negative physical impacts but no directly beneficial physical impacts. These included manifestations of lung disease and pancreatic dysfunction (enzymatic insufficiency), general decline in stamina, and toxic or distressing side effects of medications, extended hospitalizations, and other medical treatments. This was the aspect of life that was seen to have been affected in the most negative way by CF. Yet two people mentioned indirect physical benefits of having CF. One of them explained that "God used CF" to warn him to change from a self-destructive pattern of behavior. Another said that health care requirements challenged him to live in a balanced manner, thus enhancing overall well-being and physical health.

Fourteen people described the mental (i.e., intellectual and emotional) impact of having CF. Most participants (n = 13) identified this impact as negative, specifically they described negative feelings triggered by the struggle with CF, such as sadness (e.g., "discouragement, depression, grief"), and anxiousness (e.g., "fear, sense of danger, worry, distress"). Three people described feelings of anger or bitterness about having CF. Six people also mentioned troublesome thoughts related to low self-esteem, blaming oneself for sickness, pessimism, occasional suicidal ideas, or inability to set long-term goals. However, four participants identified ways that they improved mentally by responding to the challenges of having CF. They said they became stronger persons, more intellectual and self-reflective, more self-accepting, or more appreciative of life.

All participants described the effects on social relationships of having CF. This was an area in which there were both strong negative and positive impacts. Eleven respondents referred to negative impacts, such as difficulty performing tasks at workplace, school, and home and the distress of loved ones in response to the participant's having CF. Eleven people mentioned positive social impacts. Of these, 6 people mentioned that dealing with CF together with loved ones enhances feelings of mutual caring and love. Five people emphasized that they have witnessed other people being inspired and encouraged through their example of coping well with CF. Two participants said that their experience of CF has heightened their sensitivity to others' needs.

Thirteen respondents described ways that having CF directly affects their spirituality and these were mostly positive. Only 4 described negative spiritual consequences, such as "a difficult test of faith" during times of health crisis or unsuccessful faith healing cures. Thirteen participants explained that dealing with CF enhanced their spiritual lives by yielding deep insights into the meaning and purpose of life, helping them draw closer to God, witnessing to the benefits of faith to others, and stimulating overall personal growth and well-being.

Spirituality offered participants a way of living with and transcending through limits and discomforts imposed by CF. This is reflected in the contrast between the impacts of CF described for the physical aspect of life (primarily negative) and those for the spiritual aspect of life (primarily positive). Overall, benefits accrued from dealing with CF in each of the life domains were attributed to the importance of faith, spirituality, and religion. That is, according to participants, when CF and related challenges and disabilities are put in a spiritual context, it is possible to learn and to grow as a person in all realms of one's life. Spirituality is a strength that integrates and edifies the whole person.

Metaphors for the Challenges of CF

Overall, 16 people used negatively toned metaphors to describe dealing with CF and 11 used positively toned metaphors. This reemphasizes that having CF is undesirable but "not all bad" for the participants. It poses grave challenges and surprising opportunities.

Everyone used negative medical or physical metaphors, such as "disease, genetic illness, terminal illness, or handicap," and "my body is falling apart," "things are slipping away," or "I feel like I am descending into illness." There were no positive metaphors used for the physical aspect of the illness.

However, spirituality enabled people to find meaning within and beyond this physical aspect of illness. Thirteen participants used explicit religious or nonreligious spiritual metaphors to describe their coping with CF. Some of these were negative. For example, evangelical Christian respondents used metaphors relating to a battle between personified forces of good (Jesus, God, and angels) and evil (Satan, the devil). On the positive side, in response to these "trials and tribulations," they had a sense of divine protection and ultimate "Victory through Christ" (even in death) over the illness.

Ecumenical Christian respondents did not use metaphors involving battle with evil. However, some described negative metaphors such as "Dealing with CF, I feel like the survivors of the holocaust," and "CF really plays mind games with you." On the positive side, they shared the evangelical Christians' descriptions of divine protection, nurturance, and support. Some also said, "I offer up my suffering with Christ to benefit others" and "CF is a very stern teacher about life."

Challenges Associated with Spirituality

In general, participants emphasized that spirituality, faith, and religion have been of great importance in their resiliency. However, most (n = 12) reported some difficulties that arose regarding the use of spirituality in coping with illness. Ten people mentioned obstacles arising from their own religious communities. Although participants' religious communities were usually described as very supportive, some members of congregations were described as generating conflicts or tensions for the person with CF. Five of these 10 respondents said that sometimes other religious people attribute the cause of CF or the lack of successful prayer-based healing to some moral fault of the person with CF. Some have advised the person to rely only on prayer-based healing to the neglect of medical intervention. Four respondents said that certain religious teachings are too strict, rigid, or socially unjust. One explained that it is difficult to find a satisfactory minister.

Five people described skeptical, patronizing, and disparaging attitudes and comments regarding their spirituality from physicians, psychiatrists, or social workers. Four people mentioned tensions arising from differences of spiritual beliefs with significant others including family, coworkers, and friends. One person indicated that the pervasive dichotomy between medicine and spirituality in society generally inhibits patients' access to holistic, spiritually oriented health care.

Seven people described spiritual difficulties that arise from within themselves. Three of them mentioned that they sometimes have counterproductive personal qualities, such as insufficient effort in spiritual practice, being overly rational, and feeling stuck in an inner struggle over faith matters. Three mentioned that they developed self-doubts about the strength of their faith when prayers for the healing of symptoms were unsuccessful. One said that the challenges of CF keep the pressure on for constant self-reflection.

However, it is important to clarify that all these difficulties were described in the context of a predominantly positive experience of faith, spirituality, and religion. Both the interpersonal and intrapersonal difficulties were seen as challenges to overcome in the process of personal growth. For example, working through moralistic blaming from others or self-doubts led to a stronger sense of faith and clarity of spiritual perspective for participants. The ability to recognize these spiritual difficulties as challenges and opportunities for growth was another source of strength and resilience for them.

A Consensus Statement on Spirituality as a Source of Strength by Adults with CF

To convey a more detailed and comprehensive impression of the views shared by the participants, the researcher constructed the following consensus statement about the role of spirituality as a strength that supports health and well-being. This statement represents a synthesis of commonly shared views among all participants and, as previously explained, was supported by checks with hundreds of other people with CF.

> As adults with CF, we have experienced many years of health challenges, including the daily grind of numerous medications and respiratory clearance treatments, as well as times of life threatening physical crises and prolonged hospitalizations. Most of us have had to deal with symptoms of CF since childhood. Although there are many variations of onset, course, and severity of illness for people with CF, we are all acutely aware that without a lung transplant, we may die from complications of cystic fibrosis. But the very fact that we have had this challenge for so long means that we have had a powerful opportunity to learn from our experience. We have gleaned a sense of the meaning, purpose, and importance of life. And we have learned how spirituality and faith can help people with health challenges to be resilient. Since everyone must confront sickness and death eventually, we hope that what we have learned might be of some benefit to others.

The physical, mental, social, and spiritual challenges of CF give us a clear choice: We can give up and give in, or, we can learn and grow from the experience. We have found that if we approach CF as a challenge and opportunity for learning, our well-being can actually be enhanced, even if our physical condition wavers and declines. This is not easy. Sometimes we feel worn out and lose a sense of life direction. But in the long run it is much better to face the challenge than to give in to despair. The ability to find meaning through illness and to transcend the limitations of the body comes through our spirituality, including our faith in a Sacred Source of strength, our use of spiritually based healing practices to augment conventional medicine, and our sharing of a spiritual way of life with loved ones and community members.

For many of us, faith in a Sacred Source of strength means that we experience God as an active presence who helps us through the difficult times and guides us in our daily lives. Some of us feel the supportive presence of angels or the nurturing energy of nature and communion with the universe. When we share our spirituality with other members of our spiritual support community, we can help each other in our spiritual growth. At times when we are feeling down, members of the community help us; and we return the favor when we are needed. Our faith traditions also provide us with practices of individual and group prayer, reading of scripture and other inspirational texts, symbols of grace and salvation, rituals of worship, and occasions for fellowship and mutual support. All these spiritually based activities help to increase our sense of support by loved ones, friends, and sacred powers. They encourage us to be diligent in our medical care and to stay well balanced in our personal life styles. And they assist our physical health by relieving stress and providing relief for some of our symptoms of illness.

Spirituality also helps us to deal with the so-called end stage of CF and the anticipation of death. Most of us believe that death is not a terminal condition because there is a spiritual life beyond the trials and tribulations of this physical existence. And all of us recognize that approaching life and death as opportunities for insight and growth gives a sense of integrity, worth, and significance to life. So not even death can defeat us.

We have learned that it is important not to be discouraged or confused by some religious people who blame us for having CF, or who cast doubt on our faith when a miracle cure is not forthcoming, because of their own misunderstanding. And even when health care professionals ignore or depreciate our spirituality, we have learned that it is important to make our own spiritual commitments and practices clear and consistent in our own lives.

The challenges of CF remind us to set our priorities firmly according to the guidance of our Sacred Source of strength, to treasure every moment of life, to cherish our loved ones, and to use our own situation as a means to help and inspire others. Paradoxically, when we approach life and death this way, even if our physical condition worsens, our overall sense of well-being can improve.

The following two stories illustrate individual variations within this consensus view. Names and details were changed to protect confidentiality.

Gary's Story: Trying to Figure It All Out

At the time of his interview, Gary described himself as a Protestant who shares participation in his Catholic wife's religious services. For him, spirituality and faith guide all aspects of life, infuse formal religious practice with significance, and help him answer the "Why are we here?" existential questions. Persevering in the search, even when there are no clear answers, characterized Gary's resilient response to having a chronic illness.

I try to live according to the beliefs of the Christian church every day—not, of course, always successfully. And with some recent changes in my health, I feel it is even more imperative to me to really start to understand exactly what life is all about. And it's a little frustrating that I can't quite figure it all out. I'm at the point where I'm starting to feel a time pressure to try to figure it out before something drastic happens.

At church on Sundays I always pray for my health to be maintained, and if not, for the strength to deal with it, for me and my wife. I also try to pray every day for my health and the health of my wife. I guess I've given up praying for miracles. I think somewhere in the back of my mind I always figured something big would happen and that somehow I would find my way out of CF. But that doesn't seem to be in the cards.

Although I've given up on miracles, my prayer and religious activities affect my health by giving me the strength to continue with all the medical care that I've done. They give me motivation and a sense that there is a purpose out there that I've just got to figure out. And when other people pray for me, maybe the prayers are answered and it makes me feel better mentally and physically to know that other people care enough about me to pray for me.

The difficulty I have with CF is that it is a progressive disease; it only goes in one direction, and that is very difficult to deal with mentally. You have to invest so much time and effort in CF. It takes away from other things you could be doing in life. And I find that whole combination of factors to be very difficult mentally and exhausting and the inevitability of the disease is disheartening.

Having CF makes you question your faith. I'm sure you've heard it a million times. But I think it is important for all of us to figure it out. Why does God allow CF to happen? Why doesn't He cure me? You look around and see an awful lot of suffering . . . why is all this allowed to happen? Am I supposed to pray to get well? Am I supposed to pray just for the strength to deal with this? Or, is this a God who just lets things happen, and even though He loves us all, suffering is inevitable? I keep trying to evolve into a stronger faith by asking these questions. I use my faith to improve my sense of well-being, to help me deal with what's coming. And maybe sometimes there just isn't any purpose. Sometimes things just happen. And if you accept that, and I am beginning to accept that, then you have to reexamine the whole belief of what God chooses to do and not do.

I am still scared to death of death. I don't want to try it anytime in the near future. I'm having a pretty good time here. My wife and I are very happy and I like my life. And in terms of the inevitable outcome though, I'm kind of surprised at how convinced I am that when I do die, and when my wife dies, we will be reunited somewhere in heaven. And that's a comfort.

I feel if there is a purpose to life, I've got to do my best and take care of myself to stick around and figure it out. It also shows my appreciation for having this life in the first place. It makes me feel that every little bit of life is a gift and I'll stick around a little bit longer to enjoy it.

Teresa's Story: I Am Already Healed

Teresa, an African American member of a theologically conservative denomination, tells a story of certainty that contrasts with Gary's constant questioning. She described herself as a "born-again Christian." Hers is a story of confident faith and strong church community giving strength in the face of illness and death.

Spirituality and faith relate to my belief in God, a Higher Power. Faith is believing in something you can't see and the evidence of things hoped for. I put them at a 10 on a scale of 1–10. Religion (going to church every Sunday) is high up there if it is in the context of faith.

I pray daily by myself and, especially in the evening, with my daughter and husband. I also have a devotional period where I read scripture and a little daily prayer book. I may pray about my day at work. I may have prayer requests from someone. I pray for my family and their physical well-being. Being a born-again Christian, I believe that I'm already healed, it just hasn't been manifested in the natural world yet. But I just continue to pray that God continues to heal my body and make me feel better at that particular moment. All my family members pray for me and sometimes, if I am not feeling well, they come over to my house. And my sisters believe in the laying on of hands. Sometimes they place their hands right over my chest, just lay them anywhere on my body, and they'll say a prayer of healing and faith. They may anoint with oil on my forehead and pray. And sometimes I get together with a couple coworkers and we may share ideas and prayers. At church we also have a Wednesday night prayer and praise service. We share testimonies about what the Lord has done for us this week and then we'll pray for specific needs in our church or our community, pray for our school district.

These activities affect my physical health a lot. It always makes me feel better to pray and have a group of believers around who really believe that prayers are answered. My health comes and goes, but I have a belief that no matter what, I'm going to be with the Lord. And the groups from my church and my family, they just always back up that belief whenever I get depressed. I've always got that support there. And when people pray for me there's changes in my physical health, because if my mind is up and healthy and thinking the right way, I feel my body is okay.

I also know that if something ever does happen to me, I am not alone. There's community and family there that are going to step in and be with my family, my husband and daughter. Sometimes I don't even have to say anything. They can just sense that I'm not having a good day and come in with an encouraging word, or say a prayer, or I may not even need anything but a hug.

In the Bible it says that by Jesus Christ we are healed. And I believe that literally. And he said, "No weapons formed against me shall prosper." And I believe that CF is like a weapon trying to come against me; and the Bible says it won't prosper. I keep that belief and then I just wait for the natural manifestation in my body. I am pretty healthy compared to most people with CF.

Sometimes I ask myself "What is my purpose?" I've been told by others that I am an inspiration to them by how I never give up. I was always told I'll never be able to go to college and hold down a job, but I've done all that. I've had an opportunity to counsel people with chronic diseases. If my only purpose to be here is to be an example or an inspiration to somebody else, that's good enough for me. I guess my purpose is to live a positive life and try to bring somebody to Christ by example.

The most important thing I've learned is never to give up on faith. No matter how bleak it may seem. Always keep striving, keep going. And just realize that I have victory because I have a prosperous life and I know in the end I will be with the Lord Jesus Christ. That means that one day I'll be in heaven, a place where there is no sickness and no death and no sorrow. That's victorious for me. I won't have to be in this shell with pain and suffering. I'll be able to see my loved ones again one day.

Implications for Social Work

The general themes revealed in this study are most likely to be shared by other adults with CF for whom faith, spirituality, and religion are important. In addition, considering the numerous other related studies on adversity and spirituality, as identified in the introduction, it is clear that spirituality can be a tremendous resource for resilience and meaning in many situations. The stories of Gary and Teresa illustrate that common themes take on distinctive form in particular lives and contexts. This distinctness is just as precious as the commonality. Indeed, no broadly stated theme is really a strength for anybody. A person's strength is always what is specific to her or him at a particular place, time, and situation. For example, Gary channeled his tendency to doubt and question everything into an existential quest. His sense of mystery and the preciousness of life was keen. His commitment to persevere and to make the most of life was strong. In contrast, Teresa felt very sure of her beliefs and had a strong network of social support through her faith community. Teresa found comforting beliefs, healing practices, and meaning for life within her solid faith.

Participants strongly encouraged practitioners to explore the possible roles of spiritual beliefs and practices in promoting people's resilient response to chronic illness and disability. Ten of the 16 participants said that they had little or no contact with social workers, despite significant involvement with health care systems. Eleven people indicated that social workers never brought up the subject of spirituality, but rather limited themselves to practical aspects of discharge planning (exclusive of coordinating with spiritual support systems). A national survey of direct practitioner members of the National Association of Social Workers (NASW) showed that most practitioners recognize the appropriateness of assessing and utilizing religious and nonreligious spiritual supports with interested clients, but that they feel unprepared by education or training for how to do so (Canda & Furman, 1999). Perhaps that helps account for social workers' lack of attention to this topic in the experience of these participants. It is especially relevant to this study that a significant majority of survey respondents believed that it is appropriate to raise the topics of religion and spirituality with clients regarding issues of terminal illness and bereavement, and in helping clients reflect on their beliefs about what happens after death. These observations support Aguilar's (1997) call for a holistic, spiritually attuned approach to social work in health care.

To utilize spirituality as a strength in practice, social workers need to consider carefully how we use related concepts and terminology with clients. The prevailing definitions of spirituality in the social work literature provide general conceptualizations as common ground for communication among social workers regarding all religious and nonreligious spiritual perspectives (Bullis, 1996; Canda & Furman, 1999). These definitions usually present spirituality as the striving of the person for a sense of meaning, purpose, and morality in relation with the world and ultimate reality, however that is conceived. In contrast, religion refers to institutionalized patterns of spiritual beliefs, values, and practices shared by a community. Spirituality may be expressed within or outside of religious contexts. The Canda and Furman (1999) survey of NASW members demonstrated that this distinction is common among practitioners in the field as well. Spirituality is also sometimes understood as a holistic quality of the person in relationship with self, world, and the ground of being. This quality infuses and integrates all the particular bio-psycho-social and spiritual aspects of the person. As indicated by the nuances of the terms spirituality, religion, and faith found in this study, practitioners need to tailor understandings and language about spirituality based on a careful assessment of clients' own perspectives.

Study participants made a distinction between institutional religion and the spiritual aspect of human experience; they also portrayed spirituality as a holistic quality infusing all aspects of life. The similarity to social work usage suggests that professional definitions may provide a good starting point for discussion with them. However, most participants used terms, meanings, and symbols that were particular to their spiritual beliefs and experiences with health challenges. For example, most participants placed strong importance on faith, described in Christian terms, due to their religious affiliations. The prevalence of Christian affiliation among participants was probably influenced by the genetic basis of CF, since most people with CF are non-Jewish European descendents. There are a small percentage of African Americans with CF, but most European and African descendents in the United States have a Christian affiliation. Various Christian evangelical and ecumenical terminologies for faith, theology, and metaphors relating to health and illness, such as occurred in this study, are not commonly employed in social work outside of Christian religious settings. Further, each individual's story involved distinctive spiritual healing practices, religious attitudes, and imagery. This reminds us of the importance of demonstrating relevant knowledge, respect, and skill for relating to clients' religious or nonreligious spiritual perspectives, Christian or otherwise, that are unique to particular people, cultures, religions, places, times, and situations.

This study highlights the need to address spirituality as a strength in situations that are distinct to people with physical disabilities and health challenges. For example, alternative and complementary healing practices employed by clients could be coordinated with conventional medical and psychosocial care to maximize the benefits and minimize the risks of spiritual practices and support systems. This study, and the original survey of all 402 patients at the CF treatment center, revealed no medical harm from any of these practices. However, several participants described stress related to blaming or condescending messages from some members of their religious groups and health care professionals as well as personal doubts and confusions of faith. Given the evidence of benefits of spirituality for resilience, clients might be well served with assistance in addressing these challenges through self-reflection, therapeutic dialogue, and collaboration with relevant clergy and other spiritual friends and mentors.

Participants' stories of spiritual growth through adversity raise a serious caution about using conventional psychosocial and cognitive stage theories of human development in assessing clients with chronic illness. These theories have been criticized for assuming that spiritual issues of life's meaning and mortality do not emerge until middle age (Robbins, Chatterjee, & Canda, 1998). This study indicates that chronic health challenges can provoke precocious and life-long spiritual searching and growth for some people. Participants often mentioned this as one of their personal strengths. Participants did not reduce themselves to an illness, but rather expanded themselves toward wellness. Participants' use of spirituality to enhance well-being in the midst of all aspects of living and dying illuminates the human condition. While we all share mortality, we also share capacity for meaning and thriving, both within and beyond physical limitations. Issues of illness, disability, and resilience should not be limited to a special topics section of the curriculum or to specialized practice in health and hospice settings. Rather, social workers can be prepared to examine these whenever and wherever relevant to clients.

The stories of participants in this study also provide vivid realism to the strengths perspective. For them, utilizing spirituality as strength did not mean lapsing into denial of physical illness and life challenges. Rather, spiritual beliefs, experiences, and social supports provided resources for managing suffering, persevering in health care, appreciating life and loved ones, and looking into and beyond the nitty-gritty physicality of mortality.

Postscript

One of the tenets of strengths-oriented empowerment research is that researchers should conduct studies that let people speak for themselves. As I explained in the methodology section, I included myself in this study. The consensus statement reflects that this chapter is not about *they*. Also it is not just about *me*. It is really about *we*. The doing of this study has been one of the most powerfully self-transforming (and often befuddling) research projects of my career. This is because my own quandaries, challenges, insights, and stories about having CF have been inwardly recalled, questioned, stretched, and inspired as I talked with participants, analyzed their transcripts, and tried to find a realistic way of presenting them.

I became more appreciative of spiritual styles and languages very different from my own as I recognized our common themes and the inherent worth for people of their own distinctive ways. I have come to be a bit more outspoken advocate for people with disabilities and for people with cystic fibrosis. I made the choice to be public about my own disability in order to tell our stories and to advocate for us and for others. And in the process, I have achieved a little more congruity between private and professional aspects of my life. I also extended my connections and friendships in the community of people with CF. I have become stronger by doing strengths-oriented research! The process of doing this research has been a spiritual journey for me. This is how I reflected on the process during my own interview for this study:

> Deciding to do this study is part of my personal working through of issues pertaining to having CF. I can get more comfortable about the issues that participants bring up. One good thing about listening to them has been seeing how we are all in this boat together. How do they deal with it? And seeing some similarities and differences and learning from that. I don't want to tell them much about my situation (until after the interviews) because I don't want to interfere with their stories; but hearing them has helped me overcome a sense of being alone about having CF.
>
> And the idea of being of service. All right, I have CF. I am learning something from it. How can I use that as a means of helping other people? So doing a professional research project on this has been what I could do. Well, I am not just going to become detached and pretend I'm an objective observer floating off someplace, looking down at these participants, and analyzing them like bugs under a microscope. They're fellows. Just like everybody. We're all in it together, and in particular we share having this illness and I want to learn from them. I want to help distribute what they've learned to help other people. And I want to bring myself into that process, so other people can learn from my experience. And by interconnecting the participants' perspectives and mine, I'm going to learn from that too. Just having to think this through and articulate it, and when I do the analysis of the transcripts, it's going to be a lot of soul searching and reflection for me.

Dear reader, I can honestly convey the sentiments of all of the participants in this study, including myself: If this chapter contributes in some small way to your own soul searching, and to finding more strength within yourself, we will be very glad to have shared our story.

DISCUSSION QUESTIONS

1. What is spirituality? How would you define your own sense of spirituality? Has it helped you through some of the inevitable turns and troubles of life?

2. In what sense is Teresa healed even though she has a terminal illness?

3. Can you use your understanding of and struggles with your own frailties and difficulties as something that can be valuable for others as they confront adversity? How would you do it?

4. How can it be that people can improve their quality of life, expand toward wellness even though they are seriously or even terminally ill? How can you assist in that effort?

REFERENCES

Agar, M. H. (1996). *The professional stranger* (2nd ed.). San Diego: Academic Press.

Aguilar, M. A. (1997). Re-engineering social work's approach to holistic healing. *Health and Social Work, 22*(2), 83–84.

Berg, B. L. (1997). *Qualitative methods for the social sciences* (3rd ed.). Boston: Allyn and Bacon.

Braud, W., & Anderson, R. (1998). *Transpersonal research methods for the social sciences.* Thousand Oaks, CA: Sage.

Bullis, R. K. (1996). *Spirituality in social work practice.* Washington, DC: Taylor & Francis.

Canda, E. R., & Furman, L. D. (1999). *Spirituality diversity in social work practice: The heart of helping.* New York: Free Press.

Chamberlain, K., Stephens, C., & Lyons, A. C. (1997). Encompassing experience: Meanings and methods in health psychology. *Psychology and Health, 12,* 691–709.

Chesler, M. A. (1991). Participatory action research with self-help groups: An alternative paradigm for inquiry and action. *American Journal of Community Psychology, 19*(5), 757–768.

Deford, F. (1983). *Alex: The life of a child.* Baltimore, MD: Cystic Fibrosis Foundation.

Derezotes, D., & Evans, K. E. (1995). Spirituality and religiosity in practice: In-depth interviews of social work practitioners. *Social Thought, 18*(1), 39–56.

Dossey, L. (1993). *Healing words: The power of prayer and the practice of medicine.* San Francisco: HarperSan Francisco.

Dunbar, H. T., Mueller, C., W., Medina, C., & Wolf, T. (1998). Psychological and spiritual growth in women living with HIV. *Social Work, 43*(2), 144–154.

Ellor, J. W., Netting, F. E., & Thibault, J. M. (1999). *Religious and spiritual aspects of human service practice.* Charleston, SC: University of South Carolina.

Hawks, S. R., Hull, M. L., Thalman, R. L., & Richins, P. M. (1995). Review of spiritual health: Definition, role, and intervention strategies in health promotion. *American Journal of Health Promotion, 9*(5), 371–378.

Joseph, M. V. (1987). The religious and spiritual aspects of clinical practice. *Social Thought, 13,* 2–23.

Lab, D., & Lab, O. K. (1990). *My life in my hands: Living with cystic fibrosis.* Thousand Palms, CA: LabPro Press.

Lincoln, Y. S. (1992). Sympathetic connections between qualitative methods and health research. *Qualitative Health Research, 2*(4), 375–391.

Lincoln, Y. S. (1995). Emerging criteria for quality in qualitative and interpretive research. *Qualitative Inquiry, 1*(3), 275–289.

Lincoln, Y. S., & Guba, E. (1985). *Naturalistic inquiry.* Beverly Hills, CA: Sage.

Matthews, D. A., Larson, D. B., & Barry, C. P. (1993). *The faith factor: An annotated bibliography of clinical research on spiritual subjects, Vol. 1.* MD: National Institute for Healthcare Research.

Palmer, N. (1999). Fostering resiliency in children: Lessons learned in transcending adversity. *Social Thought, 19*(2), 69–87.

Rapp, C., Shera, W., & Kisthardt, W. (1993). Research strategies for consumer empowerment of people with severe mental illness. *Social Work, 38*(6), 727–735.

Robbins, S. P., Chatterjee, P., & Canda, E. R. (1998). *Contemporary human behavior theory: A critical perspective for social work.* Boston: Allyn and Bacon.

Saleebey, D. (Ed.). (1997). *The strengths perspective in social work practice.* New York: Longman.

Sidell, N. L. (1997). Adult adjustment to chronic illness: A review of the literature. *Health and Social Work, 22*(1), 5–11.

Smith, E. (1995). Addressing the psychospiritual distress of death as reality: A transpersonal approach. *Social Work, 40,* 402–413.

Staunton, V. (1991). *Gillian: A second chance.* Dublin, Ireland: Blackwater Press.

Stern, R. C., Canda, E. R., & Doershuk, C. F. (1992). Use of nonmedical treatment by cystic fibrosis patients. *Journal of Adolescent Health, 13,* 612–615.

Young, J. M., & McNicoll, P. (1998). Against all odds: Positive life experiences of people with advanced amylotrophic lateral sclerosis. *Health and Social Work, 23*(1), 35–43.

Woodson, M. (1991). *Turn it into glory.* Minneapolis, MN: Bethany House Publishers.

5 The Strengths Approach to Practice

DENNIS SALEEBEY

In Part Two, we saw the strengths and capacities of people with physical and developmental disabilities, and people from different and unappreciated cultures. The chapters in Parts Three and Four describe and discuss strengths-based practice with a number of different populations, including people with chronic mental illness, people with addictions, elders in long-term care, youth at risk, residents of economically distressed communities. While you will perceive differences among these approaches, you will see throughout the chapters a vital and unmistakable belief in the capabilities of individuals, groups, families, and communities. It comes across in many ways, but the following ideas are resoundingly clear from beginning to end:

■ People who confront stress almost always develop some ideas, capacities, traits, and motivations that may subsequently be of use to them in the search for a better life. We have been much too energetic in looking for the impediments and injuries, the deficits and desolation rather than people's compensating and transformative responses to challenges.

■ Even in the most demanding, tough, lean, and mean environments there is a bounty of natural resources—individuals, families, associations, institutions— available. While some communities are clearly more abundant than others, all neighborhoods have assets.

■ Even though individuals may have labored for years under the blame and disapproving opinions of others, or self-criticism, habitual pessimism, or unfortunate life decisions, at some level, they almost always know what is right for them.

■ As a species we surely have—or we would not have survived thus far—an innate capacity for self-righting and health.

■ Healing, transformation, regeneration, and problem solving almost always occur within the confines of a personal, friendly, supportive, and dialogical relationship (Edward Sampson (1993) calls it "a celebration of the other"). Whether friend, intimate partner, physician, social worker, shaman, or teacher, the more we entreat the power of a caring, egalitarian relationship with those we assist, the better for them and us.

■ Everybody has knowledge and talents, skills and resources that can be used for pressing forward toward a life defined in their own terms—toward their hopes and dreams, the solution of their problems, the meeting of their needs, and the invigoration of the quality of their lives—individually and collectively.

■ It is far more important to set one's gaze toward a better future, to traffic in possibility, than it is to obsess about the disappointments and injuries of a dank, dark past.

■ Even when people do injurious things to themselves and others, they are often trying to meet needs that all of us have—for respect, control, security, love, and connection.

To recognize the strengths in people and their situation implies that we give credence to the way clients experience and construct their social realities. We cannot impose from without our own versions (or those of the agency or other social institutions) of the world. This appreciation of context and construction is an acknowledgment of the special and distinctive social circumstances of each client or group (Saleebey, 1994). To hear the stories and narratives in a family or a community is one way to discover not only their preoccupations and challenges, but also to unearth their particular assets and abilities. Learning the language, the symbols, the images, and the perspectives that move clients—for good or ill—is to encounter their challenges and triumphs, over time. You will see in the chapters that follow the high level of commitment and resolve that is required to get you into the client's life-world authentically and respectfully. Other themes that abound in the following chapters include the importance of genuine dialogue; forming positive expectations of clients; helping clients participate more fully in their world of people, institutions, and communities; identifying natural resources in the clients' world; and learning from clients. One thing becomes clear in reading these chapters: Operating from a strengths perspective is good, basic social work practice. There is nothing here that is not coincidental with the core of values that energizes and drives the profession. All that we can do in these pages is to give these principles more conceptual and practical vigor.

Some Beginning Observations about Strengths-Based Practice

These observations are meant to answer some basic questions that have been asked over the years about generic practice from a strengths perspective. First of all, assume that it will take genuine diligence on your part to begin to appreciate and utilize client strengths in practice. The system is against you, the language and metaphors of the system are against you, consumers are sometimes against you because they have been inscribed with the cursor of disease, and, not insignificantly, the culture is against you. Pursuing the ideas that formulate and celebrate strengths, resilience, rebound, challenge, and transformation is difficult because they are not now natural to much of the social service, health, and mental health systems and their membership. Let us begin by examining some of the factors that are implicated consistently in salutary change and development.

The Core Conditions of Growth and Change

In his review and statistical analyses of studies done over the years on the factors that lead to constructive change in psychotherapy, Michael Lambert (1992) concluded that there are four enduring components of such change. The four ingredients for change include: factors in the matrix of clients' lives (their strengths and resources, contingent factors, etc.); the qualities of good helping relationships; positive expectations, hope and the placebo effect; and the technical operations and principles of theory. Mark Hubble, Scott Miller, and Barry Duncan offer an excellent elaboration of these four components in their 1997 book, *Escape from Babel*.

What Lambert calls extra-therapeutic factors seem to promote the greatest degree of change. These include the strengths, assets, and resources within the individual, the family, and the ambient environment. Supportive kin, determination, insights gained from intimate sources, a rising sense of hopefulness, a lessening of stresses in the environment and many other things may be involved here. Clearly important factors are contingent ones—luck, fortune, and the play of chance occurrences in one's life. All of these reflect the substance of an individual's or family's daily life—the web of resources in their surroundings, social support networks, their own wiles and wisdom, personal or collective traits and virtues, and the unforeseen in their lives. According to Lambert, the psychosocial matrix of a person's life may account for 40 percent of therapeutic change.

For years, social workers have emphasized the importance of the helping relationship and the use of self as the medium of change and growth (Shulman, 1992). Half a century ago, Carl Rogers and his associates assured us that truly healing relationships bloomed from the qualities of caring, empathy, positive regard, genuineness, and respect (1951). Over the last 30 years or so, Hans Strupp (1995) has been investigating psychotherapies of all kinds to mine the ore of real and positive change therein. He continually finds that the quality of the helping relationship is the single most important factor across schools of psychotherapy. Practitioners of the strengths perspective add to these the importance of collaboration—developing a mutually crafted project, meant to lay, brick by brick, a path to a person's or family's hopes and dreams. Charles Rapp, one of the most important figures in the development of the strengths perspective, defines the effective helping relationship as purposeful, reciprocal, friendly, trusting, and empowering (1998). Lambert reckoned that this factor might account for about 30% of the positive change in peoples' lives (1992).

Often forgotten, but truly important in promoting beneficial change are hope, positive expectations, and the placebo effect. My expectation that you can do better and prevail through your tribulations translates into the recrudescence of hope, the revival or birth of a dream—no matter how modest. A focus on possibility, an eye cast to a better future, and the creation of justifiable optimism all promote movement toward one's aspirations. Of all these, however, the most intriguing may be the placebo effect. Long known for its use in medical and pharmaceutical research, it has been virtually ignored as a force in bringing about change. The placebo (meaning "I shall please") is an inert substance or dummy procedure given to one group of randomly selected subjects. The other group gets the real pill or procedure. Typically, if a drug performs better than the placebo, that is taken to be an indication of its efficacy.

Michael Fisher (2000) reports that in the 1950s at the University of Kansas Medical Center, in order to test a new medical procedure for the treatment of angina, surgeons performed real operations on one group of patients with angina, and a placebo operation on the other group of men with angina. The placebo group was told that they were going to have heart surgery; they were given a local anesthetic, and incisions were made in their chests. But no operation was done, the surgeons just messed around a little bit, and the patients had the scars and postoperative pain to suggest that they actually had surgery. Seventy percent of the people who had the real surgery reported long-term improvement in their angina; but *all* of the placebo group did. Ethical problems with this study aside, the results are just short of amazing.

It is not at all uncommon, in tests of psychoactive drugs, for the placebo groups to show anywhere from 25 percent to 60 percent improvement (Arpala, 2000). As noted, the extent that the real drug is better than the placebo is thought to be the extent that the drug is effective. But it is unknown, for example, just how much the effect of the real drug is also a placebo phenomenon. In more recent years, people have been getting an active placebo in which they experience side effects. Side effects also occur within active placebos—look at the drug ads in your magazines and check out the data. People are more likely to get better on active placebos because the experience of side effects convinces them that they are getting a real and powerful drug. Joseph Arpala (2000) reports that a study by Fisher and Greenberg revealed that in 30 percent to 40 percent of all the studies they reviewed of antidepressant drugs and placebos, the placebo was as powerful or therapeutic as the drug.

So what is happening here? Many things no doubt. It could be—and many have proposed this—that when a person is sick and they have an expectation, thanks to a procedure or pill, that they will get better, they mobilize the healing systems within, whether it is the psychoneuroimmune system, endorphins (endogenous morphine produced by the body), relaxation response (which lowers, among other things, the level of cortisol, the production of which is related to stress), or some unknown process. But maybe even more important here is the expectation of the healer that you will get well, the mobilization of hope and possibility that things will be different in the future. We dissipate an awful lot of our possible good will, hinting or directly saying that things will not be better, that once stuck or hurt or disappointed or abused or ill, you will always suffer scars or the effects of these hurts will reverberate, in one way or another, throughout your life. It is not just the person's expectation that they will recover, rebound, do better, it is the unmistakable expectation of the social worker, physician, healer, minister, teacher, or parent that you will do better—the belief in you. As your social worker, I genuinely believe that you can make it, can leap that hurdle, climb that wall, escape that burden. You may need help, it may take time, but my belief in you is steadfast. As a child heretofore defined as at-risk, I define you, as Beth Blue Swadener (1995) suggests, as a child "at-promise." So the placebo effect harbors within it something of considerable persuasive authority.

Consider, too, that it may well be that even the group receiving a real medication may also experience a placebo effect—in some cases to the tune of 30 percent of its supposed efficacy (Brody, 2000). The emotional, nonverbal, and verbal messages that accompany the giving of a placebo appear to be extraordinarily important. Do they galvanize hope, mobilize positive expectations? Creating the expectancy of a healthy, efficacious response would seem to be a part of the potency of the placebo. But the message for practitioners is that you should never underestimate the sway of hope, the belief that things can improve. Such a prospect is vital to those individuals and groups who struggle against the tide of low expectations, little opportunity, belittled self-esteem, and thwarted justice. According to Lambert's inquiry, these factors may account for as much as 15 percent of positive, dynamic change.

That percentage is about the same as Lambert attributes to the effect of the technical operations and methods of a theory. These methods clearly are important. It is well known, for example, that cognitive behavioral techniques, and interpersonal therapy both, often in conjunction with antidepressant drugs, are effective in the treatment of moderate to moderately severe depression (Bentley & Walsh, 2001; Gitlin, 1996).[1] For people returning to the community after hospitalization for an episode of schizophrenia, the combination of a neuroleptic threshold dose[2] of antipsychotic medication and vigorous psychosocial and educational interventions is effective. It must be said, however, that in the absence of the first three factors, the techniques and methods of a theory or perspective hold less sway.

In many ways the strengths perspective builds on the mobilization of these factors, in particular the power of possibility and an unstinting and unqualified belief in the person's or group's capacity for change.

What Are Strengths?

Almost anything can be considered a strength under certain conditions, so this list is not meant to be exhaustive. Nonetheless, some capacities, resources, and assets do commonly appear in any roster of strengths.

---

[1]More evidence is mounting that the therapies without medication are quite effective.

[2]The smallest amount of medication that produces a beneficial effect.

What people have learned about themselves, others, and their world as they have struggled, coped with, and battled abuse, trauma, illness, confusion, oppression, and even their own fallibility. People do learn from their trials, even those that they seem to inflict upon themselves. People do not just learn from successes but from their difficulties and disappointments as well. For example, most people quit or moderate their drinking on their own not only because they do not like what they see in the mirror, but also because they have come to cherish other values and possibilities—some long forgotten (Peele & Brodsky, 1991). In their recent book, *The Struggle to Be Strong* (2000), Sybil Wolin and Al Desetta report the narratives of adolescents who have been subjected to enormous challenges in their lives. Consonant with Steven and Sybil Wolins' theory that resilience is forged from seven traits and capacities[3] that one might learn in the struggle against adversity, these stories reproduce evidence of those. Youniqiue Symone, living in foster care, at the age of 16 wrote this about the relationship between her and her biological mother:

> I grew up when I realized this: my mother is not going to change because I want her to. She's only going to change when she wants to. I also know deep down in my heart that we are never going to be a real family. . . . I don't want to have children at a young age to show my mother what a "real mother" is. I want to break the cycle. If I don't, I might end up doing the same thing my mother did. (p. 14)

This is an example of more than ordinary insight in a 16-year-old coming to terms with a mother who, for whatever reasons, neglected her. Out of that realization and her particular understanding about its impact on her young life, Youniqiue has determined to veer down a different passageway.

Personal qualities, traits, and virtues that people possess. These are sometimes forged in the fires of trauma and catastrophe, and they might be anything—a sense of humor, caring, creativity, loyalty, insight, independence, spirituality, moral imagination, and patience to name a few (Wolin & Wolin, 1993). These also are the products of living, the gifts of temperament, and the fruits of experience. Whatever their source, these skills and attributes might well become sources of energy and motivation in working with clients.

What people know about the world around them from those things learned intellectually or educationally to those that people have discerned and distilled through their life experiences. Perhaps a person has developed skill at spotting incipient interpersonal conflict or soothing others who are suffering. Perhaps life has given an individual the ability to care and tend for young children or elders, or it could be that a person could use an artistic medium to teach others about themselves. Maybe personal experience has motivated an individual and shaped a keen ability to help others through the grieving process. Again, we have no way of knowing what it might be without observing and asking.

---

[3]The seven possible elements of resilience are humor, insight, independence, relationships, creativity, morality, and initiative. People may develop any one or a number of these as they struggle with the challenges of their lives. They are also developmental, each undergoing maturation and sophistication with the passage of time.

The talents that people have can surprise us sometimes (as well as surprising the individual as some talents have lain dormant over the years). Playing a musical instrument, telling stories, cooking, home repair, writing, carpentry (who knows what it might be?) may provide additional tools and resources to assist individuals or groups in reaching their goals. In addition, they may be assets that can be shared and given to others to foster solidarity, to strengthen mentorship, or to cement friendship.

> Writing helped me when I was going through difficult times with my family—when they didn't or couldn't understand me, or when they didn't understand why I would cry for no reason. Writing helped me when I needed someone to talk to. Writing is like both my friend and my family, because it's always there for me whenever I need it.
>
> My mother still doesn't believe I can write on my own. She thinks I copy my poems and stories from someone else. . . .
>
> There's another reason why I would like to be a writer. I know that if someone has a problem and they read my story or poem it might make them feel a little (or even a lot) better about themselves. (Desetta & Wolin, 2000, p. 114)

Terry-Ann Da Costa, who wrote this at age 16, understands both her need to write and the gifts that her writing might bestow on others.

Cultural and personal stories and lore are often profound sources of strength, guidance, stability, comfort, or transformation and are often overlooked, minimized, or distorted. It is now often told how the stories of women have been shrouded through domination but how they are, when recounted and celebrated, sources of profound strength and wisdom (Aptheker, 1989). Cultural approaches to helping, to cite another example—whether the sweat lodge, medicine wheel, drumming, chanting, or curanderismo—may be powerful sources of healing and regeneration. Cultural stories, narratives, and myths, accounts of origins and migrations, or trauma and survival may provide sources of meaning and inspiration in times of difficulty or confusion (see Chapter 3). The exploits of cultural heroes, fictional and real, may provide instruction and guidance.

> The new mestiza [a woman of mixed Indian and Spanish ancestry born in the United States] copes by developing a tolerance for contradictions, a tolerance for ambiguity. She learns to be Indian in a Mexican culture, to be Mexican from an Anglo point of view. She learns to juggle cultures. She has a plural personality, she operates in a pluralistic mode—nothing is thrust out, the good, the bad. And the ugly, nothing rejected, nothing abandoned. Not only does she sustain contradictions, she turns the ambivalence into something else. (Anzaldua, 1987, p. 79, cited in Falicov, 1998, p. 15)

Personal and familial parables of falls from grace and redemption, of failure and resurrection, of struggle and resilience may also provide the diction, the metaphors from which one may construct a more vibrant vision of the self and world.

People have pride as well; people who have leapt over obstacles, who have rebounded from misfortune and hardship often have what the Wolins call "survivor's pride." Often this self-regard is buried under an accumulation of blame, shame, and labeling, but it is often there waiting to be uncovered. "Pride drives the engine of change; shame jams the gears!" (Wolin & Wolin, 1994).

The community is frequently overlooked as a physical, interpersonal, and institutional terrain full of riches to be tapped into (see Chapters 11, 12, and 13). The informal or natural environment is an especially rich landscape, full of people and organizations, who, if asked, would provide their talents and knowledge in the service of helping and supporting others. The work of community development (see Chapter 13) and organizing is, in part, dedicated to germinating the saplings of strength and resourcefulness in the community. The efforts of the Search Institute in Minneapolis in identifying those commuting strengths and assets that shore up the developmental infrastructure for all youth and help reduce risk behaviors is instructive in this regard. Among their many findings is that availability and vitality of community-wide institutions and neighborhood associations—youth groups, churches, synagogues, temples, ethnic associations, and schools—are critical elements of a responsive and working infrastructure for youth development (Benson, 1997).

The idea of *spirituality* is implicit, I think, in the discussions of and allusions to meaning-making. Ed Canda (see Chapter 4) has written with great wisdom about the nature of spirituality. Summarizing his perspective I would say it has three core assertions. First, spirituality refers to the essential, holistic quality of being that transcends the merely biological, psychological, social, political, or cultural but incorporates them all. This quality obliterates categorizations and dichotomies such as that between mind and body, substance and spirit (Canda, 1997). Second, spirituality reflects our struggle to find meaning, a working moral sensibility, and purposes that extend beyond selfish, egoistic concerns. Finally, spirituality refers to an essence that extends beyond the self, that defies ego boundaries, and allows us to join and revere the mysteries and complexities of life. This might be manifest in visions, peak experiences, cosmic revelations, experiences of the numinous and awe-inspiring.

For many individuals and groups, then, spirituality is a grand bulwark against the demands and stresses, both ordinary and inordinate, of life. It is also a means of discovering or creating meaning withstanding the vexing and sometimes seemingly incomprehensible events of daily life. Finally, it is a sense of the transcendent that can set the possibilities of the future in more hopeful compass.

How Do You Find out about Strengths?

Sounds difficult, but the discovery of strengths depends on some simple ideas. Look around you. Do you see evidence of client interests, talents, and competencies?

Michael

A student working with a middle-aged man with moderately severe retardation who lived in a group home was visiting "Michael" one day in his apartment and noticed some fabulous maps of the local area, the state, and the nation on the wall. They were extremely detailed, beautifully balanced, and, the student discovered, hand-drawn from memory by—Michael! He had been drawing these maps for years but no one who had worked with him had bothered to ask or show any curiosity about them. They had not looked around. Through the gradually deepening relationship between Michael and his student social worker, and through hard work and deep belief, Michael's maps eventually were exhibited at a museum, and his story was recounted in several newspapers.

Listen to clients' stories instead of zipping through an assessment protocol. Stories and narratives often contain within their plots and characterizations evidence of strengths, interests, hopes, and visions.

Bill

Bill was in his early forties, in and out of state hospitals since the age of 17 with a variety of diagnoses (chronic undifferentiated schizophrenia seemed to be the favorite). Single, living in a big city with no relatives nearby (or very interested in him), he worked as a dishwasher in a midtown bar and grill. He became hooked up with a community support program at the behest of a hospital social worker who was interested in keeping him out of the hospital. Bill was taking haloperidol. He was assigned a first-year MSW student as a case manager. The student was learning the strengths approach to practice and was anxious to try it. She began by encouraging Bill to "tell his stories"—how he got to be where he was, what interesting things he had done, and how he had survived with a serious illness. She learned many interesting things about Bill, and some of his stories clearly revealed a resourceful, motivated person. He had a serious problem with alcohol but quit drinking on his own. Yet he continued to frequent a local bar "because that's where all my buddies are," and being with his buddies was one outpost of connection and stability for him.

Bill also, on one occasion, saved enough money from his modest salary to take a trip to Oslo, Norway. He had seen some of Norway's marvelous statuary in an old *National Geographic* magazine and wanted to experience it for himself. He arranged and took the trip on his own. On his trek, he discovered a joy in flying. A dream began to form in his mind—he could see himself flying a plane.

He revealed his reverie to the social worker, who, given what she had come to learn about Bill, took it to heart. Together they began taking some modest steps toward his desire. In a few months, Bill got a job as a dishwasher at the airport, a busy international terminal, even though it involved an hour-long bus ride each way. He loved being around pilots and planes. At last account, Bill was working toward getting a job on the tarmac, perhaps as a baggage handler. Besides listening to his stories and searching within them for inklings of strength, character, and knowledge, the social worker did something else extraordinarily important to this kind of work: She let Bill know that she was genuinely interested in the hopes and dreams that he nurtured.

In trying to discover the strengths within and around, what sort of questions might one ask? There are several kinds of questions one might ask including:

Survival questions. How have you managed to survive (or thrive) thus far, given all the challenges you have had to contend with? How have you been able to rise to the challenges put before you? What was your mind-set as you faced these difficulties? What have you learned about yourself and your world during your struggles? Which of these difficulties have given you special strength, insight, or skill? What are the special qualities on which you can rely?

Support questions. What people have given you special understanding, support, and guidance? Who are the special people on whom you can depend? What is it that these people give you that is exceptional? How did you find them or how did they come to you? What did they respond to in you? What associations, organizations, or groups have been especially helpful to you in the past?

Exception questions.[4] When things were going well in life, what was different? In the past, when you felt that your life was better, more interesting, or more stable, what about your world, your relationships, your thinking was special or different? What parts of your world and your being would you like to recapture, reinvent, or relive? What moments or incidents in your life have given you special understanding, resilience, and guidance?

Possibility questions. What now do you want out of life? What are your hopes, visions, and aspirations? How far along are you toward achieving these? What people or personal qualities are helping you move in these directions? What do you like to do? What are your special talents and abilities? What fantasies and dreams have given you special hope and guidance? How can I help you achieve your goals or recover those special abilities and times that you have had in the past?

Esteem questions. When people say good things about you, what are they likely to say? What is it about your life, yourself, and your accomplishments that give you real pride? How will you know when things are going well in your life—what will you be doing, who will you be with, how will you be feeling, thinking, and acting? What gives you genuine pleasure in life? When was it that you began to believe that you might achieve some of the things you wanted in life? What people, events, and ideas were involved?

These obviously do not exhaust likely questions. And they are meant to be possibilities rather than a protocol.

---

[4]Thanks to the practitioners of solution-focused therapy for this terminology. We did not know what to call these kinds of questions (see De Jong, P. & Miller, S. D. (1995, November). How to interview for client strengths. *Social Work, 40,* 729–736).

What Are Some of the Elements of Strengths-Based Practice?

What follows is a sampler of the steps in practice. The next several chapters will approach practice in more detail.

Acknowledge the Pain.   For many individuals and families, there is real use and purpose in addressing, acknowledging, reexperiencing, and putting into perspective, the pains and trauma of one's life, especially those that seem now insistent. Catharsis, grieving, expression of rage and anxiety, and reconstruction are important in developing an understanding of where individuals have been, what their current struggles are, and what emotional and cognitive baggage they carry with them. This is also an important step in letting go of the past, and revisioning a present and future that is different and organically better. For some, it may even be beneficial to explore the roots of trauma in family, community, and culture. But the purpose is always to look for the seeds of resilience and rebound, the lessons taken away from the adversity—the cultural, ethnic, communal, and familial sources of adaptability.

Stimulate the Discourse and Narratives of Resilience and Strength.   There is often great resistance to acknowledging one's competence, reserve, and resourcefulness. In addition, many traits and capacities that are signs of strength are hidden under the rubble of years of self-doubt, the blame of others, and, in some cases, the wearing of a diagnostic label. Sometimes the problem of discovering strengths lies with the lack of words, sometimes it is disbelief, and sometimes it is lack of trust. The social worker may have to begin to provide the language, to look for, address, and give name to those resiliencies that people have demonstrated in the past and in the present (the Wolins' [1993] language of the seven resiliencies is helpful here). The daily struggles and triumphs of one's life as revealed in stories and narratives is useful (for example, what they have done, how they survived, what they want, what they want to avoid). At some point in this process, people do have to acknowledge their strengths, play them out, see them in the past and the present, feel them, and have them affirmed by the worker and others. In a sense, what is happening at this point is the writing of a better "text." Reframing is a part of this; not the reframing of so many family therapies, but adding to the picture already painted, brush strokes that depict capacity and ingenuity, and that provide a different coloration to the substance of one's life.

In a sense, then, the stimulation of a strengths discourse involves at least two acts on the part of the worker: providing a vocabulary of strengths (in the language of the client) and mirroring—providing a positive reflection of the client's abilities and accomplishments and helping the client to find other positive mirrors in the environment (Wolin & Wolin, 1994).

Act in Context: Education, Action, Advocacy, and Linkage.   The education continues about the capacities and resilient aspects of the self. Now these are linked up to the person's hopes, goals, and visions. The individual is encouraged to take the risk of acting on one's expectancies using the newly found or articulated competencies as well as already active ones. It is through action with the worker—collaborative and continuous—that individuals really begin to employ their strengths as they move toward well-formed, achievable goals. This is precarious business for many people who have been through a figurative hell. But as they decide and act, they continue to discover and enrich their repertoire of aptitudes. They also discover the limits of their resilience and the effect of still-active sore spots and scars. But, in the end, it is their decision making and activity that lead to changes in thinking, feeling, and relationship that are more congruent with their goals and their strengths. It is also vital that the individual group, or family begins to use naturally occurring community resources—from extended family to local associations and institutions—to move toward their goals.

For the social worker, this means advocacy in the form of discovering what natural or formal resources are available, accessible, and to what extent they are adequate and acceptable to the client (Kisthardt, 1993). The assumption here is that the environment is rich with resources: people, institutions, associations, families who are willing to and can provide instruction, succor, relief, resources, time, and mirroring. When people begin to plan fully to achieve their goals and to exercise their strengths, the effect is synergistic: They can do more personally, and they find themselves more connected to a community. For example, a receptionist at a physician's office begins to help an elderly woman complete her insurance forms, arrange transportation to and from the doctor's office so that she is more likely to keep appointments, and keep a level of health she believes is highly desirable. The synergistic effect is that the receptionist begins to do this for other elders as well and eventually finds other volunteers to assist them. For many of the older persons involved, this is an important support for the maintenance of relative independence—an important strength to be sure (see Chapter 9).

Move toward Normalizing and Capitalizing on One's Strengths.   Over a period of time, often short, the social worker and client begin to consolidate the strengths that have emerged, reinforce the new vocabulary of strengths and resilience, and bolster the capacity to discover resources within and around. The purpose is to cement the foundation of strengths, to insure the synergy of the continuing development and articulation of strengths, and to secure a place for the person to be. For many who have been helped through a strengths-based approach, one important avenue to normalization is teaching others what one has learned in the process. Finally, this is a process of disengagement for worker and client. Done with the assurance that the personal strengths and the communal resources are in place, disengagement is the ritual transition to normalization.

Conclusion

In summary, to assume a strengths perspective requires a degree of consciousness raising on the part of social workers and their clients—a different way of regarding

FIGURE 5.1   The Elements of Strengths-Based Practice

Risk factors		Protective/generative factors		
Challenges		*Resources*		
Damage Trauma Disorder Stress	Internal and external	Strengths Capacities Talents Gifts	Internal and external	➡
	+			
Expectations/possibilities		*Decisions*		
Hopes Dreams Visions Goals Self-righting	➡	Choices and options about paths to be taken Defining opportunities and setting directions Gathering resources and mobilizing strengths		➡
Project				

Mutual collaboration in work toward ➡ A better future

what they do together. One thing is certain, however, from reports of many of those people who apply the strengths perspective in their professional work: Once a client is engaged in building up the strengths within and without, a desire to do more and to become more absorbed in daily life and drawn by future possibilities bursts forth. As a means of visualizing the elements of strengths-based practice, the following schema may be helpful.

People are always engaged in their situations and are working on them even if they just decide to resign themselves to their fate. Circumstances can overwhelm and debilitate. We know a lot about that. But dire circumstances can also bring a surge in resolve and the blossoming of capacities and reserves. We must know more about that.

DISCUSSION QUESTIONS

1. With a friend or client, use some of the methods for discovering strengths described in this chapter. What was the outcome? How would you personalize such methods so they would be more useful to you?

2. Do you think that the way one goes about finding out about strengths has a different feel to it than methods for determining symptoms or problems? What, if any, is the difference?

3. What do you think of the role of luck and contingency in people's lives? How can it have an impact on your work with individuals, families, groups, or communities?

4. Do you know practitioners who approach clients from a strengths perspective? If so, what do you notice about their practice that is distinctive? Talk to them about how they came to practice in such a way.

5. How do you understand the placebo effect? Have you seen it at work in your professional or personal life?

REFERENCES

Aptheker, B. (1989). *Tapestries of life.* Amherst, MA: University of Massachusetts Press.

Arpala, J. (2000, July, August). Sweet sabotage. *Psychology Today, 32,* 66–67.

Benson, P. L. (1997). *All kids are our kids: What communities must do to raise caring and responsible children and adolescents.* San Francisco: Jossey-Bass Publishers.

Bentley, K. J., & Walsh, J. (2001). *The social worker and psychotropic medication.* (2nd ed.). Belmont, CA: Brooks/Cole.

Brody, H. (2000, July/August). Mind over medicine. *Psychology Today, 32,* 60–65, 67.

Canda, E. R. (1997). Spirituality. In R. L. Edwards, I. C. Colby, A. Garcia, R. G. McRoy, & L. Videka-Sherman (Eds.). *Encyclopedia of social work.* (19th ed., 1997 supplement). Washington, D.C.: National Association of Social Workers.

Desetta, A., & Wolin, S. (Eds.). (2000). *The struggle to be strong: True stories about youth overcoming tough times.* Minneapolis: Free Spirit Publishing Company.

Falicov, C. J. (1998). *Latino families in therapy: A guide to multicultural practice.* New York: The Guilford Press.

Fisher, M. J. (2000, October). Better living through the placebo effect. *The Atlantic Monthly, 286,* 16–18.

Gitlin, M. J. (1996). *The psychotherapist's guide to psychopharmacology.* (2nd ed.). New York: Free Press.

Kisthardt, W. E. (1993). A strengths model of case management: The principles and functions of a helping partnership with persons with persistent mental illness. In M. Harris & H. Bergman (Eds.). *Case management for mentally ill patients: Theory and practice.* Langhorne, PA: Harwood Academic Publishers.

Lambert, M. J. (1992). Implications of outcome research for psychotherapy integration. In J. C. Norcross, & M. R. Goldfried (Eds.). *Handbook of psychotherapy integration.* New York: Basic Books.

Miller, S. D., Duncan, B. L., & Hubble, M. A. (1997). *Escape from Babel: Toward a unifying language for psychotherapy.* New York: W. W. Norton & Company.

Peele, S., & Brodsky, A. (1991). The truth about addiction and recovery. New York: Simon & Schuster.

Rapp, C. A. (1998). *The strengths model: Case management with people suffering from severe and persistent mental illness.* New York: Oxford University press.

Rogers, C. (1951). *Client centered therapy: Its current practice, theory, and implications.* Chicago, IL: Houghton Mifflin.

Saleebey, D. (1994). Culture, theory, and narrative: The intersection of meanings in practice. *Social Work, 39,* 351–359.

Sampson, E. E. (1993). *Celebrating the other: A dialogic account of human nature.* Boulder, CO: Westview Press.

Shulman, L. (1992). *The skills of helping: Individuals, families, and groups.* (3rd ed.). Itasca, IL: F. E. Peacock.

Strupp, H. H. (1995). The psychotherapist's skills revisited. *Clinical Psychology, 2,* 70–74.

Swadener, B. B. (1995). Children and families 'at promise': Deconstructing the discourse of risk. In B. B. Swadener, & S. Lubeck (Eds.). *Children and families 'at promise': Deconstructing the discourse of risk.* Albany: State University of New York Press.

Wolin, S. J., & Wolin, S. (1993). *The resilient self: How survivors of troubled families overcome adversity.* New York: Villard.

Wolin, S. J., & Wolin, S. (1994, October). Resilience in overcoming adversity. Workshop for Employee Assistance Program members, Kansas City, MO.

6

Putting Problems in Their Place

Further Explorations in the Strengths Perspective[1]

ANN WEICK

RONNA CHAMBERLAIN

As a profession that grew out of an organized impulse to help those in need, social work has a long familiarity with human problems. While the focus of its attention has varied over time, its scope has remained wide and inclusive. Virtually every human trouble is encompassed within or touched by social work's interests. Given this investment in the well-being of society, it is worth examining what social work has brought to this history of response to problems and to ask whether its current preoccupations take advantage of the profession's wisdom and insight about the nature of human and social change.

This assessment is particularly appropriate in light of the development of a strengths perspective in social work. If social work is to more consciously focus on the strengths of people and their communities, where do problems fit? Critics claim that the strengths perspective ignores people's problems and glosses over their real pain. If we don't learn all there is to know about a person's problems, it seems that the very nature of helping is in jeopardy. Moreover, the profession's knowledge about the human condition appears to be diminished if problems are no longer the central focus of work.

Fascination with the troubled, anomalous, and paradoxical aspects of human existence is rooted in cultural phenomena that extend well beyond social work (Weick, 1992). The profession is not alone in fastening its attention on what's wrong with people and society. Other professions, social institutions, and the

---

[1]The authors wish to express appreciation to Melinda Coffman and Dianne Asher for providing case examples.

popular culture seem mesmerized by the search for fallibility. Personal and social problems appear overwhelming and obvious, while personal and social resources seem insubstantial and limited. The problems loom large; the solutions seem invisible. Our only defense seems to be an overactive vigilance in searching out, monitoring, and reporting all the ways in which people's capacity to do and endure harm is present among us.

To clarify the place of problems within the strengths perspective, it is important to develop a larger understanding about the place of problems within social work. The ways that the profession has defined its work have changed over time. Examining this history can provide a broader context for determining how social work can most appropriately view problems within its practice and how a strengths perspective can reveal the profession's essential insights about the power of our work.

The Shape of Problems

Social work has always been concerned about human problems. At the turn of the 20th century, this concern was focused on the poverty, poor health, and dangerous working conditions associated with urban life and industrial demands. Workers in charity organizations and settlement houses developed family-oriented and community-oriented strategies to help those who were caught in the jaws of this major social upheaval. In the course of this work, two general approaches to problems began to emerge.

For some social workers, the problems were squarely moral: Individuals who were poor, addicted, violent, or insane were morally and, perhaps, constitutionally defective. The character of the person was of central concern and in need of correction. But others saw the social dimensions and believed that resources such as housing, sanitation, education, neighborly assistance, and beneficient social interactions would enable people to move beyond the limits of their situations. Both of these convictions rested on the positive value of the social work relationship as the medium for constructive change.

Beginning in the 1920s, the profession's understanding of human problems began to be influenced by the burgeoning fields of psychology and psychiatry. From these perspectives, human behavior was no longer viewed as transparent or easily explained. Quite the reverse. Psychological and psychiatric theories made human actions mysterious, complex, and rarely what they seemed. The causes of behavior moved from simple categories like moral character, family origins, and social habits to a new language of explanation that only a select few knew. This language was based on ideas about human motivation, the development of personality, and intrapsychic aspects of everyday behaviors. In the world of human behavior, nothing was ever as it appeared.

The psychologizing of human behavior brought a powerful shift in the nature of the helping process. If human problems were caused not by everyday troubles but by deeply seated, complex behavioral patterns, then the persons affected could not be expected to understand their own actions. People's inner lives became both inaccessible and differently accessible. The understandings they may have had were seen as mistaken and naive. The new understanding given to them was packaged by another: Someone else became the interpreter of what one was feeling and why. A new class of experts appeared who, through professional training and perhaps through personal therapeutic analysis, were able to decipher the intrapsychic cause of one's difficulties. Moreover, the cause was thought to be connected to the cure so that no constructive action could be taken until the cause had been unearthed. The only work to be done was psychic excavation. Once the ruins were discovered, it was assumed that resolution would follow.

The redefinition of human problems has been a lasting legacy of psychologically oriented practice. What had been universal aspects of human experience throughout history evolved into new classes of behaviors, isolated from their context and viewed through the lens of pathology. Because these behaviors are removed from their larger social context, they appear to be unique failures and dangerous symptoms instead of pervasive, if frightening and puzzling, parts of human life.

What this redefinition of problems has removed from view is the idea that human troubles, in all their guises, are a normal part of social living. Saying this does not remove our responsibility or concern. What it does suggest is that our interest in why problems exist has caused us to focus on the most intriguing but least useful aspect of work. In doing so, precious energy is used to understand the problem and less attention is devoted to determining creative ways to reduce its presence and ameliorate its effects.

The quest for psychological causes has not been successful. As the title of Hillman and Ventura's (1992) book suggests, *We've Had One Hundred Years of Psychotherapy and the World Is Getting Worse.* Perhaps it is time once again to refocus our attention on results. The profession's historic commitment to working with people in the midst of their daily lives, with all their trials and cares, is a place to begin. The strengths perspective builds on this tradition by meeting people where they are and joining with them in discovering and reaffirming the talents, abilities, and aspirations that will carve a path leading beyond the problem.

Putting Strengths into Action

To join with people in the difficulties of their daily lives, one of the hallmarks of social work practice comes to the fore. An essential focus of the strengths perspective is the quality of the relationship between social workers and the people they hope to help. As social work tradition holds, the relationship is the medium for change. What the social worker brings to this relationship is one of the most important aspects of strengths-based work.

The strengths perspective depends heavily on the worker's sense of people's innate capacity to transform their lives. Stimulating this positive energy for growth begins first with an act of belief. If the social worker does not believe that people can make positive changes in their lives, no matter what their circumstances, the possibility that they will do so is greatly diminished. It is the strength of this belief that people can transform and regenerate themselves that acts as the source of positive energy to activate the process of change. The person, family, or community that is mired in the snares of trouble typically does not believe that it possesses any resources that would be useful in resolving the problem. They have already tried to fix the situation without success. The way that social workers communicate their belief in the inner strength and resourcefulness of a person, family, or community becomes the beginning step in restoring people's hope in themselves and in their capacity to influence the shape of their lives (Weick & Chamberlain, 1997).

The power of belief has been eloquently documented early by Jerome Frank (1963) in his exploration of the process of healing and later by Miller, Duncan, and Hubble (1997) in their discussion of what works in psychotherapy. But in contrast to their focus on belief in the power of the healer, the strengths perspective depends on the activation of people's belief in the power they themselves possess. This belief in people's own powers and capacities helps protect against social workers believing that they are the ones who are causing change to occur.

Fueled by the deep awareness of people's capacity for resolving their problems, socials workers practicing from a strengths perspective begin with respect for the person and the problem the person brings. Listening carefully to the story that unfolds is the opportunity to hear the pain of the problem but also to begin learning how that person survived, coped with, and tried to resolve it. Because most people who come to or are sent to a social worker have lived a long time with the problem, they have thought and worried about it extensively. They know their problem better than anyone. What they have not been able to do is find a way to get past the problem. The task of the social worker is to help people find a path beyond the problem. From the strengths perspective, the bridge to this new path will be found in the capacities, talents, and aspirations hidden in their life stories.

Doug

When Doug met with his case manager, he was a 38-year-old man with a twenty-year history of seizure disorder. He described feelings of serious depression because of his inability to find work. Although he had been able to obtain a few jobs in his life, he had always lost them due to seizures, which occurred on a daily basis. His employment problem was further compounded by illiteracy, an inability to drive due to head injury, and a criminal history of drug abuse.

Given these overwhelming obstacles to employment, many practitioners would have been tempted to side-step Doug's interest in getting a job and focus on treating his depression or helping him adjust his expectations to more realistic goals. Instead, the worker listened to Doug's wishes and concentrated on helping him find a job. She was able to locate a grocery store near his boarding home that was willing to hire people with disabilities. However, because of his seizures, Doug was unable to climb ladders, making it impossible to stock shelves or handle cutters to open cartons. Because of his brain damage, he was unable to operate a cash register. The only reasonably safe job was janitorial work and even that required that he wear a helmet while cleaning rest rooms because of the danger presented by the possibility of falling against porcelain.

Doug was thrilled to have a job. His mood rapidly improved, and, over time, his seizures became less frequent. Doug became a valued employee, and, after three years of demonstrating reliability and competence, he began training as a butcher. Through his stable income, he was able to buy a modest house. When asked to characterize these changes in his situation, Doug summed up his success by saying, "life is good."

Doug's story illustrates the major differences between a strengths and a problem approach. To focus on his multitude of problems would have been defeating for both client and caseworker. Working with Doug on goals related to his daily life, based on his interests and aspirations, helped him to find the path beyond his problem. While the problems did not disappear, a critical portion of the solution rested in minimizing them which, in turn, diminished their impact on the quality of his life.

The process of strategically minimizing or ignoring problems in strengths-based practice is often confused by practitioners with the use of positive reframing of problems. Positive reframing is a very useful tool in assisting clients to redefine problems in a manner that is understandable and non-blaming. However, even when redefined, the problem remains the focus of the work. Todd's story illustrates this difference.

Todd

Todd was a 17-year-old high school student when he was first admitted to a treatment facility for substance abuse. He had spiked hair and a preference for black clothing. As his social worker built a relationship with him, it became apparent that he believed himself to be a youth who did not fit in with most of his peers. His main contacts were with a group in which drug use was prevalent and Todd too began using drugs. However, Todd continued to spend much of his time alone and drug use was a significant feature of his isolation. His grades fell and his parents became concerned. After the accidental overdose and death of one of his group peers and the related suicide of another, Todd became frightened by his escalating drug use and, with the support of his mother, sought help.

At this point in Todd's story, many professionals might choose to engage in positive reframing by interpreting Todd's drug use as his attempt to cope with his feelings of isolation or by proposing more constructive coping strategies. While positive reframing can be a valuable tool in helping the client decrease the self-blame that often accompanies the admission of a problem, it should not be confused with a strengths approach. The use of positive reframing alone will maintain a focus on problems. Attempts to learn new, artificially constructed coping devices is a lengthy and arduous task for clients and is not always associated with success.

Fortunately, the worker used a strengths perspective to focus on Todd's capacities and interests. Throughout the crisis episode, Todd was able to maintain a quarter-time job and continue to play his saxophone. From Todd's story, it was clear that Todd enjoyed his work. He felt accepted by his boss and coworkers and believed his work was appreciated. He also derived pleasure from playing his sax. Using this as a base for their work together, the social worker assisted him in expanding the positive activities of his life. With her encouragement, he more than doubled his work hours and, seeking to expand his music, he eventually invited other students to be part of a band. By concentrating on the areas of his life in which he experienced success, his drug problems and academic difficulties began to slowly fade. Motivation to make these changes was fueled by using his strengths to develop a more satisfying life than the one that had led him to the crisis. This chance for a better future gave him an optimism and sense of accomplishment that safely carried him beyond his problems.

In some cases, a problem presents itself that is too critical to be ignored. The following case exemplifies such a dilemma.

Loretta

Loretta, age 34, was diagnosed as having a borderline personality disorder. She had multiple hospitalizations on a yearly basis following suicidal threats, gestures such as cutting of wrists, other forms of self-injury, overdosing on medications, and two more serious suicide attempts. In recent years, she had also begun to threaten to hurt other people. Loretta had been in treatment for many years. Creative social workers and psychiatrists had worked diligently with her to help her get jobs and move from her family home into her own apartments. In spite of years of treatment focused on understanding and coping with her depression and suicidal impulses and exploring different ways of managing her feelings, each job or new living arrangement ended abruptly with a dramatic crisis involving threats and/or self-destructive behaviors that required subsequent hospitalizations.

A newly assigned social worker decided that Loretta's destructive behaviors dominated not only her life but also the years of case planning. In an attempt to rid both the client and herself of the emphasis on the problem, they worked together to arrive at a detailed action plan involving a crisis team to respond to Loretta's calls and threats. Once the crisis plan was put into place, the worker's sole focus was to assist Loretta in defining her considerable talents and in helping her find ways to express them in work, her home life, and social activities. During the years following this plan, Loretta had several brief hospitalizations. These decisions to seek hospital treatment were not accompanied by the high level of drama associated with past crises, and she was able to return to her job and apartment following discharge. With the social worker's refusal to be involved in the problem, Loretta slowly learned to shift her attention to building more satisfying activities in her daily life. For Loretta, putting the problem in its place may have, in fact, saved her life.

The lesson to be learned from Loretta's situation is that, although some problems are too critical to be ignored, they need to be consigned to a position that is secondary to the person's strengths, once a crisis situation has passed. The dilemma for both the client and the social worker is that the problem is often sufficiently frightening that the details of daily life seem to be of little significance by comparison. The paradox appears to be that the problem will defy control until the client has a daily life that provides enough gratification to make it worth the arduous task of overcoming a problem as powerful as impulses toward mutilating or violent behavior. Loretta's destructive behaviors were minimized when attention to them was curtailed and she was assisted in focusing her attention on other matters.

Key Strategies in Strengths-Based Practice

Working from a strengths perspective is linked to three strategies for putting problems in their place. They require that we

- recognize problems only in their proper context.
- pay less attention to problems.
- find simpler ways to talk about problems.

Context

The strengths perspective is a vehicle for helping people identify and fulfill their own aspirations. If the problem can be seen as an obstacle to the attainment of client-determined goals, the problem becomes situation- or context-specific. Instead of becoming the whole of a person's life, it takes its place as an identifiable hurdle on the way to achieving life goals. This was exemplified by Loretta's situation. Her problem of destructive behavior needed to be handled by a very specific action plan. When her behavior precipitated a crisis, both she and her worker knew what steps would be taken to insure her and others' safety. In this way, the attention to problems was contained within a narrow focus. Helping her move beyond the crisis was accomplished by working in a single-minded, collaborative way on goals that she determined would make her life more satisfying. Deciding what she wanted for her life and having the experience of accomplishing her goals gave her reason to take medication, even with its negative side effects. Her hopes and dreams provided the larger context for her life; her mental illness became a bit player in this drama.

Paying Less Attention

Concentrating on the problems people bring creates a trap that saps both the client's and worker's energy for productive work together. Listening to the long story of how the problem began is an important starting point. But for many people such as Doug and Loretta, whose lives had been beset with chronic problems and struggles, this story takes on mythic proportions. The teller knows every nuance, every hurt, and every trial connected to the problem. Those who have had many contacts with mental health professionals can supply an astounding history of events, interventions, and diagnostic information. Their physical and emotional energy is absorbed by these tales of sorrow. If practitioners base their plans of action on even further exploration and refinement of the problem, their energy, too, will soon be drawn into this maelstrom of confusion and hopelessness. What the person needs most is to figure out how to move beyond their problem.

By paying less attention to the problem, strengths-based practice produces new energy for work. To get beyond the negativity of the problem, one must mobilize those individual, family, and community resources that make it possible for someone to create a different life. The bridge to doing so is an unrelenting focus on people's strengths. Focusing on people's aspirations, capacities, and skills is a powerful act. As we see in Todd's case, the attention itself was reaffirming. Through the eyes of his social worker, coworkers, and fellow musicians, Todd could see himself in a new light and gain energy for the difficult work of human change. Implicit in this approach is a deep respect for the reservoir of potential inherent in each person and an understanding of the approach that supports and frees that potential for use.

Everyday Language

Adopting simpler ways of talking about problems is another useful strategy for making human problems less mysterious and unmanageable. This approach harkens back to the early days of social work, when people were seen to have problems of daily living. In the works of authors such as Bertha Reynolds (1951), Helen Harris Perlman (1963), Charlotte Towle (1965), and Harriett Bartlett (1970), there was the tradition of seeing problems as ordinary aspects of human life. Even though we may use more complicated ways of defining them, people's lives are still filled with such issues and opportunities. In some cases, problems arise because basic needs are not met. People are without adequate food, housing, employment, and medical attention. In other cases, problems develop because there are insufficient social supports in areas such as child care and activities for young people or help for parents in rearing children and caring for family members whose physical or mental conditions require special assistance. Finally, there are the ongoing interpersonal challenges of life as a member of a family and in the neighborhood and workplace. By seeing these aspects of social living as part of the predictable fabric of human life, they take on a more manageable form. They move from esoteric categories of psychological diagnosis to the very real, life-size challenges that come with being human and living in human communities.

Using simple, everyday language to talk about and name the issues people bring is an important step in giving back to them a sense of control over their lives. Think about how different it sounds to hear a child described as mischievous and very active instead of having a behavior disorder or a woman described as having relationship disappointments and troubles rather than being codependent. As Kenneth Gergen (1994) said, "When the culture is furnished with a professionally rationalized language of mental deficit and people are increasingly understood according to this language, the population of 'patients' expands" (p. 161). The use of simpler, more common words is less likely to take us down the path of problem definition and more likely to begin the process of asking the client: How would you like your life to be different?

Surely there are situations in which identifying someone as having schizophrenia or hypoglycemia can lead to more, rather than less, humane ways to respond to the problem. These situations invariably involve strong biological components and require some medical or nutritional strategies. But to the extent that a diagnosis or professional label rivets attention on the problem itself and not on paths beyond the problem, then the focus of work is in the hands of the worker, not the client. Using everyday language helps ensure that the person seeking help stays in charge of her or his own process of life change.

Concluding Thoughts

As one examines the orientation to problems embraced by the strengths perspective, it becomes clear that problems are no longer in the center of the stage. Instead of being the star performer in a play, they become minor characters with small roles. The strengths perspective is anchored in the belief that a problem does not constitute all of a person's life. Whether the name of the problem is schizophrenia, addiction, child abuse, or troubled family relations, a person is always more than his or her problem.

In tandem with this belief is the acknowledgment that focusing on problems usually creates more problems. The longer one stays with a problem-focused assessment, the more likely it is that the problem will dominate the stage. Both Doug and Loretta had long and unsuccessful treatment histories where this was the case. However, problems do have a role to play. Just as actors with a few lines are important in a larger drama, problems produce uncomfortable emotions like pain, anger, shame, and confusion, which serve to get our attention and put us on notice. They are a sign that something needs to change. But the problem is not a complete signpost. It signals: "danger," "beware," "trouble ahead." It does not include directions about how to get beyond the problem. Complicated diagnoses about human problems can mask the more potent areas of strength, as well as the small victories the person experiences. A problem orientation begins to look like an exercise serving the needs of professionals, rather than the needs of the people with whom they are working.

From a strengths perspective, having the problem is not the problem. The real test comes from figuring out constructive ways to meet, use, or transcend the problem. In strengths-based practice, the goal is to mobilize personal, family, and community resources to move beyond the problem. An important ingredient in achieving this goal is to learn about what people want for themselves. Usually the problem they bring is keeping them from having the kind of life they imagine. If they did not have mental illness, an abusive partner, or a hyperactive child, they would be more satisfied and feel better about themselves. Helping people to begin talking about this vision of life without the problem taps into their aspirations, hopes, and dreams. Instead of worrying about how they came to have the problem, they can use the positive energy of the aspirations to pare the problem down to size and begin to envision a life beyond the problem.

This vision of a satisfying life, defined in their terms, and the steadfast support of social workers who believe in their capacity to achieve it, reveals the essence of the profession's long-time commitment to society's welfare. With that commitment comes a radical appreciation of people's personal potential and of the vast reservoir of supporting resources that exist within families, groups, neighborhoods, and communities. Shifting our attention to these strengths will require us to turn away from the seduction of pathology. But through this new determination, social work can reclaim its distinctive value orientation and bring its own considerable strengths to the task of improving human and social well-being.

DISCUSSION QUESTIONS

1. Can you imagine putting problems in their place—making them secondary to the work of finding and building on strengths?

2. What do you find most interesting and compelling about the examples of Doug, Todd, and Loretta? Are there ideas implicit in these examples that you can use?

3. Imagine a 10-year-old boy given the diagnosis of Attention Deficit Hyperactivity Disorder. How would you talk about him in everyday, ordinary language?

4. Paying attention to context requires us to really look at the situational elements—large and small—of a person's life. What are some of the elements of a person's immediate situation/context that you would want to understand?

REFERENCES

Bartlett, H. (1970). *The common base of social work practice.* Maryland: National Association of Social Workers.

Frank, J. (1963). *Persuasion and healing.* New York: Schocken Books.

Gergen, K. J. (1994). *Realities and relationships: Soundings in social construction.* Cambridge, MA: Harvard University Press.

Hillman, J., & M. Ventura. (1992). *We've had one hundred years of psychotherapy and the world is getting worse.* San Francisco: Harper.

Miller, S. D., Duncan, B. L., & Hubble, M. A. (1997). *Escape from Babel: Toward a unifying language of psychotherapy practice.* New York: Norton.

Perlman, H. H. (1963). *Social casework: A problem solving process.* Chicago: University of Chicago Press.

Reynolds, B. (1951). *Social work and social living.* New York: Citadel Press.

Towle, C. (1965). *Common human need.* Silver Springs, MD: National Association of Social Workers.

Weick, A. (1992). Building a strengths perspective for social work. In D. Saleebey (Ed.). *The strengths perspective in social work practice.* New York: Longman, pp. 18–26.

Weick, A., & Chamberlain, R. (1997). Putting problems in their place: Further explorations in the strengths perspective. In D. Saleebey (Ed.), *The strengths perspective in social work practice.* New York: Longman.

7

Assessing Client Strengths

Individual, Family, and Community Empowerment[1]

CHARLES D. COWGER

CAROL A. SNIVELY

Deficit, disease, and dysfunction metaphors have become deeply rooted in the helping professions, shaping contemporary social work practice through the emphasis on diagnosis and treatment of abnormal and pathological conditions within individuals, families, and communities. Yet, the proposition that strengths are central to the helping relationship appears to be slowly regaining popularity among social work educators and practitioners (Rapp, 1998). By developing a strengths-based assessment process, the profession expands the ways in which social workers can act as resources to those we refer to as "clients."[2]

Review of the social work literature on human behavior and the social environment reveals that the typical textbook now makes reference to the strengths perspective, although there is little theoretical or empirical content on this topic yet to be found in the areas of social work assessment, practice, and evaluation. The assessment literature, including available assessment instruments, continues to be overwhelmingly concerned with individual, family, and community inadequacies. Not much has changed since Rodwell's commentary on assessment in social work practice. The focus of assessment has "continued to be, one way or another, diagnosing pathological conditions" (Rodwell, 1987, p. 235). While advances have

---

[1]This chapter is based on Cowger, C. D. (1994). Assessing client strengths: Clinical assessment for client empowerment. *Social Work, 39*(3), 262–268. Copyright 1994, National Association for Social Workers, Inc.

[2]For simplicity in this discussion, the term *client* refers to those individuals, families, groups, or communities who participate in a helping partnership with a social worker.

been made in the development of strengths-based assessment instruments (Rapp, 1998), library search for assessment tools that include client strengths is still a particularly unrewarding experience, as is reviewing collections of assessment, diagnosis, and measurement instruments in book and monograph form. And, of course, various versions of the American Psychiatric Association's *Diagnostic and Statistical Manual,* from volumes I to IV have emphasized client pathology. The lack of strengths-based resources and pervasive use of deficit-based resources influences which direct practice skills are mastered in social work education.

For the most part, social workers have been negligent in documenting the application of strengths-based principles to divergent practice realms, an example of which is direct practice with families (Early & GlenMaye, 2000). Much of the social work literature in this area continues to use treatment, dysfunction, and therapy metaphors while ignoring interdisciplinary advances on family strengths.

In addition, there is very little empirical evidence indicating the extent to which practitioners consciously make use of client strengths in their practice. Maluccio (1979) found that social workers underestimated client strengths and had more negative perceptions of clients than clients had of themselves. Hepworth and Larsen (1990) highlighted this incongruity between social work ideology and practice when they stated, "social workers persist in formulating assessments that focus almost exclusively on the pathology and dysfunction of clients—despite the time honored social work platitude that social workers work with strengths, not weaknesses" (p. 157). Taking a behavioral baseline of individual, family, and community deficits and examining the ability of social workers' interventions to correct those deficits continues to be the standard for evaluating the effectiveness of social work practice (Kagle & Cowger, 1984).

It seems unlikely then that client strengths would have an impact on worker activity, considering the preponderance of deficit assessment instruments as opposed to the dearth of assessment tools that consider client strengths. However, Hwang and Cowger (1998) found that when a case that had specific strengths specified was presented to practitioners, they were likely to include strengths in their assessments, though that finding was less likely for workers in mental health settings and for practitioners who identified their theoretical orientation as psychodynamic. Not surprisingly, contemporary social workers have become more specialized, are more often held accountable for service outcomes, and, in regard to individuals and families, are more involved with managed care, which very often requires DSM diagnosis for reimbursement (Gibelman, 1999). Thus, there is pressure for social workers to be experts about pathology and demonstrate efficiency in securing remediation of problem symptoms. In light of these trends and research findings, frameworks are needed to assist social workers in creatively utilizing a strengths perspective while working within deficit-focused systems of care. In this regard, the assessment process is very important. Assessment provides an early and ongoing opportunity for the client/social worker partnership to name and rename the problem, shifting perspectives from deficit to strengths and providing the client opportunities to have voice in shaping the method for problem remediation. Evaluation of strengths-based assessments can assist in refining practice skills and provide support for policy changes related to service delivery.

There is a growing body of social work practice literature that applies the strengths perspective to individual, family, and community assessment (Cohen, 1999; De Jong & Miller, 1995; Delgado & Barton, 1998; Early & GlenMaye, 2000; McQuaide & Ehrenreich, 1997; Poole, 1997; Russo, 1999; Solomon, 1976). Notable examples of the application of strengths-based theory to practice and research is a rich body of literature that has developed a framework for understanding the experiences of minority families (Billingsley, 1968, 1992; Boyd-Franklin & Bry, 2000; McAdoo & McAdoo, 1985) and research that focuses on adolescents as competent citizens (Finn & Checkoway, 1998). Together, this body of work supports the shift in perspective needed to repoliticize social work practice. While Finn & Checkoway (1998) speak specifically about youth, their words stand as an important charge to social workers in all helping partnerships.

It is time to take the capacity of young people seriously and challenge the limits of our helping paradigms in the process. This calls for a reorientation from the therapeutic models of individual treatment to consciousness-raising models for group reflection and action. It demands a redirection from the emphasis on social work roles of counselor, case manager, and broker to those of collaborator, mentor, and animator. The process becomes one of accompaniment in which young people and adults pool their resources and join together on a new kind of journey (Wilson & Whitmore, 1995). "Changes in attitudes must accompany changes in practices. . . . This means sharing power in ways that enable young people to have a real voice in the decisions that affect their lives" (p. 344).

The Link between Assessment as Political Activity and Empowerment

This chapter is based on a mainstream contextual understanding that the primary purpose of social work is to assist people in their relationships with one another and with social institutions to promote social and economic justice (Council on Social Work Education, 1994). Practice, thus, focuses on developing more positive and promising transactions between people and their environments. However, taking seriously the element of promoting social and economic justice in those transactions may not result in conventional models of practice. Indeed, practice that recognizes issues of social and economic justice requires methods that explicitly deal with power and power relationships (see Chapter 10). This perspective understands client empowerment as central to social work practice and client strengths as providing the fuel and energy for that empowerment. Client empowerment is characterized by two interdependent and interactive dynamics: personal empowerment and social empowerment. Although social work theories that split the attributes of people into the social and the psychological have considerable limitations (Falck, 1988), such a differentiation is made in this chapter to stress the importance of each element as separate but concomitant elements in the empowerment experience.

The personal empowerment dynamic is similar to a traditional clinical notion of self-determination whereby clients give direction to the helping process, assume more control in personal decision making, learn new ways to think about their situations, and adopt behaviors that give them more satisfying and rewarding outcomes. The social worker who has personal empowerment as an objective, recognizes the uniqueness of each client and problem then assists the client in resolving the situation in a socially just manner. Clients are not personally empowered when they are learning new ways to accommodate experiences of oppression.

Social empowerment acknowledges that individual behavior and identity is "bound up with that of others through social involvement" (Falck, 1988, p. 30). Empowerment is experienced through interaction with others, a process of gaining power within and through social relationships. Persons, groups, or communities who are socially empowered have the resources and opportunity to play an important role in shaping their environment, and thus influence their own and others' lives.

Personal and social empowerments are synergistic. Each situation or problem is formed and resolved within a greater, societal context. By fortifying opportunities to achieve success for self and others, those who are gaining personal and social power help to create a more socially just environment in which to live.

Social work practice based on empowerment assumes that client power is augmented when clients are afforded the opportunity to share control in the decisions that impact their presenting problem situations and, in turn, their lives. However, empowerment-based practice assumes that social justice can be achieved, recognizing that empowerment and self-determination are dependent not only on people making choices, but also on people having available choices to make. The distribution of available choices in a society is political. Societies organize systems of production and the distribution of resources, and that affects those choices differentially. Across societies, production and distribution are based on varying degrees of commitment to equity and justice: "Some people get more of everything than others" (Goroff, 1983, p. 133). Social work practice based on the notion of choice requires attention to the dynamics of personal power, the social power endemic to the client's environment, and the relationship between the two. Therefore, both must be addressed to realize true empowerment.

One of the important obstacles to client empowerment is the traditional role that has been developed for clients to play in helping relationships. With the increasing professionalization of services, the power distance between clients and professionals becomes greater as the social worker assumes the position of expert. The process of developing a professional relationship with a person is a process whereby that person *becomes* a client and learns to play the proper client role. McKnight refers to this as a process whereby the person or community achieves "client hood" (McKnight, 1995, p. 51). This process has also been referred to as "clientilism" (Habermas, 1981) and "clientification" (Cowger, 1998). Strengths-based assessment has the potential to mitigate the imbalanced power relationship between client and professional by sharing power in the helping relationship.

Assessment as Political Activity

Assessment that focuses on deficits presents obstacles to the exercise of personal and social power for clients and reinforces those social structures that generate and regulate the unequal power relationships victimizing clients. Goroff (1983) persuasively argues that social work practice is a political activity and that the attribution of individual deficiencies as the cause of human problems is a politically conservative process that "supports the status quo" (p. 134).

Deficit-based assessment targets the client as the problem. For example, from a deficit perspective the person who is unemployed, the family who is homeless, or the residents who live in a declining community are the problem. Social work interventions that focus on what is wrong with the client—for example, why he or she is not working—reinforce the powerlessness the client is already experiencing because he or she does not have a job, a home, or a safe community in which to live. At the same time such an intervention lets economic and social structures that do not provide opportunity off the hook and reinforces social structures that generate unequal power. To assume that the cause of personal pain and social problems is individual deficiency "has the political consequences of not focusing on the social structure (the body politic) but on the individual. Most, if not all, of the pain we experience is the result of the way we have organized ourselves and how we create and allocate life-surviving resources" (Goroff, 1983, p. 134).

Personal pain is political. Social work practice is political. Diagnostic and assessment metaphors and taxonomies that stress individual deficiencies and sickness reinforce the political status quo in a manner that is incongruent with the promotion of social and economic justice. Practice centered on pathology is reminiscent of "blaming the victim" (Ryan, 1976). Practice based on metaphors of client strengths and empowerment is also political in that its thrust is the development of client power and the more equitable distribution of societal resources—those resources that underlie the development of personal resources.

Client Strengths and Empowerment

Promoting empowerment means believing that people are capable of making their own choices and decisions. It means not only that human beings possess the strengths and potential to resolve their own difficult life situations, but also that they increase their strength and contribute to the well-being of society by doing so. The role of the social worker is to nourish, encourage, assist, enable, support, stimulate, and unleash the strengths within people; to illuminate the strengths available to people in their own environments; and to promote equity and justice at all levels of society. To do that, the social worker helps clients articulate the nature of their situations, identify what they want, explore alternatives for achieving those desires, and then achieve them.

The role of the social worker is not to change people, treat people, help people cope, or counsel people. The role is not to empower people. As Simon (1990) argued, social workers cannot empower others: "More than a simple linguistic nuance, the notion that social workers do not empower others, but instead, help people empower themselves is an ontological distinction that frames the reality experienced by both workers and clients" (p. 32). To assume a social worker can empower someone else is naive and condescending and has little basis in reality. Power is not something that social workers possess for distribution at will. Clients, not social workers, own the power that brings significant change in social work practice. A social worker is a resource person, with professional training on the development, accumulation, and use of resources, who is committed to the empowerment of people and willing to share his or her knowledge in a manner that helps people realize their own power, take control of their own lives, and solve their own problems.

Importance of Assessing Strengths

Central to a strengths perspective is the role and place of assessment in the practice process (see Chapters 4, 7, and 8). How clients define difficult situations and how they evaluate and give meaning to the dynamic factors related to those situations set the context and content for the duration of the helping relationship. If assessment focuses on deficits, it is likely that deficits will remain the focus of both the worker and the client during remaining contacts. Concentrating on deficits or strengths can lead to self-fulfilling prophecies. Hepworth and Larsen (1990) articulated how this concentration might also impair a social worker's "ability to discern clients' potentials for growth," reinforce "client self-doubts and feelings of inadequacy," and predispose workers to "believe that clients should continue to receive service longer than is necessary" (p. 195).

Emphasizing deficits has serious implications and limitations. Focusing on strengths provides considerable advantages. Strengths are all we have to work with. The recognition and embellishment of strengths is fundamental to the values and mission of the profession. A strengths perspective provides for a leveling of the power relationship between social workers and clients. Clients almost always enter the social work setting in a vulnerable position and with comparatively little power. Their lack of power is revealed by the very fact that they are seeking help and entering the social structure of service. A deficit focus emphasizes this vulnerability and highlights the unequal power relationship between the worker and the client.

A strengths perspective assumes client competence and thereby mitigates the significance of unequal power between the client and social worker. In so doing, a strengths orientation implies increased potential for liberating people from stigmatizing diagnostic classifications that promote sickness and weakness in individuals, families, and communities. A strengths perspective of assessment provides structure and content for an examination of realizable alternatives, for the mobilization of competencies that can make things different, and for the building of self-confidence that stimulates hope.

Guidelines for Strengths Assessment

These guidelines for strengths assessment are presented with the understanding that assessment is a process as well as a product. Assessment as process is helping clients define their situations (that is, clarify the reasons they have sought assistance) and assisting clients in evaluating and giving meaning to those factors that affect their situations. It is particularly important to assist clients in telling their stories. The client owns that story, and if the social worker respects that ownership, the client will be able to more fully share it. The assessment as a product is an agreement, in many cases a written agreement, between the worker and the client as to the nature of the problem situation (descriptive) and the meaning ascribed to those factors influencing the problem situation (analytic and interpretative).

The following guidelines are based on the notion that the knowledge guiding the assessment process is based on a socially constructed reality (Berger & Luckmann, 1966). Also, the assessment should recognize that there are multiple constructions of reality for each client situation (Rodwell, 1987) and that problem situations are interactive, multicausal, and ever-changing.

1. Give Preeminence to the Client's Understanding of the Facts.   The client's view of the situation, the meaning the client ascribes to the situation, and the client's feelings or emotions related to that situation are the central focus for assessment. Assessment content on the intrapersonal, developmental, cognitive, mental, and biophysical dynamics of the client are important only as it enlightens the situation presented by the client. It should be used only as a way to identify strengths that can be brought to bear on the presenting situation or to recognize obstacles to achieving client objectives. The use of social sciences behavior taxonomies representing the realities of the social scientists should not be used as something to apply to, thrust on, or label a client. An intrapersonal and interpersonal assessment, like data gathered on the client's past, should not have a life of its own and is not important in its own right.

2. Believe the Client.   Central to a strengths perspective is a deeply held belief that clients ultimately are trustworthy. There is no evidence that people needing social work services tell untruths any more than anyone else. To prejudge a client as being untrustworthy is contrary to the social work–mandated values of having respect for individuals and recognizing client dignity, and prejudgment may lead to a self-fulfilling prophecy. Clients may need help to articulate their problem situations, and caring confrontation by the worker may facilitate that process. Confrontation from this perspective means sharing alternative, perhaps previously unexplored views of the situation. However, clients' understandings of reality are no less real than the social constructions of reality of the professionals assisting them.

3. Discover What the Client Wants.   There are two aspects of client wants that provide the structure for the worker–client contract. The first is, what does the client want and expect from service? The second is, what does the client want to happen in relation to his/her/their current problem situation? This latter want involves the client's goals and is concerned with what the client perceives to be a successful resolution to the problem situation. Although recognizing that what the client wants and what agencies and workers are able and willing to offer is subject to negotiation, successful practitioners base assessments on client motivation. Motivation is supported by expectations held by all involved that the client can achieve his/her/their goals.

4. Move the Assessment toward Client and Environmental Strengths. Obviously there are personal and environmental obstacles to the resolution of difficult situations. However, if one believes that solutions to difficult situations lie in strengths, dwelling on obstacles ultimately has little payoff. Client strengths are the vehicle to creatively negotiate these obstacles.

5. Make Assessment of Strengths Multidimensional. Multidimensional assessment is widely supported in social work. Practicing from a strengths perspective means believing that the strengths and resources to resolve a difficult situation lie within the client's interpersonal skills, motivation, emotional strengths, and ability to think clearly. The client's external strengths come from family networks, significant others, voluntary organizations, community groups, and public institutions that support and provide opportunities for clients to act on their own behalf and institutional services that have the potential to provide resources. Discovering these strengths is central to assessment. A multidimensional assessment also includes an examination of power and power relationships in transactions between the client and the environment. Explicit, critical examination of such relationships provides the client and the worker with the context for evaluating alternative solutions.

6. Use the Assessment to Discover Uniqueness. The importance of uniqueness and individualization is well articulated by Meyer (1976): "When a family, group or a community is individualized, it is known through its uniqueness, despite all that it holds in common with other like groups" (p. 176). Although every person is in certain respects "like all other men [sic], like some other men, and like no other men" (Kluckholm, Murray, & Schneider, 1953, p. 53), foundation content in human behavior and social environment taught in schools of social work focuses on the first two of these, which are based on normative behavior assumptions. Assessment that focuses on client strengths must be individualized to understand the unique situation the client is experiencing. Normative perspectives of behavior are only useful insofar as they can enrich the understanding of this uniqueness. Pray's (1991) writings on assessment emphasize individual uniqueness as an important element of Schön's (1983) reflective model of practice and are particularly insightful in establishing the importance of client uniqueness in assessment.

7. Use the Client's Words. Professional and social sciences nomenclature is incongruent with an assessment approach based on mutual participation of the social worker and the client. Assessment as a product should be written in simple English and in such a way as to be self-explanatory to all involved. Whenever possible use direct quotes from the client to name and describe the problem and solutions. Goldstein (1990) convincingly argued, "We are the inheritors of a professional language composed of value-laden metaphors and idioms. The language has far more to do with philosophic assumptions about the human state, ideologies of professionalism, and, not least, the politics of practice than they do with objective rationality" (p. 268). Use of the client's words shift the assessment discourse to language that reflects the client's values, places the client in the role of expert of his/her/their own situation, and places the burden on the social worker to gain an understanding of what the situation means to the client.

8. Make Assessment a Joint Activity between Worker and Client. Social workers can minimize the inherent power imbalance inherent between worker and client by stressing the importance of the client's understandings and wants. The worker's role is to inquire and listen and to assist the client in discovering, clarifying, and articulating. The client gives direction to the content of the assessment. The client must feel ownership of the process and the product and can do so only if assessment is open and shared. Rodwell (1987) articulated this well when she stated that the "major stakeholders must agree with the content" (p. 241).

9. Reach a Mutual Agreement on the Assessment. Workers should not have secret assessments. All assessments in written form should be shared with clients. Because assessment is to provide structure and direction for confronting client problem situations, any privately held assessment a worker might have makes the client vulnerable to manipulation.

10. Avoid Blame and Blaming. Assessment and blame often get confused and convoluted. Blame is the first cousin of deficit models of practice. Concentrating on blame or allowing it to get a firm foothold in the process is done at the expense of moving toward a resolution to the problem. Client situations encountered by social workers are typically the result of the interaction of a myriad of factors: personal interactions, intrapersonal attributes, physical health, social situations, social organizations, and chance happenings. Things happen; people are vulnerable to those happenings, and, therefore, they seek assistance. What can the worker and client do after blame is assigned? Generally, blaming leads nowhere, and, if relegated to the client, it may encourage low self-esteem. If assigned to others, it may encourage learned helplessness or deter motivation to address the problem situation.

11. Avoid Cause-and-Effect Thinking. Professional judgments or assumptions of causation may well be the most detrimental exercises perpetrated on clients. Worker notions of cause and causal thinking should be minimized because they have the propensity to be based on simplistic cause-and-effect thinking. Causal thinking represents only one of many possible perspectives of the problem situation and can easily lead to blaming. Client problem situations are usually multidimensional, have energy, represent multidirectional actions, and reflect dynamics that are not well suited to simple causal explanations.

12. Assess; Do Not Diagnose. Diagnosis is incongruent with a strengths perspective. Diagnosis is understood in the context of pathology, deviance, and deficits and is based on social constructions of reality that define human problem situations in a like manner. Diagnosis is associated with a medical model of labeling that assumes unpopular and unacceptable behavior as a symptom of an underlying pathological condition. It has been argued that labeling "accompanied by reinforcement of identified behavior is a sufficient condition for chronic mental illness" (Taber, Herbert, Mark, & Nealey, 1969, p. 354). The diagnostic experience reinforces the helper as expert regarding the client's situation. The preference for use of the word *assessment* over *diagnosis* is widely held in the social work literature.

The Assessment Process

The assessment process suggested here has two components, which are similar to Mary Richmond's (1917) distinction between study and diagnosis. She proposed that the social worker first study the facts of the situation and then diagnose the nature of the problem. Correspondingly, the first component here is a process whereby a worker and a client define the problem situation or clarify why the client has sought assistance. The second component involves evaluating and giving meaning to those factors that impinge on the problem situation.

Component 1: Defining the Problem Situation

Defining the problem situation is only the beginning of the helping process and should not be confused with evaluation and analysis of the problem situation. It is particularly important at this time to assist the client in telling his/her/their story. The following list outlines what the worker and client might do to define the problem situation. Items 2, 3, and 4 are based in part on guidelines developed by Brown and Levitt (1979) and later revised by Hepworth and Larsen (1990, p. 14).[3]

Defining the Problem Situation or Discovering Why the Client Seeks Assistance

1. *Brief summary of the identified problem situation.*

This should be in simple language, straightforward, and mutually agreed on between worker and client. If written, it should be no more than a brief paragraph.

---

[3]Hepworth and Larsen use items 2, 3, and 4 as questions to identify other people and larger systems that are involved in the problem situation and/or interacting with the problem. These questions are given more assessment import in this paper as they are seen as defining the problem rather than simply identifying involvement or interaction with the problem.

2. *Who (persons, groups, or organizations) is involved including the client(s) seeking assistance?*
3. *How or in what way are participants involved? What happens between the participants before, during, and immediately following activity related to the problem situation?*
4. *What meaning does the client ascribe to the problem situation?*
5. *What does the client want with regard to the problem situation?*
6. *What does the client want/expect by seeking assistance?*
7. *What would the client's life be like if the problem were resolved?*

This outline assumes clients know why they seek assistance. With a little help from a worker, a client can clarify, or perhaps discover some new insight, and articulate the nature of the problem situation. These questions are based on a model of practice whereby social workers believe their clients, trust their clients' judgment, and reinforce their clients' competency. The orientation also assumes that when dealing with problem situations, what you see is what you get—that hidden, deep-seated, intrapsychic, and/or unconscious phenomena, if real, are irrelevant. In situations in which the client consists of more than one person (e.g., a family, group, or community), multiple definitions of the problem will exist based on the various members' understanding of the situation. In these cases, it is the role of the social worker to find the common ground in problem definitions.

The word *situation* has a particularly important meaning because it affirms that problems always exist in an environmental context. To focus on the problem situation is to avoid a perception and subsequent definition of the person as pathological that may lead, for the client, to a self-fulfilling prophecy and, for the worker, to ascribing blame. However, using the word *problem* does not suggest that one therefore assumes environmental or situational pathology and continues with a pathological model by simply redirecting pathological assessment to the relevant environment. *Problem* here means only that there exists a mismatch or disequilibrium between the client's needs and environmental demands and resources that is causing difficulty, puzzlement, and often pain. Focusing on the client alone is inappropriate and may hinder problem solution. Problem situations have a life of their own and are generated by combinations of unpredicted contingencies, incongruities, and systems disequilibrium. Understanding problem situations in this way allows the worker and client the freedom to capitalize on personal and environmental strengths to resolve the problem.

Component 2: Framework for Assessment

The second assessment component involves analyzing, evaluating, and giving meaning to those factors that influence the problem situation. The model proposed here revolves around two axes. The first axis is an environmental factors versus client factors continuum, and the second is a strengths versus deficits continuum (see Figure 7.1).

Concerns about emphasizing either end of the deficits-strengths axis were discussed previously. A new theoretical interest in how environmental factors

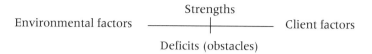

FIGURE 7.1   Assessment Axes

affect practice has been increasingly evident in the literature since the early 1970s. However, like renewed interest in client strengths, this interest has not been fully realized in actual practice as practice guidelines and specific practice knowledge have lagged behind theoretical development. The lack of knowledge of, or interest in, the relevant environmental factors, in actual practice, is evident when one reviews available assessment instruments.

When the axes in Figure 7.1 are enclosed, each of the four quadrants that result represents important content for assessment (see Figure 7.2).

Because assessment instruments themselves have tended to focus on the elements of quadrant 4, most practice today emphasizes client deficits. A comprehensive assessment would have data recorded in each quadrant. The version of the assessment axes in Figure 7.2 has been used as a recording tool in teaching, workshops, and agency consultation and has demonstrated that workers and clients can readily identify content for each quadrant. However, quadrants 1 and 2 are *emphasized* when practicing from a strengths perspective. Indeed, *deficits* may well be a misnomer and the end of that continuum might be better understood as *obstacles* to problem resolution.

Exemplars of Client Strengths (Quadrant 2)

Quadrant 2, client strengths, includes both psychological and physical/physiological strengths. For illustrative purposes, psychological factors are further developed here by listing a set of client strength exemplars (see the following section). The taxonomy of strengths—cognition, emotion, motivation, coping, and interpersonal relationships—is used to organize and structure these exemplars. The categories are quite traditional and are not free of conceptual problems. For example, it is important to note that although these items are designated as client factors, they do not represent intrapersonal attributes devoid of environmental and or physiological interaction (e.g., motivation is dependent on a unique set of environmental and personal dynamics). Physiological factors, which are not included in this list, are particularly important for some clients, such as the aging individuals or the disabled. Additions to this quadrant could include aspirations, competencies, and confidence as conceptualized by Rapp (1998).

The following list suggests exemplars of client strengths workers and clients might consider during the assessment process with individuals and families. These items were arrived at through literature review (for example, Brown & Levitt, 1979; Hepworth and Larsen, 1990) and workshops with agency practitioners.

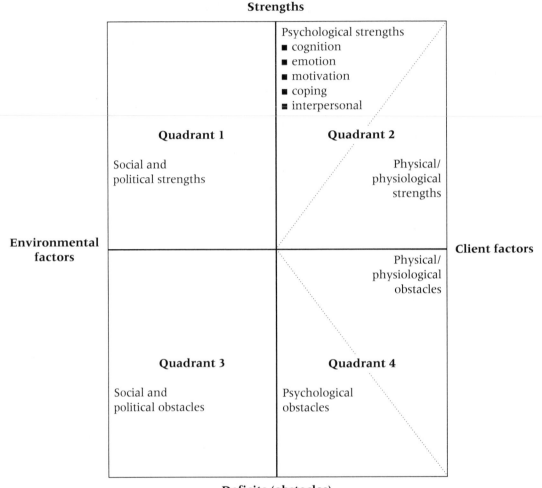

Strengths

Psychological strengths
- cognition
- emotion
- motivation
- coping
- interpersonal

Quadrant 1

Social and
political strengths

Quadrant 2

Physical/
physiological
strengths

**Environmental
factors**

Client factors

Physical/
physiological
obstacles

Quadrant 3

Social and
political obstacles

Quadrant 4

Psychological
obstacles

Deficits (obstacles)

FIGURE 7.2   Framework for Assessment

Assessment of Client Strengths
(Quadrant 2 of Assessment Axes)

A. Cognition
    1. Sees the world as most other people see it in own culture.
    2. Has an understanding of right and wrong from own cultural, ethical perspective.
    3. Understands how one's own behavior affects others and how others affect him/herself. Is insightful.

4. Is open to different ways of thinking about things.
5. Reasoning is easy to follow.
6. Considers and weighs alternatives in problem solving.

B. Emotion
   1. Is in touch with feelings and is able to express them if encouraged.
   2. Expresses love and concern for intimate others.
   3. Demonstrates a degree of self-control.
   4. Can handle stressful situations reasonably well.
   5. Is positive about life. Has hope.
   6. Has a range of emotions.
   7. Emotions are congruent with situations.

C. Motivation
   1. When having problematic situations, doesn't hide from, avoid, or deny them.
   2. Willing to seek help and share problem situation with others he/she can trust.
   3. Willing to accept responsibility for his/her part or role in problem situations.
   4. Wants to improve current and future situations.
   5. Does not want to be dependent on others.
   6. Seeks to improve self through further knowledge, education, and skills.

D. Coping
   1 Is persistent in handling family crises.
   2. Is well organized.
   3. Follows through on decisions.
   4. Is resourceful and creative with limited resources.
   5. Stands up for self rather than submitting to injustice.
   6. Attempts to pay debts despite financial difficulty.
   7. Prepares for and handles new situations well.
   8. Has dealt successfully with related problems in the past.

E. Interpersonal
   1. Has friends.
   2. Seeks to understand friends, family members, and others.
   3. Makes sacrifices for friends, family members, and others.
   4. Performs social roles appropriately (e.g., parents, spouse, son or daughter, community).
   5. Is outgoing and friendly.
   6. Is truthful.
   7. Is cooperative and flexible in relating to family and friends.
   8. Is self-confident in relationships with others.

9. Shows warm acceptance of others.
10. Can accept loving and caring feelings from others.
11. Has sense of propriety, good manners.
12. Is a good listener.
13. Expresses self spontaneously.
14. Is patient.
15. Has realistic expectations in relationships with others.
16. Has a sense of humor.
17. Has sense of satisfaction in role performance with others.
18. Has ability to maintain own personal boundaries in relationships with others.
19. Demonstrates comfort in sexual role/identity.
20. Demonstrates ability to forgive.
21. Is generous with time and money.
22. Is verbally fluent.
23. Is ambitious and industrious.
24. Is resourceful.

These exemplars of client strengths are not intended to include all the assessment content and knowledge that a social worker must use in practice. Indeed, important topics such as assessing specific obstacles to empowerment, assessing power relationships, and assessing the relationship between personal empowerment and social empowerment of the individual client are not considered. Also, community strengths, such as social cohesiveness, social networks, economic investment by community institutions, and community improvement initiatives are not included. In regard to communities, Kretzmann and McKnight (1993, 1997) provide a useful framework for identifying and mapping community assets. The use of these exemplars depends on given practice situations, and professional judgment determines their specific applicability. They are proposed to provide an alternative approach to existing normative and deficit models of intrapersonal diagnosis and treatment. The exemplars may also be of interest to practitioners who wish to use them to supplement existing assessment paradigms they do not wish to give up.

The framework and outline is proposed as a resource to assist workers and clients in considering those client strengths to be exploited in coping with the problem situation presented by individuals and families. In the initial contact, the worker should be able to begin identifying client strengths. Workers may wish to have a copy of the exemplars list readily available during an interview. Other workers may find a review of the list helpful during case reflection, recording, and planning. One worker reported to the author that he has used the list by going through it item by item with the client. Workers may use the list to (1) stimulate thinking about strengths and their importance in the practice process, (2) assist in identifying strengths that otherwise would not be thought of, (3) assist in identifying and selecting positive and supportive content to be shared with clients, (4) provide a foundation for a case plan that is based on client competency and capability rather than inadequacy, and (5) bolster worker confidence and belief in the client. The list is intended to be suggestive and heuristic in nature by illustrating the wide range of strengths that any given client might have. Early and Glen-Maye (2000) provide a valuable case example, reflecting some of the items in the assessment profile above, describing the process by which family strengths are named and explored. It is important to note that the language in the list is somewhat contaminated with professional and middle class notions of reality and the desirable, and therefore will require either interpretation or revision when the assessment process is shared with clients, especially those from different cultures.

When using these exemplars, an additional qualifier needs to be emphasized. Realistically, many clients at risk and those most vulnerable in our society simply are no match for the environmental intrusions and disruptive external impingements on their lives. The use of this list, to the exclusion of a thorough assessment of environmental strengths and obstacles (quadrants 1 and 3, Figure 7.2), provides little advantage over deficit models of practice. Indeed, focusing on individual strengths in the face of overwhelming environmental odds may be no less cruel than a practice model that reinforces client deficits. A comprehensive assessment would include content from all four quadrants. However, a strengths perspective would emphasize quadrants 1 and 2, elements often missing from assessment.

Conclusion

Inherent in the assessment guidelines is the recognition that to focus on client strengths and to practice with the intent of client empowerment is to practice with an explicit power consciousness. Whatever else social work practice is, it is always political, because it always encompasses power and power relationships.

Social work literature has emphasized philosophy and theory that presents a strengths perspective, but is lacking in practice directives, guidelines, and know-how for incorporating this perspective into practice. Assessment based on a strengths perspective places environmental and client strengths in a prominent position. Environmental and client obstacles that hinder a resolution to a problem situation are viewed only as obstacles, and as such they are not considered the primary content of assessment. Guidelines for assessing client strengths have been presented in an attempt to bridge the gap between philosophy and theory, which supports client strengths, and practice knowledge, which ignores it. Believing in client strengths can generate self-fulfilling prophecies.

DISCUSSION QUESTIONS

1. Choose a client (individual, family, or community) that you have worked with and, using the model in Figure 7.2, fill in the quadrants as best you can. Does this arrangement give you a different picture of your client?

2. What is meant by the politics of assessment? Have you seen it in operation in your practice, agency, or community?

3. How can you use assessment to empower clients? Can you recall a time when you empowered a client? What was it that you did that leads you to think so?

4. Why is it important to give preeminence to the client's perspective and to believe the client? Does this level of belief in clients exist in your agency? How do you know? If the client is the expert on her or his own life, what happens to your role as a professional helper?

5. What are the advantages of focusing on client strengths? Do you see drawbacks?

REFERENCES

Berger, P. L., & Luckmann, T. A. (1966). *The social construction of reality.* Garden City, NY: Doubleday.

Billingsley, A. (1968). *Black families in White America.* Englewood Cliffs, NJ: Prentice-Hall.

Billingsley, A. (1992). *Climbing Jacob's ladder: The enduring legacy of African American families.* New York: Simon & Schuster.

Boyd-Franklin, N., & Bry, B. H. (2000). *Reaching out in family therapy.* New York: Guilford Press.

Brown, L., and Levitt, J. (1979). A methodology for problem-system identification. *Social Casework, 60,* 408–415.

Cohen, B. Z. (1999). Intervention and supervision in strengths-based social work practice. *Families in Society, 80*(5), 460–466.

Council on Social Work Education. (1994). Curriculum policy statement for master's degree program. In *Handbook of accreditation standards and procedures.* Washington, DC: Author.

Cowger, C. D. (1998). Clientism and clientification: Impediments to strengths based social work practice. *Journal of Sociology and Social Welfare, 25*(1), 24–36.

De Jong, P., & Miller, S. D. (1995). How to interview for client strengths. *Social Work, 40*(6), 729–736.

Delgado, M., & Barton, K. (1998). Murals in Latino communities: Social indicators of community strengths. *Social Work, 43*(4), 346–356.

Early, T. J., & GlenMaye, L. F. (2000). Valuing families: Social work practice with families from a strengths perspective. *Social Work, 45*(2), 118–130.

Falck, H. S. (1988). *Social work: The membership perspective.* New York: Springer.

Finn, J. L., & Checkoway, B. (1998). Young people as competent community builders: A challenge to social work. *Social Work, 43*(4), 335–344.

Gibelman, M. (1999). The search for identity: Defining social work–past, present, future. *Social Work, 44*(4), 298–310.

Goldstein, H. (1990). Strength or pathology: Ethical and rhetorical contrasts in approaches to practice. *Families in Society, 71*(5), 267–275.

Goroff, N. N. (1983). Social work within a political and social context: The triumph of the therapeutic. In S. Ables & P. Ables (Eds.), *Social work with groups: Proceedings of 1978 symposium* (pp. 133–145). Louisville, KY: Committee for the Advancement of Social Work with Groups.

Habermas, J. (1981). *Theorie de kommunikativen handelns.* Band 2. Suhrkanp. Ausgurg.

Hepworth, D. H., & Larsen, J. A. (1990). *Direct social work practice.* Belmont, CA: Wadsworth.

Hwang, S. C., & Cowger, C. D. (1998). Utilizing strengths in assessment. *Families in Society, 79*(1), 25–31.

Kagle, J. D., & Cowger, C. D. (1984). Blaming the client: Implicit agenda in practice research? *Social Work, 29,* 347–351.

Kluckholm, C., Murray, H. A., & Schneider, D. M. (Eds.). (1953). *Personality in nature, society, and culture.* New York: Alfred A. Knopf.

Kretzmann, J. P., & McKnight, J. L. (1993). *Building communities from the inside out: A path toward finding and mobilizing a community's assets.* Chicago: ACTA Publications.

Kretzmann, J. P., & McKnight, J. L. (1997). *A guide to capacity inventories: Mobilizing the community skills of local residents.* Chicago: ACTA Publications.

Maluccio, A. (1979). The influence of the agency environment on clinical practice. *Journal of Sociology and Social Welfare, 6,* 734–755.

McAdoo, H. P., & McAdoo, J. L. (Eds.). (1985). *Black children: Social, educational and parental environments.* Beverly Hills, CA: Sage.

McKnight, J. (1995). *The careless society: Community and its counterfeits.* New York: HarperCollins.

McQuaide, S., & Ehrenreich, J. H. (1997). Assessing client's strengths. *Families in Society, 78*(2), 201–212.

Meyer, C. H. (1976). *Social work practice* (2nd ed.). New York: Free Press.

Poole, D. (1997). Building community capacity to promote social and public health: Challenges for universities. *Health and Social Work, 22*(3), 163–170.

Pray, J. E. (1991). Respecting the uniqueness of the individual: Social work practice within a reflective model. *Social Work, 36,* 80–85.

Rapp, C. A. (1998). *The strengths model: Case management with people suffering from severe and persistent mental illness.* New York: Oxford University Press.

Richmond, M. (1917). *Social diagnosis.* New York: Russell Sage Foundation.

Ripple, L. (1964). *Motivation, capacity and opportunity.* Chicago: University of Chicago Press.

Rodwell, M. K. (1987). Naturalistic inquiry: An alternative model for social work assessment. *Social Service Review, 61*(2), 231–246.

Russo, R. J. (1999). Applying a strengths-based practice approach in working with people with developmental disabilities and their families. *Families in Society, 80* (January-February), 25–33.

Ryan, W. (1976). *Blaming the victim.* New York: Vintage Books.

Schön, D. A. (1983). *The reflective practitioner: How professionals think in action.* New York: Basic Books.

Simon, B. L. (1990). Rethinking empowerment. *Journal of Progressive Human Services, 1*(1), 27–40.

Solomon, B. (1976). *Black empowerment: Social work in oppressed communities.* New York: Columbia University Press.

Taber, M., Herbert, C. Q., Mark, M., & Nealey, V. (1969). Disease ideology and mental health research. *Social Problems, 16,* 349–357.

Wilson, M., Whitmore, E. (1995). Accompanying the process: Principles for international development practice. *Canadian Journal of Development Studies* (special issue), 67–77.

8

Strengths-Based Case Management[1]

Enhancing Treatment for Persons with Substance Abuse Problems

RICHARD C. RAPP

This chapter focuses on the practice of strengths-based case management (SBCM) with persons who have substance abuse problems and findings that support the use of this intervention. Readers who are familiar with this chapter from earlier editions of *The Strengths Perspective in Social Work Practice* will note that the earlier emphasis on implementation issues is gone. This change is based on the assumption that many, if not most, readers are versed in the unique hurdles that come with incorporating a strengths approach into substance abuse treatment. For those not familiar with the impact of SBCM on substance abuse clients, staff, and the service delivery system I refer you to the second edition of this book (Saleebey, 1997) and to other sources that emphasize implementation issues (Rapp, Kelliher, Fisher, & Hall, 1994; Siegal, Rapp, Kelliher, & Fisher, 1995). While the practice of SBCM may also be familiar to many readers the specific description of case management activities is retained here, primarily because it so closely informs the findings presented. This chapter also presents findings, both from qualitative and quantitative studies, that address two questions: "Does strengths-based case management improve retention and outcomes in substance abuse treatment?" and "If so, what is it about the intervention that leads to that improvement?" While some social work practitioners may be inclined to skip over the "research stuff" I would encourage them to read these sections closely. They are user friendly and

[1]Acknowledgment: The research presented in this chapter was supported by the National Institute on Drug Abuse (Grant No. DA06944).

intimately relate to practice activities incorporated in strengths-based case management with persons who have substance abuse problems.

Strengths-Based Case Management: Addressing Two Aspects of Substance Abuse Treatment

The opportunity to systematically examine the effects of strengths-based case management (SBCM) presented itself through a 1990 National Institute on Drug Abuse (NIDA) initiative, the goal of which was to enhance substance abuse treatment, specifically by reducing attrition from treatment and otherwise improving treatment outcomes. The Enhanced Treatment Project was created by addictions researchers in Wright State University's School of Medicine to test the ability of SBCM to enhance traditional substance abuse treatment conducted in a large Veterans Administration Medical Center in Dayton, Ohio. The study population consisted primarily of males experiencing crack cocaine–related substance abuse problems. In 1996 the project was extended as the Case Management Enhancements Project, emphasizing the relationship between SBCM and field-based substance abuse aftercare treatment. Details surrounding the development of both projects can be found elsewhere (Rapp, 1997; Siegal, Rapp, Fisher, Cole, & Wagner, 1993; Siegal et al., 1995).

Initially, the intervention proposed for improving treatment participation and outcome was to be a generalist model of case management. Widely described and defined, case management was seen as an intervention that could assist clients in identifying and accessing the resources they needed to function independently. The need for such assistance was unmistakable; persons experiencing substance abuse problems are generally lacking in many of the basics of successful living (e.g., appropriate housing, occupational and educational opportunities, etc). Case management, as part of an overall treatment program, was to assist clients with very real needs, such as for housing and employment. It was hypothesized that whatever a client's acceptance of a substance abuse problem, or whatever the degree of motivation, clients would stay involved in treatment because of the assistance provided to them in these other areas.

Three requirements were imposed on the selection of a model of case management. First, the model was to have demonstrated value with similar populations. Out of necessity researchers had to settle for similar populations since at that time little actual work had been conducted with case management and substance abuse. Second, because of the prevailing attitudes regarding substance abusers there was to be a strong advocacy component to any model we selected. Third, case management would focus on resource identification and acquisition as opposed to providing counseling, therapy, or treatment.

All three of these conditions were met in a strengths-based approach to case management developed at the University of Kansas School of Social Welfare. Strengths-based case management was originally implemented with persons being discharged from long-term hospitalization for mental illness (Modrcin, Rapp, & Chamberlain, 1985). The spirit of the intervention is found in five principles.

1. *The use of client strengths, abilities, and assets is facilitated.* Central to SBCM is the belief that clients are most successful when they identify and use their strengths, abilities, and assets. The process of enumerating and using personal strengths allows clients to appreciate their own past efficacy, encourages motivation, and sets the stage for identifying and achieving goals.

2. *Client control over goal-setting and the search for needed resources is encouraged.* All goal-setting is guided by the client's perceptions of their own needs. The role of the case manager is to assist the client in making goals specific, to discuss alternatives, and to identify available resources. Underlying this principle is the belief that clients will participate most fully in treatment if they are in charge of goals that are really theirs, as opposed to goals that are dictated by others.

3. *The client–case manager relationship is promoted as primary.* The case manager serves as the consistent figure in the client's treatment experience and is thereby able to coordinate fragmented and poorly coordinated resources. A strong relationship allows the case manager to advocate for the client as necessary. Far from being an exclusive relationship, the client and case manager will involve many other persons in the search for resources.

4. *The community is viewed as a resource and not a barrier.* SBCM assumes that a creative approach to use of the community will lead to discovery of needed resources. In working with formal resources—housing agencies, job training programs—case managers assist clients by modeling and practicing behaviors that increase the likelihood of a successful contact. Whenever possible case managers will encourage clients to explore informal resources—friends, neighbors, other clients—as sources of assistance.

5. *Case management is conducted as an active, community-based activity.* Office-based contacts are minimized; case managers meet with clients in the community—in their home, at their work site, etc. For the case manager, this activity will inevitably lead to an increased appreciation of the challenges clients face in making changes. For the client these meetings provide an opportunity to develop and master skills where they actually live. In turn, this focus helps clients to break an often powerful reliance on institutional settings for assistance.

The Practice of Strengths-Based Case Management

Accurate implementation of SBCM entails maintaining the spirit of strengths-based principles and at the same time incorporating them into diverse practice settings. While this section describes how SBCM was implemented in the Enhanced Treatment and Case Management Enhancement Projects, it should provide useful ideas for how the intervention can be implemented in other settings as well.

As a first step toward accomplishing the dual goals of resource acquisition and building a positive relationship with treatment, *case managers were discouraged from reading the client's substance abuse assessment or medical record prior to their first meeting with the client.* By not doing so, case managers were encouraged to not predefine the client in terms of their diagnosis and problems. While ignoring the problems and needs of clients would be negligent, it was an assumption of strengths-based practice that the most appropriate place to hear about those needs was directly from the client and not through the filter of records passed down from previous treatment episodes.

The case manager's initial contact with a client was usually a brief meeting in which the overall project was explained and the worker introduced the concepts of case management, advocacy, and strengths approach. The case manager described examples of activities appropriate for case management, (i.e., employment searches, assistance with housing, etc). The case manager attempted to end this first contact by offering to assist the client in some immediate, tangible manner, such as helping the client's family avoid having electric service disconnected or retrieving clothing from a temporary housing situation.

Also during the first meeting with a case manager, clients rated themselves in each of nine domains: life skills, finance, leisure, relationships, living arrangements, occupation/education, health, internal resources, and recovery. Specific behavioral anchors define functioning on a nine-point scale in each of these domains. These scales, the *ETP Progress Evaluation Scales (PES),* were adapted from earlier work with mental health clients and incarcerated substance abusers (Ihilevich & Gleser, 1982; Martin & Scarpitti, 1993).

During the next several contacts clients participated in an extensive strengths-based assessment. The *ETP Strengths Assessment* is the antithesis of most assessments. The aim of this assessment was to reacquaint clients or, in many cases, acquaint clients for the first time with their strengths and assets. Discussions were focused on a client's ability to accomplish a task, use a skill, and have or fulfill a goal in the nine life domains. Discussions of topics such as arrest record, drug use, and failures were avoided. A strengths-based assessment provided clients with the opportunity to examine their personal abilities and the role those abilities can play in solving problems. Furthermore, case managers themselves were able to avoid being drawn into the skepticism and hopelessness that almost inevitably becomes attached to a recounting of real or imagined failures.

On completion of the strengths assessment clients once again rated their functioning in each life domain. At that time the case manager also rated the client's functioning. Clients were encouraged to compare their self-ratings before and after completion of the strengths-based assessment. This comparison was intended to involve the client in a discussion regarding their strengths and abilities. Next, client and case manager determined a consensus rating for each life domain, a rating that came from a comparison of the case manager and clients' ratings. Clients then decided on a goal rating for each life domain. This rating reflected their desired level of functioning in 90 days and was reviewed at that time.

These numerical goal ratings were translated into specific action plans through use of the *ETP Case Management Plan (CMP)*. From an open-ended question, "What do you need/want to accomplish?" clients began to identify goals in various life domains. Goal statements were written as broad, general, and perhaps never fully attainable, such as "Improve my opportunities to get the job I'm interested in." Objectives were always measurable, specific steps that led the veteran toward his goal. Two specific objectives for the previous goal might include, "Objective 1: Take and pass the Graduation Equivalency Degree (GED) exam" and "Objective 2: Complete a course on identifying job interests at Smith Vocational School." Strategies were specific activities that led to accomplishment of an objective. Examples of strategies used to accomplish Objective 1 included obtaining a GED application, studying a GED work guide 10 hours each week, and scheduling an appointment for taking the GED. The establishment of target and review dates for each objective and strategy prompted periodic review of client progress. While work on goals was always guided by the client's wishes, the case manager lent support to the process of goal-setting by reminding the client of identified strengths, assisting in making objectives specific, discussing alternatives, contributing a knowledge of existing resources, and by advocating for the client as they attempted to access those resources.

The detailed attention to the creation of objectives and strategies and systematic review of their outcome was powerful at two levels. First, clients learned an approach to solving problems that was easily transferable from the treatment setting to their lives outside the treatment milieu. Second, clients had the opportunity to evaluate their own progress in very personal, specific terms. Even in not completing some of their identified tasks clients had the support and feedback to learn from the experience. One former client discussed his work with his case manager: "I had a case manager who had me write every little step down, plan out every day what I was gonna do. I was so used to planning on big things and never seein' 'em get done. It was great to see some progress every day." The overall effect of this goal setting process specifically and the strengths-based approach generally was that clients were in the position to take responsibility for their own treatment. This personal responsibility, while a stated intention of traditional medical model substance abuse treatment, is unwittingly negated by the way in which that model is frequently implemented (Rapp et al., 1994).

Strengths-Based Case Management: Measuring Its Impact

The goal of two NIDA-funded companion projects, the Enhanced Treatment Project (ETP) and Case Management Enhancements Project (CME), was to assess the impact that a strengths-based model of case management had on (1) improving treatment retention among persons with substance abuse problems and

(2) improving treatment outcomes. Besides substance abuse problems, these primarily crack cocaine–involved Vietnam-era males suffered from many of the problems that case management has traditionally been expected to address. These problems included homelessness, lack of adequate employment, and uncoordinated involvement with numerous social service agencies.

The initial project (ETP) was designed to have case managers meet with veterans immediately following their entry into primary substance abuse treatment. These contacts with 632 veterans, enrolled between September 1991 and December 1994, were intended to promote clients' continued involvement in the early stages of treatment and establish a relationship between them and their case managers that could then serve as the basis for work during the aftercare (post-primary) treatment period. Case managers in the second project, CME, met with more than 400 clients in the latter stages of primary treatment and conducted their work with them from a community-based site rather than medical center grounds. Case management and post-primary services were highly integrated.

Eligibility for both projects was based on the veteran's use of any cocaine or heroin in the preceding 6 months or being a regular user of other drugs during that time and not being in treatment in the preceding 3 months. Veterans experiencing substance abuse problems were assigned randomly at entry to treatment to receive one of two treatment conditions, traditional 12 steps, medical model–oriented treatment, *or* traditional treatment and a case manager using a strengths-based approach. Follow-up interviews, generally conducted in 6-month waves, took place with both samples, for 5 and 2 years with ETP and CME subjects, respectively.

The following findings primarily provide results from the ETP and some tentative results from the CME. Three areas are covered: case management-mediated retention in treatment, outcomes associated with case management, and the characteristics of strengths-based case management that appear to influence retention and outcomes.

SBCM and Retention in Treatment

One of the reasons for implementing strengths-based case management had been the belief that the approach would encourage clients to continue their participation in treatment activities, activities related both to primary treatment and aftercare. While a complete discussion of case management's role in retaining clients in treatment is beyond the scope of this chapter, several points warrant mention.

Retention in the Enhanced Treatment Project.   Most ETP clients completed a 4-week course of *primary inpatient* treatment (N = 349/394; 89%) with little difference between clients receiving strengths case management (N = 180/201; 90%) and non–case-managed clients (N = 169/193; 88%). In contrast, attrition was quite high from *primary outpatient* treatment with only 50 percent of case-managed clients completing a 6-week course of treatment as compared to 36 percent of non–case-managed clients (31/62 vs. 21/58).

Similarities persisted between the two groups when examining participation in *post-primary* treatment. Case-managed clients were only somewhat more likely to start relapse prevention treatment than non–case-managed clients (52 percent versus 49 percent) and on average stayed slightly longer (5.45 weeks versus 4.54 weeks). In summary, case management did not seem to significantly enhance treatment retention, at least when retention was viewed in the context of participation in relapse prevention. A closer examination of the case management group during the aftercare period revealed an interesting phenomenon.

Case-managed clients demonstrated a strong tendency to select participation in case management services during the post-primary period over participation in relapse prevention services. As noted above only 52 percent of clients in this group attended at least one session of relapse prevention following their discharge from primary treatment. In contrast, 66 percent of the clients in this group attended at least one session with their case manager after completion of primary treatment. As Figure 8.1 demonstrates, the gap between attendance at relapse prevention activities and case management activities grows significantly as time progresses. Thirty-five percent of clients reported up to 20 weeks of contact with their case managers while only 11 percent of clients attended the same amount of relapse prevention activities. A similar gap, up to 21 percent, between case management and relapse prevention attendance persisted until the end of the 6-month follow-up period.

Clarifying Retention among Case-Managed Clients

A subsequent analysis attempted to determine what characteristics of the case management group (N = 313) were related to the selection of case management

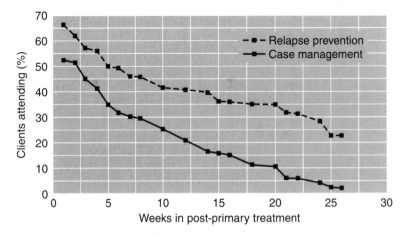

FIGURE 8.1   Participation in Post-Primary Treatment Activities Among Case-Managed Clients

during the post-primary treatment period. To do this, a cluster analytic technique was used to describe the clients in the case-managed group and their use of services following primary treatment (Siegal, Rapp, Li, Saha, & Kirk, 1997). Two variables, weeks in case management and weeks in aftercare treatment, were used to cluster the subjects. Descriptive comparisons among the clusters were conducted using such baseline measures as (1) demographic characteristics, such as age, marital status, ethnicity, gender, and educational level; (2) measures of psychosocial functioning, including drug use, employment status, and criminal justice involvement; and (3) scales measuring motivation for treatment. Psychiatric status was measured using the Global Severity Index (GSI) of the SCL-90 (Derogatis, 1977). Eight items from the Readiness for Treatment scale of the Texas Christian University Self-Rating Form were used to compute a score that measured motivation for treatment, and seven other questions were used to compute the Desire for Help scale (Knight, Holcom, & Simpson, 1994).

Clusters were also compared on nine indicators representing three dimensions of treatment outcomes: drug use, ongoing help to sustain abstinence, and improved social functioning. Cocaine and marijuana use were selected as measures of substance use, given their status as the two most abused drugs (excluding alcohol) among subjects. Attendance at self-help group meetings was chosen as a help variable as it reflects a goal of treatment, namely one that encourages clients to independently continue their recovery efforts. Two measures of social functioning chosen to compare the clusters were (1) self reports of illegal activities and incarceration and (2) employment. Both recent—30 days—and more distal—six months in most cases—measures of the three dimensions were utilized.

The analysis revealed the presence of three distinct groups of clients: (1) those who quickly dropped out of post-primary treatment services, i.e., both aftercare and case management (N = 133); (2) those who stayed in both aftercare and case management for most of the follow-up period (N = 44); and (3) those who retained significantly longer contact with their case managers during the post-primary treatment period (N = 81).

Three findings were of particular significance in addressing why some individuals elected to participate in case management and not relapse prevention activities during the post-primary treatment period. First, all three groups were remarkably similar at the time of admission to treatment on demographic characteristics, level of motivation, and the severity of substance abuse, psychiatric, and other problems. This suggests that the search for reasons for treatment retention differences were likely related to what happened during treatment and not on a priori differences in clients. Practically, this also suggests that there are no obvious preexisting characteristics that would lead treatment programs to preselect clients as more or less appropriate candidates for successful treatment.

Second, our data suggest that had it not been for the case management enhancement an additional one-third of the overall sample—those who retained significantly longer contact with their case managers—would have dropped out after primary treatment. Last, at 6 months following entry into treatment clients who retained contact with only case management services demonstrated outcomes as favorable as clients who remained with *both* case management and aftercare regimens. While case management was implemented as an enhancement, or adjunct, to traditional aftercare services, this finding suggests that case management services may also be useful alternatives to traditional aftercare.

Together these findings suggested that the case manager's time would be spent more productively in improving participation during the post-primary treatment period and assisting veterans in reintegrating into the community. As a result, case management in the successor CME project was attached directly to the aftercare component in a community-based, as opposed to medical center–based, location.

Retention in the Case Management Enhancements Project

Data collected in the second project, CME, also suggested some of the important elements of strengths-based case management. As in the earlier project initial analyses focused on the issue of retention, retention being defined as involvement in post-primary treatment or any scheduled treatment activities either at the medical center–based program or at the CME's community site. Data on aftercare attendance during the first month after discharge were collected at the 30-day follow-up interview, while data for the second and the third month were obtained through the 90-day follow-up. In a similar fashion, average contacts of aftercare for both groups were calculated for the first, second, and third month after discharge, respectively. These contacts included personal visits and telephone calls during which aftercare issues were discussed.

Post-treatment contacts were reported by 68 percent of non–case-managed clients in the first month after discharge. This figure fell to 54.8 percent in the second month and 52.4 percent in the third month, while the contacts were reported by 93.5 percent of the case-managed clients consistently over the 3-month period. During the first month after discharge the average number of post-treatment contacts by case-managed clients was 9.4, compared to 4.3 for the non–case-managed group. A similar decline pattern was found for both groups over the 3-month period. However, the average number of contacts in the third month after discharge reported by case-managed clients was triple the average number reported by the non–case-managed group—8.3 and 2.6, respectively.

SBCM and Critical Outcomes

Three areas—drug use, employment functioning, and criminal justice involvement—are consistently considered measures of the success of clients' recovery from substance abuse problems and thereby important areas that treatment should address. Consequently we examined the impact that SBCM had on these three areas of client functioning.

Drug Use Severity

Multivariate analyses were conducted to explore the relationship between strengths-based case management and drug use severity, a key outcome of substance abuse treatment (Rapp, Siegal, Li, & Saha, 1998). A standardized measure of post-primary treatment contact was created to represent the length of time subjects spent in services following their discharge from primary treatment, either inpatient or outpatient. This variable was developed from subjects' self-reported contacts with either aftercare or case management during the 6-month period following discharge from primary treatment. For clients who did not receive case management (NCM) the variable equaled the number of weeks they reported attending aftercare treatment. Since case-managed clients (CM) could participate in aftercare treatment, case management, or both, the variable was identified as the longer stay of either in aftercare or in case management. In both instances, the possible range for the measure was 0 to 30 weeks. Drug use severity, as measured by the Addiction Severity Index (ASI), was computed based on 13 questions that determine the frequency and consequences of recent (last 30 days) drug use (McLellan et al., 1992).

Bivariate analysis demonstrated a significant positive correlation between length of post-primary treatment contact and case management (r = .408). In other words, those who received case management services seemed more likely to stay longer in services after completion of primary treatment than those clients in the control group. Both case management and post-primary treatment contacts were negatively correlated with drug use severity (r = .117 and r = .151, respectively), indicating that clients who received post-primary case management services or stayed longer in post-treatment aftercare reported a lower level of drug use at follow-up 6 months after treatment.

Based on findings from bivariate analyses, two multiple regression models were constructed to identify factors independently associated with post-primary treatment contact and drug use severity at follow-up. Two of the findings of those analyses are instructive for the purposes of examining the role of SBCM in reducing drug use. First, consistent with the bivariate findings, case management remained a significant factor in predicting length of post-treatment aftercare when other variables were controlled (ß = .399). Second, the relationship between longer time spent in services after primary treatment and lower drug use severity remained significant when other factors were controlled (ß = -.120). Receipt of case management did not demonstrate a direct impact on drug use severity.

This study supports our expectation that participation in strengths-based case management is important in leading to positive outcomes among substance abusers who enter treatment. Unlike previous studies that have attempted to explain case management's role in terms of its direct effects on outcomes, we find that its value may lie in encouraging substance abusers to remain longer in treatment during the critical period after primary treatment is completed. The positive relationship between time spent in post-primary treatment and better outcomes, drug use severity in this study, is also confirmed in this study.

Employment

Beyond assisting individuals to reduce their involvement with harmful substances, a central goal of case management lies in helping individuals to become more productive in their employment functioning (Siegal, Fisher, Rapp, Kelliher, Wagner, O'Brien, & Cole, 1996). To determine the impact of case management on employment functioning, veterans entering substance abuse treatment were asked to indicate how interested they were in assistance with employment-related issues. The Patient Rating Scale from the ASI was used to allow clients to rate their interest in counseling for employment problems on a five-point scale. Those veterans from both case-managed and non–case-managed groups who indicated they were extremely interested in assistance with employment problems were selected for comparison. This grouping was used to eliminate clients who were already successfully employed and those who were not considering employment by virtue of a disability or other reason.

The extremely interested group consisted of 247 veterans who differed from veterans who were not extremely interested at intake in that they were more likely to be unemployed (81 percent versus 64 percent) and less likely to be employed full-time (13 percent versus 26 percent). In addition, those veterans who expressed extreme interest worked fewer days in the last 30 days and had applied for twice as many jobs during the last year. Of these 247 veterans, 193 completed the 6-month follow-up interview and were included in this analysis.

Among the 193 subjects expressing extreme interest in employment issues significant differences were found between NCM and CM clients. Using ASI data, case-management clients worked more days than the comparable group of NCM clients (15.6 versus 12.1). Beyond working more days, CM clients also reported fewer days of employment problems, feeling "less troubled" about their employment status, and seeing "less need" for employment counseling. The latter two findings, less troubled about employment and less need for employment counseling/assistance were based on client self-ratings on a patient self-rating scale of perceived need for assistance. The ASI severity ratings (an interviewer assigned rating of severity of employment problems) and composite scores focusing on functioning in the preceding 30 days also indicated greater average improvement for persons in the CM group with respect to employment.

Criminal Justice Involvement

In an as yet unpublished study (Seigal, Li, & Rapp, in press), case management, retention in post-primary treatment services, and a reduced level of criminal justice involvement have been linked. Given that criminal justice involvement is often regarded as an indicator of treatment outcomes, legal problem severity measured by the Addiction Severity Index and self-reported new arrests during the 12 months following treatment entry were selected as dependent variables to gauge treatment effect.

In this study two multiple regression models were constructed to identify factors independently associated with post-primary services (aftercare or case management) and legal problem severity. First, the length of aftercare participation contact was regressed with all independent variables. Secondly, legal severity was regressed by all independent factors, including aftercare participation. In the first model, case management was a significant factor in predicting length of post-treatment aftercare when other variables were controlled. Subjects who received case management services appeared more likely to stay longer in aftercare services after completion of primary treatment than those subjects in the control group.

The length of aftercare participation was introduced to the second regression model with the legal severity composite index at the 12-month follow-up as the dependent variable. Among all baseline variables in the model, only legal severity at admission was significantly predictive. The relationship between the length of time in aftercare and decreased severity of legal problems at follow-up was also significant, consistent with the finding between post-primary treatment and number of new arrests. In summary, we see that case management had a direct, positive impact on post-primary treatment participation, and that longer treatment participation was associated with better criminal justice outcomes.

Explaining the Impact of SBCM

The previously cited studies have encouraged researchers and practitioners alike to identify the process by which strengths-based case management exerts an influence. Two areas inherent in the strengths approach merit consideration. The first area is the client-driven nature of goal-setting facilitated by case managers' assistance in teaching clients *how* to set goals. Direct control over the goals they set and the steps taken to accomplish these goals may provide clients an opportunity to mobilize their heightened awareness of personal strengths. A second factor that may impact on encouraging substance abusers to remain in treatment and be successful is the nature of the therapeutic relationship formed between case manager and client. In addressing strengths, encouraging client control over their own treatment, and teaching a process of goal-setting case managers are likely to develop a particularly strong relationship with clients.

Client Driven/Case Manager
Facilitated Treatment Planning

The SBCM case management plan proved to be an especially powerful tool that provided clients an opportunity to identify those areas they saw as most immediate to their well-being and a structure in which to operationalize their abilities as the vehicles for accomplishing that work. As discussed earlier development of the case management plan was guided by clients' perceptions of their own needs. Goals were operationalized through the establishment of specific target dates for the objectives and strategies that comprised each goal. In addition client and case manager affixed an outcome of "completed" or "not completed" to each objective and "used" or "not used" to each strategy. "Revised" was used when either an objective or strategy was altered before its termination date. Table 8.1 summarizes the frequency of goals, objectives, and strategies created within each of the nine life domains and the percentage completed or used.

Most evident in an examination of Table 8.1 is the high rate of objective and strategy completion that took place overall and within each life domain. Almost two-thirds of objectives (64 percent) and strategies (65 percent) were accomplished by clients. Ranges for completion rates for both objectives and strategies were quite similar ranging from 58 percent (leisure) to 77 percent (living arrangements) and 57 percent (leisure) to 76 percent (living arrangements), respectively. On average 2.4 objectives were completed for each goal and 2.7 strategies developed for each objective. No comparable measure of goal attainment was available for the work undertaken by clients with other treatment staff, including their substance abuse counselor. While treatment plans were developed as a part of relapse prevention activities, the goals were not created or reviewed in such a way that allowed for systematic measurement of completion.

Another source of information that spoke to the value of creating case management plans came from clients' views of what was beneficial in their work with case managers and with other treatment staff. As part of a series of questions administered at the 6-month follow-up interview clients were asked to respond to the question, "What is the single most helpful topic you worked on?" The question was asked of all clients about their work with their substance abuse counselor and, for those clients who were assigned a case manager, for work with them as well. Client responses were recorded verbatim by project interviewers and then independently classified by two members of the project's scientific team. The raters then arrived at a consensus classification for each response. Although clients were asked to identify a single topic, they sometimes identified more than one. In these cases multiple classifications were assigned.

Originally the responses were to be placed into one of the nine life domains or one of two other categories of interest to the team. These two additional categories focused on (1) neutral presentation of cognitive, emotional, or psychological functioning or (2) presentation of negative or deficit-oriented cognitions, emotions, or psychological functioning. In other words, the terms clients used in presenting their own perceptions of what was helpful to them. It should be noted that positive, healthy, or constructive terms were coded under the internal resources life domain. In addition three other categories developed from client responses. These three categories included (1) relationship with their case manager or substance abuse counselor, (2) no topic seen as most helpful, and (3) assistance in learning how to set goals. Of significance to our discussion here is the frequent mention of assistance in developing goals relative to work with case

TABLE 8.1   Strengths-Based Goals, Objectives, and Strategies by Life Domains (Clients Represented = 263)

Life Domains	Goals	Objectives		Strategies	
Life Skills	33(5%)	Completed (67%)	34	Used (73%)	96
		Revised	2	Revised	11
		Not Completed	15	Not Used	24
		Total	51	Total	131
Finance	41(6%)	Completed (70%)	50	Used (75%)	126
		Revised	8	Revised	18
		Not Completed	13	Not Used	25
		Total	71	Total	169
Leisure	15(2%)	Completed (58%)	21	Used (57%)	48
		Revised	1	Revised	5
		Not Completed	14	Not Used	31
		Total	36	Total	84
Relationships	27(4%)	Completed (53%)	21	Used (60%)	85
		Revised	1	Revised	11
		Not Completed	27	Not Used	45
		Total	49	Total	141
Living Arrangements	117(18%)	Completed (77%)	204	Used (76%)	625
		Revised	14	Revised	25
		Not Completed	47	Not Used	175
		Total	265	Total	825
Occupation/Education	192(30%)	Completed (61%)	293	Used (60%)	776
		Revised	33	Revised	91
		Not Completed	158	Not Used	426
		Total	484	Total	1293
Health	46(7%)	Completed (57%)	56	Used (66%)	164
		Revised	4	Revised	9
		Not Completed	39	Not Used	75
		Total	99	Total	248
Internal Resources	21(3%)	Completed (71%)	40	Used (63%)	82
		Revised	3	Revised	6
		Not Completed	13	Not Used	42
		Total	56	Total	130
Recovery	148(23%)	Completed (60%)	257	Used (61%)	729
		Revised	11	Revised	21
		Not Completed	160	Not Used	452
		Total	428	Total	1202
Total	640(100%)	Completed (64%)	987	Used (65%)	2731
		Revised	77	Revised	197
		Not Completed	486	Not Used	1295
		Total	1550	Total	4223

managers. Thirty-six percent of clients identified working on goals, setting life goals, etc. as the most helpful topic they worked on with their case managers. In contrast only 1 percent of clients recognized this type of assistance in their work with their substance abuse counselor.

These two findings, rate of objective and strategy completion and client perception of the value of goal-setting, illustrate the practical importance of clients' controlling their own course of treatment. Simply put, clients were likely to complete those plans that they have been instrumental in creating and seemed to value the skills they had learned (goal-setting) as well as other forms of assistance (i.e., accessing resources). Obviously, the ability to systematically set goals and successfully accomplish them, is a skill that can be used independently by the client. Of course, some limitations in these findings exist given the inability to compare the outcomes between plans created under SBCM and under the disease concept.

Nature of the Case Manager–Client Relationship

A series of ethnographic interviews provided additional information about clients' perceptions of the important elements of strengths-based case management (Brun & Rapp, in press). The emphasis on individuals' strengths and abilities is the most important principle of strengths-based work and emerged frequently in individuals' stories although strengths became *positives* in the lexicon of these individuals. At the same time positives were not always readily accepted by these individuals, although for a different reason than previously anticipated. A practice implication is that strengths-based practitioners have generally assumed that individuals would be uncomfortable with looking at evidence of their own abilities because of guilt and a lack of familiarity with considering their strengths. At least one individual suggested that trusting the positive things that someone says may leave one vulnerable to being taken advantage of by persons in a drug-using culture.

In describing their treatment experience individuals found room for both a discussion of negatives and positives, of pathology and assets. While the remaining presence of pathology in individuals' perceptions about themselves may be disconcerting to strengths-based practitioners, individuals suggest otherwise. The balance that comes from the presence of both approaches—strengths and disease—results from what one client related was the ability to heal after "put[ting] it [negatives about one's use] out on the table." A practice implication is that it is possible that strengths-based staff underestimated the useful role that reflecting on problems, at least problems related to the use of substance abuse, may play in the treatment process.

Individuals described reactions to being asked to remember a time in their life when they were doing well and acting on their strengths. Individual comments included: "I can be creative," "I'm more confident," "I can weigh the positives and negatives," "It gives me my choices back," "I can be a winner," "An addict needs to hear he's doing good," "I haven't been asked about strengths in a long time," and "It [the strengths assessment] showed what I accomplished." One client in particular summed this up best:

> You have to bring out the negatives in order to start healing. But there's a time to stop all that negative stuff, too. You know treatment is to get you to put it on the table. . . . After it's brought out, you've talked about it, it's kicked around, and it's out in the open, it gets better. You have to get that stuff out before you heal.

The second important principle of the strengths-based intervention discerned in this study was the importance of the professional relationship between individuals and the case managers. References to the case manager as a "big sister" who will "check on me" cast the relationship in friendly, intimate terms. Individuals in this study, like the consumers of mental health services noted by Kisthardt (Rapp, Shera, & Kisthardt, 1993), indicated that the relational aspects of case management were important in helping them make changes in their lives. Even individuals who were not successful had positive feelings about the assistance they had received from their case manager.

Similarly, clients described the case manager relationship in ways that seem to indicate an intense joining together to accomplish specific tasks: "Someone else is seeing what I need to do," "I don't have to keep it (goals) all in my head," "She becomes a piece of my conscience," "She helps me keep my train of thought," "Hearing her voice motivates me," and "I didn't know nobody would care that much." One client shared the impact that the case manager's commitment had on him:

> She is like a big sister. She is there checking on me. She says, "So, you behavin' yourself?" I say, "Yeah." She says, "I haven't heard from you. Are you okay?" That helps that she calls and checks on me like that. I got to keep my nose clean.

An appreciation of the strengths process and sense of a strong positive relationship with their case managers combined at times to create a personal dissonance for individuals. On the one hand they wanted to embrace their own strengths and the relationship with their case manager while at the same time they were being pulled away from both by internal and external pressures. Internal events, such as depression and substance abuse, combined with external forces, such as friends and family, can wear away the gains made early in the process.

The three findings noted here—individuals' recognition of the strengths process as valuable, an emphasis on the relational aspects of the intervention, and conflict between recognizing these elements and effectively implementing them—all have significant implications for social workers who practice strengths-based case management. Perhaps most significantly social workers need to reexamine the professional detachment that frequently characterizes the relationship between social worker and client. There is no reason to believe that the warm, genuine, and mentoring relationship noted by individuals in this study cannot be maintained within the context of appropriate professional boundaries and the realities imposed on social work practice in contemporary settings.

Social workers implementing strengths-based practice must persist in emphasizing strengths throughout the relationship. It is not enough to conduct a strengths assessment early in the intervention and expect that it will effectively support an individual through challenges to their perceptions of personal competency and effectiveness. Social workers should be prepared to integrate the emphasis on strengths into all interactions with individuals, especially during the course of goal-setting activities. The most effective means of maintaining the focus on strengths lies in the social worker's fundamental examination of personal and professional beliefs about those individuals we typically refer to as difficult and resistant. The two themes that emerged from individuals' stories, the value of the helping relationship and a focus on personal strengths, begin to establish a link between the principles of strengths-based practice and the implementation of the intervention.

Conclusion

Several tentative conclusions can be drawn about strengths-based case management implemented with substance abusers. First, it seems that positive outcomes accrue to those clients who receive strengths-based case management, particularly in the areas of drug use, employment, and criminal justice involvement. More specifically the relationship between strengths-based case management and at least two of the positive outcomes—drug use and criminal justice involvement—seems to be accounted for by the ability of case managers to keep clients involved in services, specifically case management services, following primary treatment. Interestingly, case managers were not particularly effective in keeping clients involved with traditional relapse prevention activities.

Indirect evidence for allegiance to SBCM comes from (1) the high rate of success that clients experience in completing resource acquisition objectives and strategies and (2) the importance that clients ascribe to the goal-setting process. When given the opportunity to choose, case-managed clients elected to participate in strengths-based case management activities following primary treatment as opposed to medical model–oriented relapse prevention. Additional reasons for the longer involvement in the case management relationship may be related to case managers' willingness to meet clients in their homes, etc. as opposed to only in an office setting. Quite possibly clients may have found that a focus on strengths and the opportunity to direct their own treatment in a highly individualized fashion were more attractive than relapse prevention activities that focused on pathology.

In addition, clients had the opportunity to address recovery and multiple other life domains with their case manager. This one-stop shopping reflects a strengths perspective principle that encourages the case manager to be a central point in clients' search for resources. This would seem to be a welcome relief to clients who typically have been involved with numerous, disparate resources at any one time.

DISCUSSION QUESTIONS

1. We don't often think that the treatment of people with substance abuse problems is best done by exposing them to a relatively lengthy strengths-oriented treatment approach. But this chapter suggests that this type of approach has some potency. What are the elements that you see that make this approach viable?

2. The ETP Strengths Assessment is "the antithesis of most assessments." In what ways is that so?

3. How can encouraging clients to reflect on and consider problems be of benefit in a strengths-based approach like the one described in this chapter?

4. What is the importance of the relationship between the case manager and the individual in bringing about positive change?

REFERENCES

Brun, C., & Rapp, R. C. (in press). Strengths-based case management: Individuals' perspectives of strengths and the case manager relationship.

Derogatis, L. R. (1977). *SCL-90-R administration and scoring procedures manual.* Baltimore: Clinical Psychometrics Research.

Ihilevich, D., & Gleser, G. (1982). *Evaluating mental health programs: The progress evaluation scale.* Lexington: Lexington Books.

Knight, K., Holcom, M., & Simpson, D. D. (1994). *Texas Christian University psychosocial functioning and motivation scales: Manual on psychometric properties.* Fort Worth, TX: Texas Christian University.

Martin, S. S., & Scarpitti, F. R. (1993). An intensive case management approach for paroled IV drug users. *Journal of Drug Issues, 23*(1), 43–59.

McLellan, A. T., Kushner, H., Metzger, D., Peters, R., Smith, I., Grissom, G., Pettinati, H., & Argeriou, M. (1992). The fifth edition of the Addiction Severity Index. *Journal of Substance Abuse Treatment, 9*(3), 199–213.

Modrcin, M., Rapp, C., & Chamberlain, R. (1985). *Case management with physically disabled individuals: Curriculum and training program.* Lawrence, KS: School of Social Welfare, University of Kansas.

Rapp, R. C. (1997). The strengths perspective and persons with substance abuse problems. In D. Saleebey (Ed.), *The strengths perspective in social work practice.* New York: Longman.

Rapp, C. A., Shera, W., & Kisthardt, W. (1993). Empowerment of people with severe mental illness. *Social Work, 38*(6), 727–735.

Rapp, R. C., Kelliher, C. W., Fisher, J. H., & Hall, F. J. (1994). Strengths-based case management: A role in addressing denial in substance abuse treatment. *Journal of Case Management, 3*(4), 139–144.

Rapp, R. C., Siegal, H. A., Li, L., & Saha, P. (1998). Predicting post-primary treatment services and drug use outcome: A multivariate analysis. *American Journal of Drug and Alcohol Abuse, 24*(4), 603–615.

Saleebey, D. (1997). *The strengths perspective in social work practice.* New York: Longman.

Siegal, H. A., Fisher, J. A., Rapp, R. C., Kelliher, C. W., Wagner, J. H., O'Brien, W. F., & Cole, P. A. (1996). Enhancing substance abuse treatment with case management: Its impact on employment. *Journal of Substance Abuse Treatment, 13*(2), 93–98.

Siegal, H. A., Li, L., & Rapp, R.C. (in press). Case management as a therapeutic enhancement: Impact on post-therapeutic criminality. *Journal of Addictive Diseases.*

Siegal, H. A., Rapp, R. C., Fisher, J., Cole, P., & Wagner, J. H. (1993). Treatment dropouts and noncompliers: Two persistent problems and a programmatic remedy. In J. A. Inciardi, F. M. Tims, & B. W. Fletcher (Eds.) *Innovative approaches in the treatment of drug abuse: Program models and strategies.* (pp. 109–122). Westport, CT: Greenwood Press.

Siegal, H. A., Rapp, R. C., Kelliher, C. W., & Fisher, J. H. (1995). The strengths perspective of case management: A promising inpatient substance abuse treatment enhancement. *Journal of Psychoactive Drugs, 27*(1), 67–72.

Siegal, H. A., Rapp, R. C., Li, L., Saha, P., & Kirk, K. (1997). The role of case management in retaining clients in substance abuse treatment: An exploratory analysis. *Journal of Drug Issues, 27*(4), 821–831.

9 The Strengths Model with Older Adults

Critical Practice Components

BECKY FAST

ROSEMARY CHAPIN

Ann

Ann Karlin got her wish. She went home after discharge from the cardiac care unit at a large inner-city hospital 75 miles from her small rural community. Ann is a 75-year-old African American woman whose husband died last year. All of Ann's children moved out of the state shortly after their high school graduations. She lives on a small Social Security check and retirement pension that resulted from her husband's factory work in the city. Ann arrived home weak, depressed, and anxious about how she was going to manage, given her failing health resulting from congestive heart disease. Francis, Ann's neighbor, who is herself frail, also was deeply concerned about Ann and decided to contact the Area Agency on Aging (AAA) on her behalf.

Ann received a call from the social worker and refused the offered help. Despite Ann's unwillingness to accept or request formal services, the social worker from the social services agency for the aging decided to contact Ann again. The social worker was persistent in reaching out to Ann to see how she was doing and to find out if she needed any additional help. The precariousness of Ann's condition worried the social worker. She knew that a fall, insufficient nutrition, or lack of medication adherence could necessitate a nursing home admission. Slowly, a relationship developed between the two. Ann began to trust the social worker and believe that she was not secretly trying to put her in a nursing home. After being homebound for a week, Ann asked the social worker to find her a cleaning lady and someone to pick up some groceries for her at the local store. From Ann's perspective, she wanted to be sure that the social worker would respect what she wanted and needed before she agreed to any type of service arrangement.

Ann has entered into the complex and confusing web of long-term care services. Luckily, she has a seasoned social worker who uses a strengths-based practice model and understands the importance of developing rapport. When such an approach is absent, many older adults like Ann will not even consider looking at service options. The strengths model of case management is designed for people like Ann who will require different types of help and levels of intensity in caring and service provision as their health improves or deteriorates. Respect for the dignity and uniqueness of individuals like Ann is operationalized through the model's practice principles and methods. Furthermore, social workers using the strengths model are alert to the additional barriers to service access that African American women may face. Workers operating from a strengths approach are interested in building on the strengths that have helped older adults overcome previous difficult times in their lives.

This chapter describes how the strengths model of case management is implemented in the long-term care of older adults, specifically in the provision of home- and community-based services. The application of the strengths model of case management with seniors living at home in the community has not yet been empirically tested; however, initial data gathered from consumers and long-term care social workers trained in the strengths model supports its applicability to older adults. The responses and observations the authors have received from social workers while providing training on and technical assistance for the strengths approach have been instrumental in identifying and developing those components of the strengths model that seem essential to effective practice.

The first section of this chapter presents the conceptual framework that guides and directs the helping efforts with elders. The next section delineates the critical practice components of a strengths-based case management approach to long-term care, especially practice methods designed to support older adults' autonomy and meet resource-oriented needs while promoting cost-effectiveness and efficiency. The personal stories of individuals who have received case management are included to illustrate the usefulness of the strengths approach within a system accountable for reducing unnecessary institutional costs. Finally, the potential of the strengths model in changing long-term care environments is explored.

Conceptual Framework for Practice

For nearly a decade, the professional literature has occasionally considered the effectiveness and plausibility of using a strengths-based approach with older adults, children with severe emotional disturbance, and persons with mental illness and/or substance abuse problems (Perkins & Tice, 1995; Poertner & Ronnau, 1990; Pray, 1992; Rapp, Siegal, Fisher, & Wagner, 1992; Sullivan & Fisher, 1994). Strengths-based case management for older adults is derived from the basic principles and functions of the strengths model developed in the 1980s for persons with severe and persistent mental illness living in the community (Rapp, 1992).

Case management has been a part of social work practice since its inception (Johnson & Rubin, 1983). Like all social work practice, strengths-based case management for older adults rests on a foundation of values, knowledge, and skills. But there are several distinguishing features emanating from the values and philosophy of the model that set it apart from other long-term care case management practice approaches. These distinctive features include a shift from traditional models of helping based on medical necessity to a strengths-based model that addresses the whole person in his or her environment. In the strengths framework, discovering, developing, and building on the person's internal and external resources is a focal point. In contrast to many other long-term care case management models, the strengths-based helping process emphasizes consumer participation and decision making.

Medical and rehabilitation models typically emphasize professional diagnosis and treatment of the symptomatology to eradicate or ameliorate the problem. Authority for and control over decisions lies in the hands of the professional. The unspoken premise is that persons in need of assistance lack knowledge or insight about the identified physical or mental problem and certainly about how it might be resolved. Professional expertise is needed to assess and treat the troublesome condition (Freidson, 1988).

In contrast, the primary purpose of strengths case management is to help older persons maintain as much control over their lives as possible by compensating for what they cannot do and capitalizing on what they can do. The goal of strengths case management is to normalize the older person's routine within the bounds determined by the individual, often despite advancing disability. Assessment and planning strategies are woven from the social, psychological, and physical needs and strengths of an older person. For example, in a medical model case management system, a patient with a broken hip might be hospitalized, have the hip treated, and then be released. The medical needs may have been well met, but matters such as transportation, housing modifications, financial assistance, social isolation, and some physical limitations might never be considered. For most older adults, well-being is more than a medical matter. What is equally significant is the ability to contribute and feel useful, to prevent or cope with social isolation, and to normalize the routine of daily life despite the disease or illness (Smith & Eggleston, 1989). In fact, a person might be suffering from a serious chronic condition, but if these other needs are attended to, they might experience a sense of heightened well-being.

The assumption underlying the medicalization of aging services is that older people, and especially those with chronic disabilities, require the involvement of medical professionals to protect them from further injury and debilitation. In advanced age, chronic rather than acute illnesses are, for the most part, the major medical problems. The leading chronic conditions among older people include arthritis, heart diseases, high blood pressure, asthma, bronchitis, hearing or visual impairments, and ulcers (Mader & Ford, 1997). However, these conditions merely irritate some older people as they lead relatively normal lives despite aches and pains. Others are not so lucky and are significantly limited in their ability to carry out daily activities, such as cooking, housework, yard work, and getting out of the house to socialize. Of course, many older people also are periodically afflicted with acute illnesses (that is, conditions lasting less than 3 months).

But over the long haul, the stress inherent in providing and receiving emotional support and getting help with household tasks and personal care are the most pressing challenges during later life transitions for older adults and their families. Medical problems of older persons may remain stable during long periods. The person may even experience years of relative remission, occasionally interspersed with episodes of crisis and declining mental or physical health. The day-to-day stress of aging results from dealing with functional disabilities—and fluctuations in the degree of independence in functioning a person possesses in the face of illness. The performance of activities of daily living (ADLs), such as bathing, dressing, and eating, and independent activities of daily living (IADLs), such as shopping, walking, and getting out of the house, must be addressed on a daily basis. Despite functional deficits, older people may demonstrate remarkable resiliency. They often possess an underutilized or untapped capacity for growth and change even in the context of their handicapping circumstances. Like younger persons with disabilities, some older adults need only minimal assistance to arrange and manage supports and resources so that they can remain in the community and lead the life to which they are accustomed.

The conceptual framework for the strengths model of case management with older adults places self-determination as the central value, and that directs the focus to personal goal achievement. In achieving goals, consumer authority is key to the case management relationship, and the elder as well as the community must be viewed as possessing valuable resources and strengths. Thus, the case managers' task is to help elders identify and achieve access to both formal and informal resources in order to reach the outcomes they desire. Table 9.1 presents key elements of the strengths model and delineates differences between it and traditional medical/rehabilitative models of helping.

Operationalizing the Strengths Perspective

The usual assumptions made about elders is that they are problems, are on a course of rapid debilitation, are demanding, and take from society much more than they give. Case managers cannot be truly effective with older clients unless they believe in the worth, dignity, and uniqueness of older people in the face of a society that too often relegates seniors to an inferior position. So a first step for those who work with older clients is to suspend some of their beliefs about their lack of resilience and their capacity to grow and to change. This, in essence, means adopting a new concept of the aging process; acquiring a new sense of aging from those who have faced chronic illness and loss and manage to live joyfully and fully with resolution and determination. A new sense of aging is only possible when case managers are able to confront their own fears about aging and begin to envision their future selves as competent elders, capable of finding joy in life despite losses. Such a concept of self then allows case managers to join with elders rather than making plans for people they perceive to be fundamentally different from themselves. Exercises and training materials

TABLE 9.1   The Strengths Conceptual Model Contrasted with Traditional Medical/Rehabilitative Models of Helping

Factor	Strengths Model	Medical/Rehabilitative Models
Value Base	Human potential to grow, heal, learn Human ability to identify wants Self-determination Strengths of person and environment Individuality and uniqueness	Problem resolution dependent on professional expertise Compliance with prescribed treatments Patient lacks insight and knowledge about health
Focus	Combining personal and environmental resources to create situations for personal goal achievement	Professional diagnosis to determine the specific nature of the person's problem and to prescribe treatment
Solution to Problems	Determined by consumer/environment Natural community resources used first Consumer authority and investment	Professional-oriented assessment and service delivery
Social Environment	Consumer Fosters elders taking care of themselves	Patient Fosters taking care of elders by support systems
Case Management Relationship	Client as consumer makes choices and decisions Client develops rapport and trust Case manager coaches, supports, and encourages Case manager replaces self when possible with natural helpers	Clients are passive recipients Professional contact limited to assessment, planning, evaluating functions Provider-directed decision making and interventions
Case Management Tasks	Identifying strengths and resources Rejuvenating and creating natural helping networks Developing relationships Providing services within daily routines	Teaching skills to overcome deficits Monitoring compliance Medical management of identified problems

designed to develop case managers' capacities to use strengths-based strategies with older adults can help develop this new sense of aging (Fast & Chapin, 2000).

Allowing older persons to determine for themselves where they want to go, and when and how, demands faith and belief in their ability and capacity to choose and to handle the consequences of their choices. Such attitudes affirm the dignity and worth of older adults in spite of prevalent myths and stereotypes that clearly represent bias and prejudice against elders. This is a new vision of aging.

Despite the strong preference of older adults to remain in their homes as long as possible, family and professional relationships can strongly affect the elder's sense of self and the type of long-term care they decide on. A significant step in this direction is to establish work with elders on the foundation of genuine dialogue and collaboration (Perkins & Tice, 1996). Assisting older persons with identifying and defining the problems at hand, while facilitating their participation in finding solutions, helps them to believe that continued community-based living is possible. An overarching goal of strengths-based case management, anchored in the value base of client self-determination, is facilitating consumer involvement and choice. Providing older people with plausible options and including them in decision making about possible institutional placement increases the likelihood of satisfaction with, and relevance of, the choices made. When the older consumer becomes more active in making medical and social decisions, both the consumer and the providers achieve greater satisfaction.

Asking for additional help can be extremely difficult for an older person. Motenko and Greenberg assert that "the ability to acknowledge the need for help and ask for help is evidence of mature dependence, a crucial transition in late life" (1995, p. 387). These authors suggest that older persons are better able to accept increased dependence if they are given authority to make decisions about the nature of the help needed and how it should be provided. Simply stated, being in charge or calling the shots is essential to personal pride, particularly for older adults who have been operating independently throughout their lives. The more older persons feel in control of their lives by solving their own problems, the less the likelihood of unnecessary dependency and learned helplessness—two outcomes that are too often the fate of older citizens.

In the strengths model, social workers identify consumer abilities and create or find situations to use those abilities in the achievement of personal goals. Change, we believe, can happen only when you collaborate with an individual's aspirations, perceptions, and strengths. Most consumers are competent and able to participate in the planning and delivery processes. Doing so brings renewed self-confidence and independence precipitated by moving with the elder in the direction he or she chooses and in situations and contexts in which the person feels capable and willing. If consumers are experts in defining their needs, the role of the social worker must change to reflect a greater appreciation of that consumer expertise.

Helping individuals like Ann manage their own inevitable aging process and the physical and emotional losses involved assists them in being better equipped to make sound decisions regarding what type of help they want. When considering the needs of older persons and their families, risk and security must be carefully balanced. The conflict between the two becomes even clearer for elders who are more severely disabled. The following case example, supplied by a strengths-oriented case manager, illustrates this dilemma.

Sarah

Sarah Nelson is 82 years old and lives alone on the family's farm several miles out of town with her six cats and two dogs. Since her stroke, she has fallen several times. At one point she fractured her hip. Even though Sarah is confined to her recliner during the day, she continues to create dried flower arrangements. She relies on the home health aide to get her in and out of the bath, into bed, and to help with meal preparation. Sarah calls in her grocery list each week and the grocery store delivers her groceries. Her case manager and daughters assist her with finding transportation, managing her finances, and overseeing the upkeep of her home and farm. Her daughter Mary insists that she should move into the assisted-living unit in town. Sarah replies that she would rather lie helpless on the floor for hours than have to share a room and bathroom with a complete stranger. Sarah's daughters are very concerned about her living alone on the farm. They fear that she will hurt herself and no one will be available to help her.

Over and over again, older people like Sarah state that they value freedom, privacy, and the independence to make risk-laden decisions about their daily lives far more than they value living in a safe and protective environment. Sarah, a strong-willed woman, has adamantly resisted her daughters' and her medical providers' pleas that she move into supervised housing, which would prevent her from hurting herself. In this situation, Sarah's decision to remain living in her own home has continued to be respected. Her case manager has helped make it possible by providing her with meaningful choices about long-term care. Sarah's life-long habits of self-care, preferences about daily tasks, and her considerable strength of character are respected through negotiation about the type and level of service she prefers.

Table 9.2 presents a continuum of possible behaviors available to case managers for facilitating higher or lower levels of participation and involvement by the consumer. This table is intended to provide guidance to social workers attempting to foster the participation of frail or disabled older adults who are competent in decisions about their care needs. The continuum ranges from absolute authority (having the locus of control with the case manager) to a self-directed care approach (shifting the control to an informed consumer). The midpoint indicates shared responsibility by both parties for managing the multiple effects of the consumer's disabilities and illnesses, and for individualizing the consumer's resources.

The goal of strengths-based case management is to encourage more active consumer participation in long-term care decisions. The case manager begins where the consumer is and moves with him or her on the continuum to the highest possible level of participation. Professional-directed decision making is seen as the least desirable state. The aim is to expand consumer confidence in making crucial decisions such as when to seek care and what options to select, and to move toward consumer-directed decision making. Ann had never taken care of the finances, the car, or fixing the house. She was at a loss about how to handle what she saw as traditionally male duties that her husband always had performed. In

TABLE 9.2   Continuum of Decision Making

Absolute Authority	Imposing	Joint Action	Limited Constraints	Self-Directed Care
The case manager pressures the consumer to accept the problems or solutions without input or participation in the decision. The person's understanding of the issues are solicited but the case manager retains absolute authority over decisions.	The case manager defines the problem and selects the solutions that are the most promising. Consumer preferences are taken into consideration.	Together, both parties brainstorm a possible range of solutions. The case manager and consumer are both responsible for identifying consumer strengths and resources for implementing the plan of care. Decisions are not made unless both individuals agree on them.	The consumer offers preferences about the type, role, and level of service provision. Information and counseling is given by the case manager to assist the consumer in making informed decisions. The consumer retains the final decision within limits defined by the case manager.	Consumer choices are supported through being allowed to choose the mix, frequency, duration, and timing of formal/informal service provision within organizational boundaries. In this system, the case manager becomes a consultant to and resource for consumers to help make viable arrangements.
CASE MANAGER– DIRECTED DECISION MAKING		COLLABORATIVE DECISION MAKING		CONSUMER- DIRECTED DECISION MAKING

those arenas, she initially wanted the case manager to make more of the decisions. However, she wanted to retain the responsibilities that she had during her marriage. In time, she felt more confident about managing her late husband's duties and subsequently wanted less direction from the case manager.

At the self-directed end of the continuum (see Table 9.2) consumers determine what services they need and at what level they need to support themselves in the community. The example of Sarah illustrates how a consumer participated in and negotiated her care service schedule including what service would be performed. She did not want someone coming into her house to clean on a weekly basis. Sarah thought it was unnecessary for her to have a higher standard of living now than she had known previously in her life.

Self-directed care does not preclude the case manager from developing a supportive structure that enables individuals with disabilities, with the assistance of family, friends, and community members, to take responsibility for planning their own lives. Sarah, with the support of her case manager and several women who owned small businesses, was assisted in finding a market for her dried flower arrangements.

One difficulty lies with the minority of elders whose judgment is so impaired that increased responsibility for care decisions poses a danger to self and others. Questions inevitably arise about whether the person should participate in decision making and at what level. Frail or disabled older adults have the right to be involved in decisions about their long-term care. Even consumers with cognitive or psychiatric disabilities should be afforded as many choices as possible. The challenge is to be scrupulously aware of their rights and the *real* limitations of their physical and mental conditions. Given patience and time, a relationship can be established even with a very frail older person who fades in and out mentally. Their fears can be identified, concerns expressed, trust established, and actions taken in which the elder is a willing partner to the maximum of his or her potential and capacity. Strengths-based case managers strive to understand how their relationship supports or limits the autonomy of older persons.

Critical Practice Components of Effective Case Management

The purpose of strengths-based case management is to assist seniors in identifying, securing, and sustaining external and internal resources that are needed for customary interdependent (as opposed to independent or dependent) community living (Kisthardt & Rapp, 1991). The strengths model's potential to increase case management effectiveness with older adults occurs through the following practice methods: (1) personalized assessment and planning, (2) assertive outreach to natural community resources and services, (3) emergency crisis planning, and (4) ongoing collaboration and caregiving adjustments.

Personalized Assessment and Planning

Assessment from a strengths perspective is holistic rather than diagnostic. Consumer knowledge and motivation rather than professional expertise is the basis of the assessment and planning process (Pray, 1992). A standard functional assessment does not generate a complete picture of the older person's strengths, coping strategies, motivations, and potential for change (Kivnick, 1993). Eligibility for long-term care services based on functional limitations prompts social workers to view their consumers in terms of ADL, IADL typologies. In fact, so much emphasis is placed on functional limitations that an older person's quality of life is often reduced to *nothing more* than a list of ADLs and IADLs. Vulnerable older adults soon realize that to receive help, they too must describe themselves in those terms. In Ann Karlin's case, an initial focus on the deficits in her activities of daily living could have reinforced suspicions about the social worker's intentions to find her incapable of remaining in her home. Careful attention to her desires during the initial relationship building created an environment where functional limitations as well as capacities could be acknowledged and used in the care planning process.

Strengths-based assessment and planning focuses on the optimization of the older person's strengths and resources. Applied helping strategies are implemented to support the individual's sense of control and capacity to function at home. This is accomplished through finding and trying out supports and resources that take the person's limitations into consideration but counterbalance them through discovering new and old strengths and activities that might fit with the individual's desires and interests (Sullivan & Fisher, 1994). For example, in assessing Sarah's strengths, the case manager learned of her past hobby even though it had been years since Sarah had created flower arrangements. She recultivated Sarah's interest in the hobby and helped her buy the necessary supplies. After several months, Sarah's depression lifted, probably from pursuing her hobby, and her dried flower arrangements even brought in some additional income to fund her home care. The desired resources needed to optimize the person's capabilities may or may not be available on the menu of services offered by the social worker's agency. Strengths-based care plan development strives to be unrestricted by payment sources. Care planning driven by consumer interests and assets rather than steered by reimbursement is the desired outcome.

Most social workers are indeed committed to acknowledging their consumers' strengths. However, the majority of assessment and care planning tools provide little space or incentive for recording what the older person wants, is doing, has done, and can do to maintain his or her independence. This omission hinders even the best of intentions. Rarely, if ever, are consumer strengths seen as integral to the planning process so that services are provided and activities structured to maximize and promote existing or potential strengths. Subsequently, social workers can easily fall back into old habits. They fail to get to know the older person in a holistic way, whereas an appreciation of the whole person almost always creates a positive interaction. When the necessary time is taken to develop this kind of relationship, the case manager is better able to assist the consumer in developing an individualized plan of action.

Given system barriers such as large caseloads and organizational policies, the strengths assessment and planning process with senior adults should, at minimum, cover these items:

- Exploring commonalities: shared values, experiences, interests
- Learning how the person has coped with difficulties in the past
- Visioning together what kind of life the consumer wants
- Focusing on the strengths within the person and his or her environment

Basic questions to ask include

- Who is important to you in your life?
- What do you do during a normal day?
- What makes life worth living for you?
- What is going well for you right now?
- If things could be different, what would you wish for?
- What has worked well for you in the past?

The strengths assessment process is not meant to replace existing standardized assessments for conferring and allocating benefits. However, it is unjust and arrogant to suppose that the whole picture of a person is captured in diagnostic, functional, or psychotherapeutic assessments. Only through creating *life* plans rather than care plans will an older person be able to live meaningfully in the community. The above focal points and questions can serve as guides for gathering the information needed to develop such plans. An actual strengths assessment and personal plan can be found in Kisthardt (1997, pp. 103–108).

Assertive Outreach to Natural Community Resources and Services

The strengths perspective on case management practice offers an alternative conception to resource acquisition. Before using formal paid services, the case manager is expected to determine first that naturally occurring, environmental, and community resources are not available. Natural helpers include a collective of supporters to be developed and sustained such as neighbors, apartment managers, grocery store clerks, church or youth groups, adult children, and others with whom the older client comes into contact on a daily or weekly basis. The presence of naturally occurring resources is a strength of all communities and an available resource in all communities when actively pursued (Sullivan, 1997).

The strengths model advocates employing natural helpers and resources whenever possible. From the perspective of older adults, such help may be more acceptable because it is often based on friendship or a perception of mutual need, is easily accessible, lacks stigma, and is usually much cheaper. However, many seniors would rather not encumber their existing social network. In fact, when older persons are asked to help identify their helping networks, they will often tell you that no one is around who can help them. The avoidance of acknowledging dependency, combined with pride, may prevent older people from recognizing their extensive reliance on others for their daily survival. Therefore, it is imperative for strengths-oriented case managers to identify and support these helpers without undermining the older person's self-esteem and dignity. Special assistance when it comes from family, friends, employers, and colleagues often is not recognized by the older people as help per se because it is extended in such a subtle manner. This help is given by the informal social helpers as they interact with the individual during the normal rhythms of the day. These individuals may notice that their older friend is having some difficulty with walking, eating, or shopping and, without being asked, help the person with these tasks.

Social supports take on increased significance as elders become more frail. One of the losses experienced by elders is the shrinkage of the informal support system. Many of our consumers no longer have a full social support system that can help them. One of the critical functions of the social worker is to help secure and sustain connections to informal resources. The social worker's goal is to facilitate a more adequate fit between the individual's desires and the resources in his or her environment. This includes the social worker's helping the individual and primary caregivers to recognize and map out what assets are already being used to some degree and to include other community capacities that have not yet been mobilized.

Acquisition of natural community resources is predicated on the belief that including consumers in the decision about who or what entity provides the service will further promote adherence to the form and direction of the help received. The challenge for most social workers is locating and expanding a natural support system for their consumers. In Ann's and Sarah's situations, most of their friends and acquaintances, except for their children, were equally frail. They too are limited in their physical capability to conduct heavy cleaning or lift objects, and they are not able to come and go as they please. The social worker needs to be informed about the naturally occurring resources in the wider community, as well as in the consumer's personal network. It is important to generate as many potential resources as possible with consumers and their primary caregivers. Older persons may withdraw and withhold existing support network information out of pride and a desire to protect their privacy and maintain the appearance of independence.

A useful strategy that case managers can use to identify natural helpers is to accompany the older person through a typical day to learn what help is given, by whom, and how often (Lustbader & Hooyman, 1994). By going with the person to the doctor, hairdresser, etc., and by listening to the conversations, more often than not, a social worker will discover that the older person has more social contact than the social worker realized. Or, the case manager might discover a totally different personality outside the home than that seen at home in the client role.

In developing the service mix, caregiver burden is acknowledged. Support networks of family and friends should not feel overtaxed. Assertively working to relieve primary caregiver burden is basic to developing a workable care plan. Ongoing dialogue, assessment of perceived burden, and role adjustment must occur with informal caregivers when they are providing some of the major components of care. One of the chief problems with natural helpers is finding ways to limit their involvement because they are within easy reach on a potentially unlimited basis. Many who could help would rather not get involved because they fear being overwhelmed by the needs that may eventually occur. Occasionally, some older people alienate those who could help by complaining about the help or by expecting too much help.

Despite the emotional bonds linking older adults with their families, friends, and other established caregivers, these persons often lack the expertise to provide comprehensive long-term care. Further, a previous history of caregiver abuse and neglect in a given situation may necessitate agency assistance to care for and protect the vulnerable adult from any informal assistance. However, formal providers, while often equipped with the necessary technical skills, cannot fully satisfy affective needs or deliver the kind of idiosyncratic care that reflects a lifetime of shared values and experiences.

Balancing expensive formal care with less-expensive informal resources can help control costs while ensuring necessary assistance is provided in ways acceptable to the older adult. In Ann's case, the social worker discovered that the man who rented Ann's garage to store an antique car had a daughter in high school. With Ann's agreement, the social worker hired the girl to shop for groceries. Ann prepared a list that the girl's father picked up when he drove by on his way to work (he also usually dropped in to see how Ann was doing on these occasions). When the social worker explored with Ann what her experiences as an African American woman had been in seeking formal service, Ann indicated that she was hesitant to try to negotiate a formal care system primarily staffed by white people. Her preference was to rely on friends or relatives to help her get services. The high school girl and her father were recognized both as a source of help and as trusted friends who could aid Ann in her efforts to gain access to other resources.

In addition, Ann's son, a school teacher, would spend a month with his mother in the summer. His work to keep her home repaired relieved many of his mother's concerns about basic household upkeep. The social worker had a chance to become acquainted with him during these visits. At the social worker's suggestion, he accompanied his mother to the senior center each week. This allowed time for Ann to become comfortable in the service environment. She continued to attend the center from time to time even after her son returned home. Ann's son now felt more confident his mother could continue to live in the community with the support of the social worker, the service center, and other informal resources. If he became concerned about her well-being, he knew he could turn to the social worker for help. Undoubtedly, there will never be enough paid formal services to meet the needs of a growing disabled elderly population. However, focusing primarily on the deficits and lacks in the social environment only further restricts the number of helping resources.

Emergency Crisis Planning

Most older persons come to the attention of a social worker at a time of crisis. Unfortunately, crisis frequently occurs as the result of an acute care hospitalization. This experience leaves frail older adults in a weakened state suffering from depression, anxiety, or a sense of failure if the admission was caused by a fall, medication mismanagement, or lapses in personal care. During these instances, when the person's resiliency is low, they are most ready to yield to accepting professional and caregiver choices and goals. Advocating for the person's wishes and increasing elder involvement in the decision-making process increases the likelihood that alternatives to institutional care will be chosen if available. High care costs often result because the case manager has not had time to deal with the problem before it becomes a crisis or because services are simply allocated to the consumer without trying to fully assess and resolve the situation. Kulys (1983) found that older adults typically do not plan for a health-related crisis. This potential for unwanted institutionalization precipitated by unexpected crises can be mitigated by planning ahead for crisis services.

In the strengths model, an emergency plan is discussed and negotiated with the consumer and the primary caregivers before a health crisis develops. This plan is rehearsed and reviewed. Specific behaviors are practiced to ensure that they are followed in an emergency. However, developing an emergency plan entails the careful building of a relationship, as illustrated by the following examples: Emergency planning was initiated with a man who had fallen repeatedly. He was not interested in installing a medical alert system that could potentially cause a big scene in his neighborhood. Even though his pride prevented him from using a medical alert system, he did willingly agree to have his mail carrier alert his son if his mail did not get picked up. In Ann's case, she was willing to wear a medical alert pin that linked her to the small local rural hospital. She and Francis, her neighbor, discussed alternative emergency plans for nonmedical crises. In the event of such a crisis, one of them would alert the on-call worker at the aging social service agency who would then alert the staff nurse or social worker, depending on the presenting need.

An established emergency plan takes into consideration that most frail older adults will probably need time-limited, acute-care crisis services at various times. However, at a large number of crisis junctures, either low- or high-cost rapid response mechanisms can be selected, depending on how informed the consumer and caregivers are about the existing resources and their accessibility. When a structured plan for dealing with crises involving natural and formal resources is not in place, then high-cost services become the simplest and most readily available option. The strengths approach focuses on anticipating key crisis points as a strategy for providing effective case management and helping to contain unnecessary costs.

Ongoing Collaboration and Caregiving Adjustments

In the strengths perspective, monitoring is a continuous process that begins when care goals are established. The social worker frequently contacts and collaborates not only with the older person, but also with their family members, friendly visitors, senior citizen groups, nurses, and other support networks. The social worker's role goes far beyond that of appointments secretary to that of leader, trainer, and supervisor of a cadre of paid and unpaid helpers.

Skilled and effective case management presupposes that securing resources provides minimal benefits unless they are sustained and individualized to meet consumer preferences. Even after the older person has gained access to desired services and resources, a lot of work may need to be done to sustain that person. The challenge of strengths-based case management is to resolve or at least reduce the interpersonal conflicts within the personal support networks that inevitably arise. Relationship-driven collaboration recognizes the value of each person's input and the benefits of making the helping experience mutually advantageous for everyone. The goal of continuous contact is to strengthen the consumer's self-care capacities and the caregivers' ability to help through the transfer of knowledge and skills by social and medical service providers, all coordinated by the case manager.

For example, an older consumer with hearing difficulties may become extremely frustrated when the taxi driver, whom he calls for rides to the grocery store, leaves after momentarily honking the horn. Addressing the accommodation of the resource frequently involves educating the helper. Being careful to build partnerships with providers of resources, whether volunteer or paid, is very important. Tailoring the help to meet the needs of the consumer should be done in a nonthreatening way, not only for the sake of the present consumer but for all future consumers who may use that resource.

Ongoing contacts with the consumer and their helpers enable the case manager to influence cost-effectiveness through increasing, decreasing, or terminating any or all services expeditiously. Applebaum and Austin (1990) assert that rapid responsiveness to consumer changes can have a dramatic impact on service costs. The overutilization of services typically results from not adjusting prescribed amounts of delivered services to the current situation as it unfolds. Reduction in case management costs as well as paid services can be expected in the strengths model because efforts are reduced and shifted to more frail and needy individuals as other consumers regain increased levels of self-sufficiency.

The Empowerment of Older Women

There are many emergent components to the idea of empowerment for older women. Much of feminist literature proclaims the importance of connection and relatedness in the lives of women. Whether biological or a response to oppression in patriarchal social arrangements, friendships, connections, mutual caring, and support networks are sources of power and strength for older women. This is not to say that the idea that women are natural caregivers has not led to exploitation of women's interest in being nurturing. But "[a] belief in the value of connection and relationships can result in the development of interventions that support the empowerment of the individual and can contribute to group empowerment and societal change through individual empowerment" (Browne, 1995, p. 362).

Another avenue to empowerment is to reestablish bonds with and ties to the community and neighborhood. As we have seen, far too many older people are isolated and sequestered away from the communities that they live in. Elders have much to offer communities—skills built in a lifetime of work, raising families, and meeting economic, social, and interpersonal challenges. Their knowledge and experience can lend perspective and wise counsel to members of a community—individuals, families, groups, and associations. They also may have time to give. Kretzmann and McKnight (1993) give many examples of seniors making contributions to the community. In Chicago, older citizens are involved in the Visiting Important Person program in which they assist less mobile elderly neighbors and give them help with a variety of problems and needs. They are trained to provide CPR, to recognize drug abuse, to give bed baths, and to help with daily matters like budgeting, menu preparation, and cooking. The oldest participant is an 82-year-old woman. One of the most important signs of neighborhood and community is the evidence of intergenerational relationships—projects, celebration, mentoring, and child care. In *Ordinary Resurrections* (2000), Jonathon Kozol recounts the role of the older women volunteers at St. Anne's Church in making a safe and nurturing after-school environment for the young children in an economically distressed, segregated neighborhood.

> The small dimensions of the church have much to do with the unusual experience of physical and moral safety that attracts children here, and also the feeling of protectedness and intimate religion that is so important to the older women who come here to take care of the children. Several women from the congregation, one of them a great-grandmother, Mrs. Winkle, who is nearly 83 years old, come in the afternoon to congregate around a table at the far end of the afterschool, where they can keep a close eye on the kids and be available to them in times of need. (p. 20)

Here these women provide respite for 80 young children who, for the most part, live in siege conditions. None of them think what they do is out of the ordinary, but it is a little something to keep the community's obligation to its children and most vulnerable alive.

Finally, it is often elders who preserve the distinctiveness of the culture—its meanings, tools, rituals, and practices. While youth may be driven away from their culture and adopt the ways of the dominant culture, adult children often find the bridge between the old ways and the new to be built of their elders' wisdom. Celia Jaes Falicov (1998) says this about Mexican American elderly:

> The ability to become a "tough old bird"—energetic, involved, and self-confident—and perceive old age as arriving later than for Anglo-Americans, seems to be preserved among the Mexican American elderly. This finding may stem from the Latino values on collectivism, conservation, cooperation, and continuity. (p. 254)

But the elderly are mightily responsible for preserving these important values—values that remain a symbolic and vibrant cornerstone in many communities. Recognition, celebration, and solicitation of this knowledge is a part of the empowerment of older citizens.

None of the above should be interpreted to mean that many older people do not suffer the pains and anxieties, the exclusions and snubs, the marginalization of old age. It does mean that although we have a long way to go to empower the elders in our society and its cultures, we now know more about how to do that than we once did.

It should be noted here that successful aging is always a dialectical process. It is a matter of the adaptive competence and resources of a person and her or his family and the developmental supports and resources of a society, from neighborhood to federal government. In this sense, no one ages alone.

> Successful aging of individuals is related to the functioning and maintenance of communal life as the human ecology changes over time, that is to the successful aging of society through its adaptive competence. (Featherman, Smith, and Peterson, 1990, p. 82)

Utility of the Strengths Model in the Changing Long-Term Care Environment

Traditionally, aging has been viewed as synonymous with disease, and a medical framework of care has been implemented to try to cure the problems associated with growing old. Traditional medical/rehabilitative models of helping remain the most prominent in most community-based, long-term care case management systems. Within this framework, older adults have been expected to be passive recipients of care. However, in the changing medical marketplace, the traditional roles of a passive patient and doctor as sole decision maker must be revised. Financial incentives for providers to reduce overutilization increases the need for patients to take the responsibility for seeing that their health care needs are met. As Medicaid and Medicare managed care plays a larger role in the aging system, treatment decisions will be closely monitored to conserve clinical and fiscal resources. Many of these plans have been attacked for reducing consumer involvement and authority to direct the course of their help. Clearly, a need exists for case management that focuses on both consumer empowerment and cost consciousness.

Since its inception, case management has been viewed as a potentially significant mechanism for coordinating services and controlling costs to prevent premature institutionalization. In an era of limited resources, private and public payers are demanding accountability for client outcomes and cost (Quinn, 1992). Effectiveness of a case management approach has been commonly evaluated according to its ability to reduce unnecessary institutionalization. However, much less effort has been made to define and measure effectiveness of case management from a standpoint of facilitating consumer involvement and empowerment and its subsequent impact on client outcomes and cost.

The need to first articulate and then to evaluate the effectiveness of strengths-based goals, planning processes, and tasks is imperative if fiscal control becomes the driving force behind case management. Home- and community-based care have historically been embedded in the medical model delivery system where critical social, emotional, spiritual, and supportive service needs are often overlooked. The challenge for case management and home-based care becomes one of providing quality services that are acceptable to clients and effective in maintaining functioning while keeping a cost-conscious stance (Kane & Kane, 1987).

Research demonstrating the efficacy of specific case management models is still limited. Much more needs to be learned about the effectiveness of different case management models. Particular attention needs to be focused on the varying goals, tasks, processes, case manager's role, and impact on the lives of older persons. Long-term care case managers operating strictly from a functional or broker perspective of service provision, as was the case in the Channeling Demonstration Projects, did not employ the strengths model's emphasis on mutual decision making and reciprocity, and they minimized the active pursuit and empowerment of natural helpers (Rose, 1992). Equally, the Channeling Projects failed to carry out a case management process that established a trusting relationship and a purposeful counseling approach for dealing with the emotional stresses accompanying illness and loss of functions (Austin 1987). The model of case management employed influences cost effectiveness.

Although the effects of strengths case management with older persons in the long-term care delivery system have not yet been empirically tested, anecdotal evidence from Medicaid long-term care case managers trained in the use of the strengths model indicates that older adults who participate in strengths-based case management have increased levels of informal support, a more sustainable balance of formal and informal services, and fewer transitions between home and health care facilities (Fast, Chapin, & Rapp, 1994). Case management effectiveness from a strengths approach is embedded in its ability to meet case management's dual mission in long-term care—maximizing client control, dignity, and choice while containing cost.

Conclusion

This chapter has explored the essential practice components of the strengths model of case management with older adults in need of long-term care. This model of case management supports self-determination, maximizes consumer choice and interdependence, and can potentially help contain long-term care costs. With the growing number of elderly people in our society and the accompanying concern about health care costs, the importance of self-determination and consumer choice in creating an affordable home- and community-based long-term care system should not be overlooked. Articulation, implementation, and evaluation of the strengths model of long-term care case management with older adults can help professionals focus on the capacities rather than primarily on the frailty of our elders.

DISCUSSION QUESTIONS

1. How can case managers help enhance the empowerment of older citizens? What kind of practical steps could they take?

2. What is the new vision of aging?

3. What are some effective strategies for helping older consumers come to believe in their own abilities, try out new behaviors, and set and accomplish personal goals?

4. In what ways can case managers involve frail, older consumers in the assessment and planning process?

5. What kinds of contributions can older adults make to their communities?

6. Of your older relatives, which have aged successfully? Why do you think so? What relatives have not done so well? How are they different?

REFERENCES

Austin, C. D. (1987). *Improving access for elders: The role of case management.* Seattle, WA: University of Washington, Institute on Aging.

Applebaum, R., & Austin, C. (1990). *Long-term care case management: Design and evaluation.* New York: Springer.

Browne, C. V. (1995). Empowerment in social work practice with older women. *Social Work, 40,* 358–364.

Falicov, C. J. (1998). *Latino families in therapy: A guide to multicultural practice.* New York: Guilford Press.

Fast, B., & Chapin, R. (2000). *Strengths case management in long-term care.* Baltimore: Health Professions Press.

Fast, B., Chapin, R., & Rapp, C. (1994). *A model for strengths-based case management with older adults: Curriculum and training program.* Unpublished manuscript, The University of Kansas at Lawrence.

Featherman, D. L., Smith, J., & Peterson, J. G. (1990). Successful aging in a post-retired society. In P. B. Baltes & M. M. Baltes (Eds.), *Successful aging: Perspectives from the behavioral sciences.* Cambridge, UK: Cambridge University Press.

Freidson, E. (1988). *Profession of medicine.* Chicago: University of Chicago Press.

Johnson, P. J., & Rubin, A. (1983). Case management in mental health: A social work domain? *Social Work, 28,* 49–55.

Kane, R. A., & Kane, R. L. (1987). *Long-term care: Principles, programs, and policies.* New York: Springer.

Kisthardt, W. E. (1997). A strengths model of case management: Principles and helping functions. In D. Saleebey (Ed.), *The strengths perspective in social work practice* (2nd. ed.). New York: Longman.

Kisthardt, W., & Rapp, C. A. (1991). Bridging the gap between principles and practice: Implementing a strengths perspective in case management. In S. M. Rose (Ed.), *Social work practice and case management.* White Plains, NY: Longman.

Kivnick, H. Q. (1993, Winter/Spring). Everyday mental health: A guide to assessing life strengths. *Generations, 8,* 13–20.

Kozol, J. (2000). *Ordinary resurrections: Children in the years of hope.* New York: Crowne.

Kretzmann, J. P., & McKnight, J. L. (1993). *Building communities from the inside out: A path toward finding and mobilizing a community's assets.* Chicago: ACTA Publications.

Kulys, R. (1983). Future crisis and the very old: Implications for discharge planning. *Health & Social Work, 8,* 182–195.

Lustbader, W., & Hooyman, N. (1994). *Taking care of aging family members.* New York: Free Press.

Mader, S. I., & Ford, A. B. (1997). Morbidity and mortality trends among the aged. *Generations, 12,* 5–7.

Motenko, A. K., & Greenberg, S. (1995). Reframing dependence in old age: A positive transition for families. *Social Work, 40*(3), 382–389.

Poertner, J., & Ronnau, J. (1992). A strengths approach to children with emotional disabilities. In D. Saleebey (Ed.), *The strengths perspective in social work practice.* New York: Longman.

Pray, J. E. (1992). Maximizing the patient's uniqueness and strengths: A challenge for home health care. *Social Work in Health Care, 17*(3), 71–79.

Quinn, J. (1992). Case management: As diverse as its clients. *Journal of Case Management, 1*(2), 38.

Rapp, C. A. (1992). The strengths perspective of case management with persons suffering from severe mental illness. In D. Saleebey (Ed.), *The strengths perspective in social work practice.* New York: Longman.

Rapp, R. C., Siegal, H. A., Fisher, J. H., & Wagner, J. H. (1992). A strengths-based model of case management/advocacy: Adapting a mental health model to practice work with persons who have substance abuse problems. In R. Ashery (Ed.), *Progress and issues in case management.* Research Monograph, *127,* pp. 79–91. Rockville, MD: National Institute on Drug Abuse.

Rose, S. M. (1992). *Case management social work practice.* White Plains, NY: Longman.

Smith, V., & Eggleston, R. (1989). Long-term care: The medical model versus the social model. *Public Welfare, 47,* 27–29.

Sullivan, W. P. (1997). On strengths, niches, and recovery from serious mental illness. In D. Saleebey (Ed.), *The strengths perspective in social work practice* (2nd ed.). New York: Longman.

Sullivan, W. P., & Fisher, B. J. (1994). Intervening for success: Strengths-based case management and successful aging. *Journal of Gerontological Social Work, 22*(½), 61–74.

Tice, C., & Perkins, K. (1996). *Mental health issues and aging.* Pacific Grove, CA: Brooks/Cole.

10 The Strengths Perspective in Interpersonal Helping

Purpose, Principles, and Functions

WALTER E. KISTHARDT

We do clients a disservice when we insist that they have a problem for us to pay any attention to them. Our first question to a person who comes to us for help should not be . . . "what problems bring you here today?" But rather . . . "you've lived life thus far . . . tell me how you've done it."

—Bertha Reynolds

It has been 11 years since the publication of the seminal article suggesting a strengths perspective as an overarching conceptual metaphor for social work practice (Weick, Rapp, Sullivan, & Kisthardt, 1989). Since then social work educators, providers, and administrators have refined the perspective, clarified its complex application, and evaluated its effectiveness (Kisthardt, 1993; Macias, Kinney, Farley, Jackson, & Vos, 1994; Rapp, 1998). Administrators, funders, and direct care providers continue to creatively integrate a strengths-based approach within a problems-focused system. I have worked with a wide range of programs interested in implementing the strengths approach in their work with service participants. These populations include the homeless, adults with persistent mental illness, adults with developmental disabilities, and adults with the coexisting disorders of mental illness and substance abuse. I am currently consulting with the state of Florida to use the strengths approach to integrate Temporary Assistance to Needy Families (TANF), mental health services, addictions services, and New York State's

Family Resolutions project. Much has been learned regarding the barriers to truly integrating a strengths approach in daily practice.

This chapter examines the purpose and six principles consistent with strengths-based interpersonal helping. Examples shared by service providers during my recent consultations/training sessions will be used to clarify and instruct. The chapter concludes with a brief discussion of the Person-Centered Strengths Assessment and the Personal Wellness Planning helping tools.

The Purpose of the Strengths Approach

To be effective and efficient practitioners, a clear understanding of the purpose of our helping efforts is essential. I have used the following statement of purpose with my social work graduate students and providers across the country in training seminars: To assist individuals, families, and communities within the context of a mutually enriching, collaborative partnership to identify, secure, and sustain the range of resources, both external and internal, needed to live in a normally interdependent manner in the community.

There are several key contrasts that this statement of purpose suggests to providers. First, we strive in a strengths approach to help people achieve the goals that they WANT to achieve, not the goals that someone else believes they NEED to achieve. Second, the strengths approach does not suggest that anything goes. Whatever the service participant wants is agreed to and used to fuel the helping plan. This is where the notion of normal interdependence becomes crucial. The strengths-based practitioner is keenly aware of the social/cultural/legal constraints on individual behavior within a given community. Behavior that is normally interdependent (and I use the term *normally* to suggest normatively) is tolerable, acceptable, and ultimately, legal. The provider who embraces the concept of normal interdependence, seeks to influence others, within the context of the professional helping relationship, to make choices that are likely to be healthier for them, and that are respectful of other citizens. Strengths-based practitioners also know that behavioral outcomes that are considered normally interdependent in one part of the country, may not be in another. Consider the following example.

> Let's say that you have asked a service participant, who happens to have co-occurring diagnoses of mental illness and substance abuse, and who also is living with AIDS, "What do you want in your life?" The person states that he wants to work, but that his anti-retroviral medication is causing nausea. He asks you to help him get marijuana, which helps to reduce the side effects when he smokes it. How do you respond?

This example typically engenders much discussion and even heated debate. The point is that a provider in San Francisco is more likely to ultimately help this person with a referral for medical marijuana because it is now considered normally interdependent (legal) behavior. The provider in another part of the country will probably not assist in this outcome, as they would be, in effect, assisting another in breaking the law. I have consulted with many providers who opt not to help someone with a goal because they did not believe they were ready, or because they disagreed with the outcome from a value perspective. Examples include the person with mental illness who states they want to buy a motorcycle someday, the woman with borderline personality disorder who states that she wants to gets a job dancing in a topless nightclub, the recovering alcoholic who wants to get a job as a bartender, and the person with a developmental disability who wanted to leave the sheltered workshop to get a "real" job. But in each of these instances, the decision and choices are made in the sociopolitical context of the person's life, communal values, individual capacities, and social supports.

The concept of normal interdependence should ultimately determine whether or not we affirm and support each person's own aspirations. I argue that if we choose not to help someone with a goal that is normally interdependent, then this reflects a stance of oppression and a fundamental difference of opinion regarding values. In a strengths-based approach, our task becomes to help others engage in behaviors that respect the wants and needs of other citizens in the community, while at the same time promoting personal gratification, satisfaction, and sense of accomplishment. As a supreme court judge once ruled "individual liberty ceases, where public peril begins."

Our task is not to make sure the person on parole stays out of bars. If the person becomes able to go into the bar, have a non-alcoholic drink, play several games of pool, and leave rather than get into a fight with another patron, the question becomes "What is the problem?" In a strengths perspective individuals are essentially the arbiters of their own destinies and are accountable for the natural consequences of their decisions.

The six principles of strengths-based practice serve to guide and direct the range of helping efforts related to the purpose. I have found that there is often disagreement on one or more of these principles not only between different systems, but within different components of the same agency. If providers are not able to agree on these principles, consistency and continuity of care becomes far more difficult, if not impossible to achieve. We now examine these principles, incorporating actual examples from programs for which I have provided training and/or technical assistance.

The Six Principles of Strengths-Based Helping

1. The initial focus of the helping process is on the strengths, interests, abilities, knowledge, and capabilities of each person, not on their diagnoses, deficits, symptoms, and weaknesses.

The human being who enters the life of a service provider is so much more than a collection of symptoms and an amalgam of problems. This person is a survivor. Survivors are exceptionally adaptive. Despite the effects of poverty, oppression, discrimination, illness, disappointments, public apathy, and even at times hostility, people who are described as being at-risk and/or vulnerable still resolve to live each day as best they can. They are creative, resilient, persistent, and courageous. They have not given up, but have decided to press on despite external challenges and internal conflict and pain.

People can and do decide for themselves what they want in life, even if their decision statement is something as basic as "I want to live." To be able to express one's personal aspirations and desires is an important strength. Once this statement is made, then attention to deficits and various other needs assumes meaning for them. For example, I have reviewed many treatment plans that list the goal as "medication compliance." Whose goal is this? In many instances, it is the providers' goal. They are focusing on what they believe the person needs. Most service participants I speak to would rather not take their medications. A person may ultimately decide to take their medication because it helps them to achieve something that they want. That is the goal. Medication is a means toward some other strengths-based end. One person said, "I want to keep my job. I really love it, and I know I need to take my medications to help me stay healthy." Still another person told me, "I didn't want to work anymore, so I went off my medication and I lost the job." If the fact that this person no longer wanted to work had been identified, he could have been counseled to leave the job in a normally interdependent manner by giving notice, getting a letter of reference, etc. What happened, however, was that his "illness" and "medication noncompliance" were cited as the reasons why he "lost" his job.

To focus on people's strengths challenges us to assume a stance of respect and admiration. We are challenged to assume the role of student interested in learning about this person's hopes and dreams, rather than as the expert who purports to know more about what motivates a person than the person does. We are committed to get to know each person as unique and valuable beings, to learn what things they want in their lives, what holds meaning for them, and to then collaborate on what needs to happen for them to be successful. One service participant remarked:

> Mary (social worker) was the first person I ever worked with who asked me what I wanted to do. She told me that she admired me because of how I have been able to cope with my mental illness and still get what I need each day. She told me she had a lot to learn from me. She said I have a lot of strengths, and I guess she's right . . . but I didn't see them as strengths . . . but I do now.

2.   The helping relationship becomes one of collaboration, mutuality, and partnership—power with another, not power over another.

In a strengths perspective, the notions of independence and dependence lose their utility. All people are interdependent (Derezotes, 2000). People do differ to the extent that they require the assistance of others to accomplish their personal goals and satisfy the needs related to these goals. Human service professionals and service participants each bring their own experience, knowledge, skills, emotions, and personal agendas to the helping encounter. Each is interdependent. How can there be an identity as a professional helper without another who assumes the role of client, consumer, patient, service participant, or whatever word is used to identify the recipient of care? By taking the time to develop helping relationships that model mutual satisfaction and enrichment, we are able to assist the service participant to develop mutually satisfying relationships with others in the community.

The goal of partnership challenges us to develop helping plans with people not for them. It challenges us to share power and decision making as we journey with another human being. The implications of implementing this goal in practice demand that we expand the boundaries of the helping enterprise. Who decides where meetings take place? Who decides what the treatment goal is to be? Who decides how long the meetings last? Who decides if there can be communication between regularly scheduled meetings? Who decides which questions are appropriate and which are not? Who decides whether there will self-disclosure on the part of the provider? These are but a few of the important questions to ask as we strive to make the helping relationship more collaborative and more strengths based. A service participant shared these thoughts with me regarding the power of this type of relationship:

> My case manager was more like a friend than doctors and therapists I have worked with in the past. She really seemed to care about me, and she did not force me to do things. We talked about our mothers; we smoked and laughed together. She helped me get my own place and she came to AA meetings with me. Now I go without her. She has been a gift from heaven, a real miracle in my life.

Strengths-based practitioners have realized the importance of expanding traditional boundaries of the helping relationship. As Derezotes notes, "in a reciprocal relationship the client and worker share co-responsibility for the work process . . . the worker and client view themselves as equals . . . (they) co-create the practice goals, objectives, and tasks" (2000, p. 79). The ideal situation in any helping encounter is when both workers and service participants, having been guided by the wants and needs of those helped, come away from the process enriched. Strengths-based practitioners do not have more invested in the process and outcomes than do service participants. They operate from a belief in the resourcefulness, determination, and resiliency of all people, regardless of illness, disability, or personal history.

3.   Each person is responsible for their own recovery. The participant is the director of the helping efforts. We serve as caring community living consultants.

People constantly make decisions. Do I take one drink or not? Do I change the baby now or wait until later? Do I take my medications? Do I get out of bed today? A strengths perspective recognizes that decisions are being made. The question here is not whether someone is conscious that they are making a decision. Their behavior becomes de facto an indication of the decision that has been made. If we are to influence and promote other decisions that are more normally interdependent, the first step is to help people realize that they are in fact making these decisions. And that if these decisions continue, they may not attain the goal they have articulated.

The example of the young single parent who refuses to get help for a chemical addiction is a prime example. She has stated that she *wants* her baby (who has been placed in foster care) back. This goal becomes the ultimate focus of the work. She refuses to participate in treatment and the providers, who have a duty to the baby and the larger community, petition to terminate parental rights. Although the young parent may blame social services for taking her baby, she, in fact, decided not to do what was necessary to become a more effective parent. She directed and determined the course of events. I have spoken with many providers who were convinced that what some of these young people truly wanted was to not be a parent. By making certain decisions they accomplished that goal in a manner that shifted the responsibility to the state department of children and family services. To be aware that this was, in fact, a decision may help the individual in the future make other decisions that might promote her well-being in a more affirmative way. The decision is also likely a means to meet a need or resolve a conflict. There may be other ways to do that, and these alternatives might be the basis for future decisions.

4.   All human beings have the inherent capacity to learn, grow, and change.

The human spirit is incredibly resilient. Despite the hardships, trauma, experience of repeated psychiatric hospitalizations, years of living on the streets, years of experiencing the negative effects of poverty, physical or neurological disability, structural oppression, stigma and discrimination, each person, at the time you begin the collaboration, may be on the verge of making important changes in his or her life. Appreciating the inborn urge to growth and change challenges us to harness the motivating power of positive expectations—the healing power that often is the product when the faith, hope, and love conveyed by one person ignites the fire of potentials and possibilities for another.

I have encountered service providers in training seminars who suggest that this idea is fine for those who are "higher functioning" but the majority of the people they work with have "severe disabilities" and may not even be able to tell you what they want. In these types of situations it becomes important to shift our focus from asking questions to patiently observing. A strengths perspective suggests that people will indicate their preferences by their behavior. Moreover, we should constantly attempt to try something new and different with people who, on the face of it, may seem to have very little potential to accomplish new tasks or to engage in certain behaviors. The following experience illustrated the essence of inherent capacity and it is an image I will never forget.

> I was providing two days of training for staff at Tachachale, a residential treatment facility in Gainesville, Florida. Prior to the training the staff was taking me on a tour of the cottages. In one cottage there was a young man who was strapped on a hospital

bed, face down and reclined at a 45° angle, with his head about two feet from the floor and his feet elevated. He was not able to speak, as he had experienced significant neurological impairment due to traumatic brain injury. This position assisted with postural drainage. As the staff stopped to introduce me he began to make low guttural vocalizations. It seemed clear that he heard the staff member, and was responding as best he could. Acting on an impulse, I laid down on the floor where he could see my face and said, "Hi Jimmy, it's nice to meet you." At which point Jimmy began to make much louder vocalizations, which the staff agreed was laughter! They stated that they had never heard him respond in this manner. I asked them if they had ever lain down on the floor to talk to him when he was in this position. They had not. They decided that they would start doing this, especially on those days when it seemed to them that he was having one of his "off" days.

If we believe that all people possess the capacity to learn, grow, and change, then we will constantly be seeking new and different strategies to create opportunities for this growth to occur. At every helping session we should strive to learn something about the service participant(s) that we did not know before. Each new piece of information may serve as a key that unlocks the potential that resides in all people. Sometimes when staff has worked with a person for several years they may get to the point where they think they know everything about the person. Many times, when I have done an actual demonstration of engagement, strengths assessment, and planning with a current service participant at a particular program, I have learned things about them in 20 minutes that no one at the agency knew. The following example illustrates this point.

At a recent training in Iowa, I spoke with a man who has a developmental disability at a workshop in Fort Dodge. There were more than 100 people at the seminar, and this gentleman agreed to come up front and work with me to demonstrate the engagement and strengths assessment process. During our conversation, I asked him if spirituality was an important part of his life. He hesitated, looked around the room, and then shared that he wanted to get baptized into the Lutheran faith. There was a marked buzzing in the room, and it became clear that this desire had never been shared with anyone at the program. I asked him if his family (especially his father who was his legal guardian) would be supportive of this. He said that he told his grandmother and she thought it was a good idea, but that he was afraid to ask his father as he was not sure how he would react. The staff later said they would work with him on a plan to share this desire with his father at his next circle of support meeting.

Believing that we know everything about a person serves as a barrier to integrating a strengths perspective in our work. There is always something new to learn. We must assume the perspective of an explorer and enter into a voyage of discovery. The more we learn about the uniqueness, talents, skills, accomplishments, desires, and knowledge people possess, the more creative we may be in mutually developing helping plans that are truly individualized and hold particular meaning for them.

5.   A strengths-based, person-centered approach encourages helping activities in naturally occurring settings in the community.

Three models of case management (community care) have been evaluated and proven to be effective in working with people with persistent mental illness. These are the strengths model (Kisthardt & Rapp, 1992; Rapp, 1998; Rapp & Chamberlain, 1985; Rapp & Kisthardt, 1996; Rapp & Wintersteen, 1989), the psychiatric rehabilitation model (Anthony, Cohen, and Farkas, 1990), and the assertive community treatment model (Bond, McGrew, & Fekete, 1995; Stein & Test, 1980). A common characteristic of each of these models is that case managers are expected to work with people in various locations in the community.

In my conversations with providers, we frequently note several benefits of meeting with people out of the mental health center or program building. First, we are able to observe firsthand some of the realities of the person's day-to-day living circumstances. Second, people often feel more comfortable and share more detailed personal information in the context of completing tasks together in the community. Third, people with disabilities are more visible in the community, and this serves to break down myths, stereotypes, and the discrimination that is often a result of these biases. In addition, many case managers state that they would much rather be out of the office, so there is a feeling of satisfaction and even joy that accompanies the challenges of holistic, comprehensive helping. Finally, providers often report a marked change in people's behavior when they are in naturally occurring settings in the community. People behave less like patients or clients (Holmes, 1997) and more like collaborators and partners in completing the helping tasks. The goals related to community activities should always be documented on the Personal Wellness Plan (included later this chapter) with the service participant or guardian signing off, thus signifying informed consent (Fellin, 1996).

6.   The entire community is viewed as an oasis of potential resources to enlist on behalf of service participants. Naturally occurring resources are considered first, before segregated or formally constituted mental health or social services.

This principle challenges providers to avoid the knee jerk reaction that sometimes accompanies the planning and referral process. For example, the person sets a goal of finishing their high school equivalency (GED) and the provider refers them to a GED study group at the partial hospital day program. Before this referral should be made, the provider might encourage enrollment in a review course offered by the local junior college, or see if there is a mentoring program in which the participant may study one-on-one with a retired teacher who is willing to volunteer. This may actually be more comfortable for those who do not do well in formal classroom-like settings. Seeing the entire community and the potentials and possibilities for resource development is an essential perspective of the strengths-based practitioner. The strengths perspective transcends the individual, to neighborhood, organization, and larger community (Sullivan, 1997).

One major disincentive to implementing this principle in mental health practice has been the prevailing policy of "fee for service." If the center is billing for services provided at their program and they cannot bill for services provided by a natural helper, the choice for administrators is fairly clear-cut. If they are to achieve their goal of sustaining the program, revenues are needed. The landscape of funding services for people with persistent mental illness, however, has shifted markedly in recent years.

Managed care, capitated financing schemes, and case management options through Medicaid now provide incentives for providers to expand traditional notions of therapeutic and clinical care (Fellin, 1996). For example, in a capitated arrangement providers receive a set annual dollar limit for each person who meets the criteria of persistent mental illness. Person-centered outcomes will drive the work. How each individual meets the needs related to these outcomes will vary. The point is, providers will be more likely to use a wider range of natural supports if their funding is not totally dependent on formally constituted clinical services.

The relatively new concept of supportive housing is another example of recognizing and employing community resources (Ridgeway & Zipple, 1990). Often a person desires to secure their own apartment, and others—family and/or treatment team—see this goal as unrealistic. A plan is then suggested whereby the person lives in a group home or other supervised housing arrangement as a transitional step. For some individuals, this approach works well. For others, however, it is not effective and often leads to acting-out behaviors. Anyone who has ever lived in the same space with six or more nonrelatives for a period of time knows firsthand how stressful congregate living can be.

Here, the challenge to providers is to creatively and directly identify barriers and strive to remove them so that each person may live where they want to live. As one service participant shared:

> I was in a group home and I couldn't take it. I can't be around people. I don't like people. I went back to the hospital [state psychiatric hospital], I had more freedom there. My case manager helped me to get my own place. It's not much, just one room, but it's mine.

Each of these principles serves to guide and direct strengths-based, person-centered helping. By identifying and honoring individual aspirations, skills, resiliency, resourcefulness, and potential for growth, we gain a fuller picture of the person. As Sir William Osler, a pioneering physician, once said, "it is more important to know what sort of patient has the disease, than it is to know what sort of disease the patient has." By realizing that there is more in our shared experience as human beings that makes providers like participants than different from them, we gain the courage to be warm, caring, empathic, and genuinely affirming of people's own visions (Kisthardt, 1997). In this spirit of connection, we expand the boundaries of therapy and strive to assist in ways that are therapeutic. When this happens, both provider and participant come away from the process enriched, fulfilled, and gratified. One participant became tearful as he shared his experience with his provider:

> He's like a brother to me. I know he care (sic) about me. He checks on me, comes to my place, makes sure I get my medicine . . . he send me a card at Christmas. I never got a card at Christmas . . . it meant so much. . . . I showed it to my mom. I'm gonna keep the card forever . . . Tom's (provider) gone now, but I'll never forget him.

As strengths-based practitioners we understand that the people we work with make decisions. The essence of helping is to help people bolster their internal and external resources so that more choices may be available to them. We strive, through the collaborative partnership and caring relationship, to influence decision making that may lead to healthier, more satisfying lives. We recognize that the first meetings play an important role in whether or not people choose to work with us. My research on the service participant perspective regarding the factors that promote effective engagement suggests the following strategies.

Strategies That Promote Effective Engagement from the Perspective of the Service Participant

We have entered into the era of "targeted populations." For example, people with the coexisting disorders of mental illness and substance abuse, people who are receiving TANF, people with developmental disabilities, people who are homeless, people who have been diagnosed with HIV/AIDS, or people who are mandated to receive services by order of the correctional system, may become the focus of helping efforts. Engaging these individuals, who are confronted with many challenges, not the least of which are related to poverty and institutional discrimination, is not an easy task.

By talking to people who receive services as well as to experienced community care providers across the country, the following strategies appear to contribute to effectively engaging people in the helping process. I will use examples from work with many different populations. These experiences were shared during time I spent at different service agencies providing training and technical assistance in the strengths model.

■ *Focus more on conversational skills than interviewing skills.* Service participants seem to respond more fully to providers who come across as real people. It is not possible to have a conversation with another person if I am not willing to self-disclose. I have heard from many providers who share that they have been trained not to self-disclose to a patient or client and, indeed, that many of their programs have policies that prohibit such activity. Despite this reality, many seasoned providers have learned that they will get much more information if they are willing to share personal information that is timely, relevant, and designed to foster trust and collaboration. The following example from a training session I conducted for the staff at the Department of Corrections in Kansas illustrates this point:

> After an exercise in which the people at the training were asked to spend a few minutes with a colleague identifying as many things as they could that they had in common, we reconvened. One of the uniformed corrections officers (complete with standard issue sidearm neatly holstered by his side) stood up and said, "If you are asking us to do this type of thing with prisoners we would be in direct violation of the Department of Corrections Policy and Procedures Manual, which clearly states, 'at no time disclose personal information to any of the inmates.' " After I thanked him for sharing this information I said, "Now, given that reality, may I ask if you have ever shared something about yourself with an inmate?" He hesitated, and then said, "Yes, I have." I then asked all of the other uniformed officers in the room if they had ever self-disclosed in their interactions with inmates. All of their hands went up. Our discussion then centered on how they made decisions regarding what specifically might be shared, under what circumstances, and to whom. One officer summarized our discussion by saying, "We're much less likely to have trouble with inmates if we treat them with respect, like human beings, and to affirm that we may have common interests as human beings."

■ *Send a clear message that you are not there to make negative judgments or to try to change them, but rather to affirm their own aspirations and work together toward making those dreams a reality.* This is accomplished by integrating questions from the Person-Centered Strengths Assessment (provided later in this chapter) right from the start of the work. This process seeks to identify what people want in their lives before identifying what they need in their lives from your perspective. The shift from focusing on what someone else thinks the person needs to the person's own motivation (what they really want) seems to be an essential component of effective engagement. The following example from a case manager working with a person with coexisting disorders clearly illustrates this shift. He shared this with me 6 months after going through the strengths perspective training at his agency.

> I started working with a guy who had a long history of mental illness and substance abuse. At our first meeting I asked him if he was still drinking and he said "occasionally." I asked him if he would be willing to accept a referral for inpatient detox after which we could start working on some other things in his life. He said, "I can handle it, I don't have a problem with it." My first thought was that he was clearly in denial. I then thought about shifting the focus and I said, "OK, you don't want to work on that and you don't think you need to, what is it that you do want?" He said, "I want my own apartment." I asked him to write that goal on the top of the personal wellness plan. He did. Then we talked more specifically about finances, location, etc. I agreed to meet him the following week to begin to develop the plan to achieve this goal. I then said, "OK, our meeting is at 11 A.M. You need to know that I will be sober when I get there. I also expect you to be sober, because this is your goal, not my goal, and if you really want it you have got to make some

important decisions about your drinking. If you have been drinking before I get there, I'm going to leave." He agreed. When I showed up he was ready and indeed had not been drinking. This was the first time in a long time that he had not taken a drink before noon. The weeks went by and he worked hard to complete the short-term goals related to getting an apartment. When he moved in he was so proud and said he had never really had his own place. I said, "If you want to keep it, you might think about watching how much you drink." It would have been better, I believe, if he would not be drinking at all, and working on sobriety. This however, was not his goal yet. He has been in the apartment for 3 months and seems to be doing well. He reports that he is still taking a drink every now and then, but that he has "really cut down, because I don't want to get sick again and lose this great apartment."

■ *Engage in activities you both enjoy.* Providers who work with children have known for years how important it is to get on the floor with kids and engage them through games and activities that they enjoy and that make them comfortable. What happens to that strategy when we are working with adults? Why is it some-times considered unprofessional or even unethical to engage in activities with a participant that are enjoyable, while at the same time doing an assessment, getting ideas for possible helping plans, monitoring and evaluating progress, and getting to know the participant better? When we ask people where they would like to meet, if they would like to walk while we talk, if they would like to throw a ball back and forth while we get to know each other, these are truly examples of start-ing where the client is. The following vignette, shared by an income maintenance case manager/advocate from Kansas City, is still the best example I have heard of creative use of self in an effort to engage an assertively reluctant participant.

A case manager was working with a program to attempt to engage with noncusto-dial fathers (The Futures Connection) throughout the city. Each time the case man-ager found this particular individual he was not willing to talk at any length and would not remain very long. The case manager sometimes spent hours just trying to find him, and often he did locate him at the neighborhood basketball court, where he was known for his skill. The case manager then got an idea. He told the man that he had a proposition for him. They would play one-on-one to 21 points. If the participant won, the case manager would "not bother him" any more. But, if the case manager won, the participant would become involved in the program. The person agreed. The case manager won the game! The participant, bound now by the agreement made on the basketball court, was true to his word and became involved in skill training, job readiness, and case management. When the partici-pant completed the program, he got a full-time job with benefits driving a Pepsi truck and making $14.00 per hour. He had reestablished contact with his children and was regular in his child support payments to their mother.

■ *Be sensitive to cultural factors; honor diversity and seek to assist people in involvements that hold meaning for them.* The strengths approach, by its very nature, attempts to be sensitive to the importance of culture in people's lives. A strengths-based prac-titioner is like an ethnographer. The goal is to learn about an individual's lived experience, the fund of meaning and understanding from family and culture that sustains and directs them, and the visions of the future that are culturally relevant and have value (Rodwell, 1990). When we gain an appreciation for a worldview that is different from ours, we will join people in generating plans that reflect outcomes that resonate on multiple levels. The following example shows the power of culturally sensitive engagement.

> A social worker in Lawrence, Kansas who was a case manager at a community support program for people with persistent mental illness was attempting to engage with a young man by doing outreach. During the first few visits the case manager's agenda was to influence the young man to come in to the mental health center for intake and evaluation, and to become involved for "socialization" at the partial hospital program. The young man was cordial and polite, but refused to go to the center. As the case manager grew to know him better they talked of his Native American roots. They talked of things he had done in the past related to the culture of his people. He shared that he used to get much from attending sweat lodge ceremonies. The case manager then got the idea of connecting him with some people at the Haskell Indian University located in Lawrence. He said he would agree to this plan. They both went to meet some students at the school, and he quickly became involved in a regular sweat lodge ceremony. He also eventually became more involved with the services the mental health center had to offer.

■ *Seek to incorporate humor, joy, and laughter into the helping process.* To be sure, many people we attempt to help are in very serious situations and struggle with the harsh realities of poverty, illness, addiction, sadness, and loss. Our field is becoming increasingly aware of the healing power of humor, joy, and laughter. As Sigmund Freud once said, "Like wit and the comic, humor has a liberating element. It is the triumph of narcissism, the ego's victorious assertion of its own vulnerability. It refuses to suffer the slings and arrows of reality" (1905). It is somewhat unfortunate that many service providers equate the presence of humor and laughter in the helping process as being callous, uncaring, heartless, and indifferent. I recently spoke to an emergency room nurse who was written up because her supervisor heard her laughing and the ER was "no place for laughter."

It seems clear from feedback I have gathered from people on the receiving end of our ministrations that a sense of humor, honesty, and joy are perceived as important characteristics of people who would attempt to help them. And, as one participant shared with me "this does not mean they try to do a 10-minute monologue to try to make me laugh, and it does not mean that they use humor as a substitute for knowledge, skills, and professionalism."

The Person-Centered Strengths Assessment and Personal Wellness Plan

During the engagement process providers are also gathering data and seeking to begin documenting the helping/service plan. Many providers are now incorporating the Person-Centered Strengths Assessment and the Personal Wellness Plan in their daily work with participants. This section examines these helping tools in detail.

Providers in many different venues and with many different populations have used the Person-Centered Strengths Assessment (Figure 10.1) and the Personal Wellness Plan (Figure 10.2). In consulting with providers who have worked with these tools the following points seem to be related to successful implementation.

■ *Both documents must reflect the dynamic nature of the helping process.* Many programs have become accustomed to writing a treatment plan for a service participant that often is not reviewed until some time in the future. In some programs it is an annual review. Seasoned clinicians know that gathering relevant information (assessment) and working toward goals the service participant has articulated occurs at each and every helping session. Therefore, new information regarding the person's life should be documented as the helping process evolves. Moreover, shifts in the service participant's priorities and incremental gains made toward stated goals should be recorded at each visit. I have suggested that both these tools be used when meeting with the person. Many clinicians do their paperwork after the person has left the office. Providers who have begun to use the Person-Centered Strengths Assessment and Personal Wellness Plan at each meeting report that this is an effective strategy to "draw the person in" to the collaborative helping partnership. Some providers have shared that they now complete their progress notes in the presence of the service participant. One provider observed, "This really helps me to be more descriptive and less jargony. . . . I also tend to use more strengths-based language . . . rather than stating the client is resistive, manipulative, non amenable to treatment . . . I will say . . . client continues to have strong feelings about what they want and need and has remained steadfast in his decision not to follow through on my recommendations."

■ *These documents are designed to be user friendly. Therefore, service participants should be encouraged to actually write the information and record the plans.* I have suggested that providers give people a copy of the assessment to take home with them to work on at their own pace. Many providers have reported being amazed at how much information people write when they have a chance to take the form with them. I recall an experience I had doing training at a state hospital in Kansas. A patient from one of the wards volunteered to join me in a demonstration of how I would conduct the first meeting using a strengths approach. At the conclusion of our conversation, I showed him a copy of the Person-Centered Strengths Assessment. I pointed out that I had asked him many of the questions during our talk just as they appear on the assessment. I invited him to take the form back to the ward and I encouraged him to work on it if he felt up to it. I then asked him to consider sharing it with his treatment team the next time they met. The following day at the training the group had quite a surprise. The young man had finished the entire assessment and had asked one of the nurses if he could come to the training building again to show me how well he had done. As I shared some of what he'd written the treatment team was quite impressed that he was able to concentrate for this period of time and that he had recorded meaningful information that was not included on their diagnostic, problems-based intake assessment.

FIGURE 10.1   Person-Centered Strengths Assessment

1999 Wally Kisthardt, Ph.D., UMKC Graduate Social Work Program: 816-235-1743 kisthardtw@umkc.edu

Participant _____ Case Manager _____ Date _____

Housing/A Sense of "Home":

Where are you living now?

What do you like about your current living situation?

What things don't you like about where you are living now?

For now, do you want to remain where you are, or would you like to move?

Describe the housing situation you have had in the past that has been the most satisfying for you.

Transportation/Getting Around:

What are all the different ways you get to where you want or need to go?

Would you like to expand your transportation options?

What are some of the ways you have used in the past to get from place to place?

If you could travel anywhere in the world, where would you go? Why? (use back to elaborate)

Financial/Insurance:

What are your current sources of income, and how much money do you have each month to work with?

What are your monthly financial obligations?

(continued)

FIGURE 10.1   Continued

Do you have a guardian, conservator, or payee to help you with your finances?

What do you want to happen regarding your financial situation?

What was the most satisfying time in your life regarding your financial circumstances?

Vocational/Educational:

Are you employed full- or part-time currently? If so describe where you work and what you do at your job.

What does your job mean to you? If you do not have a job now, would you like to get one? Describe why you would or would not like to get a job at this time.

What activities are you currently involved in where you use your gifts and talents to help others?

What kinds of things do you do that make you happy and give you a sense of joy and personal satisfaction?

If you could design the perfect job for yourself what would it be? Indoors or outdoors? Night or day? Travel or no travel? Alone or with others? Where there is smoking or no smoking? Where it is quiet or noisy?

What was the most satisfying job you ever had?

Is it harder for you to *get* a job, or harder for you to *keep* a job? Why do you think this is so?

Are you currently taking classes that will lead to a degree or taking classes to expand your knowledge and skills?

What would you like to learn more about?

How far did you go in school? What was your experience with formal education?

FIGURE 10.1   Continued

What are your thoughts and feelings about returning to school to finish a degree, learn new skills, or take a course for the sheer joy of learning new things?

Do you like to teach others to do things? Would you like to be a coach or mentor for someone who needs some specialized assistance?

Social Supports, Intimacy, Spirituality:

Describe your family.

What are the ways that members of your family provide social and emotional support for you, and help to make you feel happy and good about yourself?

Is there anything about your relationships with family that make you feel angry or upset?

What would you like to see happen regarding your relationships with family?

Where do you like to hang out and spend time? Why do you like it there?

What do you do when you feel lonely? Do you have a friend that you can call to talk to or do things with? If not, would you like to make such a friend?

Do you have the desire to be close to another in an intimate way? Would you like to have this type of relationship?

What meaning, if any, does spirituality play in your life? If this area is important to you, how do you experience and express your spiritual self?

Do you like nature?

Do you like animals?

Do you have a pet?

If not, would you like one?

Have you ever had a pet?

(continued)

FIGURE 10.1   Continued

Health:

How would you describe your health these days?

Is being in good health important to you? Why or why not?

What kinds of things do you do to take care of your health?

What are your patterns regarding smoking? Using alcohol? Using caffeine? What effect do these drugs have on your health?

What prescription medications are you currently taking? How do these medications help you?

How do you know when you're not doing too well? What is most calming and helpful for you during these times?

What limitations do you experience as a result of health circumstances?

What do you want and believe that you need in the area of health?

Leisure Time, Talents, Skills:

What are the activities that you enjoy and give you a sense of satisfaction, peace, accomplishment, and personal fulfillment?

Would you like the opportunity to engage more frequently in these activities?

What are the skills, abilities, and talents that you possess? These may be tangible skills such as playing a musical instrument, writing poetry, dancing, singing, painting, etc. or intangible gifts such as sense of humor, compassion for others, kindness, etc.

What are the sources of pride in your life?

FIGURE 10.1   Continued

Are there things you used to do regularly that gave you a sense of joy that you have not done in recent years?

Which of these activities would you consider rediscovering at this time in your life?

Prioritizing: After thinking about all of these areas of your life, what are the two personal **desires** that are most meaningful for you at this time?

■ *These documents honor and document the person's wants, desires, and aspirations first. Once this data has been gathered, the needs are discussed and negotiated in the helping process.* As you can see as you examine the Strengths Assessment it does not focus on what someone needs from another person's perspective. It focuses on what people have going for them now, what they *want* in the future (and for some people they write, "I want to keep things just the way they are"), and what people have accomplished in the past. The areas of people lives, or life domains, provide a holistic, comprehensive picture of person and environment. If the person is not able to write I encourage the provider to record their responses in their presence, using their own words. If the person is not able to talk, I have encouraged providers to record their observations in each of these areas, as people will tend to gravitate to activities that are enjoyable or pleasant for them.

■ One of the most frequently noted barriers to using a strengths approach, especially in work with people who suffer from neurological impairments or other developmental disabilities, is the question of safety. The following example from a workshop I provided in Indiana illustrates how we can negotiate with people around this concern once we have affirmed their agenda and motivation.

A 27-year-old woman with a developmental disability agreed to work with me to demonstrate the strengths approach in front of more than 50 of the staff as well as her mother (her legal guardian) who attended the training. I asked her what she really liked to do during the day. Before she answered, she slowly looked around the room, smiled, and then said with some conviction, "I like to go to Scott's grocery store." I heard a bit of rumbling in the room and bits of comments shared between the staff in the room. I then invited her to write that down on the assessment. The rumbling grew a bit louder. She agreed, and I gave her the letters and she wrote them on the assessment. She talked about how she liked the people at Scott's, how they make her laugh, and how she buys Twinkies. She then said, "I take the Twinkies back to my room, and eat them before my program manager gets there!" Now the group was laughing loudly. As I learned in processing this encounter, the staff was actually trying to keep her from going to Scott's through a contingency management plan. They

FIGURE 10.2   Personal Wellness Plan

1998 Wally Kisthardt, Ph.D. UMKC Graduate Social Work Program: 816-235-1743 kisthardtw@ umkc.edu (Use back for progress notes.)

Participant _____

Case Manager/Clinician _____

Participant's Aspiration (motivation—may be concrete or abstract):

Intermediate Concrete Goal Related to Aspiration (3 to 6 months):

Short-Term Goals (What NEEDS to get done to accomplish above?):

Goal/Task/Objective Target Date /// Date Achieved

_____

PARTICIPANT   PROVIDER
COLLATERAL

_____

_____

thought it was not safe, and they were concerned that she was overweight and they knew she liked to get Twinkies. What took place was rethinking her plan, and making a deal with her that they would not try to stop her from going to Scott's if she agreed to buy one Twinkie, not three, and to buy one apple. She happily agreed to this plan. I heard from the staff at this program some months later that they were working on helping her to get a part-time job at Scott's as she was unhappy at the sheltered workshop and shared that she wanted a "real job."

Closing Thoughts

This chapter has briefly examined a statement of purpose, six principles, and practical tools to aid in the integration of a strengths perspective in interpersonal helping. Concepts such as normal interdependence, personal autonomy, personal freedom, citizenship, accountability, reciprocity, community resources, the fundamental difference between what we want in our lives versus what we truly need in our lives, negotiated plans, partnership, collaboration, and mutual enrichment (provider and service participant) become essential to consider as we become more strengths-based and person-centered. For some providers, this process entails some profound shifts in perspective and practice. For others, however, these notions have served as a welcome affirmation of beliefs and helping activities that have long been integral components of their community-based helping efforts.

Policy makers and funders are challenging providers to integrate and coordinate their services on behalf of people who are involved with multiple systems—corrections, addictions, mental health, social welfare (TANF), for example. The strengths perspective has been suggested as a philosophical and conceptual bridge that may serve to span systems. I was involved with a recent yearlong SAMHSA study in Oklahoma that demonstrated that providers from different and often disparate theoretical perspectives can achieve consensus on a common purpose and set of practice principles. The growing research and anecdotal evidence suggests that further refinement, development, and evaluation of a strengths-based model is indicated. If service participants are welcomed as key informants and legitimate stakeholders in this enterprise, we will generate deeper and more valuable knowledge.

The following poem, from my book, *You Validate My Visions: Poetic Reflections of Helping, Healing, Caring, and Loving,* attempts to capture the implications of being truly person-centered in our work.

What Is Person Centered?
What is "person centered?" an important question today.
As we strive to help another, as she travels on her way.
As we try to know the spirit, that makes people what they are.
As we encourage one, whose arms are weary, to reach for one more star,

Person centered is seeing beyond labels which have been worn.
A person is more than symptoms, and the problems he has born.
A person cannot be fully understood, by calling her a name.
Schizophrenic, Borderline, or Bi-Polar . . . people are not the same.

To be person centered is a challenge, it is not an easy task.
The nature of our sharing, the questions that we ask.
What are your gifts? What are your joys? What holds meaning on your quest?
What are your dreams? What makes life real? What is it you request?

A person is a producer, a person also consumes.
A person may have more potential than prognosis may assume.
A person is entitled to express her own opinion,
Without fear of reprisals, when another holds dominion.

A person has the right to fail, as she risks something new,
Without another telling her "that goal is unrealistic for you."
A person is a fluid being, ever changing, ever free.
A person makes her own decisions, though others may disagree.

A person is a spirit, whose energy is divine.
A person is a work of art, that the brushes of life refine.
More than a "stage," more than a "phase," more than "old" or "young."
More like a song, drifting on the wind, both singer, and that which is sung.

A person may make plans one minute, and then decide to change them.
A person may order things a certain way, then turn, and rearrange them.
A person may not grasp some things, while with others, they are clever.
A person is the moment . . . a person is forever.

Person centered is being grateful, for the gifts that others share.
Person centered is valuing the opportunity to care.
Person centered is cherishing the wonder of each being.
Person centered is joyful, it is enriching, and it is freeing.

DISCUSSION QUESTIONS

1. What do you understand normal interdependence to be? Has it ever played a role in your work with service participants?

2. Which of the six principles of strengths-based helping is the most difficult for you to employ in your work? Why do you think this is so? Which seems the most natural to your way of working?

3. What is the importance of humor in a helping relationship? Has humor or play or fun ever been a part of your work? How and with what results?

4. Do the strengths assessment yourself. When you are done (be sure and take your time), review it. Are there things about yourself that are surprising? Did you discover strengths that you were not fully aware that you had?

5. Now do a strengths assessment on a service participant (if it is OK with your supervisor and it fits with your work). Any surprises?

REFERENCES

Anthony, W. A., Cohen, M. R., & Farkas, M. D. (1990). *Psychiatric rehabilitation.* Boston: Boston University, Center for Psychiatric Rehabilitation.

Bond, G. R., McGrew, J. H., & Fekete, D. M. (1995). Assertive outreach for frequent users of psychiatric hospitals: A meta analysis. *Journal of Mental Health Administration, 22*(1) 4–16.

Derezotes, D. S. (2000). *Advanced generalist social work practice.* Thousand Oaks, CA: Sage.

Fellin, P. (1996). *Mental health and mental illness: Policies, programs, and services.* Itasca, IL: Peacock.

Freud, S. (1905). *Jokes and their relation to the unconscious.* (J. Strachey, Trans.). New York: Norton. (Original work published 1960.)

Holmes, G. E. (1997). The strengths perspective and the politics of clienthood. In D. Saleebey (Ed.), *The strengths perspective in social work practice* (2nd ed.). New York: Longman.

Kisthardt, W. E. (1993). An empowerment agenda for case management research: Evaluating the strengths model from the consumers' perspective. In M. Harris and H. Bergman (Eds.), *Case management for mentally ill patients: Theory and practice.* Langhorne, PA.: Harwood.

Kisthardt, W. (1997). The strengths model of case management: Principles and helping functions. In D. Saleebey (Ed.), *The strengths perspective in social work practice.* New York: Longman, pp. 97–114.

Kisthardt W. E., & Rapp, C. A. (1992). Bridging the gap between principles and practice: Implementing a strengths perspective in case management. In S. Rose (Ed.), *Case management and social work practice.* New York: Longman.

Macias, C., Kinney, R., Farley, O. W., Jackson, R., & Vos, B. (1994). The role of case management within a community support system: Partnership with psychosocial rehabilitation. *Community Mental Health Journal, 30*(4), 323–329.

Rapp, C. A. (1998). *The strengths model.* New York: Oxford.

Rapp, C. A., & Chamberlain, R. (1985). Case management services to the chronically mentally ill. *Social Work, 30*(5), 417–422.

Rapp, C. A., & Kisthardt W. E. (1996). Case management with people with severe and persistent mental illness. In C. Austin and R. McClelland (Eds.), *Perspectives on case management.* Milwaukee: Families International.

Rapp C. A., & Wintersteen R. (1989). The strengths model of case management: Results from twelve replications. *Psychosocial Rehabilitation Journal, 13*(1), 23–32.

Ridgeway, P., & Zipple, A. M. (1990). The paradigm shift in residential services: From the linear continuum to supported housing approaches. *Psychosocial Rehabilitation Journal, 13,* 11–31.

Rodwell, M. K. (1990). Person/environment construct: positivist versus naturalist, dilemma or opportunity for health social work research and practice? *Social Science Medicine 31*(1), 27–34.

Stein, L., & Test, M. A. (1980). Alternative to mental hospital treatment. *Archives of General Psychiatry, 37,* 392–397.

Sullivan, W. P. (1997). On strengths, niches, and recovery from serious mental illness. In D. Saleebey (Ed.), *The strengths perspective in social work practice* (2nd ed.) New York: Longman.

Weick, A., Rapp, C. A., Sullivan, W. P., & Kisthardt, W. E. (1989). A strengths perspective for social work practice. *Social Work, 89,* 350–354.

11 Creating Strengths-Based Alliances to End Poverty[1]

JENNIFER C. JONES

MARY BRICKER-JENKINS

WITH MEMBERS OF THE KENSINGTON WELFARE RIGHTS UNION

If you have come here to help me, please go away. But if you have come because your liberation is bound up with mine, let us work together.
—Lila Watson[2]

The considerable literature on strengths-based practice abounds with references to the strengths of many groups of people with which social workers engage, but little on the strengths of social workers.[3] Further, little or no consideration is given to the notion that people in client status might—and most likely must—be assessing the strengths of social workers as work together begins and progresses.[4] This is

---

[1]The research study on which this chapter is based was a collaborative effort with the Kensington Welfare Rights Union and was sponsored by its education committee. Jennifer Jones, the principal researcher, also wishes to thank her advisors—Dr. Joyce Everett and Dr. Dominique Steinberg—at the Smith College School of Social Work for their support and guidance in this work. Mary Bricker-Jenkins thanks June Close, Kathy Winchester, and Kathy Hendrixson of the Justin Potter Public Library, DeKalb County, TN, for their research skills and forbearance.

[2]Lila Watson is a Brisbane-based aboriginal activist; she was speaking to social workers and other community workers.

[3]A notable exception is the literature on supervision, management, and administration (Rapp & Poertner, 1992).

[4]We prefer the terms *people in client status* or *with whom we work* or even *folks* to the objectifying terms *client* or *consumer;* in this, we agree with Cowger's (1998) important critique of a limitation of a strengths model embedded in market and professionally oriented structures.

a curiously ironic omission, one that places the people with whom we wish to form partnerships in an implicitly passive position.

This subtle contradiction is especially incongruous when working with people living in poverty, as it is self-evident that they have strengths. This chapter—along with the research project that informs it—turns the study of strengths upside down. It is part of a collaborative effort to discover and extend the ways that social workers might become more fully engaged and effective in building a movement led by the poor to end poverty. The study revealed in a most compelling way that the assessment and engagement of strengths is a mutual, two-way process and must become more consciously so if we are to achieve genuinely collaborative relationships. Moreover, without such relationships, it is unlikely that social workers can achieve our potential in our ethically mandated efforts to end economic oppression.

As social workers committed to expanding our presence and effectiveness vis-à-vis poverty and its consequences, we have been working for several years as allies with the Kensington Welfare Rights Union (KWRU). That organization has been actively building a mass movement to end poverty since 1991, when it was created by a small group of welfare mothers in the multiracial/multiethnic, deindustrialized, economically impoverished Kensington section of Philadelphia. In this chapter, we will first provide some information about the movement and the organization and then describe the collaborative study that informs this chapter. Finally we will present findings from the study related to opportunities for social workers in the movement, many of which have implications for work with the general population of people living in poverty or otherwise experiencing economic dislocations. As we shall see, this work both challenges and expands the theory and practice of strengths-based social work.

The Context: Poverty Theory and the War on the Poor

Virtually all government-sponsored anti-poverty programs of the 20th century were based on theories of the causation of poverty that deflect attention from macroeconomic forces.[5] Schiller (1998) summarizes the four explanations for or theories of causation of poverty that have underpinned American policy and, to a large extent, the popular rhetoric that shapes attitudes toward the poor: (1) an individual's *flawed character* and lack of investment in one's own future (human capital) are the primary reasons why particular people are poor in the "Land of Equal Opportunity"; (2) the poor have had *restricted opportunities* to obtain education and jobs due to economic, gender, and racial discrimination; (3) the over-indulgent Welfare State—*Big Brother*—has allowed the poor to become dependent on the government; and (4) the urban poor living in racially and economically

---

[5]We would argue that the Social Security Act of 1935—which was originally proposed as an *economic security act*—and its amendments responded to but did not correct for economic dislocations.

segregated ghettos have developed a culture of *the underclass* as a result of years of social and economic deprivation. Each of these theories or a combination of them had a turn at driving policy, and, not surprisingly, none has substantially reduced poverty, much less ended it. Thus, toward the end of the century, the combination of the following two factors played a key role in building support for the Personal Responsibility and Work Opportunity Reconciliation Act (PRWORA) of 1996: the political rhetoric and the inherent flaws and failures of programs woven from these theoretical strands and the demands of a globally expanding economy. Referred to as "welfare reform" by the media, politicians, and much of the general public, to others the PRWORA represented an all-out assault on the poor and, ultimately, on the majority of working Americans.

As we enter the 21st century, social workers appear to be traveling three broad policy and practice avenues.[6] Some are engaged in *providing a new array of social services* designed to enhance individuals' self-esteem, social skills, and other marketability factors; in light of the satisfying individual success stories, little consideration is given to the fact that these services are a new subsidy to corporations that, by and large, are participating in an elegantly devised system to acquire cheap labor and depress income levels for the majority of wage workers. Even less consideration is given to those who have disappeared into prisons, the overcrowded homes of relatives and friends, or the streets.

A second broad avenue involves *advocating for more money* for an improved welfare (or post-welfare) state; like Jencks (1996), this approach recognizes that the welfare system did not enable people to move out of poverty because it did not give women with children (the majority of the counted poor outside of prisons) enough money to live on. Such advocates—many of whom are preparing to mount a massive lobbying effort for the 2002 welfare reform reauthorization— argue that welfare reform time limits will not help people to get jobs and to move out of poverty because recipients are being forced to take jobs that do not provide an adequate income on which to raise a family. Although programs based on such restricted opportunity theories are more attentive to the structural problems that poor people face, adding more money to the welfare system—even through such devices as transitional housing programs, "micromarkets" and "enterprise" strategies—constitutes an attempt to save a failing institution and does not actually address the nature of economic dislocation and oppression in the United States, much less its global context. For this, a third approach is needed: to build a movement to end poverty.

Building a movement to end poverty does not, as we shall see, take place apart from the other approaches but is strategically distinct. Taking a "value-critical" stance reminiscent of Rein's (1971), increasing numbers of individuals and organizations led by poor and unemployed persons are questioning the values, logic, and ultimate efficacy of any market-linked welfare project. Indeed, they are challenging us to question the very need for poverty and, through intensive study of

---

[6]For a practical and tactical reasons, these avenues sometimes intersect, but they are very different in terms of overall theory of and strategy for addressing poverty.

history, challenging us to act on the values and visions espoused by most people in this country (Baptist, 1998). These values and visions, codified in the economic provisions of the United Nations Declaration of Human Rights, are at the core of the Poor People's Economic Human Rights Campaign—a nationwide coalition of poor people's groups and their allies. The KWRU was instrumental in pulling this coalition together and helps to sustain it through organizing national marches, demonstrations, and other events (Baptist, Bricker-Jenkins, & Dillon, 1999) and by hosting the campaign's Web-based University of the Poor, a primary medium of exchange of information and analysis among movement groups.

Counteracting the Psychological War: Leadership by the Poor

That the movement is being led primarily by people living in poverty is notable for many reasons, not the least of which is the way this capacity for leadership confronts prevailing stereotypes of the poor—stereotypes vigorously promoted in the media and often taken up by poor people themselves. The national rhetoric surrounding those who live on low incomes or in poverty (such as, "the only people who are unemployed and on welfare in this strong economy are lazy and taking advantage of the system") reinforces people's sense of failure, ineptitude, and isolation when they believe they alone are unable to support their families (Rose, 1990). The media does not regularly present the experiences of people living in poverty from the perspective of people who are consistently facing structural barriers to gaining access to power. Instead, two-dimensional images of drug- and violence-infested neighborhoods, abused and neglected children, and minority teen mothers are given to represent a very heterogeneous population of people who struggle daily to provide for their basic needs. The national silence surrounding the structural barriers that economically oppress millions of people only magnifies each individual's feelings of being at fault, ashamed, and socially isolated from others who are also suffering (Belle, 1990).

In our culture, typical approaches to these stresses and strains range from prayer to psychotherapy, but not collective action. Historically, people living in poverty who organize with others to demand livable wages, affordable housing, and health care are dismissed, denigrated, or rendered invisible. Thus, many people do not join those organizations that are available because they are afraid that they may experience repercussions from their employer or the welfare system. They turn to the easily accessible and often modeled solutions: going without what they need; making do with some help from the limited resources of family, friends, or their church; or avoiding thinking about their problems by numbing their pain and frustration with substances, such as crack cocaine, marijuana, and alcohol.

Seeking treatment poses another peril. Historically, people of color and people living in poverty have been overrepresented in the number of people being diagnosed with psychotic disorders (such as schizophrenia), given lengthy hospitalizations, and prescribed high dosages of antipsychotic medications (Bhugra, 1997; Bulhan, 1985). Contacts with mental health and social service systems also increase the state surveillance of families at a time when government legislation, reflecting and reinforcing institutionalized rage toward the poor, places the very existence of these families at risk. No wonder that welfare reform, the Adoption and Safe Families Act of 1997, and hundreds of state and municipal regulations that criminalize poor people are experienced as a pincer movement in a sustained war on the poor, one in which corporations pillage poor communities, and both media images and mental health theories pillory impoverished individuals and families.

It is in this landscape that KWRU leaders see and develop strength. Leadership by the poor and unemployed not only counters psychological assaults, presenting an alternative image of strength and capability, but also reduces the crippling isolation attendant on poverty in America. Through daily projects of survival and problem-solving as well as organizing movement-building events, KWRU and its allies engage in healing through struggle and organizational development. All activities are informed by ongoing study of historical and contemporary movements, economic structures, and the members' own experience of poverty. In this way, the individual experience of poverty is traced to its institutional wellsprings. As we shall see later in this chapter in the reports of the meaning of the organization to its members, the KWRU serves many of the functions of social services and support groups, but in its leadership, analysis, and movement-building function it is clearly distinguishable in its approach to poverty and its effects.

Defining Roles for Social Work in the Movement: A Collaborative Effort

What might be the appropriate roles for social workers in the movement and its organizations? This is the overarching question that motivated the study that informs this chapter. In this section we will provide an overview of the study, beginning with the underpinning suppositions that motivated and shaped it.

Study Assumptions and Propositions

Since we see research as a political, albeit rigorous and accountable, undertaking, we want to be clear about several assumptions and stances that determined the study design and process.

First is a commitment to *mutual engagement of strengths.* We assume that people are the experts on their own lives; moreover, they are capable of determining their own analyses and shaping the meaning of their lives. While this seems obvious, the dominant discourse and method in social science research places expertise primarily in the hands (or minds) of the researcher. This study assumes that the skill of the researcher in problem-posing, research design, interviewing, organizing data, and the like can and should be joined with expertise of the researched. However, much of the literature presenting potential approaches to social work practice with people living in poverty has been written by professionals and academics and not by the people themselves. Thus, the voices of people who have historically been disenfranchised continue to remain silent or to be mediated by professionals within the field of social work. Sung Sil Lee Sohng (1998) challenges social workers to engage in research that will question the dominant discourse about oppressed people and to support those who have been historically silenced to uncover, examine, and describe their own lives. This study takes up Sohng's challenge to amplify the voices of the true experts on poverty.

A second assumption is that the *research process is—and should be—a political process.* Sohng refers to research as an "empowerment strategy," when she writes, "Transformative research empowers when it enables people to create the kind of knowledge that yields power. . . . Research activity should serve the emergence of marginalized and disadvantaged groups" (pp. 196–197). No profession has more contact with the poor than social work; indeed, ours is the only occupational group that has serving the interests of oppressed populations central to its mission. Thus, an explicit goal of this project is to create a knowledge base that challenges the dominant social work theories about poverty and people living in poverty as well as the ways that knowledge is developed.

Flowing from this position is the assumption that *social workers have an ethical obligation* to develop effective ways to work with people who are economically oppressed; that we are concerned about ending injustice instead of merely helping people cope with economic oppression; that we have a range of skills, including clinical skills, that can be rewoven into practice that enhances political and structural change; and that we are ethically responsible for creating the conditions within which effective direct practice and social change can take place. Therefore, it is helpful and ethically necessary for social workers to know what people living in poverty and people organizing to end economic oppression think of them and the field of social work—what strengths they see in us and what impediments and opportunities they see to collaborative work.

Finally, we believe that the *abolition of poverty is our own issue,* essential for our own freedom from economic exploitation and necessary to create conditions that are consonant with our personal and professional values. As previously suggested, we see the war on the poor in broader terms—as a tactical assault on one segment of the larger class of people who do not have control over the means and mechanisms to meet their basic human needs. The desperate restructuring, mass layoffs, privatization and contracting of services, declassification, and falling wage scales in the social services all bear witness to the fact that our class interests lie with those we call our clients. Thus, it is in our best interests to develop an action model of practice that will enable social workers to participate with poor people to end poverty. To this new abolition movement we come not as advocates, but as allies, seeking collaboration in all dimensions of the necessary work including the development of new practice theory.

Thus we come full circle, but in an enhanced way that grounds the notion of unity of strengths in a common political and economic context. Without denying the real material power that social workers can have over the lives of people in client status, Lee (1994) offers a "conceptual framework" that is consonant with our work; she describes

> the roles of a partner, collaborator, coteacher, coinvestigator . . . coactivist and coworker. . . . The prefix *co* is used to indicate that these are roles clients share, with each partner bringing her own expertise and perspective to the processes of empowerment. . . . We are partners against oppression, but in this dance, leading and following may be fluid and interchangeable. The concept of coteaching implies that clients and worker teach each other what they know about the presenting problem and about the oppression(s) faced. (p. 29)

Like Lee, we affirm that professionals benefit from economic arrangements, but we also see social workers as partners with poor people in oppression and, potentially, in liberation. With this in mind, the authors—the social workers and the members of the Kensington Welfare Rights Union—have decided to collaboratively develop models of liberatory practice. The study was proposed to and approved by the KWRU Education Committee and then the KWRU "War Council" (the organization's policy-making body) as part of an ongoing research and action agenda between social workers and KWRU.

Study Design and Methods

In this study we wanted to explore these questions: (1) Based on their past experiences, what do people living in poverty and organizing with KWRU to end poverty think about social workers and the work that they do, and (2) considering what the participants have found helpful about working with social workers and the skills that social workers are trained to have, how do they imagine social workers participating in the movement to end poverty led by the poor?

Given the nature of the study and its mutual knowledge-building/action agenda, a modified participatory research approach was used (Brydon-Miller, 1997; Cornwall & Jewkes, 1995; McGuire, 1987; Williams, 1997; Yeich & Levine, 1992).[7] By using this approach, this study privileges the words and subjective experiences of people living in poverty, thus enabling the participants to take a collaborative role in challenging the dominant discourses that attempt to define and inevitably invalidate their lives. Signs were posted in the KWRU office announcing

---

[7]In true participatory research, all phases of the research process are designed jointly by participant and researcher. Since this study served as the basis for the lead author's thesis, certain parameters were preestablished. In particular, the research questions were developed by the lead author, though negotiated with the KWRU Education Committee. However, the methods used in this collaborative study incorporate the three primary components of participatory research: data gathering, education, and social action. Thus, we refer to the study as a collaborative one conducted in the tradition of participatory research.

the study; significantly the 10 members who responded to the invitation had developed relationships with the social workers through several years of work as allies in KWRU activities—planning meetings, marches and demonstrations; doing child care and "educationals"; and singing in the Economic Human Rights Choir.

Each participant met the following criteria:

- be a person at least 18 years old of any race/ethnicity, religion, gender, or physical ability;
- be currently or have been previously homeless, receiving welfare, and/or living near or below the official poverty line;
- have self-identify as being poor or economically oppressed;
- have had some experience working with a social worker either within public or private human services, school, child welfare, and/or mental health systems;
- have been associated with KWRU as an active member; and
- agree voluntarily to participate in an audiotaped individual interview and a group discussion and to sign an Informed Consent Form.

Profile of the Participants.   Of the 10 participants, 2 identified themselves as "black" men and 2 as "black" women; 2 identified themselves as "Latina" women of Puerto Rican descent; 1 identified herself as a "Caucasian" woman of French and Italian descent; 1 as a "biracial" woman of Caucasian and Native American (Chipowa) descent; 1 as a "white" woman; and 1 identified herself as a "Caucasian" woman who is "probably a lot of different things." The age range of the participants was 26 to 54.

Five of the participants completed high school and attended at least a year of college. The other 5 participants did not have a high school diploma or its equivalency. Nine of the participants identified their socioeconomic status as being poverty level to low income. Only one of the participants, in addition to her work with KWRU, had a full-time paid position at a not-for-profit agency, and she identified her socioeconomic status as low-middle income/working class. Four of the participants were doing unpaid work with KWRU as well as taking care of their younger children who were not yet in school full-time. Three of the participants were working with KWRU full-time without pay, 1 of the participants was working with KWRU and taking college courses part-time in addition to caring for her toddler twins with special needs; 1 of the participants was going to school full-time in addition to sharing the responsibilities of raising children with her partner and working with KWRU. Five of the participants were receiving medical assistance, subsidized housing, food stamps, and TANF/cash assistance for themselves and their children. The oldest of the participants was receiving SSI cash and medical assistance and living with her daughter, who gets subsidized housing. The other 4 participants were receiving no cash, medical, food, or housing assistance from the government. Nine of the 10 participants reported that they received government welfare at some point in their lives.

All of the participants had been homeless in the past; none was homeless at the time of the study. Seven of the 10 participants began working with KWRU while they were homeless and had their subsidized housing as a result of their organizing and demonstrating with KWRU. Three participants had been involved with KWRU since its inception in 1991; 4 participants began working with KWRU 3 years prior to the study; 2 began organizing with KWRU a little more than 5 years prior; and 1 had been involved with KWRU about a year.

Two of the participants were married to each other; 2 were committed partners and co-parenting together; 1 of the participants was living with her husband and their seven children; 1 was living alone (her child recently becoming independent); and 4 of the participants were living alone with their children.

Three of the participants had three children; 1 had one child; 1 had seven children; 2 of the participants (a couple) had three children and were expecting a fourth; 1 had two children and two grandchildren; and 2 of the participants (another couple) had two biological children and another whom they consider their son. The ages of the children and grandchildren range from 3 to 34; out of the 27 children and grandchildren, 18 of them were under the age of 13.

Data Collection and Analysis.   Each of the 10 participants chose a time and place to be interviewed for 1 to 2 hours. Although lines of inquiry were preestablished (and piloted with another volunteer), the interviews were open-ended and conversational in style. Each audiotaped discussion began with the researcher asking the participants to explain how they were involved with KWRU and what motivated them to get involved. Then participants were asked about their past experiences working with social workers, were given examples of some of the work that social workers do, and were asked if they have ever worked with a social worker in such a capacity. Participants were also asked from whom they usually sought assistance (if not from social workers) and why they turned to those person(s).

All audiotapes were transcribed, generating several hundred pages of transcripts, and were read by both social work authors. From these, themes and coding categories were developed following the data analysis protocols of grounded theory research (Glaser, 1992; Glaser & Strauss, 1967; Strauss & Corbin, 1990). The tentative findings were then presented to and discussed with a focus group consisting of the 7 participants who could be available for the meeting and with 1 individually who has a particular interest and expertise in research. Participants were asked to think about and to discuss whether the themes clearly articulate their views. Any discrepancies between the researcher's perceptions of the data and the group's were discussed thoroughly.[8] This process resulted in both clarification of the findings and elaboration of recommendations for social work practice. The process was also intended to create an opportunity for interested participants to learn more about research, thus laying a foundation for additional phases in an ongoing collaborative research and action process. The positive

[8]When differences were not reconciled through discussion, both interpretations were reported in the findings, with participants' views taking precedence.

responses of the members toward participation in this kind of study were reflected in a comment by one member, with others nodding in agreement: "I'm 50 years old and no one's ever asked me what it's been like living in poverty or working with social workers."

Doing the Work: Findings and Recommendations

In this section we summarize the participants' responses. Relying primarily on their words and the collective analysis of the focus group, we present findings and recommendations in three areas: the experience of poverty and welfare, the KWRU response, and the ways that social workers have hindered and helped them.[9] Analysis of the last part generated a set of guidelines for practice for social workers who would be allies in the movement led by the poor to end poverty. All three parts are represented in summary form in Table 11.1.

Experiencing Poverty and Welfare

Poverty and welfare experiences are often linked, but distinguishing between them is increasingly important when so many jobs available to former recipients of welfare-state programs and services leave them in poverty. In this section we present participants' perspectives on the costs of survival in poverty, their experiences of welfare ("The System"), and their perceptions of the institutionalized roles of social workers vis-à-vis poverty and welfare.

Living in Poverty: The Costs of Survival.   While claiming their strengths and efficacy, participants cautioned not to romanticize the notion of survival or underestimate its costs. They described some of the material, moral, and psychological costs of survival in poverty.

Material Costs: Hunger and Homelessness.   One participant summed up a core challenge of poverty: "Trying to figure out everyday, on a daily basis, how they're going to feed their children, how they're going to keep the lights on, their gas on, pay their rent at the beginning of the month, have nice decent attire for their kids, you know." Under these circumstances, it takes only one tug at a linchpin for a family to end up on the street. The following account also highlights the utter failure of the ultimate safety net, the shelter system:

> I had started out, before I became homeless, I was living in an apartment, in a little room that I was paying $275 every two weeks. So, just a little room with a kitchen and I had to share the bathroom. I had three kids, my two babies that I had to buy

---

[9]For the purpose of this chapter, we have summarized and reorganized some of the findings of the Jones (2000) study, and we focus primarily on those pertaining to positive social work practices.

TABLE 11.1   A Framework for Liberatory Practice with People Living in Poverty

Experiencing Poverty and Welfare	The KWRU Response	Guidelines for Practice
Living in Poverty: The Costs of Survival	*Building a Movement to End Poverty*	*Critique of Existing Practices*
	Organizing at the base	Punitive, coercive, and
Material costs:	Education and action vs. social	paternalistic
hunger and homelessness	service delivery	Decontextualized and
Moral costs:	Healing through struggle	depoliticized
daily compromises	Changing hearts and minds	Individualistic and elitist
Psychological costs:	*Commitment to Collaboration*	*Helpful Practices*
self-blame	*and Collectivity*	Support self-liberation
questioning	Collaboration vs. isolation	warn and inform
competence	Collective action	engage knowledge
isolation	Mobilizing strengths and skills	and strengths
frustration		Support healing
undermined relationships	*Leadership Development*	attunement
rage	Historical imperative	engagement
	Leaders versus "clients"	egalitarianism
Living on Welfare: The System		do conscious therapy
Suppression of individuality	*Social Work Functions of KWRU*	release shame and
Workfare: the illusion of	Service roles	blame
inclusion	Counseling roles	contextualize
The work of welfare		politicize assessments
Caseworkers: demeaned and		collectivize
demeaning		experiences
		[Re-]politicize social work
Social Workers and Poverty		structurally situate
Social workers = welfare workers		practice
Institutionalized inequality		make common cause
Institutionalized powerlessness		Build the movement
Institutionalized degradation		connect
		collaborate
		share skills and
		relationships
		research
		range of roles
		alliances
		organize other social
		workers

and I had to share the bathroom. I had three kids, my two babies that I had to buy diapers [for] and stuff like that. But my rent was taking all my money.

So one day the lady came up to me and said we're putting the security up and it's going to be $300. $300 every two weeks. So where was I going to come up with $300, you know. I only was getting $247 by that time . . . She [the landlady] said well if you're not paying, you're going to have to move out. One day I came home, there was a padlock on my door. So, I took my kids to a friend's . . . but it was too crowded, then I moved to another friend's house, and another. . . . You know, I tried to get to the shelters, but the shelter system turned me away.

For most people living in poverty today, employment alone is not the answer: "I'd never been homeless before. I'd been a worker all my life, and I'd worked hard in my lifetime. But because of my health and being sick, I wasn't able to do that anymore." A participant who had been turned away from the city shelters with her toddler twins underscored the need for action: When she became involved with KWRU, protesting on the streets and participating in housing takeovers, the public agency helped her find housing.

Moral Costs: Daily Compromises.   This story illustrates another dimension of living in poverty: Moral people are pushed outside the "arc of legitimacy"—sometimes breaking the law—to survive. As on participant stated, poor people "have to make a lot of concessions in order to continue to eat and stay alive." Not reporting occasional work, using the accounts of dead people to get the electricity turned on, sharing a license plate—such acts of individual survival are undertaken by people who would rather obey the law. Collectivizing acts of survival through KWRU enables people to highlight that the immorality lies in the system that forces them to break the law and not in the acts of the people themselves.

Psychological Costs.   These flow inevitably from being poor in a land of plenty, especially where the popular, policy, and professional message is one: "It's your fault." Participants described *self-blame/low self-esteem, questioning their own competence* (especially as parents), *isolation, frustration, undermined relationships* with family, friends, and community, and—ultimately—*rage*. One participant summed up the psychological costs to self and others when explaining what it felt like to be poor.

Like shit. [pause] Like shit, always, constantly blaming yourself. You might even result in taking your problems out on your children. . . . I'm not saying that's it for me. But, like, I've seen people that want to kill themselves because of their situations, you know. I've seen people abuse their children, and they don't even mean to, it's just their frustration and like not knowing how to handle it, you know. . . . I also notice, like, a relationship deteriorate because of it.

Explaining the importance of political education in KWRU, participants said that poor people's rage is often directed inward and released on family, friends, and neighbors when they cannot identify the enemy or who is oppressing them. It's easier to blame each other than an amorphous, invisible, distant system.

Living on Welfare: The System.   Participants referred to the range of government programs that they had experienced as "The System." This personification of
programs attests to their pervasive power over people's lives. It also underscores
the role they have in perpetuating myths about poor people and, ultimately, in
disciplining them. Participants described how the system works toward these
ends.

Suppression of individuality.   "Immediately when you get on welfare . . . you cease
to be a person and you become a case number," said one participant. Another
elaborated: "The System doesn't really talk to individuals to find out what they
need to get out of poverty. Instead, they put them in classes about what clothes to
wear and how to put on make-up for work."

Workfare: The illusion of inclusion.   The following description of a welfare-to-work
program reveals the gulf between the participants' realities and the "world of
work" being promoted under contemporary policy.

> It was about 50 of us that had to go every week to these sessions and then we had
> to, through the week, pursue a certain task. . . . They had us go on this kind of rig-
> orous program of job search . . . where they put a magnifying glass on you, you
> know; you have to really just concentrate your efforts. So, you have to really fill
> out these slips of paper and show that you've been to these places. And they can
> check on it, because there's a number they can call and spot check. So we all par-
> ticipated in, you know, diligently [and] went on out to places; and we came back
> and here's these guys up there, you know lecturing us and going over our different
> sheets and stuff, and [they] realized that none of us really had been able to find any
> jobs. And so, then they began to try to have a discussion as to why we weren't able
> to find a job. And so they were asking different people, and people were going
> around saying different things; but basically, people were saying fundamentally
> there ain't no jobs, you know. [pause] There ain't no jobs out there, or the jobs that
> they're giving us are just part-time situations. They are not enough for us to sus-
> tain our families and stuff like that. And despite the overwhelming result and dis-
> cussion, a consensus almost, these guys began to get into the problem of body
> language, you know, how you dress. I mean, they were just programmed, you
> know, to go to their next step, which was this is how you sign an application, how
> you dress, and how you talk. And we'd be, everybody would be looking at each
> other saying there's no jobs out there, ain't no job; they don't care how you dress.
> And it wasn't so much that . . . they would take us through these ridiculous situa-
> tions for us to meet the requirements to get our welfare check, and there was no
> real appreciation of the situation that we were dealing under. . . . The social work-
> ers had this mentality that we were next to animals, you know. . . . They were just
> going through the motion. It had nothing to do with the reality of our lives and the
> realities that we were confronted with.

The work of welfare.   As this account indicates, being on welfare (or food stamps, or
subsidized housing, or medical assistance, etc.) is hard work. Those who advocate

for a work solution to poverty are not aware of the nature and costs of the work already being done. To illustrate:

> They [caseworkers] have you running all over the place, you know. Uh, I want a birth certificate, you know, you don't give me a birth certificate, then you don't get . . . TANF or AFDC. . . . Now, if you're a poor person, you ain't got the $10 to go get a birth certificate . . . you know, you don't have the carfare; and they don't want to hear it. They're going to take you off the check.

Caseworkers: demeaned and demeaning.   Despite their criticism of the attitudes and behaviors of the caseworkers, participants were clear that these were shaped by the demands of The System on the workers. Caseworkers were seen as overwhelmed with paperwork, punitive policies, and a lack of the services that people need—in essence, they were seen as victims as well as agents of The System.

Social Workers and Poverty.   Participants affirmed the common class interests of workers in the social welfare system and the poor, but they were also clear that The System institutionalized relations between the groups that disadvantaged the poor and concealed those common interests. Moreover, participants' views of professional social work were shaped by their experiences with public welfare workers.

Social workers = welfare workers.   Even though the KWRU participants and the social work researchers had worked together for a long time, participants generally thought of public welfare workers and social workers as the same. Moreover, they indicated that this was the prevailing perception in poor communities. However much the profession might protest and promote an alternative view, social workers must first work with and through such perceptions as suggested by participants that social workers "take people's kids" and that poor people are "at the mercy of the [caseworker's] decisions to sanction or penalize them."

Institutionalized inequality.   A core dimension of the structured relations between worker and client is inequality.

> I kind of only understood [caseworkers] as somebody that I had an unequal relationship with, almost as a boss–worker relationship, because they determined whether or not I'd get my welfare check, or have any, you know, food, or you know, housing or whatever. So the relationship was always one of kind of unequals.

Institutionalized powerlessness.   Moreover, when working as individuals, poor people have little or no power in The System—not even the power to speak their truths: A participant spoke of feeling threatened by her welfare caseworker's control over her cash benefits when she said, "I was so scared to tell her that I'm homeless because I thought that she was just going to cut my check off. . . . It was just like I'm scared of you. It was like a cat and a dog . . . that's how I felt."

Institutionalized degradation. The last speaker intimated the feelings of degradation devolving from work within the system. Most were clear that the source of degradation was the policies and the structure of the welfare (or post-welfare) system, and not the individual worker, but the worker was the instrument and agent of a suffocating structure nonetheless.

> I came with my application; my application was empty. The food stamps, it said all the benefits, health, food stamps, and checks—cash, I'm sorry. And I told them, listen, I cannot read. She told me, oh, well you should have got somebody to do it, now you're making me do all this. I'm like, excuse me, I'm asking you just to tell me, and I know how to write, and I know how to write the streets whatever, and I'll do it. And she told me, "I sent it to you already," which is true. She sent it to me like four days, but I don't know nobody and I don't trust nobody to let people know that I don't know how to read. You know, and so I'm trusting her as being a caseworker. She should have the courtesy to say, well, don't worry about it, we'll fix this problem. No . . . no, she just like, "what's your name, what's your this, you know, real snotty. And my self-esteem was so low, that I felt so cheap, I was like oh my God, I've got to do something. I even told her like this, "can you make me a copy of this so I will learn so that next time you all send me my 6-month check-up or my year check-up, I'll know how to fill it out." She said, "I don't have time." And I felt like, like I was so low. I just went and cried.

Even when a worker might try to help, participants said, it was difficult to trust a person who is invested with the authority to take your children or decide whether they will eat on a given day.

The Kensington Welfare Rights Union Response

The KWRU response to these conditions is to build a movement to end poverty. Participants explained how and why they were doing this, focusing on that strategic objective and on two major implementing objectives: (1) commitment to collaboration and collectivity and (2) development of leadership from the ranks of the poor. While patently not a social service organization, KWRU was seen as performing certain social work functions in the lives of its members. In this section, we elaborate on each of these themes.

Building a Movement to End Poverty

Organizing at the base. All of the participants were involved in (1) going to welfare offices to advocate for people who have had their benefits cut and to hand out flyers about the organization and its actions; (2) giving out food to engage other poor families; (3) helping people with utility and housing issues; (4) educating themselves and others about their economic human rights, how economic systems oppress people throughout the world, and how past movements have been built; (5) discussing strategies for furthering the growth of the movement; (6) planning and participating in protests, marches, housing takeovers, and tent cities; (7) talking to other poor people to encourage them to grab hold of their rights and grab hold of their dignity again.

Education and action versus social service delivery.   Given this integration of education, action, and meeting basic needs, one participant noted that KWRU "is not just a social service agency. It's actually poor people taking a stand, you know, fighting against—fighting for economic human rights and having a voice." Another participant made a similar distinction: "So, we engage ourselves in activities that seek to get people housing, food, and get the various services, get the needs met immediately through collective efforts. But, at the same time, we do it in such a way as to commit them to social change, to deal with the root of the problem."

Healing through struggle.   By providing safety, solidarity, and opportunities for people to experience their agency, KWRU addresses some of the psychological costs of poverty as well:

> I think KWRU's even, it's more than just about ending poverty. I think it's about letting people know that they are human beings, letting people know that it's okay to feel the way you feel, you know, and letting people know that this is a place you can go to, people you can talk to, and people that do find, people that do find ways to figure out what to do.

Changing hearts and minds.   To achieve its purpose, KWRU seeks to change hearts and minds—both those of people living in poverty and of those who are not:

> [We are] really focusing on this problem of changing people's minds and getting people who have been subjected to 20 to 30 years of concentrated propaganda to the effect that they are subhuman, that they're less than human,—that they're nobodies, lazies, and crazies or something like that—to get them to feel they're human again and feel like they can think for themselves, speak for themselves, and really rise to the level of leadership, not just of themselves, but of the country.

Although their study of social movements instructs that leadership must come from those most directly affected by the particular form of oppression, KWRU members are clear that others not living in poverty also are affected and are potential allies. Just as the enslaved and the free united to abolish slavery, KWRU calls for a new Underground Railroad committed to ending the economic institution of poverty. As one participant pointed out, through this network of allies, KWRU "brings people together that, under other circumstances, would never be in relationship," including students, professors, professionals, and members of other national and international organizations.[10] One member explained that by bringing into dialogue people with similar beliefs but with different

---

[10]In social work, KWRU has an ongoing relationship with the Social Welfare Action Alliance (formerly the Bertha Capen Reynolds Society); for information on the cosponsored "Partners in Crime" project, contact the Underground Railroad—Temple Depot at URR@blue.temple.edu.

resources, skills, and educational backgrounds, KWRU enables individuals who are often kept separate by structural barriers to share their knowledge, ideas, and other resources with one another. While groups and individuals might have very different perspectives on how to end poverty, the joint movement-building objective of KWRU and URR is to convince people that it should—and can—be done.

Commitment to Collaboration and Collectivity.   Through their work, members come to realize about poverty, that "it's got to be something not just wrong with me. It's got to be something wrong in the world, in the system." That being the case, there are no individual solutions to institutional problems.

Collaboration versus isolation.   Isolation is seen as a consequence of and a primary mechanism for maintaining institutional poverty; KWRU counters with "bringing people into a relationship with each other to solve their own problems." As a participant explained, both within the membership and through its alliances, KWRU affirms that "you're just much stronger to deal with questions and understand things through organization than you are as an individual." All of the participants voiced the feeling that being a member of KWRU and being a part of a collective movement has helped them to break their sense of isolation, lessen their feelings of self-blame, and increase their sense of self-efficacy.

Collective action.   Countering the individualist solutions promoted in the mainstream, KWRU's collaborative analyses promote collective action. One participant recounted how she learned the power of collectivity after she was fired from a low-wage job:

> They just gave me a letter and sent me to unemployment. From unemployment, they sent me another letter and told me to go to welfare. When I went to the welfare, they just add up all my pay stubs. . . . And they just said, no, you got to go. They told me I had to be unemployed for 3 months more. They don't know that I lived day-by-day, in a one-bedroom apartment with all these kids, three kids. And I mean I have to feed them and everything. I cried to them. I pleaded. They said no. When I met the organization [KWRU], we went on protests and everything and they [DPW] gave it to me. Like the third day, we went back to the welfare and we complained to them, and before I left out of there, they was giving me food stamps. That showed me that a person by herself cannot do a lot of things. Now, if you be, like, an organization—to let you know how you feel about yourself, I felt great.

Mobilizing strengths and skills.   KWRU does not, however, rely primarily on mobilizing numbers, but on mobilizing the skills and strengths of its individual members and their allies. As described by one participant, strengths are assumed and developed.

> There's a lot of people that we've dealt with, you go back into their histories and you see in the course of their lives the things that they do. There's real strengths and there's real things that are affirmative, but society doesn't give affirmation or

acknowledgement of it. So, we have to find out in activities and educationals a way to give acknowledgement and confirmation to that aspect of people's history, psychology, and personality that reflects their strength and their decency and their dignity as people. We need to bring that out.

A collectivist perspective promotes the valuing of all kinds of skills. The words of another participant underscore this. By no means are [we] from KWRU doctors or social workers. It's just every one of us has so much to give, every one of us has knowledge of so many different things. Some people are great talking with others, some people are great babysitting . . . each one of us has our own thing and some of us are good at organizing—which makes us KWRU.

Referring both to the members and the allies, another participant spoke of the organization's skills transfer methods.

I think that there is a lot that we can learn from each other and share experiences and train each other and stuff. I think that there's a lot of things that, you know, people may be good at or have a certain bent at, and they should contribute what they can and what they like, you know, but with the spirit of us kind of learning from each other and training each other. Because any skill, to me, is transferable— any kind—and that's what we got to be about, is trying to educate each other and to help kind of diversify our skills and our knowledge.

Leadership Development.   As noted, KWRU members' interpretation of history directs their emphasis on leadership of the movement coming from the ranks of the poor, and leadership development pervades the organization's activities.

A historical imperative.   A member explained the emphasis as follows:

I think that all of history corroborates that when social change . . . came to be necessary, it was brought about by the forces that were most dislocated or most devastated by the status quo. . . . And when their position was consolidated in the forefront of the movement, social movement—when they were organized, and their program was placed at the forefront of that social movement—that movement brought about social change successfully.

Leaders versus clients.   Thus, leadership development is integral to the mission of the organization. Another participant explained the way the mission is reflected programmatically.

We don't use a service mentality; we have a leadership mentality. When somebody comes into the office, we try and see that person as a potential leader, as opposed to somebody that we could potentially service. And so that is a very different approach to an individual. Immediately, we see them as somebody that has their own individual needs that gotta be met, but their individual needs only gotta be met because they have an overall responsibility to larger society. So they gotta be treated as a potential leader. And so they have to be a part of trying to solve their own problem as well, which is very different than "you sit here and I'll hook you up" or something.

Social Work Functions of KWRU.   Nevertheless, KWRU clearly performs several functions for its members that social workers think of as theirs. Given a list of typical social work functions, one participant encapsulated the sentiment of most: "Then the people at KWRU are social workers—without paychecks." In particular, members assume service roles and counseling roles.

Service roles.   According to the participants, members of KWRU provide advocacy for individuals with various systems, problem solve, meet people's basic needs, teach values, raise people's political consciousness, write grants for funding, conduct their own educational and research projects, emotionally support their fellow members, and "see people within their whole context, not just in the welfare office."

Counseling roles.   In addition, several of the participants indicated that KWRU fulfills their emotional needs by creating a sense of family and by encouraging them to tell their own stories and talk about their hurt and pain. Illustrating this, one participant said she helps members with "family planning—abortions and birth control," and "I also do one-on-ones constantly where I go out with different individuals. . . . We call it 'lunch.' "

This does not mean that social work is irrelevant in the organization and movement. However, a relevant social work practice would look rather different than most prevailing models.

> The ideal situation is that we are gonna get in this office one or two politically savvy social workers that really help develop the individual from the inside out to be connected to a bigger process. Somebody who thinks and studies and relies upon the collective process.

Such social workers would be most welcome at KWRU. Having learned about the range of social work functions, one focus group participant exclaimed with relief, "Then they could do some of the things I have to do now!" In the final section of this chapter, we turn to the participants' guidelines for the kind of liberatory social work practice they need and want.

Guidelines for Practice

This section is based on an analysis of participants' testimony about experiences they had had with social workers. A summary of the critique of existing practices provides a grounding for their guidelines for helpful practice—social work that will meet their needs. While the group's frame of reference was their work in the movement, the guidelines have clear implications for work with all persons living in poverty.

Critique Of Existing Practices

Punitive, coercive, and paternalistic.   This characterization was sometimes attributed to individual workers, but—as indicated earlier—was more often viewed as a function of the constraints of the social welfare system.

Decontextualized and depoliticized. Participants felt that most social workers were not aware of the realities of poor people's lives, nor of the sociopolitical functions of social work agencies and systems. Thus, social workers "have the privilege not to 'get it,' " as one participant said. Another illustrated: [They give people] "a couple of canned goods when they don't have a can opener to open them." Most participants credited social workers with good intentions; as one said,

> I think that social workers used to have ideals but have changed and now they work within the system and don't change it. Instead they convince the people that need the services that the problems they have are because they made bad choices, instead of understanding the bigger issue that is underlying the problem.

Reminding us that the American economy of abundance is being fueled by expansion and exploitation of low-wage work sectors here and abroad, another spoke to the drift in social work functions propelled by this economic context.

> As time goes on and the economy gets worse [for poor and working class people], more social workers are having to play more and more horrible roles on behalf of the state. That's just going to be like devastating, ya know, in terms of the taking of kids. . . .

Finally, another participant reminded us that not to act is to act.

> A social worker who, in a period of social change, is only seeing their task as to maintain the status quo and keep people coping, accepting the status quo and not become a part of that social change, I think that social worker is not doing real social work.

Individualistic and elitist. As one participant stated, KWRU's model posits that individualism is antithetical to social change and that practice rooted in individualism "teaches [people] to be individuals and just worry about their own problems and separates them from the rest of their community and society," not to see "their struggle bound up with others." Once connected with each other, people can begin to come up with their own collective solutions, but elitism within social work limits collaboration. As one participant said, some social workers think that because "they went to school and what they learnt," they can ask "someone what's the problem and they'll [social workers] come up with the solution." Again, this tendency was seen by many as manifesting a structural relationship more than a personal characteristic.

> It was always underneath even those so-called caring ones, this kind of paternalism. And I think, you know, within the code of ethics, there's this notion of the client, you know, it's like this lawyer-with-the client-relationship. And it says "you have nothing, you have no knowledge of law or nothing like that, you're just this kind of client." You know, I think that that notion translated to a kind of paternalistic kind of relationship.

Helpful Practices. Despite their critiques, most participants were able to recount some positive experiences with social workers.[11] Their accounts generated a profile of helpful practices that was presented to the focus group and, as revised by the group, is presented here. To us, the profile represents a union of the strengths of social workers and of people living in poverty. The practices fall within three categories: support self-liberation, politicize practice, and build the movement.

Support Self-Liberation. In essence, participants said they wanted to be seen as experts on their own lives "in the process of liberating themselves." This stance translates into specific prescriptions: *warn and inform, engage knowledge and strengths, support self-healing, and provide conscious therapy.*

Social workers have a great deal of information about rules and regulations that, rigorously enforced, can result in sanctions and penalties being applied. One participant illustrated the duty to *warn and inform* by referring to a worker she had had:

> I remember her actually kind of warning me, kind of what to do and what not to do in terms of reporting income or reporting, like so-and-so gave me $10 for my birthday, or something like that, what had to be reported and what didn't and how to really get around things. She's the only one that I recall ever really trying to, you know, educate me in terms of how the system worked. . . . You know, she at least seemed to want to relate as human beings.

Helpful workers will also assume and *engage knowledge and strengths.* All participants indicated that the only way social workers can avoid being paternalistic is if they acknowledge that people living in poverty have life experiences and skills that give them a unique perspective from which social workers can learn. Social workers "could be educated. . . . They can open their eyes and see that every poor person that depends on them or needs them is not dumb, is not stupid . . . that they are articulate." Trusting strengths leads to engaging strengths. This participant recounts her experience with "good" child welfare workers:

> They make me feel better, because when they come out to the house, they come out and they talk to you. They don't check your house. . . . They'll just come to check out if everything's okay with the kids and if there's any problems, and I tell them no. *If there's something wrong they would tell me and then I would straighten it out.* [emphasis added]

Another described the best mix of collaboration and supportive services: "They ask people what is best for dealing with their situation instead of telling them, and then help them follow through to meet their needs."

---

[11]Although the participants were aware that the researchers were indeed social workers, most of them thought of our work with KWRU as not falling within our definitions of social work, but rather as something we do because we are "good people." Naturally, the participants with whom we work most closely in the organization held views of social work more like ours.

Given the ravages of poverty, many participants had been in counseling or therapy. Good practice in this realm is built on a foundation of *support for healing*. One participant said her social worker helped her "to identify ways in which I could begin to deal with tremendous amounts of shame that was locked in and to do a whole lot of really good internal work." Another stated that, even though he found his social workers to be condescending, they helped him to build his self-esteem. Participants described specific helpful techniques such as "attunement"—"they're there; they give you a hand in case you're down, they, you know, they know how to pull you up"; "engagement"—participants prefer to talk to a social worker involved with KWRU because "[she's] been around me a long time. . . . If you've been around that person for so long, you know, it's like you got more (pause) comfort"; and "egalitarianism"—social workers who join their specialized expertise with that of people living in poverty help the latter overcome feelings of shame and low self-worth.

On this foundation of support for healing, social workers can construct an approach that one of the participants called *conscious therapy*. To do conscious therapy, participants suggested, social workers must (1) release shame and blame, (2) contextualize people's issues, (3) politicize their assessments, and (4) collectivize experiences. A participant attested to the importance of "releasing shame and blame" as a foundational step:

> I think social workers . . . can play a tremendously powerful role in assisting people in not internalizing their misery and blaming themselves or their kids or their loved ones or their neighbors for whatever they have to endure.

This statement suggests another element of the practice—"contextualizing" or helping people see the ways their behaviors reflect (and can reinforce) objective conditions. Another participant elaborated on this point, and also suggested the need to "politicize assessments" developed in dialogue.

> Poor people need conscious therapy, as opposed to just therapy—an explanation as to why the counselor is suggesting that they look at this, this, and this or do this and this because it relates to the political always, because it's all political.

She continued by pointing out the need to "collectivize experiences."

> So when social workers get poor people to do stuff around self-esteem or more stuff around the individual, they got to simultaneously do more stuff around the group.

Social workers who work with people within the movement to end poverty need to help focus the goals of the therapy around the needs of both the individual and the collective. Participants voiced the concern that social workers who lack a sociopolitical understanding of poverty may conduct individual therapy in a way that does not help people liberate themselves but instead perpetuates self-blame, isolation, and individualism. A social worker, by conducting therapy with KWRU members without having a sociopolitical framework, could inadvertently sabotage the movement building process. But as one participant recommended, social workers can "open their eyes to the sociopolitical realities of poverty and the system" and transform their practice.

[Re-]Politicize Social Work.   Not only therapy, but all practice needs to be politicized—or re-politicized—in two ways: as social workers view and work with people in client status and as they view themselves and function in the sociopolitical arena. First, all practice must be *structurally situated*—that is, social workers need to open up their eyes to the whole social structure and to see how the welfare mom deals with things, and understand the stresses in our situation. They need to

> understand what poor people have to go through just to get to an appointment with kids. They need to take the information they have about society *and act on it.* [emphasis added]

A primary way of acting on it is to *make common cause*—seeing the ways that social workers and poor people alike are targets of the current economic policies, to engage in shoulder-to-shoulder political work, to expect and work for fundamental change.

> I think with the enactment of welfare reform and the coming reenactment, I think a certain polarity is beginning to develop among social workers who are beginning to rethink their relationship with their so-called clients. And I think a real partnership is beginning. People are beginning to think about partnership, and I think that's the combination of the impact that a certain section of organized poor is having on the welfare, to the degree that people are exposed to that kind of experience of poor people organizing themselves to make an impact, to articulate their issues. Social workers who have been in contact with that process, many are beginning to question their ethics and their approach and their relationships. And I think you're seeing some people who are more concerned with being social workers with the small "s" and small "w" than many that's kind of enamored with their degrees and their profession, their so-called professionalism.

Quite possibly the one thing that social workers have most in common with each other is being affected by poverty and economic dislocation, and no sector of the labor force has more daily contact with people living in poverty than social workers. If social workers are willing to make common cause with their natural allies, they can take the next step.

Build the movement.   When asked how social workers could be most helpful, one participant responded, "End poverty with us." Nearly all participants spoke of the importance of social work involvement in the movement to end poverty. Sometimes small acts of solidarity that *connect* people with each other and the movement can make a big difference.

> If social workers really want to be out there helping people, then they'd slip them the paper that says KWRU and tell them the number to call. So many people would listen to them and call that number. That would lead to a way of the person really getting what they need without hurting the social worker's job.

As this statement implies, participants were aware of job constraints; they also realized that not every social worker could commit long hours to movement work. But to the degree possible, participants hoped that social workers would *collaborate* in all aspects of the movement work, "you know, organizing, outreach, helping out with food, helping out with clothing, helping out with child care, everything." Supporting participants' involvement in the movement was seen as helpful, but it was seen as more helpful when social workers joined in the activism, because not only does that show that this is their struggle as well, but if people really heal through struggle, then they are modeling what they believe.

The importance of some form of collaboration is evidenced by reports of all the participants that they would work with social workers if they were allies or members of KWRU; they would be less likely to go to other social workers because they wouldn't trust the social worker to work with them in a helpful, collaborative manner.

An excellent way to collaborate is to *share skills and relationships*. A participant described an ideal social worker as one "that has a holistic approach and helps in the facilitation of somebody's liberation—and sees themselves as coming into a relationship with a particular amount of *skills that can be transferred and utilized.*" [emphasis added] "Research" skills were mentioned as particularly useful, as KWRU members wanted to develop their own knowledge base. All of the participants indicated that the voices of the poor need to be heard to challenge the dominant messages that do not represent their realities. Therefore, participatory research has great potential, because

> it's not just research for research sake, but it's something that arms and equips all the members of Kensington Welfare Rights Union to speak intelligently about things, to develop strategies on what needs to be done and why. . . . So, research becomes, it turns over into a living thing, more than just kind of an academic question. And I think that, in turn, [it] gives something to the people who do the research, as well as to the rest of the people in the organization.

Naturally, participants were aware of the social work research role because of their participation in this project and their contact with social work academics, but many were surprised to hear of the "range of roles" in which social workers were schooled. When told that social workers are trained to do community organizing and to fight social injustice, one participant replied, "Whoa! Where have I been? (laughs) Oh, sorry, I've been in poverty. I didn't know all this was going on." As we noted earlier, many will not see what social workers do in the movement as social work, but as valued labor. Members of the focus group suggested that social workers advertise more about what they do—not as a public relations or marketing tactic, but to make all their skills available even as they do what needs to be done in the organization.

Participants also mentioned the sharing of relationships as significant in movement building. Social workers can and do help craft "alliances" that are significant in the lives of people living in poverty.

> I've been really impressed with the level of organization and connections that they [KWRU social work allies] use. I mean the social workers that are involved with national social work organizations that put the entire organization in relationship with organizations like KWRU. . . . If it starts out from the standpoint of a connection with a social worker, you better believe there will be welfare recipients involved.

Finally, it is clear from this project that there is, in fact, a movement and a model for organizing it that is based on the leadership and unity of the poor. This is not a movement or model that relies on professional organizers for its information, analysis, or efficacy. But there is a place for social workers in the movement, both working directly with groups led by the poor and *organizing other social workers*. Participants emphasized the need for allies who understand the basis for unity with the poor, are willing to convey this to their colleagues, and are able to bring them into relationship with the movement.

In Conclusion, A New Beginning

Reading this chapter, many social workers will recognize that elements of this practice framework already exist in social work. Indeed, the framework was developed primarily from the participants' accounts of their positive experiences with social workers. The framework is especially consonant with some implementations of strengths-based, feminist, empowerment, structural, and generalist models, and it evokes Bertha Capen Reynold's famous dictum—that the best social work is done "on the highways and byways of life." Listening deeply to the voices of these participants, blending them with the lessons of social welfare history, we can hear clearly the challenge and the hope for social work. One of the participants encapsulated both in a closing reflection.

> I think that we're in a period of social change. I think that the dismantling of the welfare state is only an indication of that change. Because I think the change is much more encompassing than that. And I think in periods of social change, the meaning of social work changes too; it has to change. And that means many of the principles or techniques and approaches of social work have to be looked at again in light of the question of whether we're going to be midwives to this change or we're going to just become those who participate in aborting that change. I think that's the challenge before social workers. . . . They have to see . . . how they're affected, too. . . . These so-called welfare reforms are not restricted to welfare recipients. . . . There's a direction that the economy is heading toward, a polarization

between wealth and poverty that is beginning to affect everybody, including social workers. . . . [T]hey can understand the change and see all these ramifications and see how they fit in with regard to the needs of building the movement to help effect that change in the right direction, them understanding their role in terms of change and also understanding that they themselves are affected by it.

DISCUSSION QUESTIONS

1. How have social workers contributed to the oppression of the working class and people in poverty? Have you seen instances of this in your work?

2. What are some of the material, psychological, and moral costs of living in poverty?

3. Why, in a country as a wealthy as this one, is the problem of poverty so persistent and the lives of those who live in poverty (even though they may be working two jobs) made so miserable and abased? What is your obligation as a social worker to confront this inequality and oppression?

4. What are the strengths and assets of people living in poverty? How can you tap into these as a social worker?

5. What does it mean to really work in collaboration with any group of people who happen to be clients? How is that different from being the expert.

REFERENCES

Baptist, W. (1998). *On the poor organizing the poor—The experience of Kensington.* [On-line]. Available: *http://www.libertynet.org/kwru/educat/orgmod2.html*

Baptist, W., Bricker-Jenkins, M., & Dillon, M. (1999). Taking the struggle on the road: The New Freedom Bus—freedom from unemployment, hunger, and homelessness. *Journal of Progressive Human Services, 10,* 7–29.

Belle, D. (1990). Poverty and women's mental health. *American Psychologist, 45,* 385–389.

Bhugra, D. (1997). Setting up psychiatric services: Cross-cultural issues in planning and delivery. *International Journal of Social Psychiatry, 43,* 16–28.

Brydon-Miller, M. (1997). Participatory action research: Psychology and social change. *Journal of Social Issues, 53,* 657–666.

Bulhan, H. (1985). *Frantz Fanon and the psychology of oppression.* New York: Plenum.

Cornwall, A., & Jewkes, R. What is participatory research? *Social Science & Medicine, 41,* 1667–1676.

Cowger, C. D. (1998). Clientism and clientification: Impediments to strengths-based social practice. *Journal of Sociology and Social Welfare, 25,* 25–37.

Glaser, B. (1992). *Basics of grounded theory analysis.* Mill Valley, CA: Sociology Press.

Glaser, B., & Strauss, A. (1967). *The discovery of grounded theory.* New York: Aldine.

Jencks, C. (1996). Can we replace welfare with work? In M. Darby (Ed.), *Reducing poverty in America: Views & approaches.* Thousand Oaks, CA: Sage.

Jones, J. (2000). *Doing the work: A Collaborative study conducted with members of the Kensington Welfare Rights Union, Philadelphia, PA.* Northampton, MA: Smith College School for Social Work.

Lee, J. (1994). *The empowerment approach to social work practice.* New York: Columbia University Press.

McGuire, P. (1987). *Doing participatory research: A feminist approach.* Amherst, MA: University of Massachusetts.

Rapp, C., & Poertner, J. (1992). *Social administration: A client-centered approach.* White Plains, NY: Longman.

Rein, M. (1971). *Social science and public policy.* New York: Penguin.

Rose, S. (1990). Advocacy/empowerment: An approach to clinical practice for social work. *Journal of Sociology & Social Welfare, 17,* 41–51.

Schiller, B. (1998). *The economics of poverty and discrimination* (7th ed.). Upper Saddle River, NJ: Prentice Hall.

Sohng, S. (1998). Research as a empowerment strategy. In L. Gutiérrez, R. Parsons, & E. Cox (Eds.), *Empowerment in social work practice: A sourcebook.* Pacific Grove, CA: Brooks/Cole.

Strauss, A., & Corbin, J. (1990). *Basics of qualitative research: Grounded theory procedures and techniques.* Newbury Park, CA: Sage.

Williams, L. (1997). *Grassroots participatory research: A working report from a gathering of practitioners.* Knoxville, TN: Community Partnership Center, University of Tennessee.

Yeich, S., & Levine, R. (1992). Participatory research's contribution to a conceptualization of empowerment. *Journal of Applied Social Psychology, 22,* 1894–1907.

12 Turnaround People and Places

Moving from Risk to Resilience

BONNIE BENARD

Do most young people from high-risk situations such as abusive homes, alcoholic or drug-abusing parents, multiple foster care placements, overcrowded and under-funded schools, and/or poverty-stricken communities end up in trouble as adults? Are there any personal strengths that assist a young person in navigating these environmental risks all around them—including an exploitive media and public policies that would rather incarcerate than educate or rehabilitate? Are there any environmental resources that protect a young person exposed to these prolonged and pervasive risks?

These are precisely the types of research questions that have resulted in the new and growing field of resilience, the study of how individuals throughout the human lifespan have successfully transformed serious and multiple risks and adversity to become, in the words of the premier resilience researcher Emmy Werner, "competent, confident, and caring adults" (Werner and Smith, 1982, 1992).

Resilience research is a true gift to the fields of education, youth services, and strengths-based social work. It gives all who work with children, youth, and families a research-based answer to the questions: What works to prevent negative developmental outcomes? How best can we intervene to promote positive youth development in *all* children and youth, especially those with the odds stacked against them? Resilience research provides the answers by identifying the specific *protective factors,* the developmental supports and opportunities that have facilitated young people's healthy and successful development—even in the face of stress, adversity, and trauma.

This research also identifies the specific strengths, the positive developmental outcomes that have resulted from youth experiencing critical protective factors in their families, schools, and communities. Resilience research then provides a research-based *language of* strengths—both environmental and personal—for grounding and pursuing the *strengths perspective* in social work practice and the

youth development approach in prevention services. This language gives practitioners the vocabulary needed to look for and name youth's strengths and mirror their
strengths back to them, and to perform program evaluation.

The following three short stories illustrate not only the nature of protective
factors and personal strengths but also some major messages for practitioners, policy makers, and the American public. These stories will frame our discussion of
resilience practice.

The other evening I entered the C train at 59th Street. I immediately became
absorbed in a book when I heard a voice say, "Gary, is that you?" I looked up and
saw the face of a young man whom it took me a moment to place. Finally, I said,
"Jimmy, how are you doing?"

It had been 7 years since I had seen him last at Green Chimneys Children's
Services. He told me that he was living in his own apartment and had just celebrated his 22nd birthday. Jimmy was one of the most difficult kids that I had
worked with and I hadn't forgotten him. As we talked he said, "You know I made
a lot of mistakes when I was at Green Chimneys. I made even more mistakes when
I left. I had a big drug problem. But I went to rehab for 19 months and I'm doing
great now. I've been clean for over 2 years. I have two jobs. I'm supporting myself
and I have a really nice girlfriend."

To be honest, he was doing much better than I ever would have predicted.
Indeed, I've often talked about him over the years precisely because he was so difficult. But it was Jimmy's next comment that will stay with me now: "Gary, even
though I was a real pain when I lived at Green Chimneys, I want you, and any of
the other staff who are still there, to know that I really did learn from all of you.
Some days when I was really down, I remembered what you all told me and it
really helped me. And I'm not just saying that. I really mean it." It was a "reward"
I'll carry around for awhile. (Mallon, 1995)

Carmella was a recipient of multiple social services while growing up. One of them,
the foster care system, placed her at a boarding school, which dropped her off at the
Salvation Army at the age of 18. Homeless, and with no family, Carmella began
volunteering at her homeless shelter, while finishing her high school diploma.
Carmella's courage and tenacity led her to become a board member of a grass-roots
advocacy organization; to be the first woman selected for the city's midnight basketball league; and to be adopted by the volunteer director of a homeless advocacy
group. As an ally, Carmella organized a youth council in the housing development
where she played basketball. The council suggested to city leaders ways in which
the housing development could be improved for residents. The young people also
created a video about their lives in the development. Carmella is now finishing college and continuing to work full-time with young people. (Kretzmann & Schmitz,
1999)

I [Alexandra] first moved away from my father the day before I started high school.
As I headed toward my new home . . . I remembered the many times I had to cook
and eat alone, waiting for my dad to remember me and come home. I knew I
deserved better. Since that day, however, I have become too familiar with moving
from household to household. . . . In the middle of my junior year, I found myself

without a home, a steady source of income, or a family. . . . I almost lost my sense of identity and any motivation. . . . During these difficult times, I found the stability that was lacking in my personal life at school. I went to the Peer Resource Center . . . because I needed support. . . . I became very active in the Peer Resource Center, where I was able to form close ties while helping others with difficulties like mine. . . . Although I have had an overwhelmingly stressful past, my experiences have been essential in my growth as a person and as a friend. I am proud of the fact that my forced independence empowered me to find the initiative and strength to provide for my own well-being. (Kent, 1995)

The messages embedded in these stories clearly reveal to practitioners, policy makers, and the public critical truths that fly in the face of media hyperbole, political propaganda, and the personal beliefs of many who work with young people.

The Core Beliefs of Strengths/ Resilience Approach to Youth

1. Most High-Risk Youth Make It.

When tracked into adulthood, resilience researchers worldwide have documented the amazing finding that at least 50 percent and usually closer to 70 percent of these children and youth from high-risk environments grow up to be not only successful by societal indicators but have personal strengths usually falling into the following categories: social competence and connectedness, problem-solving and metacognition skills, a sense of autonomy, and a sense of purpose and future. These skills and feelings particularly stand out in the stories of Carmella and Alexandra.

This finding belies the pubic perception or myth that youth with multiple risk factors are doomed and don't make it. Certainly all of the youth in the above stories would have been considered lost causes. The preoccupation with risk factors and high-risk youth over the last decade has played into a general societal loss of belief in the capacities of *all* young people. For example, a survey conducted by the Public Agenda in June 1997, *Kids These Days: What Americans Really Think About the Next Generation,* identified high levels of antagonism towards teenagers with two-thirds of the American public using only negative adjectives to describe them: rude, irresponsible, and wild, to name a few. And nearly half of those polled had a negative view of children and characterized them as spoiled and lacking discipline. These attitudes play right into the current anti-youth political climate and support the further criminalization and incarceration of young people despite the overwhelming evidence to the contrary—*that most youths do better than we think, even in the face of adversity.*

2. All Individuals Have Innate Resilience.

Many researchers and practitioners have latched onto the personal strengths of resilient youth found in the research. They see the need to create a myriad of social-emotional and life skills programs to directly teach these resilience skills.

The strong message in resilience research, however, is that these strengths and competencies are outcomes—not causes—of resilience. Werner and Smith (1992) refer to resilience as an innate "self-righting mechanism" (p. 202) and Lifton (1994) identifies resilience as the human capacity of all individuals to transform and change—no matter what risks *they face and challenges they endure.*

We are genetically hardwired to form relationships (social competence), to problem-solve (metacognition), to develop a sense of identity (autonomy), and to plan and hope (a sense of purpose and future). These are the growth capacities that have enabled survival throughout human history. The perspective of resilience as a gift we all have also challenges the myth of scarcity, that resilience belongs to only a few super-kids as well as the myth that, somehow, to have it we have to be good enough, old enough, white enough, or male enough. It also means that, like Jimmy in the foregoing story, even though a young person may not presently be acting in a healthy way, his resilient nature recognizes health and healthy people and messages and stores these away as a future possibility.

3. People and Places Make A Difference!

So what does all this mean for social workers? A common finding in resilience research is the power of one person—often unbeknownst to him or her—to tip the scale from risk to resilience. Werner and Smith (1989) found that these "turn-around" people played many roles: neighbors, friends, ministers, youth workers, extended family members, siblings, a parent, a teacher. In Dave Pelzer's accounting of his horrific captivity by his abusive mother, his savior was Pam, his social worker, who "hugged [him] and never let go first" (1995). Barbara Staggers, the director of adolescent medicine at Oakland Children's Hospital, states, "With all the kids I know who make it, there's one thing in common: an individual contact with an adult who cared and who kept hanging in with the teen through his hardest moments" (Cited in Foster, 1994).

Repeatedly, these turnaround people are described as providing, in their own personal styles and ways, the three critical protective factors consistently identified in the research: caring relationships, high expectation messages, and opportunities for participation and contribution (Benard, 1991).

They are described, first and foremost, as *caring*. They convey *loving support*— the message of being there for a youth and the declaration of trust and unconditional love. Resilient survivors talk about relationships characterized by "quiet availability," "fundamental positive regard," and "simple sustained kindness"—a touch on the shoulder, a smile, a greeting (Higgins, 1994, pp. 324–325). Higgins' subjects (all sexual abuse survivors) "strongly recommended that those of you who touch the life of a child constructively, even briefly, should *never* underestimate your possible corrective impact on that child" (p. 325). *Respect,* having a person "acknowledge us, see us for who we are—as their equal in value and importance" also counts critically in turnaround relationships and places (Meier, 1995, p. 120).

These caregivers also convey a sense of *compassion*—nonjudgmental love that looks beneath a youth's negative behavior and sees the pain and suffering. They do not take the youth's behavior personally. They understand that no matter how negative a young person's behavior, the youth is doing the best she or he can given how she or he *sees* the world. Sandy McBrayer, founder of an alternative school for homeless youth and 1994 National Teacher of the Year, declares, "People ask me what my 'methods' are. I don't have a method. But I believe one of the things that makes me an adequate or proficient teacher is that I never judge" and "I tell my kids I love them every day" (Bacon, 1995, p. 44).

Finally, being *interested in, actively listening to,* and *getting to know the gifts* of young people conveys the message, "You are important in this world; you matter." Alice Miller's account of resilient survivors of childhood sexual abuse and trauma validates the healing power of youth being able to tell their story to someone who believes them: "It turns out in every case [of successful adaptation] that a sympathetic and helpful witness confirmed the child's perceptions, thus making it possible for him to recognize that he had been wronged" (1990).

At the core of caring relationships are *positive and high expectations* that reflect the adult's deep belief in the young person's innate resilience and self-righting capacities. Werner (1996) states, "One of the wonderful things we see now in adulthood is that these children really remember one or two teachers who made the difference . . . who looked beyond outward experience, their behavior, their unkempt—oftentimes—appearance and saw the promise" (p. 24).

A consistent description of turnaround youth workers is their *seeing the possibility:* "They held visions of us that we could not imagine for ourselves" (Delpit, 1996, p. 199). These teachers, youth workers, counselors, and social workers follow up this belief message with a challenge message: "You can make it; you have everything it takes to achieve your dreams; and I'll be there to support you." This message is consistently documented by young people of color who have survived poverty, poor schools, and discrimination to become highly successful adults (Clark, 1983; Gandara, 1995). These adults not only see the possibility and communicate the challenge message, they *recognize existing strengths, mirror them back,* and help young people see where they are strong (see Figure 12.1).

FIGURE 12.1   Strengths Practice

- Listen to their story
- Acknowledge the pain
- Look for strengths
- Ask questions about survival, support, positive times, interests, dreams, goals, and pride
- Point out strengths
- Link strengths to client's goals and dreams
- Link client to resources to achieve goals and dreams
- Find opportunities for client to be teacher/paraprofessional

Effective youth workers are *youth centered:* They use the young person's own strengths, interests, goals, and dreams as the beginning point for learning and helping. Thus, they tap young people's intrinsic motivation, their existing, innate drive for learning and personal growth. John Seita, who grew up in multiple foster homes, tells the story of his turnaround social worker: "Mr. Lambert, who was a recent graduate of college when he first met me, had no training in bonding with relationship-resistant youth. Few of us do. But he reached me through the back door. He doggedly attempted to find a *special interest* of mine, namely my dreams of being a sports hero. Although I did not trust other adults, he connected with me through a special interest" (1996, p. 88).

Turnaround people assist youth, especially those who have been labeled or who have suffered oppression, in understanding their personal power to reframe their life narratives from damaged victim to resilient survivor. Turnaround people help youth see the power they have to think differently about and construct alternative stories of their lives. They help them (1) to not take personally the adversity in their lives ("You aren't the cause, nor can you control, your father's drinking/your friend's racist remarks"); (2) to not see adversity as permanent ("This too shall pass"); and (3) to not see setbacks as pervasive ("You can rise above this"; "This is only one part of your life experience") (adapted from Seligman, 1995).

Creating the opportunities for youth participation and contribution is a natural outgrowth of working from this strengths-based perspective. Werner and Smith (1992, p. 205) found that while their resilient survivors weren't unusually talented, "They took great pleasure in *interests and hobbies* [my emphasis] that brought them solace when things fell apart in their home lives. They also engaged in activities that allowed them to be part of a *cooperative enterprise,* [my emphasis] such as being a cheerleader for the home team or raising an animal for the 4-H Club [as well as] active involvement in a church or religious community"— activities that connected them to a group that became a surrogate family.

It is through having the opportunities to be heard, to voice one's opinion, to make choices, to engage in active problem solving, to express one's imagination, to work with and help others, and to give one's gift back to the community that youth develop the attitudes and competencies characteristic of healthy development and successful learning: social competence, problem solving, and a sense of self and future. Giving youths real choices and decision-making power characterized the successful neighborhood organizations in the nationwide study conducted by McLaughlin, Irby, & Longman (1994). In the long-term evaluation of Big Brothers/Big Sisters mentoring efforts, "The longest lasting and most regularly meeting matches were those in which the adult took a developmental approach to the relationship—allowing it to proceed at its own pace as the pair engaged in recreational activities that the youth had a voice in choosing" (Tierney, Grossman, & Resch 1995).

Infusing the power to make choices and decisions into the life of the classroom, school, community organization, after-school program, treatment program, and so on does not necessarily require any special add-on programs but rather requires adults to let go of their control orientation, to see youth as a valuable resource, to willingly share power with youth, to create a system based on reciprocity and collaboration rather than on control and competition. Asking questions that encourage critical, reflective thinking; making learning more hands-on and experiential; involving youth in curriculum and program planning; using participatory evaluation strategies; and letting youth create the program/group norms and agreements are all ways to invite the participation and encourage the motivation of youth on an ongoing basis.

Creating ongoing opportunities for reflection and dialogue around issues that have meaning for youth—especially those related to sexuality, drug use, and family communication—is continually identified by youth as what they want in youth programming (Brown, D'Emidio-Caston, Kauffman, Goldsworthy-Honner, & Alioto, 1995). When youth are given the opportunity, especially in a small group context, to give voice to their realities, to discuss their experiences, beliefs, attitudes, and feelings, and are encouraged to thoughtfully question societal messages—those from the media and their own conditioned thinking around these issues—we are empowering them to be critical thinkers and decision makers around the important issues in their lives.

Werner and Smith (1992) also found that "acts of required helpfulness" (p. 205) such as caring for younger siblings or managing the household when a parent was incapacitated were associated with all these positive developmental outcomes. Programmatic approaches built on this concept, on providing the opportunities to give one's gift back to the community—whether in a cooperative learning or peer support group, a cross-age/peer helping, or community service—have also documented these positive outcomes (Melchior, 1996, 1998; Slavin, 1990).

This giving back was clearly a powerful hook for both Carmella and Alexandra in the preceding stories. The experience changed their self-perceptions from being a problem and *recipient* of services to being a resource and *provider* of services.

4. It's How We Do What We Do That Counts.

The major message from long-term studies of human development as well as successful schools and community youth-serving organizations (McLaughlin et al., 1994; Rutter, Maughan, Mortimore, Ouston, & Smith, 1979) is that it's how we do what we do that counts. These three protective factors are so powerful because they are precisely what meet our basic human needs for love and belonging, respect, power, accomplishment, challenge and learning, and, ultimately, meaning. No matter what official role we play in a young person's life (teacher, parent, neighbor, social worker, youth worker, minister, coach, extended family member), we can do it in the caring and empowering way that describes turnaround people—and at no extra cost!

It is what we *model* that makes the final difference. Social learning theorists tell us that most of our learning comes from the modeling around us. If we are caring and respectful, if we help our youth discover and use their strengths, if we give them ongoing responsibilities as active decision makers, they will learn empathy, respect, the wise use of power, self-control, and responsibility.

Moreover, when we ourselves model this invitational behavior, we are creating a *climate* in which caring, respect, and responsibility are the behavioral norms. Schools, classrooms, programs, groups, services, and community-based organizations that have been turnaround places for young people are continually described by them as being like "a family, a home, a community"—even "a sanctuary": "School was my church, my religion. It was constant, the only thing that I could count on every day. . . . I would not be here if it was not for school" (Children's Express, 1993). Our most challenging youth—disconnected and disempowered youth—must be invited back in through relationships and responsibilities.

5. It All Starts with Our Belief in Innate Capacity.

Certain programmatic approaches have proven particularly effective at providing the structure for developing caring relationships as well for providing opportunities for active participation and contribution: small group process, cooperative learning, peer helping, cross-age mentoring, and community service. However, the key point from resilience research—and from our own life experience—is that successful development and transformative power exists not in programmatic approaches per se but at the deeper level of relationships, beliefs, and expectations, and the willingness to share power. Asa Hilliard (1991) advises that, "To restructure [our programs, services, etc.] we must first look deeply at the goals that we set for our children and the beliefs that we have about them. Once we are on the right track there, then we must turn our attention to the delivery systems, as we have begun to do. Cooperative learning is right. Technology access for all is right. Multiculturalism is right. *But none of these approaches or strategies will mean anything if the fundamental belief system does not fit the new structures that are being created*" (p. 36, my emphasis).

The bottom line and starting point for creating youth-serving organizations, programs, services, classrooms, and schools that tap young people's capacities is the deep belief on the part of adult staff that every youth has innate resilience. This means every adult in the program, school, service agency, and organization must personally grapple with questions like: What tapped my resilience? What occurred in my life that brought out my strength and capacity? How am I connecting this knowledge to what I do in my program?

Believing in our young people's capacities requires foremost that we believe in our own innate resilience, our own capacity to transform and change. It means too that to teach our youth about their internal power, we first must see we have the power to rise above our past and our current life stresses, to let go of our conditioned thinking, and to access our innate capacities for compassion, intuition, self-efficacy, and hope. We must also reframe the stories we tell ourselves about who we are: We must not define ourselves only through our problems but through our strengths as well, and we must not take our own stressors as personal, permanent, or pervasive. We cannot teach this to our young people unless we live this ourselves: Our walk always speaks louder than our talk. When we believe in and tap our own innate resilience, it follows that we also believe this capacity exists in the young people we work with. And only once this belief is in place are we able to model the caring, positive expectations, and invitational behavior that engages the innate resilience in our young people and promotes their positive development.

Thus, nurturing the staff becomes the bottom line for promoting the resilience in the young people we serve. Resilience applies to all of us: What has sustained youth in the face of adversity is also what enables social workers, teachers, and youth workers to overcome the incredible stresses they face in working in schools and communities that have few resources and many environmental stresses. Staff need supportive caring relationships with their colleagues, high expectations on the part of their administrators and managers, and time and opportunities for professional development and to work collegially together to build a sense of professional community and a learning network for sharing their expertise. We, too, long for love and belonging, for recognition for our work, for personal power and control, for challenge, and, ultimately, for meaningful work that makes a difference. Strengths-based social work practice offers this promise and possibility.

Conclusion

Whether parents or professionals, classroom or community, we can become turnaround people and turn the environment into a turnaround place. Figure 12.2 summarizes the critical steps for creating turnaround places. Figure 12.3 is a checklist that allows you to assess to what degree you and your agency or school creates a place that nourishes and nurtures those keys to resilience: caring and connection, positive and high expectations, and participation. The message here is, "It can be done."

FIGURE 12.2 Creating Turnaround Places

■ **Reflect personally and engage in dialogue as a staff about your beliefs in innate resilience.** What does it mean in my program if *all* kids have it? Coming to this belief as a social worker is the first step in creating resilience-enhancing relationships.

■ **Form a resiliency study group.** Read the research on resiliency, including the studies of successful community-based organizations and youth programming. Share stories—both personal and literary—of successful overcoming of the odds. "It is important to read about struggles that lead to empowerment and to successful advocacy, for resilient voices are critical to hear within the at-risk wasteland" (Polakow, 1995, p. 269). Working against the dominant risk paradigm means we need the support and "shelter of each other."

■ **Build caring relationships.** This includes not only social worker to youth relationships but youth to youth, staff to staff, and staff to parent. This rapport is the critical motivational foundation for successful learning and development. A major role of social workers in promoting resilient young people is to not only connect youth to formal mentoring programs but to help link them to and nurture their relationships with the naturally occurring mentors in their lives.

■ **Play to young people's strengths.** Starting with young people's strengths—instead of their problems and deficiencies—enlists their intrinsic motivation and their positive momentum, and keeps them in a hopeful frame of mind to learn and to work on any concerns.

(continued)

FIGURE 12.2   Continued

■ **Teach youth they have innate resilience.** Show them they have the power to construct the meaning they give to everything that happens to them. Help them recognize how their own conditioned thinking—the environmental messages they've internalized that they're not good enough, smart enough, thin enough, and so on—blocks access to their innate resilience. Metacognition, the recognition of how their thinking influences their feelings and behaviors, is the most powerful tool we can give our youth. In a Miami, Florida, study, the dropout rate for youth from a public housing community fell to nearly zero when they were taught they have this power (Mills, 1991).

■ **Provide ongoing opportunities for young people to develop relationships, use their strengths, follow their interests and imagination, help others, and make decisions.** Remember to ask them and they'll tell you what they want and need. Social workers can assist youth in connecting to naturally occurring supports and opportunities in their schools and communities: afterschool programs, community-based organizations focused on their respective interests, apprenticeships, advocacy groups, and leadership programs. The young people you work with deserve the best society has to offer.

■ **Be an ally to young people.** In our current anti-youth climate it is imperative that social workers speak out for and on behalf of young people at every opportunity. Working in adult-youth partnerships for causes you—and they—believe in is not only fun but a powerful expression of the intergenerational support and guidance so lacking in our society.

■ **Try an initial experiment using the resiliency approach.** Choose one of your most challenging youth. Look for and identify all her strengths. Mirror back her strengths. Teach her she has innate resilience and the power to create her own reality. Create opportunities to have her participate and contribute her strengths. Be patient. Focus on small victories (they often grow into major transformations).

■ **Relax, have fun, and trust the process!** Working from our own innate resilience and well-being engages the innate resilience and well-being of our youth—and any other clients for that matter. Thus, counseling becomes much more effortless and enjoyable. Moreover, resiliency research gives us all the proof we need to lighten up, let go of our tight control, be patient, and trust the process.

■ **Know that you are making a difference.** When you care, believe in, and invite back our disconnected and disempowered youth, you are not only enabling their healthy development and successful learning. You are, indeed, creating social change from the inside out—building compassionate and creative citizenry with a sense of social and economic justice.

FIGURE 12.3 Environmental Strategies for Tapping Resilience Checklist

[Circle the degree to which each protective factor is present.]

Caring and Support

1	2	3	4	5	Creates and sustains a caring climate
1	2	3	4	5	Aims to meet basic developmental needs
1	2	3	4	5	Is available/responsive
1	2	3	4	5	Has long-term commitment
1	2	3	4	5	Creates one-to-one time
1	2	3	4	5	Actively listens/gives voice
1	2	3	4	5	Uses appropriate self-disclosure
1	2	3	4	5	Pays attention
1	2	3	4	5	Shows interest
1	2	3	4	5	Believes/sees the innocence
1	2	3	4	5	Checks in
1	2	3	4	5	Gets to know hopes and dreams
1	2	3	4	5	Gets to know life context
1	2	3	4	5	Gets to know interests
1	2	3	4	5	Shows respect
1	2	3	4	5	Fundamental positive regard
1	2	3	4	5	Is nonjudgmental
1	2	3	4	5	Looks beneath "problem behavior"
1	2	3	4	5	Reaches beyond the resistance
1	2	3	4	5	Uses humor/smiles
1	2	3	4	5	Flexibility
1	2	3	4	5	Patience
1	2	3	4	5	Uses community-building process
1	2	3	4	5	Creates small, personalized groupings
1	2	3	4	5	Creates opportunities for peer helping
1	2	3	4	5	Uses cross-age mentoring

Creates Connections to Resources

1	2	3	4	5	Education
1	2	3	4	5	Employment
1	2	3	4	5	Recreation
1	2	3	4	5	Health and social services

(continued)

FIGURE 12.3   Continued

High Expectations

1	2	3	4	5	Sustains a high expectation climate
1	2	3	4	5	Models innate resilience
1	2	3	4	5	Believes in innate resilience of all
1	2	3	4	5	Believes in innate capacity of all to learn
1	2	3	4	5	Strives to develop holistic competencies
1	2	3	4	5	Sees culture as an asset
1	2	3	4	5	Shows common courtesy
1	2	3	4	5	Respects others
1	2	3	4	5	Challenges and supports ("You can do it; I'll be there to help.")
1	2	3	4	5	Connects learning to interests, strengths, experiences, goals, and dreams
1	2	3	4	5	Encourages creativity and imagination
1	2	3	4	5	Conveys optimism and hope
1	2	3	4	5	Affirms/encourages the best in others
1	2	3	4	5	Attributes the best possible motive to behavior
1	2	3	4	5	Articulates clear expectations/boundaries
1	2	3	4	5	Models boundary-setting/adaptive distancing
1	2	3	4	5	Uses rituals and traditions
1	2	3	4	5	Recognizes strengths and interests
1	2	3	4	5	Mirrors strengths and interests
1	2	3	4	5	Uses strengths and interests to address concerns/problems
1	2	3	4	5	Uses a variety of instructional strategies to tap multiple intelligences
1	2	3	4	5	Employs authentic assessment
1	2	3	4	5	Helps to reframe self-image from at-risk to at-promise
1	2	3	4	5	Helps to reframe problems to opportunities
1	2	3	4	5	Teaches healthy thinking process
1	2	3	4	5	Sees students as constructors of own knowledge and meaning
1	2	3	4	5	Teaches critical analysis
1	2	3	4	5	Encourages self-awareness of moods and thinking

FIGURE 12.3   Continued

Opportunities for Participation

1	2	3	4	5	Sustains a democratic climate
1	2	3	4	5	Provides opportunities for planning
1	2	3	4	5	Provides opportunities for decision making
1	3	3	4	5	Provides opportunities for problem solving
1	2	3	4	5	Empowers group to create rules

Infuses Communication Skills

1	2	3	4	5	Reading
1	2	3	4	5	Writing
1	2	3	4	5	Relationship

Creates Opportunities for Creative Expression

1	2	3	4	5	Art
1	2	3	4	5	Music
1	2	3	4	5	Writing
1	2	3	4	5	Storytelling/drama
1	2	3	4	5	Invites the strengths, interests, goals, and dreams of each person
1	2	3	4	5	Gives meaningful responsibilities

Welcomes Marginalized Groups

1	2	3	4	5	Girls/women
1	2	3	4	5	Persons of color
1	2	3	4	5	Persons with special needs
1	2	3	4	5	Infuses service/active learning
1	2	3	4	5	Uses adventure/outdoor experience-based learning
1	2	3	4	5	Offers community service
1	2	3	4	5	Offers peer-helping
1	2	3	4	5	Offers cross-age helping
1	2	3	4	5	Offers peer support groups
1	2	3	4	5	Uses facilitative teaching style
1	2	3	4	5	Uses cooperative learning
1	2	3	4	5	Provides ongoing opportunities for personal reflection
1	2	3	4	5	Provides ongoing opportunities for dialogue/discussion

DISCUSSION QUESTIONS

1. Reflecting back on your life, what personal attitudes and competencies have especially helped you succeed and grow? What relationships, messages, experiences, and opportunities have made you strong?

2. Can you identify a special mentor, teacher, or helping professional that made a difference in your life? What was it about him/her that influenced you? What impact has this had on your career choice and other decisions?

3. Is your agency or field placement a turnaround place? If it is, why do you think so? If it is not, how could it become such a place?

4. As social worker or helper, what would you have to do in your approach to your work to become a turnaround worker? Could you apply these ideas to an individual or family or community you might be working with?

REFERENCES

Bacon, J. (1995). The place for life and learning: National teacher of the year, Sandra McBrayer. *Journal of Emotional and Behavioral Problems, 3,* 42–45.

Benard, B. (1991, August). *Fostering resiliency in kids: Protective factors in the family, school, and community.* Portland, OR: Northwest Regional Educational Laboratory.

Brown, J., D'Emidio-Caston, M., Kauffman, K., Goldsworthy-Honner, T., & Alioto, M. (1995). *In their own voices: Students and educators evaluate California school-based drug, alcohol, and tobacco education programs.* Bethesda, MD: Pacific Institute of Research and Evaluation.

Children's Express (1993). *Voices from the future: Children tell us about violence in America.* New York: Crown.

Clark, R. (1983). *Family life and school achievement: Why poor Black children succeed or fail.* Chicago: University of Chicago Press.

Delpit, L. (1996). The politics of teaching literate discourse. In W. Ayers and P. Ford (Eds.), *City kids, city teachers: Reports from the front row.* New York: New Press.

Foster, D. (1994, July/August). The disease is adolescence. *Utne Reader, 64,* 50–56.

Gandara, P. (1995). *Over the ivy walls: The educational mobility of low-income Chicanos.* Albany: State University of New York Press.

Higgins, G. (1994). *Resilient adults: Overcoming a cruel past.* San Francisco: Jossey-Bass.

Hilliard, A. (1991). Do we have the will to educate all children? *Educational Leadership, 49,* 31–36.

Kent, A. (1995). The power of peer helping. From the Fourth Annual University of California–Berkeley Incentive Awards Dinner Program and Activities Report, San Francisco, June 18.

Kretzmann, J., & Schmitz, P. (1999). It takes a child to raise a whole village. *Resiliency in Action, 1,* 3.

Lifton, R. (1994). *The protean self: Human resilience in an age of fragmentation.* New York: Basic Books.

Mallon, G. (1995). Letter to the editor. *Youth Today, 4,* (November/December), 46.

McLaughlin, M., Irby, M., & Langman, J. (1994). *Urban sanctuaries: Neighborhood organizations in the lives and futures of inner-city youth.* San Francisco: Jossey-Bass.

Meier, D. (1995). *The power of their ideas.* Boston: Beacon Press.

Melchior, A. (1996, 1998). National evaluation of Learn and Serve America School and Community-Based Programs: Interim and final reports. Washington, DC: Corporation for National Service.

Mills, R. (1991). A new understanding of self: The role of affect, state of mind, self-understanding, and intrinsic motivation. *Journal of Experimental Education, 60,* 67–81.

Pelzer, D. (1995). *A child called It: One child's courage to survive.* Deerfield Beach, FL: Health Communications.

Polakow, V. (1995). Naming and blaming: Beyond a pedagogy of the poor. In B. Swadener and S. Lubeck (Eds.). *Children and families at promise: Deconstructing the discourse of risk.* Albany: State University of New York Press.

Rutter, M., Maughan, B., Mortimore, P., Ouston, J., & Smith, A. (1979). *Fifteen thousand hours.* Cambridge, MA: Harvard University Press.

Seita, J. (1996). *In whose best interest? One child's odyssey, a nation's responsibility.* Elizabethtown, PA: Continental Press.

Seligman, M. (1995). *The optimistic child.* Boston: Houghton Mifflin.

Slavin, R. (1990). *Cooperative learning: Theory, research, and practice.* Englewood Cliffs, NJ: Prentice Hall.

Swadener, B., and Lubeck, S. (Eds.). (1995). *Children and families at promise: Deconstructing the discourse of risk.* Albany: State University of New York Press.

Tierney, J., Grossman, J., & Resch, N. (1995). *Making a difference: An impact study of Big Brothers/Big Sisters.* Philadelphia: Public/Private Ventures.

Utne Reader, (1994). Today's teens: Dissed, mythed, and totally pissed: A generation and a nation at risk. *Utne Reader, 64,* 50–56, July/August.

Werner, E. (1996). How kids become resilient: Observations and cautions. *Resiliency in Action, 1,* 18–28.

Werner, E., & Smith, R. (1982; 1989). *Vulnerable but invincible: A longitudinal study of resilient children and youth.* New York: Adams, Bannister, and Cox.

Werner, E., & Smith, R. (1992). *Overcoming the odds: High-risk children from birth to adulthood.* New York: Cornell University Press.

13 Community Development, Neighborhood Empowerment, and Individual Resilience

DENNIS SALEEBEY

The profession of social work has gradually withdrawn much of its interest in, and emphasis on, community development and community organization as areas of practice, education, and inquiry. Some 30 years ago, nearly every school of social work had curricula, if not tracks, devoted to community organization. Today, few schools have a robust curriculum in any aspect of community, theory or practice. In this chapter, I would like to explore three interlocking, although rudimentary, developments that might have significant importance for the profession—in the restoration of theory and practice around community and the extension of the strengths perspective.

First, in a variety of fields outside of social work, there seems to be renewed interest in community phenomena, especially community development (Delgado, 2000; Hanna & Robinson, 1994; Kretzmann & McKnight, 1993; Mills, 1995; Specht & Courtney, 1994). This rediscovery of community has brought refinements in thinking and action that have implications for the direction of the profession in the future. In addition, they provide some new language and perspectives with which to address the nettlesome problems of oppression, isolation, and marginalization that too many clients of social workers face.

Second, there has been a virtual explosion of knowledge in the field of individual, family, and community resilience (see, for example, Benson, 1997; McQuade & Ehrenreich, 1997; Walsh, 1998). Like the strengths perspective, these various literatures, developed somewhat independently, are founded on the idea that each individual, family, and community has capacities, knowledge, and means that enhance revitalization and these are usually interlocking and interdependent. Likewise there are factors, some operating, others imminent, that elicit and sustain resilient behavior, relationships, and institutions. Furthermore, there is thought to be a complex and abiding calculus of resilience—that community and individual or family resilience are inextricably bound together (Kretzmann & McKnight, 1993; McGoldrick & Carter, 1999; Mills, 1995; Schorr, 1997).

Finally, the notion of empowerment, favored these days by so many groups within the spectrum of political beliefs and by many professions, can be put into dramatic relief by some of the ideas we will discuss. A noble ambition or sentiment, empowerment as a practice sometimes falls far short of its intention. Nonetheless, the idea of empowerment as a framework for practice is regaining considerable ground in social work (Gutierrez & Nurius, 1994; Kondrat, 1995; Lee, 1994; Simon, 1994).

Some of the concepts of the emerging approaches to community development are discussed later in the chapter and then illustrated with reference to a number of current programs that operate from a strengths- and assets-based framework. But first, I would like to address an emerging sense of the notion of context—interpersonal, built, physical, and natural.

The Power of Context: What You See Is How You Get

Social workers have known for years, or at least claimed, that the environment is an important piece of the ecological or systems perspective. We speak blithely and often about person/environment in this profession. While there have been critiques of the whole idea (Wakefield, 1996), generally we have accepted the sense of this transaction. Often we speak of environment in fairly grand terms: community, economic dislocation, housing blight, etc. This is fine. But there is another sense of context—smaller, more immediate, more personal, even symbolic—that influences how people feel and act. Malcolm Gladwell, in his intriguing book, *The Tipping Point* (2000), reports on the "Broken Windows Theory" of crime epidemics put forward by criminologists James Q. Wilson and George Kelling. The basic idea is that crime blooms when signs and signals of disorder reign. Windows broken and unrepaired lead to more broken windows and ultimately the sense that no one cares and no one is in charge. There are many equivalents of broken windows—graffiti, ramshackle structures, empty houses and apartments, effusions of trash and litter. Gladwell quotes Wilson and Kelling:

> Muggers and robbers, whether opportunistic or professional, believe they reduce their chances of being caught or even identified if they operate on streets where potential victims are already intimidated by prevailing conditions. (p. 141)

From a very different point of view, Judith Rich Harris argues that context is a powerful determinant of behavior. While we think of personality as something rather solid and persistent, the fact is our behavior can change dramatically depending on context. Ask any parent. The dutiful and decorous son at home becomes a jokester and prankster par excellence with peers after school. The picky eater at home is highly likely to eat well away from home. In one study, 33% of all kids were picky eaters either at home or at school, but only 8% in both places (Rydell, Dahl, & Sundelin, 1995, cited in Harris, 1998). Behavior is not necessarily transferred from place to place. It varies in terms of setting, the people in that setting, and the messages of the context (this is what happens here).

The point? We often look inward or to the family to explain and understand behavior, but the immediate context—interpersonal, built, and physical—is a powerful influence on how we feel, think, and act. So the environment—be it school, neighborhood, or playground, and its people and structures—can be a major force in helping people to turn around their lives (see Chapter 12). And it may not take much to turn that environment from one in which deficits, disorganization, and destruction discourage and deflate everybody to one where people have hope and pride. Terry Woodberry, CEO of United Way in Kansas City, Kansas, said that he and a bunch of his colleagues tried to figure out what made a good neighborhood. After discussions with many neighborhood residents from different parts of the county (Wyandotte County), well-to-do and economically depressed alike, he and his group developed the following criteria: (1) Hopeful housing stock: A critical mass of apartments, houses, and grounds, whether in wealthy areas or poor, that show signs of being cared for, kept up, or refurbished.[1] (2) Symbols of community: These might be anything around which the community gathers, works, takes pride, or celebrates—sculptures, buildings, murals, community gardens, events. (3) Intergenerational relationships: These are a visible manifestation of the richness of the immediate interpersonal context, and of caring, connected relationships between older and younger residents. (4) Good neighbor stories: People tell and retell stories of good deeds, supportive acts, and acts of beneficence and the passing on of these stories is as important as the original event itself, providing a kind of poignant message and narrative structure to the livability of the context.

So the context, however modest and small, can be a force for regeneration, healing, and transformation. And the good news is it may not take much to turn the context from despairing to hopeful.

Community Development: Emerging Ideas and Practices

Let us turn now to some of the emerging themes and practices around community development. A conviction that social workers have long prized but often forget in practice is that individual troubles and successes must be framed within the larger

[1]HUD finally has this idea. They are tearing down high-rises and replacing them with more home-like structures and grounds, and people take some pride in their care.

context of family, community, and society. To decontextualize individuals and groups as we attempt to help them is to strip away much of the essence of their identity. Community development harks us back to the time-honored belief in the importance of the person–environment interplay. Community work also has ties to social work's abiding interest in social justice as well as a recently diminished collectivist view of the world. In the collectivist view of human development, for example,

> development is perceived to be [a process] in which individuals learn to become participants in the organized social life around them—the family, neighborhood, school, work, voluntary associations, government, and so on. (Specht & Courtney, 1994, pp. 138–139)

Some Basic Ideas about Community Development

A few simple ideas bespeak the basics of community development in the 1990s and into this new century. One of the most basic of these ideas is that the community has the capacity to deal with many of the problems of individuals and families. Voluntary associations, clubs, leaders, institutions, all kinds of interest groups, and self-help groups are at the ready to help. Thus, many of the conceptions of community development focus interest on making an accounting of and using the assets, resources, and strengths available in the community. In this view, the beginning steps in community development involve assaying what resources exist in the community; what human and physical capital underwrite community life; what competencies and resources the people who live and work there possess; what organizations and associations having roles to play contribute to community wealth (Benson, 1997; McKnight, 1997). As in the strengths approach to practice with individuals, the first steps in the development process do not focus on the problems, deficits, and conflicts of the community. Rather, the emphasis is on first discovering the assets in the community.

Because practitioners are looking for and making an accounting of the resources, assets, and capacities of the community, they necessarily begin their work from within the community. External forces do exist and may even be crucial for community vitality. These factors ultimately will be addressed, but by searching for the assets, problem-solving capacities, and leadership in the community, practitioners stress the importance of locality, neighborhood, interdependence, and context, as discussed previously.

Being serious about appreciating and stimulating the resources, capacities, and assets that abound in the community requires that community development workers constantly be on the lookout to build or reconfigure relationships between themselves and residents and formal resident associations (Kretzmann & McKnight, 1993; Mills, 1995; Shaffer & Anundsen, 1993). As one volunteer community developer in an inner-city program for the community's youth said, "I love it when somebody tells me, 'You can't change those kids. Those kids are no good.' They're never *our* kids, it's *those* kids. And my philosophy is that they're *our* kids. They're *my* kids and they're *our* kids, as a community" (McLaughlin,

Irby, & Langman, 1994, p. 97). The fundamental principle abides that the community and its surround may have the internal resources to propel the residents to a place of increasing energy, synergy, growth, prosperity, and progress, but the vehicle is often the development of trusting, caring, and responsible relationships.

For a variety of reasons, these ideas have been devastated in the 1980s and 1990s thanks, in part, to the forces of segregation, isolation and alienation, the separation of work and residence, and, importantly, the increasing inequity in the distribution of wealth and other social resources (McKnight, 1997). So "the sense of efficacy based on interdependence, the idea that people can count on their neighbors and neighborhood resources for support and strength has weakened. For community builders who are focused on assets, rebuilding [and building] . . . local relationships offers the most promising route toward successful community development" (Kretzmann & McKnight, 1993, p. 10). Regrettably, individuals and communities, especially those struggling against poverty, oppression, and isolation, often do not think of themselves as having an accessible fund of assets. Those outside the community, too often service providers as well as other institutions and individuals, act on stereotypes, myths, unquestioned assumptions about who people really are, and clearly do not regard them as having strengths and competencies. As Paula Wehniller says, "When there are walls of ignorance between people [and communities], when we don't know each other's stories, we substitute our own myth about who that person or community is. When we operate with only a myth, none of that person's or people's truth will ever be known to us" (cited in Benard, 1994, p. 380). What assumptions, for example, do we make about the people who live in a given public housing complex and about the environment itself? And where did we acquire those suppositions? To operate as a professional seeking assets, searching out resilience is to turn your back on stereotypic, certainly class-based, and often media-induced, misunderstanding. In community development, a strengths- and assets-based orientation can induce optimism, hope, and motivation for both clients and workers.

From all this we may conclude the following about community and about community development: "A community is a dynamic whole that emerges when a group of people

- participate in common practices,
- depend on one another,
- make decisions together,
- identify themselves as part of something larger than the sum of their individual relationships,
- commit themselves for the long term to their own, one another's and the group's well-being" (Shaffer & Anundsen, 1993, p. 10).

In this somewhat idealized view (there *are* other views of community—especially from those who live in particular neighborhoods and communities), community development involves helping unleash the power, vision, capacities, and talents within a (self-defined) community so that the community can strengthen its internal relationships and move closer toward performing the important functions of solidarity and support, succor and identification, and instructing and socializing. The community must also be helped to strengthen its relationship to outside institutions, associations, and organizations. These can be the lifeblood that allows the community to find its heart, solve its problems, and reach its goals. But the primary resources to be found and employed are the strengths and resiliency, the skills and talents of the residents and members of the community.

Coming Together: Community and Individual Resilience

Let us review here some of the ideas and conclusions from the varied fields of resilience research. We will see, as we do, that there is a growing sense that individual and familial resilience and the characteristics of the communities in which people live are inseparable.

A number of communal factors seem to be related to individual and familial resilience. The developmental infrastructure of communities, beyond caring and attentive families, is strengthened to the extent that it (1) has caring adults or surrogate caregivers who provide safety, support, guidance, comfort, and mentorship; (2) invites the gifts of, and supports youth involvement and participation in, community-building projects and in the moral and civic life of the community; and (3) has high expectations of all youth with respect to their roles and responsibilities in community and family life (Benson, 1997). In this regard, decades of research continue to show that resilience is a process and an effect of *connection*. In Rutter's words, "Development is a question of linkages that happen within you as a person and also in the environment in which you live. . . . Our hope lies in doing something to alter these linkages, to see that kids who start in a [difficult] environment don't continue in such environments and develop a sense of impotency" (Benard, 1994, p. 8). To Emmy Werner and Ruth Smith, who have done the most ambitious longitudinal study of resilience and vulnerability, effective interventions (including natural ones) in every arena must reinforce the natural social bonds between young and old, between siblings, between friends, "that give meaning to one's life and a reason for commitment and caring" (1982, p. 163). Ernesto Cortes, an organizer for the Communities Organized for Public Service (C. O. P. S.), a community-organizing and community-building project in San Antonio for the last 20 years, emphasizes the importance of relationships and sharing stories in community projects of all kinds (Crimmins, 1995). John McKnight (1995) observes that a generative community relies on the gifts of everybody, not just the few. That includes groups seen as deviant. Melvin Delgado (2000) says that a strategy predicated on strengths and community capacity enhancement involves the following assumptions:

1. The community has the will and resources to help itself;
2. it knows what is best for itself;
3. ownership of the strategy rests within, rather than outside, the community;

4. partnerships involving organizations and communities are the preferred route for initiatives;
5. the use of strengths in one area will translate into strengths in other areas—in short, community capacity enhancement will have a ripple effect (p. 28).

The research on resilience challenges us to build this connectedness, this sense of belonging—by helping to transform families, schools, and communities to become "psychological homes" where people can find caring and support, respect, and opportunities for meaningful involvement, and, not insignificantly, where people can defend themselves against incursions and stresses of all kinds. Everyone has the potential for self-righting, the self-correction of life course, but it doesn't operate in a vacuum; it operates when environments challenge and support, and provide protective and generative factors. McLaughlin and colleagues (1994) after their research into the inner city and effective leaders and programs for youth, quote former gang-banger Tito as summing it up most aptly, "Kids can walk around trouble, if there is someplace to walk to, and someone to walk with" (1994, p. 219).

In a very important sense, then, fostering resilience and capitalizing on and extending strengths and capabilities is about building community and creating opportunities for belonging and participation. This is where the paths of community development and resilience cross. As social workers we know this and we certainly claim it: We work both sides of the psychosocial street, the individual and the environment, and the transactions between them. In fact, however, our recent history suggests that we have turned away—not completely, but too frequently—from our community obligations and the contextual side of practice. "Most important, social work's objective is to strengthen the community's capacity to solve problems through the development of groups and organizations, community education, and community systems of governance and control over systems of social care" (Specht & Courtney, 1994, p. 26).

According to Rapp (1998), strengths-based case management with individuals who have severe and persistent mental illness, depends mightily on the availability and use of supportive, instructive, and integrative natural resources within the community. The guiding presumption is that every community, no matter how burdened by economic dislocation or other social stresses, has an array of often untapped resources—people, institutions, and associations—that are potential collateral in insuring genuine integration into the community. These words bespeak the importance of caring and support across the life cycle and within the community.

Another important protective, maybe even generative, factor in a community—and this seems especially relevant for youth—is the existence of normatively high but not inappropriate expectations, seeing "potential not pathology" (McLaughlin et al., 1994, p. 96; see also chapter 12, this volume). "Loving agendas [sic] and positive missions with productive and healthy purposes" for youth in trouble in communities are essential (McLaughlin et al., 1994, p. 97). Unfortunately, many communities see only gangs, drug abuse, delinquency, truancy, and violence, and shrink from providing youth the expectations of possibility and the connections to health-promoting people, places, and programs. The community and its membership, manifest in its face-to-face relationships, are powerful media for developing, sustaining, and enforcing expectations and norms. Those expectations that are communicated explicitly through the values, actions, and relationships within the community are the most durable and potent. Such expectations also encourage involvement in the community, imply membership, and foster the development and use of the capacities, strengths, and assets of individuals and families.

Related to the persistent communication of high expectations is the creation of *opportunities for people to be contributing members* of their community; opportunities for valued and consequential ways to be involved in family, work, school, associations, and the community at large. High expectations make no sense unless there is the prospect of becoming a collaborating community member, a real citizen with portfolio. A tragedy today in neighborhoods at all socioeconomic strata is that many people have little real chance for participation in the life of a given community whether we are talking of political concerns, economic development, social/associational relationships, or helping to confront the challenges that face a community. This is often true of elders and certainly of people who are viewed as deviant, but it is particularly true in the case of youth.

> The unique energy and creativity of youth is often denied to the community because the young people of the neighborhood are all too often viewed only in terms of their lack of maturity and practical life experience. Categorized as the product of "immature" minds, the legitimate dreams and desires of youth are frequently ignored by the older, more "responsible" members of the community. . . . Given the proper opportunities, however, youth can always make a significant contribution to the development of communities in which they live. What is needed for this to happen are specific projects that will connect youth with the community in ways that will increase their own self-esteem and level of competency while at the same time improving the quality of life of the community as a whole. (Kretzmann & McKnight, 1993, p. 29)

Exemplars of Community Development Practice

In this section we take a brief look at two community development programs and philosophies. Although the language is different in each of them, both are clearly assets and strengths based. Following presentation of these programs, we draw some lessons for social work community development practice.

Building Communities from within: The Assets-Based Approach

Recognizing that many communities in the United States are either devastated physically and civically or deeply disturbed, John Kretzmann and John McKnight of the Center for Urban Affairs and Policy Research at Northwestern University have said this:

> In response to this desperate situation, well-intended people are seeking solutions by taking one of two divergent paths. The first, which begins by focusing on a community's needs, deficiencies and problems, is still by far the most traveled, and commands the vast majority of our financial and human resources. By comparison with the second path, which insists on beginning with a clear commitment to discovering a community's capacities and assets, and which is the direction [we] recommend, the first and foremost path is more like an eight-lane superhighway. (p. 1)

In the view of Kretzmann and McKnight (1993), each community has a surfeit of assets and resources, often unrecognized or underutilized. This is especially true of marginalized communities where individuals and groups have had to learn to survive under difficult and often rapidly changing conditions. These assets should be accounted for and mapped as a basis for working with and from within a community. The resources to be weighed are not just those of individuals but include local citizens' associations, those informal organizations in which citizens come together for the purpose of problem solving and/or building solidarity. More formal institutions—schools, government entities, businesses, churches, health and welfare organizations, colleges and universities—should likewise be included in the mapping of human and social capital within a community.

Three principles define this approach. First, it is *assets and strengths based.* Community workers start with what resources are present in the community and not with what is missing, what is wrong, or what the community needs. Second, this approach to community development is *internally focused.* That is, it is very important to know what is going on within the community, what assets are available, and what individual and group capacities exist. The role of external factors and institutions is, for the time being, ignored. Rather the focus on the inner life of the community demonstrates the centrality of local control, local capital, local vision, and local ownership. Finally, if the first two elements of the assets-based scheme are to hold, then the process must clearly be *relationship driven.* If people are to be pulled into the life of the community and share their capacities, it will be done through the medium of relationship. A gift is given from hand to hand.

A significant part of assets-based community development occurs in the beginning with taking a capacity inventory, a strengths assessment, or a catalogue of community assets. The inventory is not a formal research tool. Its primary purpose is to gather information about, say, a specific person (it could also be family, organization, association, or institution) to see what they might give to a community resource bank and to help that person make a contribution to the community. But, this is a two-way street and that person should receive the gifts of resource and skill development, perhaps even education, income, and employment as well. What is actually done to help an individual contribute and receive the gifts of involvement, resource acquisition, and skill development? The practitioner must know how to

- assess the individual's skills and strengths, and then link them to the needs and aspirations of other residents or groups.
- add up the cumulative resources of individuals and groups in the community and, with the residents, combine them in the development of programs and resources the community genuinely wants and needs (for example, a food pantry, or a child care service).
- ensure that all those who make a contribution to the human and resource capital of the community have the opportunity, through connection with others, to move toward achieving personal and familial goals, to create or develop an enterprise, or to solve problems.
- help residents strengthen their sense of community through the development of activities that symbolically and practically cement ties between individuals and groups (for example, a street fair, a mini-grants program).
- help ensure that individual well-being and resilience are a part of all community activities; that there is real work, real responsibility, real opportunity to produce income, and genuinely positive expectations of success and accomplishment (Benard, 1991; Kretzmann & McKnight, 1993; McLaughlin et al., 1994; Mills, 1995).

While the idea is to *connect* people as well as local associations and groups through the bartering of their capacities and resources, strengths, and competencies for mutual benefit, clearly none of this happens without the full involvement and direction of residents. Important, too, is the necessity to link residents with local businesses, local institutions and service providers, and other sources of capital and credit. Recognition of resident and community assets may be obscured by the shadow of labels such as "ex-con," "mentally retarded," "mentally ill," "dropout," or, in the case of associations and communities, "gang," "problem group," or "target population." But the root idea of community development is to identify local capacities and mobilize them, which involves *connecting people with capacities to other people, associations, institutions, and economic resources* (Kretzmann & McKnight, 1993): "[E]very living person has some gift or capacity of value to others. A strong community is a place that recognizes those gifts and ensures that they are given. A weak community is a place where lots of people can't give their gifts and express their capacities" (p. 27). A true community, then, is inviting and encourages participation. The Foundation for Community Encouragement puts it this way, "A true community is inclusive, and its greatest enemy is exclusivity. Groups who exclude others because of religious, ethnic, or more subtle differences are not communities" (Shaffer & Anundsen, 1993, p. 12).

In the case of older residents, for example, their potential is augmented by the fact that they may have time, they have history and experience and often economic resources, and they are very likely to be a part of a larger peer group that can be mobilized. To release seniors' capacities, making an account of the resources of elders in a given community or association is essential; but then an inventory of the resources of local individuals, associations, and institutions must be either completed or, if complete, consulted. Following that, the building of strong and mutually beneficial partnerships between local seniors and other individuals, associations, and institutions is requisite. Finally, having established strong connections, bonds, and alliances within the community, additional affiliations with resources outside the community may be built. Kretzmann and McKnight (1993) offer some examples:

- Seniors are involved in the Visiting Important Persons Program in which they visit less mobile elderly and try to assist with any practical problems. Seniors are trained to be able to provide CPR, to recognize drug abuse, to give bed baths and first aid, and to help with practical daily matters like budgeting and food selection and preparation. The oldest participant is an 82-year-old woman.
- Latch key kids who are feeling lonely, experiencing a crisis or just want to chat, can call on the telephone from their homes to senior citizens through the "Grandma Please" program.
- Seniors are recruited and trained to acquaint them with the local police station and other citywide departments. As a result, seniors visit other seniors in a door-to-door campaign in order to provide security evaluations and advice (pp. 59–60).

Assets-based community development work, although not always known by that name, is occurring around the country. The West Philadelphia Improvement Corps and Atlanta Clark University's Partners in a Planned Community program are just two examples of programs that have their focus, among other things, on the capacity of the community to invigorate itself.

Health Realization/Community Empowerment

The work of Roger Mills (1995) and the Health Realization Institute (2000) has led quickly to broad application in a number of fields including addictions, education, community policing, community development, and public housing, among others. Although the principles began evolving from work with individuals and groups, the first community demonstration project began in two Dade County, Florida, public housing communities (Modello and Homestead Gardens) in the 1980s, communities like many others beset with the results of poverty and racism—hopelessness, lack of opportunities and skills, high rates of violence, drug dealing, domestic violence, teen pregnancy, and school failure (even though these problems did not characterize many families and individuals in the community). The program began, as have subsequent ones, with community leadership training (normally 36 hours) and training for staff of agencies working with the residents. The training is oriented around Psychology of Mind (POM) principles that emphasize the power of creating life experience from thoughts; honoring and getting in touch with the health and wisdom within; learning how an external world of expectations and visions has obscured individuals' own inside world of possibility and calm. The essential feature of this is that those who have been taught now become teachers. Lest this all sound like some 1-900 nostrum, consider the following: After three years, comparative analysis of the results of pre- and post-tests of 142 families and 604 youths revealed improved parent–child relationships in 87 percent of the families; more than 60 percent of residents became employed from a baseline of 85% on public assistance; a 75 percent reduction in delinquency and school-related problem behaviors; a 65 percent decrease in drug trafficking; more than a 500 percent increase in parent involvement in schools; and only one student from these communities was failing from a baseline 64 percent failure rate (Mills, 1995, pp. 128–139; Health Realization Institute, 2000, pp. 9–10). These findings have been replicated in dramatic fashion in other community empowerment/health realization projects. Coliseum Gardens in Oakland, California, was beset not only by economic distress, but ethnic and racial divisions and hostility, crime, and gang-related violence. To cite just one of many amazing statistics, this community had the highest homicide rate of any in Oakland for a number of years. After 7 years, there has not been one homicide. Mills and his staff did all the "right stuff" at the outset: They fostered community ownership early on and developed collaborative relationships across many systems. The following quote gives some of the flavor of the program.

> We did everything we could to reduce sources of stress when we began our public housing programs in 1987. We helped our clients with emergency rental needs, paid utility bills, and provided supplementary food, clothing, and physical security. We offered job training and day care assistance. We worked hard to make circumstances easier for our clients. . . .
>
> At the same time, we never lost sight of the bottom line. . . . We wanted to see what could happen when people learned some practical ideas about how they could take charge of their own thinking. We hypothesized that they would begin to handle adversity with more hope and self-respect and find ways to improve their circumstances both as a community and on their own. We trusted that our clients' innate intelligence would surface as soon as they could drop their attachment to alienated or insecure patterns of thinking. We suspected and hoped that the buoyancy of the human spirit would deliver the resiliency they needed to frame their prospects and capabilities in a more hopeful light. (Mills, 1995, p. 128)

First, the principles that guided the program were consonant with some of the findings of the resilience research: the idea that resilience (the capacity to be relatively healthy despite exposure to a variety of severe risks and stresses) is *innate*; the idea that resilience is *directly accessible*; and that organismic wisdom, intelligence, and common sense inhere, to some degree, in all individuals even though buried by years of negative expectations, or the destructive and disheartening imagery and responses of others in one's life.

Second, the goal of "health realization," according to Mills, is to "reconnect people to the health in themselves and then direct them in ways to bring forth the health in others. The result is a change in people and communities which builds up from within rather than being imposed from without" (Benard, 1994, p. 22). Again the importance of the idea of connection surfaces: For communities to make themselves more resilient, there has to be a critical mass of individuals and families who become attached to one another and committed to the community.

Third, the methods of health realization are based on the idea that people construct meaning in their lives. This meaning is expressed in thoughts, manifest in behavior, and fateful for the resilience and energy of the individual. Two sources of meaning (or thoughts) are (1) those that are primal and indigenous—the immanent wisdom of the body/mind, the things that we appear, given a chance, to intuitively understand and know about ourselves and our world; and (2) those that are socialized—thoughts that are engendered in us over time by others, by social institutions, by media, by the very culture itself. For too many people, these latter accretions of meaning add up to assumptions of fear, inadequacy, and discouragement. These conditioned networks of thoughts weave the imagery of victimization, a symbolism of blame, and an array of negative expectations (Mills, 1995). Feelings of anger, depression, and despair are the unfortunate progeny of these constructions. Such feelings often are expressed in victimizing or abusive behavior toward the self and others.

Fourth, health realization is based on teaching one to listen and hear the message of health, resilience, possibility, and hope. But this teaching (which will eventually be done by residents for each other) can only be done after creating a positive, caring, collaborative, egalitarian relationship. Mills puts it this way, "Perhaps the most vital ingredient is the establishing of empowering relationships" (1993, p. 29). He refers to "being in a state of service" in which "[w]e have no personal agenda other than what's in the client's best interest" (1993, p. 30).

Fifth, once you live the principles with your clients and in your professional life, then community organizing principles come to the fore, such as enlisting a core group of people, creating a forum for them to meet regularly in small groups, and facilitating the establishment of collaborative relationships with other residents, service providers, government agencies, and the marketplace.

Sixth, this model builds at the grass-roots level a critical mass in each community, and then between communities, that will help create change and put pressure in the right places to move toward policy changes that support human well-being and individual and collective efficacy.

The approach to members of the community occurs individually and in groups and is educative and informative as well as therapeutic, intending to help people discover the strength, capacity, and wisdom within. Establishing a respectful, collaborative, light-hearted relationship with residents—a relationship that sees clients as equals and as having the potential for insight, change, and growth—is essential. Furthermore, all individuals and groups are seen as potential teachers and therapists for other constituents of the community. Most important, it requires that helpers be in the real world of residents, in real time, and teach the power of hope. "The process of building rapport, of listening deeply to someone else's world, of assisting them to learn how to use their own common sense and innate wisdom, are all part of any empowering relationship. . . . We usually have . . . permission to be a teacher, but it helps to remember always that what we really are is a facilitator. We are facilitating the other person realizing the resources they already have in them for health, insight, and wisdom" (Mills, 1995, p. 121).

Notes on Community Building and Programs That Work

Community Building

Community building refers to the reality and possibility of restoring or refurbishing the sense and reality of community in neighborhoods. It involves among other things helping neighbors—individuals, families, and associations—in a community strengthen relationships with one another usually around mutually crafted projects. The idea is to replace the notion that they must be completely dependent on outside or professional organizations and institutions for help with the assumption that they have internal assets and capacities that can be developed and used in increasing the human and social capital of the community. The upshot of this is an increase in the sense of self-efficacy and power in the individuals, families, and associations of the community—they believe that they can make things happen!

Kingsley, McNeeley, and Gibson (1999) in their report on the growth of community building initiatives outline several successful efforts in economically distressed communities including the tenants of a Washington, DC, public housing community who assumed management of the project and, in the initial years, with the involvement of many residents and resident associations, set up its own educational, social service, and economic development initiatives. As an example of their effectiveness, over the first few years they decreased the vacancy rate from 18 percent to 5 percent (vacancies are critical to these communities because the more vacancies there are, the more they are likely to be commandeered by drug dealers, etc. and/or the more likely the local housing authority may decide to cut back support or, in extreme cases, even close down the project). They also created more than 100 jobs for residents and helped 132 residents get off welfare. And, in 15 years of the program some 700 youths from the community have gone on to college and three-fourths of them have graduated. Stories like this are becoming more common. We can see several themes and appreciations that bind them together.

1. They center interest on specific and doable community projects and initiatives that improve the community, invite participation, and increase the human and social assets (capital) of the community. Whether the project is a community mural, the development of a block watch, improving relationships with local schools, starting a parenting group, taking over maintenance of the grounds, or developing cooperative relationships with local police to confront the drug problem, the most important outcome is the building of connections between neighbors, developing

capacities, trust, and the symbolic ownership of the community. These make future projects more likely and more likely to be successful.

2. They are driven by communal interests, concerns, and hopes, and typically have extensive involvement of residents. Through these projects, members of the community discover that their interests, values, beliefs, and skills are tools to be used in making their neighborhood the kind of place they want to live in. This does not mean that they must foreswear help from outside agencies or the infusion of outside resources (such as funded local projects), but that the project and the encompassing community-building process are primarily an internal process involving as many residents as possible to avoid the development of a local "oligarchy."

3. They are assets based. The shift is away from focusing on problem solving or even meeting needs to the development and employment of the residents' individual and collective strengths—knowledge, skills, tools, and resources—to evolve the kind of community that they want, and on their own terms. The basic idea here reflects one of the essential strengths principles: All communities, no matter how distressed, have an array, often untapped, of human, associational, natural, built, and institutional resources. These are to be used in the building of community— symbolically, practically, and experientially.

4. They are comprehensive and vision based. These community-building efforts may begin with an accounting of the assets and resources of a community and then employing them on one or two doable but visible and important projects. But from there, as the vision of the community is articulated, more goals are enunciated and projects to meet those goals developed. More alliances within and without the community are nourished and the community is in motion. Part of the idea of comprehensiveness is to end the isolation from external institutions and organizations that these communities often suffer. Businesses, schools, social service and health agencies, law enforcement agencies, foundations, recreational institutions, etc. are seen as potential partners in helping the community achieve their goals, but also in helping the institutions meet their needs. Businesses need customers and employees; law enforcement agencies need local help in fighting crime; schools need parental involvement. On the other hand, many residents need jobs, more avenues to opportunities, and more protections, and want to be players in the marketplace and local government.

5. In keeping with the ideas about context and locality discussed earlier in the chapter, these initiatives are best tailored to discrete neighborhoods at the start where residents have some geographical proximity and identity, and daily face-to-face interactions. Thus the sinew of connection has already developed to some degree. However, it is conceivable that there may be umbrella institutions (also resident-driven) that bring together initiatives in various neighborhoods in terms of sharing ideas and resources.

6. Finally, these community-building enterprises must be aware of the continuing racism and barriers to full citizenship that exist in many institutions and

agencies. The idea of collaboration—bringing people and groups together—contains within it the dangers of racial, ethnic, class, and cultural conflict. But being mindful of these realities and always keeping the "eyes on the prize," the outcomes that may be mutually beneficial to all involved, may allow the parties to surmount those historic barriers and hoary conflicts. A part of this, too, is to recognize the strengths inherent in different cultures and groups—to celebrate those, to educate about them, to share differences, but most importantly to use them in moving toward the vision of community (Delgado, 2000; Kingsley et al., 1999; McKnight, 1995)

Programs That Work

Lisbeth Schorr (1997) in her continuing efforts to understand and detail the elements of programs for economically distressed individuals, families, and communities has gathered up what seem to be the characteristics of many programs that work. In particular, she has been interested in educational, family, and child welfare programs in communities where poverty, unemployment, and debilitating physical conditions abound.

Successful programs are almost always community based, nested in a neighborhood—of it, not just in it. They involve residents as well as professionals in common interests and pursuits, like helping our teenage mothers take care of their children or educating adolescents about sexuality and responsibility. Successful programs are adaptable, responsive to changing community conditions, and broadly conceived. They are in the game for the long haul, and will do what needs to be done—going way beyond professional and bureaucratic limitations. These are programs that think on their feet. Whatever needs to be done, they are willing to do it. While they acknowledge the real problems of individuals, families, and the whole community, they are as interested in, no, more interested in, the assets, strengths, and resources in the community. These are the tools for building programs that work. These programs thrive on the uncertainty but look to the possibility inherent in community-based work.

These programs think ecologically. They see children in the light of their families. But they see the families in the context of the community and the culture. Families that are sustained and supported in the raising of their children are essential to the developmental infrastructure of any community. And the reverse is true—strong communal ties and neighborhood institutions, and esprit, cultural tools, and rituals are the key to strong families. These programs involve the residents, young and old, the excluded and the influential, in significant, power-sharing ways. They are neither "rule-bound" nor "hidebound." "Successful programs are shaped to respond to the needs of local populations and to assure that local communities have a genuine sense of ownership. . . . These programs are both of the community and in the community" (Schorr, 1997, p. 7, 8).

The organizational culture (see the earlier discussion in this chapter of the health realization program) of these programs is one of health, energy, commitment, experimentation, innovation, collaboration, and excitement. Their mission is clear and based on a communal vision. The organization is committed to the vision, nurtured by common beliefs and values, but is flexible about the strategies that are required to achieve the mission. But the overriding value for the staff is competence, funded by the administrative assurance that they will have the tools, training, and resources to become competent and maintain that capacity.

Perhaps the most important aspect of successful programs is their dedication and ability to form trusting, mutual, credible, and respectful relationships with their clients and the community and its institutions. Staff will play many roles: confidant, advocate, counselor, partner, guide, and teacher. They will not be solely or even often guided by time-tested or shopworn theory, but are willing to act on their intuitions, their sense of what is needed, the urgency of the problem they face, and the clarity of their vision (Schön, 1987; Schorr, 1997).

Conclusion

I hope I have been able to convey the excitement of some of the developments in thinking about the relationship between community and individual resilience and putting them into practice. For our profession, these developments are affirmations of a noble and honorable legacy about which we may have become amnesic. The social work profession, over the years, has positioned itself to champion the cause of the underdog, the oppressed, and to envision and promote the idea of a world worth living in for all. We cannot do it alone, obviously, but we are becoming in danger of not doing it at all. The long traditions of community organizing and activism, of liberation theology, of radical confrontational politics, of Marxist transformation, have often looked askance at community development activities that do not address the sociopolitical sources of oppression. The approaches described here might seem to some to be engaged in selling out. But while we await the revelations of ultimate social metamorphosis, let us fortify ourselves and our communities to meet the daily struggles and challenges that life brings. John McKnight (1995) puts it this way:

> Community is about the common life that is lived in such a way that the unique creativity of each person is a contribution to the other. . . . Our goal should be clear. We are seeking nothing less than a life surrounded by the richness and diversity of community. A collective life. A common life. An everyday life. A powerful life that gains its joy from the creativity and connectedness that come when we join in association to create an inclusive world. (p. 123)

When transformation comes, we will be ready to seize the moment. We would do well to be guided by the words of sixth-century Chinese philosopher Lao-tsu.

> *If there is radiance in the soul, it will abound in the family.*
> *If there is radiance in the family, it will be abundant in the community.*
> *If there is radiance in the community, it will grow in the nation.*
> *If there is radiance in the nation, the universe will flourish.*

DISCUSSION QUESTIONS

1. How would you describe the relationship between the resilience of the individual and that of the community? Can you think of an example in which a community did or did not help promote the resilience or competence of an individual? What were the key factors?

2. Which of the exemplars of community development practice provides a model that you, as a social worker, would find most compatible with your values and methods? Why?

3. Even if you do not work in a community-building agency or organization, can you see how your agency might be able to employ some of these ideas or models to better serve the residents of the surrounding community?

4. To what extent do you think that social workers are obligated to understand the context of their clients' lives? What difference does that understanding make in your practice?

REFERENCES

Benard, B. (1991). *Fostering resiliency in kids: Protective factors in the family, school, and community.* San Francisco: Western Regional Center.

Benard, B. (1994, December). *Applications of resilience.* Paper presented at a National Institute on Drug Abuse conference on the role of resilience in drug abuse, alcohol abuse, and mental illness, Washington, DC.

Benson, P. (1997). *All kids are our kids.* San Francisco: Jossey-Bass.

Crimmins, J. C. (1995). *The American promise: Adventures in grass-roots democracy.* San Francisco: KQED Publications.

Delgado, M. (2000). *Community social work practice in an urban context: The potential of a capacity-enhancement perspective.* New York: Oxford University Press.

Gladwell, M. (2000). *The tipping point. How little things can make a big difference.* Boston: Little, Brown.

Gutierrez, L., & Nurius, P. (Eds). (1994). *Education and research for empowerment practice.* Seattle: University of Washington School of Social Work: Center for Policy and Practice Research.

Hanna, M. G., & Robinson, B. (1994). *Strategies for community empowerment: Direct-action and trans-formative approaches to social change practice.* Lewiston, NY: EmText.

Harris, J. R. (1998). *The nurture assumption: Why children turn out the way they do.* New York: Free Press.

Health Realization Institute. (2000). *The understanding behind health realization: A principle based psychology.* Long Beach, CA: Author.

Kingsley, G. T., McNeeley, J. B., & Gibson, J. O. (1999). *Community building coming of age.* Baltimore: Development Training Institute

Kondrat, M. E. (1995). Concept, act, and interest in professional practice: Implications of an empowerment perspective. *Social Service Review, 69,* 405–428.

Kretzmann, J. P., & McKnight, J. L. (1993). *Building communities from the inside out.* Evanston, IL: Institute for Policy Research, Northwestern University.

Lee, J. A. B. (1994). *The empowerment approach to social work practice.* New York: Columbia University Press.

McGoldrick, M., & Carter, B. (1999). Self in context. In B. Carter & McGoldrick (Eds.). *The expanded family life cycle: Individual, family, and social perspectives.* (3rd Ed.). Boston: Allyn & Bacon, pp. 27–46.

McKnight, J. L. (1995). *The careless society: Community and its counterfeits.* New York: Basic Books.

McKnight, J. L. (1997). A 21st-century map for healthy communities and families. *Families in Society, 78,* 117–127.

McLaughlin, M. W., Irby, M. A., & Langman, J. (1994). *Urban sanctuaries: Neighborhood organizations in the lives and futures of inner city youth.* San Francisco: Jossey-Bass.

McQuade, S., & Ehrenreich, J. H. (1997). Assessing clients strengths. *Families in Society, 78,* 201–212.

Mills, R. (1993). *The health realization model: A community empowerment primer.* Alhambra, CA: California School of Professional Psychology.

Mills, R. (1995). *Realizing mental health.* New York: Sulzburger & Graham.

Rapp, C. A. (1998). *The strengths model: Case management with people suffering from severe and persistent mental illness.* New York: Oxford University Press.

Schön, D. A. (1987). *Educating the reflective practitioner: Toward a new design for teaching and learning in the professions.* San Francisco: Jossey-Bass.

Schorr, L. B. (1997). *Common purpose: Strengthening families and neighborhoods to rebuild America.* New York: Anchor/Doubelday.

Shaffer, C. R., & Anundsen, K. (1993). *Creating community anywhere.* New York: Tarcher/Perigree.

Simon, B. (1994). *The empowerment tradition in American social work: A history.* New York: Columbia University Press.

Specht, H., & Courtney, M. (1994). *Unfaithful angels: How social work has abandoned its mission.* New York: Free Press.

Taylor, J. (1997). *Niches and practice: Extending the ecological perspective.* In D. Saleebey (Ed.). *The strengths perspective in social work practice* (pp. 217–227). New York: Longman.

Wakefield, J. C. (1996). Does social work need the eco-systems perspective? Parts I & II. *Social Service Review, 760,* 1–32, 183–213.

Walsh, F. (1998). *Strengthening family resilience.* New York: The Guilford Press.

Werner, E., & Smith, R. S. (1982). *Vulnerable but invincible.* New York: McGraw-Hill.

14 Environmental Context, Opportunity, and the Process of Recovery

The Role of Strengths-Based Practice and Policy

W. PATRICK SULLIVAN

CHARLES RAPP

Research on the process of recovery from serious and persistent mental illness is currently at a nascent stage, yet few areas of inquiry in the field have drawn as much interest and enthusiasm among consumers and professionals alike. This excitement is predictable insofar as the work embodies a hopeful view of the future for those facing serious mental illnesses and suggests modes of intervention that reflect humanistic values and principles of social justice.

Much of what we know about the process of recovery has been gleaned, appropriately enough, from first-person accounts—and the vivid words of consumers will be used liberally in this chapter. These accounts are consistent with Anthony's (1993) description of recovery as "a deeply personal, unique process of changing one's attitudes, values, feelings, goals, skills and/or roles" (pp. 559–560). The narratives illustrate the heroic struggles and efforts by people with severe mental illness to transcend the limits imposed by the illness and its social sequelae. Listening to these stories shatters the myth that those affected by mental illnesses are by definition only emotionally fragile, for these recovery stories speak to the determination and resilience needed to survive day to day.

However, unlike the tales of heroes in yesterday's dime novels, people rarely go it alone and succeed solely on their personal grit. Human development and growth is a transactional process that occurs within a social and interpersonal context. In the best of all circumstances young children are reared in environments where the meeting of basic needs is guaranteed, and families can secure the additional resources and supports necessary for a child to thrive. Successful adults are also usually adept in the art of acquiring and accessing resources central to improving their overall quality of life, especially in environments that they are familiar with and that are favorable.

Unfortunately, a wide range of converging forces seemingly conspire to restrict access to life-enhancing resources for those burdened with serious mental illnesses. Oftentimes, the stress and press of the illness hamper the ability of affected individuals to interact effectively with the outside world. Furthermore, social resources are often withheld from those facing unique challenges, the result of impulses as wide-ranging as fear and the desire to protect. Stigma also trumps the transactions with the world of people and resources.

To deny access to genuine interaction and participation in community life, as well as the enriching resources the social environment can offer, thwarts the process of recovery. It sequesters individuals in a world demarcated by physical and emotional barriers both real and perceived. Here individuals become labeled and entrapped, and they may lack the necessary tools, opportunities, and supports essential to their escape and recovery.

We assert in this chapter that the environment is the second factor in the recovery equation, and therefore we explore some of the dimensions of the surrounding environment that constrain and boost a person's quest for recovery. Strengths-based practice models are predicated on the central premise that all people should have access to the social resources necessary to optimize growth and development. Therefore, professional services guided by strengths-model principles and practices are ideally positioned to advance the process of recovery. Professionals often serve as bridge for consumers to the life-enriching resources the social environment has to offer. Yet, practitioners and consumers cannot go it alone. Alterations in social policy are needed to produce a supportive context that boosts the efficacy of strengths-based practice and unveils new opportunities for those on the journey to recovery.

Environment and Mental Illness

In many respects the mere presence of the term recovery in the lexicon of consumers and professionals reflects an evolutionary journey both in our understanding of the challenge presented by serious and persistent mental illness, and the social response to those afflicted. As we begin the new millennium, few question the biophysical roots of severe mental disorders, but nonetheless, similar to other potentially chronic conditions, mental illness is defined and shaped by the sociopolitical and cultural context as well as the local places where people live—the neighborhoods, streets, homes, and shelters. Thus, the individual experience of mental illness cannot be understood solely as a matter of neurotransmitters and receptor sites. Indeed, the role of stigma and poverty, the forces of oppression, social ignorance, and discrimination contribute mightily to the perception and experience of disability. Dembo (1982) drew a similar conclusion when considering the term *handicap* noting that "handicapping conditions are *between* people, rather than *in* people, that is, the handicaps are located in interpersonal relations. A handicap requires at least two people in a certain relationship in which one person *considers* the other handicapped" (p. 133).

By extension, Dembo's (1982) observation extends to collective or cultural responses whereby entire classes of persons are labeled, stigmatized, ostracized, and expelled overtly or covertly from community life or compelled to participate in limited activities, based on their identity as mentally ill. Such exclusion is often excused as necessary for the good of the person. Indeed, there are times when the expression of the illness, whether internally or externally induced, overwhelms nearly everyone. In such cases, regardless of the presumed stimulus for the occurrence, the external world is deemed toxic to the suffering individual and, thus, some life opportunities are denied.

There have also been times in history when the very institution designed to offer asylum, the psychiatric hospital, has been viewed as an unsavory milieu. Here the concern rises from the prevalence of abuse in these settings and/or the squalid and impoverished conditions of the facilities. It has also been argued that psychiatric hospitals have an iatrogenic impact on people when they become accustomed to, and most comfortable in, the regimented life of total institutions (Goffman, 1961). Thus, it would appear that from the simplest of interpersonal interactions to the complex behaviors required in daily life that most environmental settings, at one point or another, have all been hypothesized to exert a negative and powerful influence on individuals facing mental illnesses.

Any reasonable model of human behavior must account for the influence of extra-individual forces on development. Indeed, the reciprocal relationship between people and the environment, however construed, is a fundamental precept in social work and most professions concerned with the well-being and health of people. Yet, while general systems theory and ecological models may provide excellent templates for understanding human development and behavior, it is decidedly more difficult to use this knowledge to affect desired change (Thyer & Myers, 1998; Wakefield, 1996).

An enduring principle of the strengths perspective, a model largely hailed for its congruence with social work values, is that behavior is a function, at least in part, of the resources available to people (Davidson & Rapp, 1976). It is also true that people shape the environments in which they function, setting forth a continuous stimulus-response loop. Failure to understand this reciprocity can result in explanations of behavior and events that, to use an analogy, draw on only half the available data. It is clear, however, that the feedback loop is unbalanced in the case of people who are oppressed, isolated, and marginalized.

In the examples above, a diverse range of environmental settings have been implicated in the development and maintenance of troubling conditions and behaviors. For the purpose of this chapter the term *behavior* encompasses more than the simple observable actions of people, for as Thyer and Myers (1998) note, "behavior is whatever the body *does*, regardless of whether it can be publicly observed" (p. 36). Here, behavior includes cognitions, and emotions, vitally important issues for understanding the experience of mental illness as these concealed states often provide the impetus for the observable actions that raises concern among others.

The discussion offered thus far follows a familiar path and reflects the pervasive tendency to focus on deficits and pathology not only in people, but also in the surrounding environment. The ability to survive and even thrive is impossible without many of the supports provided by the surrounding world. If environmental inputs and transactions have an impact on the expression, experience, and trajectory of an illness, then it stands to reason that these same forces can be marshaled to support the process of recovery.

Environment Defined

It is important to begin by considering the term *environment*, a concept that proves to be more elusive than it would appear. For some, the term quickly conjures up images of nature and the increasing concerns about the degradation and depletion of the earth's resources. For some, the built environment, particularly the condition of inner cities, comes quickly to mind. Historically, social policies such as urban renewal were launched on the assumption that environmental conditions contributed to the pathological behavior of individuals and major social problems such as crime. More specific to mental health, there have been periods in the past and even today where environmental conditions have been seen to cause or elevate a person's susceptibility for mental illness (Faris & Dunham, 1939; Torrey & Yolken, 1998). Furthermore, in the case of more restricted and smaller localities, the potential power of environmental manipulation in treatment has influenced the physical design of psychiatric hospitals and alterations in the treatment process inside the walls as reflected in past innovations such as the introduction of therapeutic communities and ward government.

Environment is defined in *Webster's New World Dictionary* (1979) as "all the conditions, circumstances, etc. surrounding and affecting the development of an organism." This definition indicates that environment can not be understood monolithically—that in reality all people function in a wide range of environments each day. Consider those individuals considered socially adept. As a society we tend to admire people who can operate comfortably and with facility in a host of settings—from a rural bar to a boardroom of a Fortune 500 company. Some seem to have an almost innate knack for social engagement and the negotiation of a variety of social surroundings. But it is more likely that they honed this skill through encouragement, exposure and experience. As we will explore later, many who confront mental illness face isolation and, so, the impoverishment of opportunities to traverse in many social circles. As a result, they lack the necessary experience and opportunity to develop social aptitude in a variety of milieux.

The developmental process described here is one that many people have experienced at various points in their life, and it is equally likely that most of us could find ourselves in social contexts for which we lack preparation. To illustrate, few of us have attended a state dinner, or visited the pope or the queen of England—hence, we would need instruction on proper protocols. However, despite the novelty of the present task, past experience and confidence can be drawn upon to navigate unfamiliar terrain. Unfortunately, mental illness often compromises the ability to process information, and this, coupled with lack of experience in a range of social settings (e.g., the world of work), only confirms others' misperceptions of the nature of mental illness and the abilities of those who are challenged by it. This often sets forth a negative cycle that erodes a person's confidence and reinforces the inclination to avoid new experiences.

The Social Niche

One useful framework that can be used to explore the transactional nature of human development and the recovery process is the concept of the social niche as devised by Taylor (1997). Much like Thyer and Myers (1998), Taylor argues that the ecological metaphors present in social work provide an important framework for thought and possibilities for action. Ecological models, he observes, "draw attention to person-environment transactions . . . and [they emphasize] holistic thinking and interactive process" (p. 217). Human beings are social creatures, and as such the niche they occupy is a function of complex forces that go well beyond those needed for mere survival. Taylor's (1997) construct of "social niche" reflects this distinction and underscores the reality that humans

> need social support, help in the construction of social norms and social skills, aid in setting socially meaningful goals, group feedback to establish and maintain concensus on social reality, and reciprocal ties of mutual aid. The variety and need for such social and intangible resources is uniquely human. (p. 219)

If these social inputs are necessary for humans to grow and develop they are naturally critical to the process of recovery. Tragically, these opportunities are lacking in the lives of many that face serious mental illnesses. Instead, social support networks shrink with each hospitalization leaving the individual and family to survive by their wits. Social rejection is omnipresent despite sustained efforts to enlighten the populace about the realities of mental illness. Many are relegated to special environments, notable in their differentiation from the world of most adults' membership, segregated spatially and emotionally from others. They suffer, in Taylor's words, from "niche entrapment," becoming totally defined by their social category, in highly stigmatized environments with others of "their kind," and afforded few opportunities to obtain the feedback, skills, or opportunities to escape.

Figure 14.1 provides a theoretical representation of the factors that shape the social niche one occupies. While few people use the term *niche* in daily life, there are indications that we do think about our relationship with the surrounding environment with some regularity. For example, a job may be considered a good fit, or a relationship gone astray is often deemed a poor match. Similarly when we immediately

Individual strengths   **Environmental strengths**

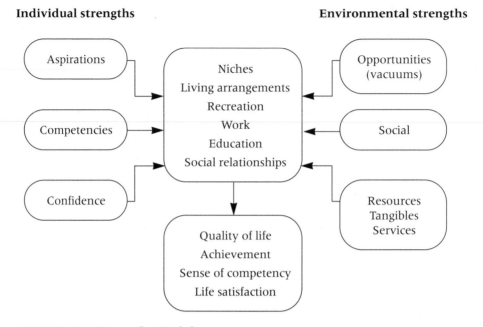

FIGURE 14.1   Strengths Model

feel comfortable in new surroundings, it is deemed to feel like home or we simply note that we feel at ease. Good fits or matches require fewer emotional or physical adjustments, and when we land in an ideal setting or situation we tend to perform at our best, enjoy greater confidence, and feel protected and supported. When those blessed with resources and opportunities believe that key elements of their life are less than ideal they may, in everyday parlance, decide to make a change. A new job may be secured, a better home purchased, a new neighborhood sought, or the search for a new mate initiated. As is depicted in Figure 14.1, the wants, confidence, skills, opportunities, resources, and social relations are all aligned for success.

Contrast this with the experience of many who face serious and persistent mental illness. In the worst scenario, some are left rootless through homelessness or live in settings that increase their chances of being victimized and exploited. While it is fortunate that most people do not confront such dire circumstances, many have felt the anxiety of landing in surroundings that are frightening or threatening. At these times, the ability to think logically and coherently is greatly compromised. Even normalized events, such as extended vacations or work that takes one from home can be disquieting and leave one longing for the familiar. Unfortunately, when pressed with undesirable circumstances many mental health consumers cannot make a change. Not only are the resources needed to facilitate escape from entrapping niches lacking, but oftentimes others (e.g., professionals, families) choose the niche they must occupy. The desire of consumers to feel at home is not a criterion for placement in a congregate living facility, nor is a good match the primary concern in the assignment of a roommate. So there are endemic aspects of the helping enterprise that may impede recovery, not the least of which is the sequestering of those who suffer serious mental illness in entrapping niches. Certainly, there are pragmatic considerations, primarily economic, that shape the structure and process of helping. However, there are also opportunities to forge new partnerships with the consumer and community that may prove to be both clinically and economically efficacious.

Niche Enrichment and Recovery: Mobilizing Personal and Environmental Strengths

This section will explore a range of environments and environmental factors from the most basic to the most complex and link them to a consumer's quest for recovery. While it is recognized that many individuals challenged by mental illness travel through life and recover without the aid of professional services, for the purposes of this chapter professional involvement is assumed. Accordingly, we will begin this exploration with a discussion of one basic environmental interchange, but one vitally important to consumers—the helping relationship.

Professional–Consumer Relationships

When mental health consumers are involved in professional services it is commonly a difficult time in their life. Being under care reflects a sentiment held by self or others that, at the present, it is impossible for the individual to carry forth on her or his own volition. For many consumers the period is marked by one of the most profound of human emotions—despair. Despair is the feeling of being cast adrift on a sea turbulent with the darkest of emotions and without means of finding safe harbor.

A ubiquitous element in the recovery matrix is hope—a feeling at the polar opposite of despair. As an emotional state hope reflects a bedrock belief in a better future and that cherished goals can be realized (Snyder, 2000). First person accounts of the recovery process confirm that hope is an indispensable ingredient for success:

> When one lives without hope, (when one has given up), the willingness to "do" is paralyzed as well. (Deegan, 1988, p. 13)

> Hope is crucial to recovery, for our despair disables us more than our disease ever could. (Leete, 1993, p. 122)

> My mood changed—I was happy and hopeful once again. (Fergeson, 1992, p. 29)

> I find myself being a role model for other clients and am only a bit uncomfortable with this. For the first time, I begin to feel real hope. (Grimmer, 1992, p. 28)

> Success will never be realized if it cannot be imagined. (Leete, 1993, p. 126)

Ideally, an encounter between a professional and a consumer should be hope provoking and hope sustaining. So many consumers have faced a constant string of disappointments and have been dissuaded from goals that they have held dear. How might hope be reactivated? An exhaustive discussion of interpersonal practice will not be attempted. Instead a few basic themes will be introduced with the prospect that this short discussion will stimulate further inquiry into this essential phase of helping.

Virtually all methods of assessment in the helping professions focus on exploring the contours and textures of a person's problems, deficits, maladies, and pathology (Cowger, 1997). This process, in which clients have to recall their inadequacies, is not only not hope inducing but can actually increase despair. Recently, the development and use of specialized assessments geared to capture the competencies, goals, and dreams of consumers (Cowger, 1997; McQuaide & Ehrenreich, 1997; Rapp, 1998) have been developed. Without question these assessments direct the attention of consumers (and practitioners) to different aspects of the consumer's life. It gives consumers a chance to reveal what has gone well in their life, what they enjoy, and what they still hope to do. The magic is not, however, in the completion of a form or task, it is in the essence of the interaction. One serendipitous finding from a previous study on the recovery process was the great joy consumers gained from having someone even consider them to be successful (Sullivan, 1994a).

Certainly, instilling or sustaining hope with consumers may come via entirely new paradigms for helping, like the strengths perspective, but a range of simple tools or even the basic attitudes professionals hold about consumers can help rejuvenate a hopeful view of life. One promising approach in interpersonal practice is the use of the "miracle question" (De Jong & Miller, 1995; De Shazer, 1988; Miller, 1997). The miracle question can take on a variety of forms, but in essence asks consumers to consider how their life would be different if their primary problems were to vanish, and further, how they would recognize that their life had changed. Miller (1997) notes that it is difficult to consider miracles when you are constantly focused on problems. Getting consumers to even consider the possibility of a miracle is an important first step, but as Miller (1997) asserts "the task at hand is figuring out how the miracle can be made to happen or . . . figuring out how the miracle is already evident in clients' lives" (p. 81).

While there are those who eschew any contact with mental health professionals (and sometimes for good reason) it seems fair to assert that, for many, these relationships are vitally important. It is not surprising that what appears to matter greatly to consumers is that professionals treat them with respect and dignity. Disrespect is demonstrated in team meetings and progress notes rife with phrases such as "lacks motivation," "non-compliant," "manipulative,"or "resistive." Disrespect occurs when professionals discount a consumer's goal as "unrealistic" or deem that its acceptance will "set them up to fail." Disrespect is manifest when professionals deny a client's experience, the knowledge they have, and their narratives of struggle and redemption. Actually, there is evidence that consumers are quite knowledgeable about mental illness and learn how to monitor the cycles of illness and their own behavior accordingly (Spaniol, Gagne, & Koehler, 1997).

Facilitating Purpose

While hope may be the core ingredient to the recovery process the next step is perhaps the most crucial—translating this renewed optimism into action. Accordingly, a critical ingredient of recovery is purpose, and a formidable but critical task for professionals is to help facilitate the sense of purpose in the lives of consumers.

For those facing the most stringent of challenges the intrinsic desire to attack each day has been weakened. Consider this bleak portrait of mental illness: "I have nothing to live for, no drive but to just exist. . . . Sometimes I sleep 12 to 14 hours because there's nothing else to do. No zest" (Stanley, 1992, p. 25). This individual's observation is shared by many struggling through mental illnesses, but the steps taken by many of these individuals to begin the process of recovery are particularly instructive.

> And so I took my dreams off the backburner and claimed as my personal goals, understanding, writing and doing something to help others who were afflicted. Doing so was neither grandiose or magnanimous. It was survival. (Keil, 1992, p. 6)

> One short term goal was to further myself educationally, and I took buses to get to college. (Reilly, 1992, p. 20)

> You can live through any kind of a situation, if you find a reason for living through it. We survivors were daily living through impossible situations precisely by finding reasons for living. (Fergeson, 1992, p. 30)

> With Mark's death, I was snapped into a new awareness that resulted in my not only caring about others, but having a cause worth fighting for. (Risser, 1992, p. 39)

Mental health programs vary widely in the degree to which they facilitate or suppress purpose. In many environs, our programs and interventions are directed towards survival and maintenance. People with severe mental illness are asked to adopt "clienthood" as their primary role. Today, it is not uncommon for consumers to spend their days in some form of psychosocial program and their nights in some congregate setting where staff establish the rules and direct the activities (even the term *consumer* connotes taking not giving).

Other programs create environments rich with opportunities to contribute and have purpose. Any review of the success of clubhouse models, support groups, or consumer-directed programming point to ability to offer people important and meaningful roles—oftentimes focused on helping others. In some situations people are pressed into service because there are more important roles to be filled than people to fill them. Rappaport, Reischl, and Zimmerman (1992) use the term *underpopulated* to describe such settings.

Returning to Figure 14.1, a key force in niche enrichment comes from the expansion of individual talents and skills. Historically, the prime vehicles to help consumers in this life domain have been structured skill building exercises and groups, day treatment, and other in-house educational efforts. It is certain that these efforts have been helpful to many. On the downside, teaching people skills in a laboratory is similar to teaching history as a series of facts and dates without proper context. Education, strictly speaking, works better when there are chances to practice in real life.

In previous work, parallels were drawn between the concept of underpopulation and the social context found in some developing countries—and this is most evident in the area of work (Sullivan, 1994b). Because of the nature of work in some of these countries, and the need for all available people to contribute, there are built-in incentives that encourage participation by all—even those commonly excluded in more technologically developed lands. This constitutes a naturally occurring normalization process. Beyond the obvious mathematical reality that there are increased opportunities to work, it is argued here that this constitutes an increased pathway to recovery. The idea is straightforward and self-evident: Work provides meaning and a chance to contribute, enhances self-esteem, and provides a connection with other people and the community. As in some developing countries, in many consumer-operated services, there is the necessity to encourage the involvement and labor of others. Similar to volunteer organizations, people are needed to fill key roles and do important tasks. When this happens, people often must stretch, that is, assume unaccustomed responsibilities that impel them to learn additional skills. In daily life, people often speak of "growing with the job." Such risk taking helps people gain a sense of mastery and prepares them to consider future challenges that will aid in their personal development.

This method of self-enrichment, and by extension, niche enlargement is only possible if people are afforded opportunities. The deficit perspective pivots on the identification of real or perceived inabilities. Staying with the current example, such deficits are seen as insurmountable barriers to work and when coupled with an inflexible and inhospitable social milieu, one avenue toward recovery is blocked. Note that the traditional vocational programming found in many health programs, captured by the phrase "food, filth, and folding," does not mitigate this issue. For work to significantly contribute to recovery it must provide a connection to mainstream cultural activities and symbols. Traditional work programs, such as in-house services, or enclaves, *may* be important steps towards recovery but they can do so *only* by building confidence and skills and by providing structure and modeling opportunities. The argument here is that these traditional work programs should not routinely be considered an end or desired state.

Work not only offers purpose but also helps people afflicted with mental illness to transform their self-concept from "I am schizophrenic" to "I have schizophrenia but it is only one part of me." For many people, the mental illness becomes their principle source of identification thereby reifying the problems and the perceived limits that accompany them. On the occasion of meeting a new person, we often first ask, "What do you do for a living?" Because of their status, most people with mental illness are answer-less. Even an unemployed person can respond, "I'm an unemployed fork-lift operator". Work allows a consumer to say, "I'm a cook, an artist, a teacher, etc." and build an identity beyond the illness.

It may well be that there are some cultural contexts in which people with a range of physical and mental challenges are more freely accepted and, thus, are afforded more access to resources and opportunities. In America, there are undoubtedly places where this is true. But the overall fabric of our society, while changing, is threaded with ambivalence about people with challenging conditions, particularly serious and persistent mental illness. Our society is predicated on predictability and standardization. McDonald's is popular *because* the food is always the same. There are now a host of standardized services staffed by professionals who perform functions that were once considered the domain of the family. But the reality is, too, that our population is mobile and the structure and nature of family life is evolving. Thus, the cultural and environmental context that can support persons with mental illness will not readily occur naturally, it must be created.

"Choose, get, and keep" models of services, in the area of work, home, education, and leisure, are examples of strengths-oriented models of service (Anthony & Blanch, 1988). By focusing on the necessary supports needed for success, rather than the impediments to success created by mental illnesses, one by one, business by business, home by home, the niches of consumers are enlarged. Therefore, returning to Figure 14.1, key environmental factors, opportunities, and supports are linked. But in the end, programs such as these will need the proper social and fiscal policy context to survive, and ultimately, to alter the prevailing views on the life chances and competencies of citizens.

Social Policy

Social policy helps create the social, political, and economic environment where professionals and consumers come together and work toward a better life. Social policy effects wealth and its distribution, opportunity structures, personal control, and human and civil rights, and the shape of services offered to assist. Much of current social policy has been based on a belief that major mental illness is a chronic, life-long illness with little chance of escape. Furthermore, implicitly and explicitly the message is clear: Those facing serious mental illnesses need protection and social care, and until deemed stable, they shall remain socially segregated.

Current policy reinforces the oppression that people with serious mental illness suffer. Most live in poverty and, at best, can merely survive on a SSI check. Since reimbursment to service providers is commonly based on the amount of service provided, the day-to-day life of many consumers is dominated by contact with mental health programs. Since group interventions are more lucrative, individualized services suffer. Opportunities afforded many of us in work, living arrangements, recreation and social activities, and social relationships are severely constricted by the double jeopardy of poverty and mentalism (the institutionalized and interpersonal bias and discrimination against people with mental illness).

Recovery-oriented policies would be based on a different set of assumptions. First, it would recognize that more than 50 percent of people with severe mental illness actually do recover to a substantial degree, and that number likely would be even higher with more vigorous supports and incentives (Harding, 2000). Second, it would recognize that oppressed people need more choices and power to choose rather than less (Rappaport, 1978). Third, it would not allow spirit-breaking practices like restraints, isolation, sequestering, and physical force to occur.

The suggestion is that social policy should be based on a strengths perspective (Chapin, 1995). Two of the most successful pieces of social legislation have been the Social Security Act and the G. I. Bill. The Social Security Act's "old age benefit" was not based on a derogatory view of the elderly but rather that their lifetime of contribution should entitle them to a minimum income at retirement. This act has been the most successful antipoverty effort in the United States. Similarly, the G. I. Bill recognized the debt owed by other Americans to the soldiers of World War II. In the form of assistance in housing, job training, and college, the G. I. Bill underwrote opportunities for a decent life for veterans, many of whom suffered the physical and emotional ravages of war.

The following is a sample of policy initiatives that would reflect the application of a strengths-based, recovery-oriented perspective to social policy on behalf of people with severe mental illness.

1. Prohibit Abusive Practices.

The use of physical restraints, isolation, and other forms of physically coercive practices should be banned or further limited. In contrast, advanced directives in which clients define how they are to be treated and by whom during difficult crisis situations should be required.

2. Strengthen Antidiscrimination Law.

Although discrimination in housing based on disability is illegal, discrimination based on source of income is legal in all states but Massachusetts. It should be illegal to deny a person housing based on whether they have a voucher.

3. Establish Bridge Tenant Based Assistance (TBA) Programs.

HUD Section 8 housing vouchers have allowed many people the opportunity to afford decent living arrangements, but the number of people needing them far outstrips the supply. A combination of increasing HUD vouchers and states establishing transitional voucher programs until HUD vouchers are available would open up housing opportunities to many more people. A Texas program has produced significant outcomes in this regard (Burek, Toproc, & Olsen, 1996).

4. Fund College Scholarships.

Adults learn in college not in psychosocial programs. College is a primary path to a better life. No person with mental illness should be denied the opportunity because of lack of money. A modest scholarship fund for college or vocational school would open this opportunity.

5. Establish Asset-Matching Accounts.

The accumulation of assets rather than income seems a more powerful force for moving out of poverty (Page-Adams & Sherraden, 1997). States could establish a pool of funds to match (2 to 1) any money saved by consumers for the purpose of home ownership, education, business start-up, or buying a car.

6. Defund Segregated Programs and Fund Recovery-Oriented Programs.

A few examples are proposed. Abolish or dramatically decrease HUD 611 funds that promote segregated housing and reallocate those funds to increase vouchers. Reduce reimbursement rates to psychosocial programs and replace them with increased funding for consumer-run programs, supported work, and supported education programs.

7. Realign the Incentive Structure.

The incentives contained in most mental health financing schemes produce the current maintenance orientation of services. The suggestion is to realign monetary incentives so that service providers are rewarded for recovery-oriented outcomes like competitive work, independent living, improved educational status, and client satisfaction with the services they receive.

These policy recommendations are hardly exhaustive, in part because the adoption of the recovery model for mental health services has not been universally embraced. Using recovery as a benchmark for success in day-to-day practice will undoubtedly expose a new list of important policy initiatives and alternations that can help create a context within which consumers can flourish.

Conclusions and Recommendations

The recent interest in the process of recovery has put the consumer back into the equation for success. While there is little doubt that pharmaceutical breakthroughs and the refinement and development of community-based models of care have been important for success, the efforts of consumers cannot be overlooked. Through their own drive and determination and the use of available supports, the ability of many consumers to surmount the potentially devastating effects of mental illness is an established fact.

Recovery is also an interactive process that requires a supportive environmental context. Such environments extend from the intimate and face-to-face interactions with family, friends, and professionals, to the resources and responsibilities of community life and the provisions of public policy. The exploration of the dimensions of the recovery experience must ascertain the effects and contributions of such environments. When recognized, all phases of professional service, from direct practice, to program design, to public policy must be fashioned to buttress and support consumers on the road to recovery. We argue here that when the mission of mental health services is shaped by the vision of recovery that professional practice at all levels will be informed by the principles of the strengths model. From the reports of consumers and the research conducted to date on successful community-based programs, several recommendations are offered.

If the professional–consumer relationship has a basic role in the process of recovery it is in the potential for this interchange to be hope provoking. A bedrock principle requires that practitioners believe deeply that consumers can continue to transcend the impact of serious mental illness and recover. Expectations must be set high and communicated. Simultaneously the small steps taken by consumers must be celebrated. The professional, at minimum, must be consumer focused, empathic, steadfast, genuine, and trustworthy (Rapp, 1998).

In conjunction with the first principle, social agencies must endeavor to *put the consumer center-stage* and ensure that programs and policies are designed for the benefit of those they serve, not simply for their convenience. Consumer input will be gathered on all fronts and this data will be used to alter the day-to-day operations of the agency. These agencies should clearly articulate a mission and vision that reinforce the expectation of recovery. Importantly, the attitude and actions of all staff must speak to their commitment to the mission.

Professional services and agency involvement must also be viewed as *a way station, not a destination.* All efforts are directed to helping consumers take incremental steps towards active engagement in community life. Professional staff seek to secure community collaborators, peer support programs, and other people or services that can replace the functions and activities they are providing. Providers should seek to build "programs without walls" (Sullivan, 1989). This is an important step in reversing the seemingly implacable journey towards perpetual clienthood.

The first encounter between a consumer and professional sets the stage for the journey that follows. It is for this reason that the assessment phase of helping must involve the discovery of individual and environmental strengths. Intriguingly, *the process of strengths discovery may be more valuable* than the initial document that is generated. The ability of the practitioner to tease out the dreams, desires, and wishes of consumers is indispensable to recovery. From here the consumer–professional team explores past activities and interests in key life domains and begins an initial inventory of community resources that are essential for consumers to realize their goals and dreams.

As a dynamic tool the strengths assessment should aid the delineation of consumer goals in key life domains (work, housing, health, leisure, etc.). These goals should be tailored to the specific needs of the clients ranging in degree of difficulty and level of specificity. In essence these goals are the steps that force the action and move the consumer back towards full community citizenship. Recovery involves both challenges and risks, often the very things that professional services seek to avoid. Yet, as research has demonstrated, when pressed into important roles consumers are often equal to the task (Rappaport et al., 1992). At times additional supports are needed, like job coaches or mentors, but these services are still geared to buttress consumer strengths, and reflect an appreciation of the innate ability of all consumers to work.

The job of providers and consumers would be enhanced by *enlightened social policy that reduces despair and instills hope* producing practices and reallocating funds to recovery-oriented lives. Funds should be available to increase a person's opportunities and resources for a decent adult life, not just a life as a service recipient.

By simple modifications in the environment a context is created for the individual to experience success. So at each successive step—beginning at the level of the one-to-one relationship, to involvement with social agencies, to the first steps back into community—the supports, feedback, and experience of interested others interact with the drive and will to succeed of consumers and lay the paving stones of the recovery journey.

Pain and frustration often mark the recovery process, and it is rarely linear. This fact alone can be discouraging to those who care about consumers including family members and professional helpers. Yet, this fact alone provides little justification for turning our back on those who have shown an amazing ability to persevere in spite of enduring a host of biophysical and social insults. The task that lies before us is to craft a supportive environmental context for recovery to flourish. It is well within our power and resources.

DISCUSSION QUESTIONS

1. How is the recovery movement different from our usual way of thinking about the future of people with severe and persistent mental illness?

2. If you worked in a community support program (CSP) what steps would you take as a social worker to enhance the recovery possibilities of some one with, say, a diagnosis of chronic undifferentiated schizophrenia?

3. What is a good and enabling niche? How would you recognize one? Do such places exist for people with mental illness?

4. Discuss the role of hope in recovery from mental illness (and others of life's troubles).

5. What role can social policy play in making life better for people who struggle with serious life problems? What can you as a social worker do to influence social policies?

REFERENCES

Anthony, W. (1993). Recovery from mental illness: The guiding vision of the mental health system in the 1990s. *Psychosocial Rehabilitation Journal, 16*(4), 11–23.

Anthony, W., & Blanch, A. (1988). Supported employment for persons who are psychiatrically disabled: An historical and conceptual perspective. *Psychosocial Rehabilitation Journal, 11*(2), 5–23.

Burek, S., Toproc, M., & Olsen, M. (1996, February 11–13). Third year outcomes of supported housing in Texas: Measuring the long-term effects of system change. Paper presented at the sixth annual national conference of *State Mental Health Agency Services Research and Program Evaluation,* Arlington, VA.

Chapin, R. T., (1995). Social policy development: The strengths perspective. *Social Work, 40*(4), 506–514.

Cowger, C. (1997). Assessing client strengths: Assessing for client empowerment. In D. Salee-bey (Ed.), *The strengths perspective in social work practice* (2nd ed.), (pp. 59–73). New York: Longman.

Davidson, W. S., & Rapp, C. (1976). Child advocacy in the justice system. *Social Work, 21*(3), 225–232.

Deegan, P. E. (1988). Recovery: The lived experience of rehabilitation. *Psychosocial Rehabilitation, 11,* 11–19.

De Jong, P., & Miller, S. (1995). How to interview for client strengths. *Social Work, 40*(6), 729–736.

Dembo, T. (1982). Some problems in rehabilitation as seen by a Lewinian. *Journal of Social Issues, 38*(1), 131–139.

De Shazer, S. (1988). *Clues: Investigating solutions in brief therapy.* New York: Norton.

Faris, R., & Dunham, H. W. (1939). *Mental disorders in urban areas.* Chicago: University of Chicago Press.

Goffman, E. (1961). *Asylums: Essays on the social situation of mental patients and other inmates.* Garden City, NY: Anchor Books.

Gowdy, E., & Rapp, C. (1989). Managerial behavior: The common denominators of effective community-based programs. *Psychosocial Rehabilitation Journal, 13*(2), 31–51.

Grimer, D. (1992). The invisible illness. *The Journal, 3,* 27–28.

Harding, C. (2000). *Overcoming the persistent resistance within the helping professions to ideas of recovery in serious mental illness.* Lawrence, KS: The University of Kansas School of Social Welfare.

Keil, J. (1992). The mountain of my mental illness. *The Journal, 3,* 5–6.

Kretzmann, J., & McKnight, J. (1993). *Building communities from the inside out: A path towards finding and mobilizing community assets.* Evanston, IL: Center for Urban Affairs and Policy Research, Neighborhood Innovations Network, Northwestern University.

Leete, E. (1993). The interpersonal environment: A consumer's personal recollection. In A. B. Hotfield & H. P. Lefley (Eds.), *Surviving mental illness.* New York: Guilford Press, pp. 114–128.

McQuaide, S., & Ehrenreich, J. H. (1997). Assessing client strengths. *Families in Society, 78*(2), 201–212.

Miller, G. (1997). *Becoming miracle workers.* New York: Aldine De Gruyter.

Page-Adams, D., & Sherraden, M. (1997). Asset building and community revitalization strategy. *Social Work, 42,* 423–434.

Rapp, C. (1998). *The strengths model.* New York: Oxford University Press.

Rappaport, J. (1977). *Community psychology.* New York: Holt, Rinehart, & Winston.

Rappaport, J., Reischl, T., & Zimmerman, M. (1992). Mutual help mechanisms in the empower-ment of former mental patients. In D. Saleebey (Ed.), *The strengths perspective in social work practice* (pp. 84–97). New York: Longman.

Reilly, S. (1992). Breaking loose. *The Journal, 3,* 20.

Riusser, P. A. (1992). An empowering journey. *The Journal, 3,* 38–39.

Roach, J. (1993). Clinical case management with severely mentally ill adults. In M. Harris, & H. Bergman (Eds.), *Case management for mentally ill patients* (pp. 17–40). Langhorne, PA: Harwood.

Saleebey, D. (1997). Community development, group empowerment, and individual resilience. In D. Saleebey (Ed.). *The strengths perspective in social work practice* (2nd ed.), (pp. 199–216). New York: Longman.

Snyder, C. R. (2000). Hypothesis: There is hope. In C. R. Snyder (Ed.), *Handbook of hope: Theory, measures, and application.* San Diego: Academic Press.

Spaniol, L., Gagne, C., & Koehler, M. (Eds.). (1997). *Psychological and social aspects of psychiatric dis-ability.* Boston: Sargent College of Allied Professions, Boston University.

Sullivan, W. P. (1989). Community support programs in rural areas: Developing programs with-out walls. *Human Services in the Rural Environment, 12*(4), 19–24.

Sullivan, W. P. (1994a). A long and winding road: The process of recovery from severe mental ill-ness. *Innovations and research, 3*(3), 19–27.

Sullivan, W. P. (1994b). Recovery from schizophrenia: What we can learn from the developing nations. *Innovations and Research, 3*(2), 7–15.

Taylor, J. (1997). Niches and practice: Extending the ecological perspective. In D. Saleebey (Ed.), *The strengths perspective in social work practice* (2nd ed.), (pp. 217–227). New York: Longman.

Thyer, B., & Myers, L. (1998). Social learning theory: An empirically-based approach to understanding human behavior in the social environment. *Journal of Human Behavior in the Social Environment, 1*(1), 23–32.

Torrey, E. F., & Yolken, R. (1998). Is household crowding a risk factor for schizophrenia and bipolar disorder? *Schizophrenia Bulletin, 24*(3), 321–324.

Young, S., & Ensing, D. (1999). Exploring recovery from the perspective of people with psychiatric disabilities. *Psychiatric Rehabilitation Journal, 22*(3), 219–231.

Wakefield, J. (1996). Does social work need the eco-systems perspective? Part 1. Is the perspective clinically useful? *Social Service Review, 70*(1), 1–32.

15 The Strengths Perspective

Possibilities and Problems

DENNIS SALEEBEY

Focusing and building on client strengths is not simply a counterweight to the prevalence of the deficit model. It is an imperative of the several values that govern our work and the operations of a democratic, just, and pluralistic society including distributive justice, equality, respect for the dignity of the individual, inclusiveness and diversity, and the search for maximum autonomy within maximum community. There has been some criticism of the strengths perspective that turns on its blithe ignoring of the realities of structural poverty, institutional inequality, and the reality of oppression and discrimination.

John Longres (1997) makes the case that devotion to the strengths perspective may lead to the scrapping of those sociological and political ideas (e.g., Marxism, symbolic interactionism, and functionalism) that give an invaluable slant on the withering realities of oppression, alienation, and anomie. This is a serious criticism, if true. I do not think that there is anything in the strengths approach that requires ignoring the viewpoints and insights of any number of theories. I do think, however, that many of those theories have been misused to only illuminate the nether regions of the human condition, something that is not necessarily inherent in their character. And those theories are formed around essential values. Some are founded on the belief in the altruistic and valorous core of the human condition and human nature. Others are funded by the belief that human nature is self-interested and acquisitive. Some are driven by the essential value of libertarianism (the highest value is individual rights), others by communitarian spirit (the highest value is interdependence). Some focus on human nature as basically economic, often political; others focus on human nature as grounded in the commons—the shared possibilities that only come forth in interaction, each person with the other (O'Toole, 1995). The point? That all theories have an inclination or two that prepares the ground for their evolution and that theories are often conflicted about the basic qualities of human nature and the human condition. The strengths perspective, not as grand as a theory, nor as evolved, by any means, recognizes the fallibilities of people and the grinding problems that they face, but it is an attempt to restore, beyond rhetoric, some balance to the understanding of the human condition such that we recognize and honor the strengths and capacities of people as well as their afflictions and agonies.

In a sense, everything depends on the vitality and fairness of the developmental and social infrastructures of the community and state. In Walzer's (1983) view, justice and equality do not call for the elimination of differences, but the elimination of certain kinds of differences—those defined or created by people in power that are the bedrock of their domination of fellow citizens, whether the differences are couched in the language of race, class, gender, sexual orientation, or religious belief. In his words:

> It's not the fact that there are rich and poor that generates egalitarian struggle but the fact that the rich grind the faces of the poor. It's always what one group with power does to another group—whether in the name of health, safety or security—it makes no difference. The aim, ultimately, of the fight for equality is always the elimination of subordination . . . no more toadying, scraping and bowing, fearful trembling. (p. xiii)

For us, the message is that many models and institutions of helping have become pillars of this kind of inequality. They have evolved into means of domination through identity stripping, culture killing, status degradation, base rhetoric, and/or sequestering. We dominate, sometimes benignly with a velvet glove, and we may do it in the name of good, welfare, service, helping, or therapy. What we have finally done, *by emphasizing and assigning social status to a person's deficiencies, differences, and defects is to rob them of some of their inherent powers and motivations.* Or at the least we steal from them the opportunities, the courage, and the audacity to use those powers. In a sense, in the name of helping sometimes we have impoverished, not empowered. All of our knowledge (theories, principles) and all of our technical orientations must be examined, "critiqued, challenged, or corroborated in the light of their relationships to power and interest" (Kondrat, 1995, p. 417). Whether we discover that we are serving corporate interests, malign political claims, or benighted professional frameworks, if they, in any way, obfuscate or distort local knowledge, ignore and suppress personal and communal strengths and powers (cognitive, moral, behavioral, political), then we, too, have committed a root act of oppression.

Whatever else it is, social justice is understood only in terms of domination—domination of the distribution of social goods, those resources essential for survival, growth and development, transformation, simple security and safety. Welfare, communal support and connection, commodities, goods, health, education, recreation, shelter, all underwrite identity as well as personal resourcefulness and strength—the tools for becoming as human and competent as possible. A more just and equitable distribution system is at the heart of the development and expression of individual and collective powers and capacities. As social workers, we confront and promote the idea of strengths at two very different levels—policy (philosophy) and practice (principles)—but they always meet in the lives of our clients.

In the 1960s, we talked of "power to the people." That apothegm had many different meanings. Not the least of these was that a government or social movement must dedicate itself to returning social, economic, material, and political goods to the people who had been systematically denied them. The idea of returning power to ordinary and oppressed citizens alike raised nettlesome questions. What, in fact, do people need? What are citizens entitled to? Whose claims to scarce social goods shall prevail? How shall these goods be distributed? When the ardor of the 1960s was stanched in the mid-1970s, these questions had not been answered. Today, in the debate over balanced budgets, the size of the federal government, welfare and health care reform, we seem no closer to answers.

In the 1980s, the New Federalism—Reaganomics, for some—made the idea that these social resources could be disbursed through the devices of the marketplace exceedingly attractive. But the marketplace, at best, can provide only limited resources, often on quite a selective and preemptive basis. And, it should be obvious to anyone who shops, trades, sells, or invests, that the marketplace is no venue for the pursuit of justice, equity, or recompense. Unless it might sell beans, philosophic assertions about fertilizing the roots of democracy seem frightfully out of place in the private, for-profit sector of the economy. One would think, however, judging by all the books, talk shows, workshops, infomercials available that the marketplace distribution of social and psychological capital has been a tremendous success. I think, rather, that this procession of pop-psych, pop-soc nostrums indicates that we have failed through conventional socializing institutions to help many individuals develop a sense of autonomy, personal mastery, or communal connection and failed to assist neighborhoods, communities, and cultures to retain their sense of value and distinctiveness.

As we lurched toward the millenium in the 1990s, the impetus for slicing the traditional ties between government and vulnerable people, between workers and corporations gained momentum. The welfare reforms of 1996 (the Personal Responsibility and Work Opportunity Act), all gussied up in the language of familial responsibility and participation in the workplace, still leave almost 14 million children poor. And while officials chortle at the success of getting people on welfare back to work, they ignore some obvious facts. First, most people (usually women and their children) used welfare as it was intended: as a temporary socioeconomic respite when work was not available. Roughly 70 percent of all AFDC recipients fell into this category. The other 30 percent had much more tenuous ties to the workplace because of lack of skills, personal difficulties, searing intergenerational poverty, mental and physical illness. Even given that, the total time spent on AFDC by all who ever received it is 6 years. Second, it is unlikely at this point that welfare reform will touch the dire circumstances, the problematic motivation, the dearth of ways into the opportunity structure of the latter group. The other 70 percent will do as they have done in the past (Albelda & Folbre, 1996; Edelman, 1997). This is not to say that AFDC was a smashing success. But it is to say that the values that originally inspired it were closer relatives of the considerations and necessities of social justice. Finally, the debate that led to these changes turned on old stereotypes of the poor; ignored many of the structural foundations of enduring poverty; smelled more than a little bit of racism; and ignored the fact that a dead-end job with few or no benefits, or a transient one, is worse in some ways than welfare, in that it does not assure, to as great a degree, the health and security of the children and other dependents involved.

We have argued in this book for a subtle change in the basic equation between equality, justice, community, and autonomy and asserted that there is power in the people and their environments. No matter how subordinated, marginalized, and oppressed individuals and communities may appear, people, individually and collectively, can find nourishment for their hopes and dreams, tools for their realization somewhere. These tools may be damaged, hidden, or out of circulation, but, whatever their condition, they are there awaiting discovery and/or expression. When we talk of building on client strengths, of respecting people's accounts of their lives, of regard and respect for a people's culture, we are, in a sense, giving testimony that, in spite of injustice and inequity, people do have prospects. People do show a kind of resilience and vitality that, even though it may lie dormant or assume other guises, is inward. In some ways, the work of the strengths perspective is a modest form of locality justice: aligning people with their own resources and the assets of the neighborhood or community. In the end, this work is about citizenship: helping individuals, families, and communities develop a portfolio of competencies and resources that more fully allows them to enact the duties and receive the rights of full citizenship. The quest for social resources and justice should never end, but we do not have to wait for the Godot of ultimate justice to do this work well.

Questions and Cautions about the Strengths Perspective

Those of us who have been involved in practice, education, research, and training using the strengths perspective have encountered a number of concerns expressed by practitioners and students. I will present these in the form of questions.

Isn't the strengths perspective just positive thinking in another guise? The United States has a long and honored tradition of positive thinking that even today is alive and well. From Mary Baker Eddy to Norman Vincent Peale to Anthony Robbins, our society has enjoyed an array of positive thinkers purveying their own nostrums and panaceas on television, in books, in workshops, from the pulpit, and through other media. My view is that the strengths perspective is not the mindless recitation of uplifting mantras or the idea that relief and surcease from pain and trauma is just a meditation or glib reframing away. Rather, it is the hard work of helping clients and communities build something of lasting value from the social wealth and human capital within and around them. There is little else from which to create possibility and prospects where none may have existed before.

Your expertise as a professional social worker is obviously one of the resources to be used, but by itself professional cunning and craft is not enough; social services are not enough. We must help find, summon, and employ the resources of the client or community. But people, especially people living against the persistent rush of dire circumstance, are not prone to think of themselves and their world in terms of strengths or as having emerged from scarring events with something useful or redeeming. In addition, if they also happen to be or have been clients of the health, mental health, or welfare systems, they may have been indoctrinated in the ideology of weakness, problems, and deficiencies. They are not easily dissuaded from using these ritual symbols to understand themselves and their situation. The strengths perspective requires us, as well, to fashion collaborative, appreciative client relationships that we have been taught are the basis for effective, principled work with clients. Establishing such relationships obliges us to a strict and accurate accounting of client assets. Finding these and utilizing them compels arduous and careful work.

Aren't you ignoring the real problems and difficulties that people have especially when they are at the point of seeking help? I don't think that there is anything in this book or inherent in the perspective itself that requires being heedless of the serious problems of living and relationships that people have. Case management with people who have serious and persistent mental illness—say, schizophrenia of one sort or another—begins with these assertions: that these individuals have had and do suffer from a serious human condition that has biopsychosocial and spiritual components; that they have had or do have hallucinations or delusions; that they have probably experienced serious ruptures in the tempo and pace of their lives; that they may need medication and support for a lengthy period of time. But the strengths perspective is driven by the idea that each of these individuals has prospects and possibilities. The essential presumption is that they will recover and that there are a variety of internal and external resources still available to them. In a pilot study of the recovery of people with serious mental disorders, the 71 consumers who were interviewed identified several factors critical to recovery. The most important elements, in order, were the ability to have hope; developing trust in one's own thoughts and judgments; and enjoying the environment—basking in the warmth of the sun, listening to the sounds of the ocean, sitting in the shade of a tree. Simple pleasures and ready possibilities (Ralph, Lambric, & Steele, 1996).

If practitioners using a strengths framework do disregard the real problems that afflict clients and those around them and, thus, end up contributing to the damage done to people's lives, that is capricious, perhaps even reckless. There is nothing, however, in the strengths approach that mandates the discounting of the problems of life that people bring to us. In each of the chapters of this book, authors call for a responsible, balanced assessment and treatment plan, seeking to undo the too-often imbalanced deficit or problem assessments. All helpers should evaluate and come to a reckoning of the sources and remnants of individual and family troubles, pains, difficulties, and disorders. Often, this is where people begin, this is what they are compelled to relate, these are matters of the greatest urgency. There may well be the need for catharsis, for grieving and mourning, for the expression of rage or anxiety. We may also need to understand the barriers, both presumed and real, to the realization of hopes, dreams, and expectations. As Norman Cousins (1989) suggested, we shouldn't "deny the verdict" (diagnosis/assessment) but "defy the sentence" (prognosis/outcome).

Once having assessed the damage and the disappointment, we must ensure that the diagnosis—the assessment—does not become the cornerstone of an emergent identity. To avoid that possibility, we want to calculate how people have managed to survive in spite of their troubles, what they have drawn on in the face of misfortune or their own mistakes. We want to understand what part of their struggle has been useful to them. We want to know what they know, what they can do, and where they now want to go. Whatever else the symptoms that so bemuse us are, they are also a sign of the soul, of the struggle to be more fully alive, responsible, and involved (Moore, 1992). For social workers, the goal may not be the heroic cure, but the constancy of caring and connection and working collaboratively toward the improvement of day-to-day living, in spite of, or because of, symptoms. So what is of interest to us is how people have taken steps, summoned up resources, and coped. People are always working on their situations, even if just deciding for the moment to be resigned. As helpers, we must tap into that work, elucidate it, find and build on its promise. In some contexts, even resignation about or acceptance of one's condition may be a sign of strength.

It is well, too, to keep in mind that labels always bespeak the reality of an outsider, they collectivize and abstract real experience, and make the client's own experience and stories seem alien and contrived. We must use labels judiciously if at all, and with a profound respect for their distortions and limitations, and also with an equally profound respect for their potential to "mortify" individuals (Goffman, 1961), stripping them of their distinctive identity, and overwhelming them, through a variety of rituals and social processes, with their new and exotic identity. It may be useful, however, to think of a label as a designation given too quickly, without sufficient biopsychosocial assessment, and delivered through the efficacies and efficiencies of the power inequality between professional (and institution) and client.

Why is it that people do not look as though they have strengths? Why do they seem beaten, angry, depressed, and rebellious? Dominated people are often alienated people; they are separated from their inner resources, external supports, their own history and traditions. People struggling with cruel circumstance, the betrayal of their bodies in disease, or foundering in the larger social and economic world also find themselves isolated, alienated from their own resources and sense of self and place. One of the key effects of alienation is identification with the oppressor. Such identification may assume many forms but it is, regrettably, common. One of its forms is the assumption of the self-identifying terms of a diagnostic label: Or, in other words, to be what the oppressor says I am (Freire, 1973). Herb Kutchins and Stuart Kirk (1997) remind us that the mental health enterprise turns on the administration of people's minds and the bureaucratization of their health. Both depend on the power to define. The more specific the definition, as in DSM IV, now the DSM IV TR (Text Revision) (American Psychiatric Association, 2000), the more the authenticity of inner experience and perception, the more the availability of capacities becomes lost. Consider, Joel Kovel (1981) says, ADHD (Attention

Deficit Hyperactivity Disorder)—a disorder manifested by the fact that some kids, usually male, move around too much, that is, at least too much for school authorities (this is not to deny that there is a *much smaller* group of youth who do seem to have complex neurobiological abnormalities underlying what some would label their hyperactivity). The child occupies the wrong kind of space in too little time and is thus considered to have a disease. Once the child is so defined, the system can control and administer. Once defined, the child also has the beginnings of a new identity so that some years down the road, he might define himself as a hyperactive adult.

   Isn't it true that the strengths perspective simply reframes deficit and misery? Some people have claimed that what proponents of a strengths-based approach really do is simply reconceptualize the difficulties that clients have so that they are sanitized and less threatening to self and others. In this way, someone with paranoid schizophrenia is regarded as having an extraordinary and acute sensitivity to other's meanings and motives. Or a person gripped by addiction is attempting to rediscover that lost creativity within. Thus, clients and workers do not do the hard work of transformation, normalization, and amelioration, risking action and building bridges to a larger world. But, again, the strengths approach does honor the pains of what has been called schizophrenia. The approach's tenets, principles, and methods were forged in intense work with people thought to have severe and persistent mental illness. In every case, to the extent that they apply, the authenticity of symptoms, delusions and hallucinations, the neurochemical and structural abnormalities and the necessity of medication are acknowledged and become part of the work of constructing a world of possibility and opportunity for the individual and family. We are not in the business of talking people out of painful realities. Remember, *it is as wrong to deny the problem as it is to deny the possible!* But there is a kind of reframing to be done—to fashion an attitude, a vocabulary, a story about prospects and expectation, and a four-color glossy picture of the genuine individual lurking beneath the diagnostic label. This is work—creating access to communal resources so that they become the ticket to expanded choices and routes to change.

   How does practice from a strengths perspective change what social workers do? If we are to believe advertisements for ourselves, maybe not much. But both loudly and implicitly, the chapters herein have decried the hegemony of the medical model, the caricature of the helper as sly and artful expert, as applied technologist, the idea that the world of the professional social worker travels a different orbit than the clients'. So, must we surrender our status as experts, our esoteric and practical knowledge and lore? While we might want to reexamine the notion of expert, especially the implicit paternalism nestled within it, we do have special knowledge and would be foolish to deny that. But, it might be very important to critically analyze and rethink the assumptions and the consequences of the use of our knowledge, as well as their cultural, racial, class, and gender distortions and biases. Many have commented on the attractive alternative to the usual construction of professional intervention developed by Donald Schön and Chris Argyris (Schön, 1983)—reflective practice (see discussion in Chapter 1). Opting for relevance rather than rigor, Schön's description of the reflective practitioner not only highlights the considerable artistry, intuition, and extemporaneousness of practice, but also a radically different contract between client and professional, very much in keeping with the strengths perspective.

A reflective contract finds the practitioner with obvious knowledge and skills to offer for service but also recognizes that the professional is not the only one in the contractual relationship with the capacity for enlightenment. The professional defines the work as a mutual quest in which the client is joined in a search for solutions, surcease, and success. Both parties to the contract have control: In a sense, they are independent but bound together. The professional asks the client to continually judge the work that is done and to revise its content and course as necessary. In any case, the core of the contract is in the establishment of an authentic connection to the client. In Schön's (1983) words,

> the reflective practitioner's relation with his [sic] client takes the form of a literally reflective conversation. Here the professional recognizes that his technical expertise is embedded in a context of meanings. He attributes to clients, as well as to himself, a capacity to mean, know, and plan. . . .He recognizes the obligation to make his own understandings accessible to his clients, which means he often needs to reflect anew on what he knows. (p. 295)

The nature of the contractual relationship changes in the direction of power equalization, mutual assessment, and evolving agreements. In a sense, the worker is the agent of the individual, family, or community. This may put the social worker in direct conflict with the agency, as discussed further in this section.

Perhaps the biggest change in practice will be a change in vision, the way in which we see and experience clients, even the most disreputable and frightening clients. Suspending skepticism, disbelief, and even our cynicism about clients and client groups will probably not be difficult for many social workers. We are of good heart, after all. But beyond that, to see in the internal and external environments of misery, pain, self-delusion, even self-destruction, the glimmer of potential, the glint of capacity, virtue, and hope asks of us a significant deepening of our consciousness of, and openness to, clients' worlds.

How can I work from a strengths orientation if my agency is riddled with the deficit model? We can hardly be about the business of empowering clients if we feel weak, powerless, defenseless, and alienated from our own work because of agency policies, philosophies, and attitudes toward clients. There is little doubt that in agencies where social control trumps the socialization of clients, deep pessimism about client motives exists. Negative expectations of clients hold thrall, work is defined in terms of controlling damage, and clients are defined in terms of degrees of manipulation and resistance, and the health of workers is compromised (Benard, 1994; Duncan, Hubble, & Miller, 1997). Burnout, turnover, dissatisfaction, and fatigue are too often the fruits of work conducted under these conditions. In my own experience, these conditions exist far more commonly than we think. They create an atmosphere polluted with negative or shrunken expectations of clients, and shrouded in a fog of anger, disappointment, and cynicism on the part of professionals.

If you work in such an agency, must you succumb to the blandishments and protective seductions of such a view of clients? We think not. There is always choice. For example, you can choose how you will regard your clients. You can take the time and make the effort to discover the resources within the client and in the environment. You can choose how you will interpret and use information about the client as well as deciding what information you will seek. Over the years, in a class on the biopsychosocial understanding of mental health and mental disorder, two suggestions from students stand out. In our state, as in many others, to be licensed as a social worker at the highest level, you must have had a course in psychopathology (understanding and making diagnoses using the DSM IV). The document itself is unremittingly negative and, as was observed before, turns each individual into a case. A student suggested that the five axes of assessment should be expanded to six. Axis VI would be a detailed accounting of the resources and strengths of the individual. She added that in every staffing you would be obligated to declare and demonstrate the positive attributes and environmental resources of the client—no matter how modest.

A second student once asked why there wasn't a diagnostic strengths manual—an attention-grabbing suggestion to say the least. With the suggestions of students, I embarked—somewhat tongue in cheek—on such an endeavor (Saleebey, 2001). This comes from the observation that it is difficult to employ a strengths perspective if you do not have a language or lexicon for doing so. One example: Under the section, 300.00 Estimable Personal Traits, we find 301.00 *Trustworthiness.*

> Criterion A.   For at least 6 months, nearly every day, the individual has exhibited at least three of the following:
>   1. Did what he or she promised
>   2. Kept at a task that had many snares and difficulties
>   3. Did not reveal a confidence
>   4. Stuck by a relative, friend, or colleague during a rough time
>   5. Did more than expected
>
> B.   This is not better explained by codependency or a pathological desire to please.
>
> C.   Such behavior must have improved the lives of other people.
>
> D.   Rule out the possibility of a self-seeking desire to cash in on these loyalties later.

How can I and why should I give up the disease or deficit model of the human condition when it is so acceptable and widespread in our culture, generally, and the culture of helping, in particular? Even though the devolution of health and mental health care toward managed care, the rise of third-party payments and vendorship, licensing, and the spread of private practice all play a part in the amplification of the disease model, it is, ultimately, an act of individual intention and purpose to renounce it. To do so you must examine it critically, examine the consequences of its employment in your work, and consider the advantages that the substitution of a strengths-based approach would confer on your professional work and on the welfare of your clients. The disease model has reigned in many fields, in some of them since the 19th century (psychiatry, for example), but it has produced very little in the way of positive results. By almost any measure, the problems we oppose with the tools and dispositions of the disease/medical model remain rampant and poorly understood, except at the most general level (Peele, 1995). As Hillman and Ventura (1992) claim, in a different arena, "We've had one hundred years of psychotherapy and the world is getting worse!"

The disease framework has reproduced itself over and over again in many different contexts. In spite of notable failures in treating common human frailties and conditions, more and more behavior patterns, habits, life transitions, life dilemmas, and personal traits—from excessive shopping to extremist thought, from persistent sexual activity to adolescent turmoil—are regarded as illnesses. This is not to ignore some successes. The neurobiological understanding (and psychopharmacological treatment) of some major mental disorders; the gradual unraveling of the mystery of the genetic components (and their interactions with the environment) of temperament; and the neuropsychological bases of emotions, memory, cognitive states of all kinds, as well as those of mental disorders, all have been remarkable. But the impudence and truculence of the human condition, in all its astonishing variety, still remains.

The disease framework, whatever else it is, is a kind of cultural discourse or conversation. It is a vocabulary that has consequences for those who are designated or defined under its lexicon. Kenneth Gergen (1994), taking a social constructionist[1] view of the situation, comments on the power of the deficit discourse promoted in the mental health field: to encourage social hierarchies (doctor/expert knows best and has the power to act on that knowledge) heightens the erosion of community (we focus almost always on individuals and ignore the context of their suffering or struggles), and fosters what he calls "self-enfeeblement."

> Mental deficit terms . . . inform the recipient that the "problem" is not circumscribed or limited in time and space or to a particular domain of his or her life; it is fully general. He or she carries the deficit from one situation to another, and like a birthmark or a fingerprint, as the textbooks say, the deficit will inevitably manifest itself. In effect, once people understand their actions in terms of mental deficits, they are sensitized to the problematic potential of all their activities, and how they are infected or diminished. The weight of the "problem" now expands manyfold; it is as inescapable as their own shadow. (pp. 150–151)

Yes, but . . . many social workers and agencies claim that they already abide by a strengths regimen. A review of what their practices actually involve often reveals applications that stray from an orientation to client strengths. The question is, "How would you know if you or your agency was practicing from a strengths perspective?"

---

[1]Roughly, social constructionism is an emerging point of view that emphasizes the role of interpretation, discourse, and language in understanding and making sense of human experience.

To be able to answer this, as Charlie Rapp has commented, would move everyone along in the articulation and use of this perspective. Let us give it a try. First, the emotional atmosphere in the agency and your own emotional state would be more passionate and buoyant. The expectations of both clients and staff would be more heartening and hopeful, creating a more uplifting ambience in the agency. Second, clients and their families would be more actively involved in their own journey to a better life, but also in the agency, participating as real partners and collaborators in program, policy, and helping (e.g., mentorship) to the extent that they wished. Third, the language and ethos of the agency (and the records and archives) and everyone in it—clients included—would be abundant with terms, phrases, metaphors, and categories that directly refer to the resources and capacities of clients and communities, the range of possibilities in people's lives, individually and collectively, and the shades and facets of enriched and collaborative helping relationships. It would also reflect clients' native languages and discourse metiers. Fourth, the realization and expression of health and hopefulness would be intense and embracing. Finally, the level of expertise of social workers would be expansive and balanced as they work to understand the continuing interplay of problems and possibilities in people's lives. This is a minimal list but perhaps a beginning. So, look around the agency or organization where you work or have a field placement. What do you see? Feel?

Get real! There is evil in the world; people can do horrible things to each other and to innocent victims. Isn't that true? It would be naive and disingenuous to deny the reality of evil. Apart from any philosophical efforts to define what it is, there is little doubt that there are individuals (and groups) who commit acts that are beyond our capacity to understand, let alone accept (see Chapter 1). But writing off such individuals and to circumscribe certain behaviors as irredeemable is an individual moral decision that you must make. Such a decision is not always rendered with clarity or certainty. For example, would you agree with George Bernard Shaw that "[t]he greatest of our evils and the worst of our crimes is poverty"? Or would Sophocles' cry, "Anarchy, anarchy! Show me a greater evil!" be more compelling? Certainly the world has endured, on both small and large scales, horrendous destruction of both spirit and life itself. Everyday brings with it another disclosure of tyranny of the soul and body—the capture of the minds and bodies of others. But in terms of our work, there are at least three things to consider in answering this difficult question:

1. There may be genuinely evil people, beyond grace or redemption, but it is best not to make that assumption about any individual first, even if the person has beaten his spouse or if she has sold crack to school-age kids.
2. Even if we are to work with someone whose actions are beyond our capacity to understand or accept, we must ask ourselves if they have useful skills and behaviors, even motivations and aspirations that can be tapped in the service of change to a less destructive way of life.
3. We also must ask if there are other more salutary and humane ways for these individuals to meet their needs or resolve their conflicts. We cannot automatically discount people without making a serious professional and moral accounting of the possibility for change and redemption.

Finally, in my experience when the judgment of clients as being beyond hope is made, it often relates more to the rendering of them as manipulative, threatening, or resistant within the treatment process.

In Erich Fromm's view, there is an uncanny commonality underneath those behaviors that destroy and demolish human spirit and those that uplift and assert it. Each individual or group bent on either the destruction or the affirmation of humankind does so from the requisite meeting of basic existential needs—for something to be devoted to, for roots, a place, and affective ties to others, and for a sense of coherence and integration, among others. These essential and compelling needs can be met through the blandishing of weapons, or the extension of the hand of friendship and care (1973).

Does the strengths model work? We can argue about what constitutes evidence but given our usual methodological appetites, both quantitative and qualitative research shows that the strengths perspective has a degree of power that would suggest its use with a variety of clients. The most current research summary compiled by Rapp (1998) does imply that the strengths model, when evaluated on its own or compared to other approaches, is efficacious in working with people with severe and persistent mental illness. If we examine various outcome measures—hospitalization rates, independence, health, symptoms, family burdens, achievement of goals, degree of social support among others—between and within studies, the strengths model consistently shows that it delivers results with populations that typically, over time, helped with more conventional methods, do not do as well on these measures.

It must be stated that modesty is appropriate here. The studies that Rapp (1998) cites include only two experimental studies, one quasi-experimental study and three nonexperimental studies involving a total of 783 people. These results, however, do not include any of the studies reported in this volume. Likewise, it does not include the substantial research done from other but related vantage points, such as the health realization work reported in Chapter 13. Nor does it include the research done on the factors that make helping, regardless of school, theory, or perspective, efficacious. (See Chapter 5.) It does not include the newly emergent studies of the recovery process for people with serious mental illness. Much remains to be done. But if we add to these studies the reports of practitioners around the country, the testimony of clients, and the witness of our own experience (these are data, too), there is no compelling reason to shrink from the strengths approach to practice.

Whatever else it might be, however else it might be construed, the strengths perspective, like other perspectives, is a manner of thinking about the work you do. The test of it is between you and those with whom you work. Do they think the work has been relevant to their lives? Do they feel more adept and capable? Have they moved closer to the hopes, goals, and objectives that they set before you? Do they have more connections with people and organizations, formal and informal, where they find succor, a place, occupation, project, time well spent, or fun? Do they have more awareness and respect of the energy and aptitude that they have forged in the fires of anguish and trauma? Do they have the sense that you will be with them and for them as they try to construct a better life for themselves? Do they know that you trust them eventually to continue on a path without your help, guidance, and good will?

In the end, the superordinance of the disease model should be foresworn because it discourages two facets of good social work practice:

- searching the environment for forces that enhance or suppress human possibilities and life chances
- emphasizing client self-determination, responsibility, and possibility so cherished in the rhetoric of social work practice

An unthinking and monolithic devotion to the disease model undercuts, in the broadest and deepest way, the possibility of personal autonomy and community responsibility by sparing no human behavior from the lash of disease, no group of human beings from the rack of illness. Even when we acknowledge the reality of an illness, we are not absolved from finding resources within that person, her environment, and her relationships, and assisting her in capitalizing on those in living beyond the disease and improving the quality of her life.

Of Paradigms and Prospects: Converging Lines of Thought

In many different places and through many different means, it is claimed that Western culture, perhaps the world, is undergoing a fundamental paradigm shift. If we define a paradigm as a framework crafted of symbols, concepts, beliefs, cognitive structures, and cultural ethos so deeply embedded in our psyches that we hardly know of its presence, the crumbling of an existing paradigm and the rise of another can be a deeply disturbing phenomenon. While there is profound disagreement and even conflict about what the old paradigm is, and what it is being replaced with, some have seen the hegemony of the rational, linear, scientific worldview challenged by the rise of a perspective that is more interpretive—a paradigm that claims that, when it comes to the human condition and human nature, there are no singular, objectively wrought truths to be had. No perspective is final and maybe even no perspective is superior to another. All are deeply rooted in a particular social context and linguistic and discourse tradition (psychiatrists talk differently than car salespeople or nuclear physicists who talk differently and see a different world than school teachers, and so forth) and, thus, make sense therein, but might appear as sheer lunacy in another time and place.

There is comfort here for voices that have struggled too long to be heard, for cultures and peoples whose understanding of the world has been thrust aside or debased, for all those who have something to bring to the intellectual, moral, and spiritual marketplace. There is also encouragement here for other paths of knowing and being in the world. Others would disagree with this perspectivalism. But, it does seem to many that "for better or worse, the world is in the midst of the torturous birth throes of a collective emergence of an entirely new structure of consciousness" (Wilber, 1995, p. 188). It may be that we are moving in the direction of some sort of integration of the spheres of life, seeing and expressing the intricate and still-evolving connections between the body, mind, and environment; the earth, cosmos, and spirit. None of this will occur without tremendous upheaval and resistance, and no one can be certain, if the older paradigm is shattering, what will appear in its place.

What has all this to do with the strengths perspective? In a modest way, the strengths perspective moves away from the disease paradigm that has dominated much of the professional world, the scientific and technological realms. That model, described in various ways throughout these chapters, assumes a different viewpoint on clients and our work with them than the strengths model does. So to begin to surrender it can be a wrenching experience—in a moderate fashion, as disruptive as larger, more cosmic shifts in consciousness. But it is nonetheless a shift in consciousness, a change in the way that we see our clients and regard our work. Fortunately, we are not alone in this transformation of our professional consciousness. In other disciplines and professions, fault lines have appeared, and new conceptual and practical structures are becoming visible. Some of these have been alluded to in the previous chapters. There are four that I want to briefly emphasize in this concluding chapter.

Resilience

In the fields of developmental psychology and developmental psychopathology in particular, it has become clear that children exposed to risk in their early years do not inevitably consummate their adult lives with psychopathology or sink into a morass of failure and disappointment. The field is not of one mind here, but after arising out of the presumption that there are specific and well-defined risks that children will face, and these will always end in some sort of developmental disaster, it now seems clear that most do not; most children surmount adversity and, while bearing scars, do better as adults than we might have predicted. Yes, some children do face trauma, institutional and interpersonal, so toxic that to emerge unscathed or relatively functional would be miraculous. But even here, there are miracles. We need to understand better what makes them happen. Consider alcoholism and children growing up in homes where alcohol abuse and its attendant profligacy on the part of one or both parents is a frequent phenomenon. The literature has it that these children are at serious and elevated risk for alcohol abuse as adults as well as other assorted personal struggles and failings. But most children of parents who have serious alcohol problems do not become alcoholic drinkers; many deliberately structure and restructure their lives to avoid such an eventuality. Identical twins show a discordance rate for alcoholic drinking of 40–50% (meaning that about half the time, when one twin has clearly documented drinking problems, the other twin *does not*). Many people who end up struggling with alcoholism have no family history of it at all. And our common assumption that *all* families where there is alcoholism are disorganized and dysfunctional could stand closer scrutiny.

So the picture is a very mixed and confusing one (Peele & Brodsky, 1991; Wolin & Wolin, 1995). But one thing is clear from the research, not just on children growing up under these circumstances but other stressful and challenging ones as well: These children, when they become adults, most of the time (½–⅔) do not succumb to the particular risks and vulnerabilities that supposedly inhered in their childhood experience. That they suffered is clear, but it is not the issue here (Wolin & Wolin, 1995).

Any environment is a welter of demands, stresses, challenges, and opportunities, and these become fateful, given a complex array of other factors—genetic, constitutional, neurobiological, familial, spiritual, communal—for the development of strength, resilience, hardiness, or diminution of capacity. We are only now learning what factors lead to more hopeful outcomes. Clearly in almost every environment, no matter how trying, there lurk not only elements of risk, but protective and generative factors as well. These are people, resources, institutions, and contingencies that enhance the likelihood of rebound and recovery, or may even exponentially accelerate learning, development, and capacity. To learn what these elements of the body/mind/environment equation are, we have to go to the community, the family, and the individual and learn from them how transformation or resilience developed.

One of the more celebrated studies, mentioned previously, of the development of resilience in children as they grow into adulthood was the longitudinal research begun in Kaua'i, Hawaii, in 1955 by Emmy Werner and Ruth Smith (1992). In their earlier report (1982), they reported that 1 out of every 3 children who were evaluated by several measures to be at risk for adolescent and adult problems developed, as it turned out, into competent and confident youths at age 18. In their follow up, Werner and Smith (1992) found that a surprising number of the remaining two-thirds had become caring and efficacious adults at ages 32 and 40. A more specific and telling example: Only one-third of the children who had developed serious emotional and behavioral problems in adolescence had some continuing midlife problems. More surprising yet, by age 40 only 4 percent of the delinquent youths in the study had committed additional crimes (Werner, 1998). One of their central conclusions is that most human beings have self-righting tendencies and are able to effect a change in life trajectory over time, but this tendency must be supported by internal and external factors. One of the many factors that contributes to that is the presence of a steadfast, caring adult (or peer in a few cases). It need not be a parent nor need the relationship be an everyday affair. Other factors included a sense of faith and coherence of meaning, even during times of turmoil and trouble; schools that fostered and encouraged learning and the development of capacities and that had a buoyant, optimistic spirit in the classroom; teachers and mentors who instructed, guided, supported, and acted as protective buffers to the incredible stresses that some of these children faced. The children themselves often showed problem-solving abilities and a persistent curiosity.

But as discovered in Werner and Smith's study, over the past few years, elements of communities and neighborhoods have emerged as important in the balance among risk, protective, and generative factors. In those communities that seem to amplify individual and familial resilience, there is awareness, recognition, and use of the assets of most of the members of the community, through informal networks of individuals, families, and groups. Social networks of peers and intergenerational mentoring relationships provide succor, instruction, support, and engagement (Benson, 1997). These are "enabling niches" (Taylor, 1997), places where individuals become known for what they can do; where they are supported in becoming more adept and knowledgeable; where they can establish solid relationships within and outside the community; where they are, in fact, members and citizens in good standing. In communities that provide protection, generate growth, and minimize risk, there are many opportunities for participation in the moral and civic life of the community. In this way, the most abundant resources for the promotion of resilience, health, and self-righting are natural and available in most every community, to one degree or another. But if we do have programs designed to enhance capacities and the rebound from adversity, Lisbeth Schorr (1997) in her review of programs that work (see Chapter 13) to prevent poor or "rotten" developmental outcomes for children found they typically had seven qualities: (1) they were comprehensive, flexible, and responsive to local needs and interests; (2) they crossed traditional professional and bureaucratic boundaries; (3) they saw the child in the context of the family; (4) they saw the family in the context of the community; (5) they had a long-term commitment to prevention; (6) they were managed by competent and caring individuals; (7) their services were coherent and easy to use.

There is also a relationship among health, adversity, and resilience. In a comprehensive review of studies that have documented how people may benefit from adversity, McMillen (1999) culled out and fashioned from the data the following factors. First, a difficult, even traumatic event, once faced, may lead to greater confidence that another challenge can be met, bringing with it an increase in the perceived efficacy of one's ability to handle adversity, making future stressful events seem less toxic. Second, as many people have discovered, a seriously adverse event may encourage a deep review of one's values, beliefs, priorities, commitments, relationships, and pastimes. Such changes may really enhance one's health and lifestyle. Third, when trouble surfaces, a person may discover unrealized sources of support from other people, as well as realizing their own vulnerability. Both of these may, in turn, lead to a revised and more positive, balanced view of other people. Finally, in the struggle to cope with an aversive and forbidding event, a person may find the seeds of a new or revised meaning. The questions, "Why me? Why now?" may lead to an authentic existential shift of gears.

So resilience is dependent on the interaction of factors at all levels, from biological to personal, to interpersonal, and environmental. Not only do children and adults learn about themselves and develop strengths as they confront challenge and adversity, if they are lucky they find and make connection with compatriots in the making of a better life, and they find themselves in a community where natural resources are available, no matter how sparse they might seem.

Health and Wellness

Health and wellness are artifacts of a complex, reticulate relationship among body, mind, and environment. Generally speaking, the body is built for health maintenance. Much of Western medicine is predicated on fighting illness when it occurs, often with substances that are, even when carefully employed, toxic (for example, cortisone). Natural or spontaneous healing, on the other hand, depends on the resources that lie immanent in the body, as well as psychological readiness and environmental encouragement. To realize health, to experience regeneration after trauma or disease, to achieve levels of functioning unimagined earlier, some of the following factors are essential and understood.

- People do have the innate capacity and wisdom for health and healthy living. The possibility of soundness and wholeness lie within (Mills, 1995; Pelletier, 2000; Weil, 1995).
- Positive beliefs about oneself and one's condition—hopefulness—seem indispensable for recovery and regeneration (Synder, 2000).
- Health-promoting positive emotions probably support, or elevate, the functioning of elements of the immune system because whatever else they are, they are hormonal events (Restak, 1995).
- The community plays an important role in health sustenance. The connections between people, important mutual projects, the mentoring and support, the common visions and hopes that occur in vibrant and vital communities are important to health and recovery. Hope always has a collective element (Snyder & Feldman, 2000).

The resilience and health and wellness literature run parallel in many regards. Both assert that individuals and communities have native capacities for restoration, rebound, and the maintenance of a high level of functioning. Both suggest that individuals are best served, from a health and competence standpoint, by creating belief and thinking around possibility and values, around accomplishment and renewal, rather than focusing on risk and disease processes. Both indicate that health and resilience are, in the end, communal projects—an effect of social connection, the pooling of collective vision, the provision of guidance, and the joy of belonging to an organic whole, no matter how small.

Story and Narrative

The constructionist view, in its many guises (see the discussion of perspectivalism earlier in this section), urges us to respect the importance of making meaning in all human affairs. Human beings build themselves into the world, not with their meager supply of instinct, but with the capacity to construct and construe a world from symbols, images, icons, language, and ultimately stories and narratives. While culture provides these building blocks, we impart, receive, and revise meanings largely through the telling of stories, the fashioning of narratives, and the creation of myths. Many are given by culture, some are authored by families, individuals, and subcultures. And there is always some tension between the culture and the self in this regard. But individuals and groups do tell their own stories. Stories serve many purposes. They are about dreams, discovery, redemption, trouble, courage, love, loss—every element of the human experience and condition. They instruct, chasten, guide, comfort, and surprise. They provide a sinew of connection between those who share them. They survive because they have human value and humane consequences. We are prepared by our own history as a species and as individuals to respond to the medium of stories. Good stories grounded in our experience can elevate us or put us firmly in the bed of familial, intimate, and cultural relationships in ways of our own making, not somebody else's. Children are socialized in large part by stories and narratives. For children today, however, the stories are not so much rooted in family and culture, neighborhood and community, but in the media and the marketplace. Mary Pipher (1996) says this:

> Now the adults who are telling stories [read: the media] do not know the kids who are listening, do not love them and will not be there to comfort them if they are confused and upset by their stories. Another problem is that the stories that are told are designed to raise profits, not children. Most of the stories children hear are mass-produced to induce them to want good things instead of good lives. . . . We need stories to connect us with each other, stories to heal the polarization that can overwhelm us all and stories to calm those who are frightened and who hate. These stories would offer us the possibility of reconciliation. (pp. 270–271)

Some single mothers in a public housing community were encouraged to relate their stories of survival under what were often siege conditions (O'Brien, 1995). Reluctant at first, they often reiterated the public's and media stories about people like themselves, and their initial attempts were not very flattering. But once they got into it, they all had distinctive, sometimes buried, stories to tell about survival. These stories were often about courage, wiles, faith, relationship, struggle, and uniqueness. These women were not saints; they were simply human beings who, facing the enormous difficulties of being poor, isolated, often unemployed, and raising children alone, had somehow managed to make it. If there was a persistent theme in these stories, it was resilience. And it was important for these women to share their stories. Most times, no one cared how they happened to see their worlds. Without encouragement to tell, some of their world was unconstructed, or not of their making. It was, they said, important for their children to hear these stories. These were in some ways cautionary tales admonishing the listener—children, too—on the dangers out there and how to avoid them. They were ennobling as well. Listeners were instructed on the managing of hardship and ordeals, and the mounting of internal and external resources in its face.

Groups who suffer under the domination of the larger culture and social institutions frequently do not have their stories told or heard in the wider world nor, regrettably, sometimes in their own world (Rosaldo, 1989). One of the human costs of being oppressed is having one's stories buried beneath the landslide of stereotype and ignorance. This means, then, that one of the genuine strengths of people(s) lies in the fabric of narrative and story in the culture and in the family. These are generative themes (Friere, 1996), and they capture the hopes and visions, the trials and tribulations, the strengths and virtues of a people, of a family. It is part of the work of liberation, renewal, and rebuilding to collaborate in the discovery, projection, and elaboration of these stories and accounts. A story told and appreciated is a person, family, or culture affirmed. While we understand that there is an innate capacity or urge toward health in the human body, we may not understand as well that in a story or narrative may be the health of a culture.

Solution-Focused Approaches

Coming from the work and philosophy of Steve de Shazer, the clinical work and writing of Insoo Kim Berg and Peter De Jong, and the recent work of Scott Miller, Mark Hubble, and Barry Duncan, the solution-focused approach to helping has gained ground, both in terms of its clinical use, but also in terms of increasing empirical support. Although it does not attend pointedly to strengths, it does have an implicit and abiding interest in the strengths of individuals and families (De Jong & Miller, 1995). And, as yet it has not, in my view, really concentrated on the resources and solutions in the environment. John Walter and Jane Peller (1992) say the basic question asked by this approach is "How do we construct solutions?" And such a question, they argue, harbors certain assumptions: there are solutions; there is more than one solution; solutions can be constructed; that therapists and clients do the constructing; that constructing means the solutions are invented or made up not discovered; and how this is done can be said and shown (Walter & Peller, 1992). From the outset, in solution-focused work, the eye is always on the goal, the end, and the solution and the thinking, imagining, motivating, and relating that takes place around solution development is independent of the processes that sustain problems. Furthermore, the emergence of solutions obscures and trumps the further development of problems.

Of great importance to the practitioners of this approach is this question: How do theories, methods, and practitioners actually contribute to the elaboration and intensification of the problems presented to them by clients? Duncan and others (1997) suggest the following: (1) Certain conditions invite the expectancy of difficulty or impossibility (think of borderline personality disorder or urban ghetto youth) and "attribution creep"—the expansion of negative impressions based on the expectancy that things will not get better, probably worse. These impressions are hardy blooms and difficult to prune. (2) Theories often have within them negative countertransference. That means that they create word pictures of groups of clients that are often pessimistic or invalidating (the psychodynamic view of schizophrenia, for example, or the at-risk view of certain groups of children and their neighborhoods). Likewise, they mute the theories and language of the individual and culture. (3) Often, when solutions of one kind or another do not work or the problem turns out to be refractory, practitioners (parents, teachers, all of us sometimes) do more of the same. And as more of the same produces a hardening of the problem, we do even more of the same. Think of parents and their adolescent children. A midnight curfew on the weekend doesn't do it? How about an 11:00 P.M. curfew? Not effective? How about a 10:00 P.M curfew for the whole week? Or consider a psychiatrist with little time to see each patient. One antidepressant doesn't do it? How about another? And another? (4) It is common to think of many individuals or families as unmotivated or treatment resistant if they do not respond to our blandishments. Sometimes we make things worse by overlooking or misunderstanding the client's motivation. The fact is that every client has some range of motivations. They just may be out of the purview of our approach and intent.

Jim Kreider, a skilled social work practitioner and accomplished educator, gives the following example of the blending of solution-focused and strengths-based work.

> Bill (not his real name) looked dejected as he slumped in his chair and talked about feeling demoralized because he had never been able to hold a job for more than a week. He was to start a new job the next week, but was afraid he'd repeat what had happened with the 30 or more jobs he'd had since high school. He'd force himself to apply for one job a day, which was all the stress he could tolerate, until he got one. But after several days of working, he'd feel so overwhelmed by his "worries" (such as whether or not he was doing the job well enough) that he'd become physically ill, have to go home, and not return the following day. Bill would then feel so ashamed about "failing again" that he wouldn't go back to pick up his check: Sometimes he'd feel so discouraged that he wouldn't even get out of bed for as much as a week.
>
> Even as a young adult of 25, Bill had already had substantial experience with both inpatient and outpatient psychiatric care. He, like his mother and sister, had been prescribed a variety of psychotropic medications for severe depression. Unfortunately, Bill only found the medications moderately helpful, but extremely unpleasant due to their various side effects. He found that drinking helped him feel less anxious and depressed, but was afraid he might become an alcoholic, so he avoided self-medicating with alcohol.
>
> When asked what he most hoped for in his life, he was emphatic that he just wanted to be able to get and keep a job. He was certain he would "struggle with depression" for the rest of his life, like others in his family; but he also thought that if he could just keep a job it would give him something to do other than focus on his substantial worries. He also hoped that holding a job would help him feel like a success rather than a failure, with the implications reflected in his statement that, "Even if I have to suffer from depression, at least I won't have a depressing life."
>
> Even though Bill's personal and family histories looked rather bleak, I wanted to explore any work-related strengths he had by asking about when he'd been most successful at keeping a job. He looked puzzled at first, perhaps by my asking about when he was *successful*, even though he viewed himself as a complete *failure* in terms of his work experience. After waiting silently for what seemed a long time, Bill hesitantly began his response, "Well, I . . . uh . . . this sounds kinda weird . . . but it has to start at the beginning of the day. I have to stop myself before I make up things to worry about: I have to tell myself to 'Just get out of bed and only think about the first thing to do, then the next, and the next, and the next. Just take a small step and don't make anything a big deal. Don't think about what can go wrong or how crappy you feel.' It helps if I use a clock radio, too, instead of an alarm clock: It's not

so harsh." When I asked Bill how this helped, he responded, "It's so easy to think about all of what can go wrong, and then I get so overwhelmed that I just want to pull the covers over my head. When I just concentrate on what's right in front of me, the day passes and I can look back and say 'Whew: I made it. I did it!" When I asked Bill how frequently he used this strategy in the past, he again paused for a long time then replied, "I don't think very much. I didn't really think about it before . . . I mean before you asked . . . probably not very much.

Since Bill was very demoralized and fearful of failing again, I suggested that he might try using what worked for him in the past on his new job. Bill obviously had many challenges to overcome in his life, but this simple strategy was enough for him to maintain that new job for six weeks, the longest he'd ever managed! Doing so gave him hope that he might be able to keep a job for even longer the next time. Did this mean Bill's troubles were over or his psychiatric symptoms were "cured"? Obviously not: It was merely a small yet significant step toward discovering how to write a life story that included competence rather than only failure.

Among other things, this is a story, as are most strengths-based stories, about possibility—the possibility of overcoming an ordeal, a fear, a roadblock, and the possibility of achieving, in some small way, a dream. But it is also a story that begins with discovering a capacity, talent, strengths within (or around)—something that someone already has done, or knows but may not have used it or even seen it as a basis for change.

Clearly there is a convergence in these approaches of appreciations, perspectives, and points of view. While differences remain, the union of certain assumptions and standpoints is heartening to say the least.

Conclusion

The contributors to this volume—most of whom are practitioners as well as scholars and educators—hope that you find something of real value here that can be translated for use with the individuals, families, and communities that you serve. We all believe that the initiatory act in employing a strengths perspective is a commitment to its principles and underlying philosophy—a credo that, in many regards, is at serious odds with the approach we have variously labeled the deficit, problem, or pathology orientation. We firmly believe that once committed you will be surprised, even amazed, at the array of talents, skills, knowledge, and resources that you discover in your clients—even those whose prospects seem bleak. In a nutshell, that is, for us, the most convincing rationale for embracing a point of view that appreciates and fosters the powers within and around the individual. The authors also hope that you have found some tools to assist you in the promotion of the health, resilience, and narrative integrity of your clients. But, in the end, what will convince you to stay with this perspective is the spark that you see in people when they begin to discover, rediscover, and embellish their native endowments. That spark fuels the flame of hopeful and energetic, committed and competent social work.

DISCUSSION QUESTIONS

1. You have finished the book. Where do you stand now on the utility and relevance of the strengths perspective? How will you understand problems that people bring to you now?

2. Do you think that you can practice from a strengths perspective no matter what sort of organization or agency you work at?

3. If you do assume a strengths perspective what will you say to people who think you are being Pollyannaish?

4. What are the limits and weaknesses of the strengths perspective?

REFERENCES

Albelda, R., & Folbre, N. (1996). *The war on the poor: A defense manual.* New York: New Press.

American Psychiatric Association (2000). *Diagnostic and statistical manual of mental disorders IV TR.* Washington, DC: American Psychiatric Association.

Benard, B. (1994, December). *Applications of resilience.* Paper presented at a National Institute on Drug Abuse conference on the role of resilience in drug abuse, alcohol abuse, and mental illness, Washington, DC.

Benson, P. L. (1997). *All kids are our kids: What communities must do to raise caring and responsible children and adolescents.* San Francisco: Jossey-Bass.

Cousins, N. (1989). *Head first: The biology of hope.* New York: Dutton.

De Jong, P., & Miller, S. D. (1995). How to interview for client strengths. *Social Work, 40,* 729–736.

Duncan, B. L., Hubble, M. A., & Miller, S. D. (1997). *Psychotherapy with 'impossible' cases: The efficient treatment of psychotherapy veterans.* New York: Norton.

Edelman, P. (1997, January). The worst thing President Clinton has done. *Atlantic Monthly, 282,* 43–58.

Friere, P. (1973). *Pedagogy of the oppressed.* New York: Seabury.

Freire, P. (1996). *Pedagogy of hope.* New York: Seabury.

Fromm, E. (1973). *The anatomy of human destructiveness.* New York: Holt, Rinehart, & Winston.

Gergen, K. J. (1994). *Realities and relationships: Soundings in social construction.* Cambridge: Harvard University Press.

Goffman, E. (1961). *Asylums.* New York: Doubleday/Anchor.

Hillman, J., & Ventura, M. (1992). *We've had one hundred years of psychotherapy and the world is getting worse.* San Francisco: HarperSanFrancisco.

Kondrat, M. E. (1995). Concept, act, and interest in professional practice: Implications of an empowerment perspective. *Social Service Review, 69,* 405–428.

Kovel, J. (1981). *The age of desire: Reflections of a radical psychoanalyst.* New York: Pantheon.

Kutchins, H., & Kirk, S. A. (1997). *Making us crazy: DSM: The psychiatric bible and the creation of mental disorders.* New York: Free Press.

Longres, J. (1997). Is it feasible to teach HBSE from a strengths perspective? No! In M. Bloom & W. C. Klein (Eds.), *Controversial issues in human behavior and the social environment.* Boston: Allyn & Bacon.

McMillen, J. C. (1999). Better for it: How people benefit from adversity. *Social Work, 44,* 455–468.

Mills, R. (1995). *Realizing mental health.* New York: Sulzburger & Graham.

Moore, T. (1992). *Care of the soul.* New York: HarperCollins.

Ornstein, R., & Sobel, D. (1989). *Healthy pleasures.* Reading, MA: Addison-Wesley.

O'Toole, J. (1995). Goods in common: Efficiency and community. In M. Adler (Ed.), *The great ideas today: 1995.* Chicago: Encyclopedia Britannica.

Peele, S., & Brodsky, A. (1991). *The truth about addiction and recovery: The life process program for outgrowing destructive habits.* New York: Fireside Books/Simon & Schuster.

Pelletier, K. R. (2000). *The best alternative medicine: What works? What does not?* New York: Simon & Schuster.

Pipher, M. (1996). *The shelter of each other: Rebuilding our families.* New York: Ballantine Books.

Ralph, R. O., Lambric, T. M., & Steele, R. B. (1996, February). *Recovery issues in a consumer developed evaluation of the mental health system* (pp. 1–13). Paper presented at the 6th annual conference of *Mental Health Services Research and Evaluation Conference.* Arlington, VA.

Rapp, C. A. (1998). *The strengths model: Case management with people suffering from severe and persistent mental illness.* New York: Oxford University Press.

Restak, R. M. (1995). *Brainscapes.* New York: Hyperion.

Rosaldo, R. (1989). *Culture and truth: The remaking of social analysis.* Boston: Beacon Press.

Schön, D. A. (1983). *The reflective practitioner.* New York: Basic Books.

Schorr, L. B. (1997). *Common purpose: Strengthening families and neighborhoods to rebuild America.* New York: Anchor/Doubleday.

Snyder, C. R. (2000). Hypothesis: There is hope. In C. R. Snyder (Ed.), *Handbook of hope: Theory, measures, and applications.* San Diego: Academic Press.

Snyder, C. R., & Feldman, D. B. (2000). Hope for the many: An empowering social agenda. In C. R. Snyder (Ed.), *Handbook of hope: Theory, measures, and applications.* San Diego: Academic Press.

Taylor, J. (1997). Poverty and niches: A systems view. In D. Saleebey (Ed.), *The strengths perspective in social work practice* (2nd. ed.). New York: Longman.

Walter, J. L., & Peller, J. E. (1992). *Becoming solution-focused in brief therapy.* New York: Brunner/Mazel.

Walzer, M. (1983). *Spheres of justice.* New York: Basic Books.

Weil, A. (1995). *Spontaneous healing.* New York: Knopf.

Werner, E. E. (1998). Resilience and the life-span perspective: What we have learned—so far. *Resiliency in Action, 3,* 1–8.

Werner, E. E., & Smith, R. S. (1982). *Vulnerable but invincible.* New York: McGraw-Hill.

Werner, E. E., & Smith, R. S. (1992). *Overcoming the odds.* Ithaca, NY: Cornell University Press.

Wilber, K. (1995). *Sex, ecology, and spirituality: The spirit of evolution.* Boston: Shambhala.

Wright, B., & Fletcher, B. (1982). Uncovering hidden resources: A challenge in assessment. *Professional Psychology, 13,* 229–235.

INDEX